POLICY STUDIES FOR EDUCATIONAL LEADERS

POLICY STUDIES FOR EDUCATIONAL LEADERS

AN INTRODUCTION

Second Edition

Frances C. Fowler
Miami University, Oxford, Ohio

PEARSON

Merrill
Prentice Hall

Upper Saddle River, New Jersey
Columbus, Ohio

KH

Library of Congress Cataloging in Publication Data

Fowler, Frances C.
   Policy studies for educational leaders : an introduction / Frances C. Fowler.
      p. cm.
   Includes bibliographical references and index.
   ISBN 0-13-099393-X
   1. Education and state—United States. 2. Politics and education—United States.
   3. School administrators—United States. I. Title.

LC89.F69 2004
379—dc21

                                                                2002044475

Vice President and Executive Publisher: Jeffery W. Johnston
Executive Editor: Debra A. Stollenwerk
Editorial Assistant: Mary Morrill
Production Editor: Kris Robinson
Production Coordination: Carlisle Publishers Services
Design Coordinator: Diane C. Lorenzo
Cover Designer: Jason Moore
Cover image: SuperStock
Production Manager: Pamela D. Bennett
Director of Marketing: Ann Castel Davis
Marketing Manager: Darcy Betts Prybella
Marketing Coordinator: Tyra Poole

This book was set in Janson Text by Carlisle Communications, Ltd. It was printed
and bound by R. R. Donnelley & Sons Company. The cover was printed by The Lehigh
Press, Inc.

Pearson Education Ltd.
Pearson Education Singapore Pte. Ltd.
Pearson Education Canada, Ltd.
Pearson Education–Japan

Pearson Education Australia Pty. Limited
Pearson Educación North Asia Ltd.
Pearson Education de Mexico, S.A. de C.V.
Pearson Education Malaysia Pte. Ltd.

PEARSON
Merrill
Prentice Hall

10 9 8 7 6 5 4 3 2
ISBN: 0-13-099393-X

11/22/04

To my parents, George Robertson and Louise Cate Fowler.
With love.

Foreword to the First Edition

William Lowe Boyd

As I was perusing an issue of *Education Week*, I came upon a remarkably sophisti-cated and insightful commentary article on the problems of school reform (Fowler, 1985). What made it remarkable was not only its insights but a fact I dis-covered at its conclusion: Rather than having been composed by an exceptionally perceptive academic or policy analyst, it had been written by a sixth-grade teacher in Tennessee! I wondered, How did an elementary school teacher find the time and wherewithal to do this? This very exceptional teacher turned out to be Frances Fowler, author of this book. Because of the extraordinary quality of her writing and analytical ability, I contacted her and, despite her relatively un-known status at the time, invited her to contribute a chapter on the politics of school reform for the first *Yearbook of the Politics of Education Association*, which Charles Kerchner and I were then editing (1988).

Since that time, Frances Fowler has become a distinguished scholar of the politics of education. With the publication of this important book, she has reached a new level in an already impressive career. Few textbooks on the poli-tics of education have been published and none has offered the remarkable com-bination of qualities found in this book: a rich and comprehensive introduction to the field of educational policy and politics for educators and lay persons; a re-markable blend of theoretical analysis and practical advice and guidelines; and a message and writing style that appeal to a wide audience, not only lay persons and educators uninitiated to the political world but also experts and scholars.

Teachers and school administrators will welcome this book because the au-thor genuinely understands their situation and speaks directly to their interests and concerns. Scholars also will welcome this book, not only because it will be enormously useful for teaching purposes but also because it accomplishes more than just didactic objectives: It makes a significant contribution to the literature on the politics of education in several ways. First, it achieves a balance and rein-tegration of the relationship between policy studies and politics. Scholars of the politics of education who have been worried that the recent trend toward policy studies has led to a de-emphasis or even neglect of the politics associated with ed-ucational policy making will be gratified by the balance Fowler achieves here.

William Lowe Boyd is a Distinguished Professor of Education at The Pennsylvania State University.

Second, Fowler draws together the themes and analysis in her book through a sustained concern for the competing values at play in educational politics and policy making. She illuminates the resulting tensions with many examples throughout the book. Then, in a significant and original concluding chapter, she uses the lenses of four theoretical frameworks to consider likely future trends in American education policy in light of our political culture and competing values.

Fowler's sensitivity to competing values here is not surprising. One of her most important contributions to date has been her demonstration that the American school choice debate has been framed very narrowly and has neglected a number of important policy values. In large part, the debate has been dominated by neoconservatives utilizing economic models and public choice theory. Opponents of school choice proposals have generally been at a disadvantage, relative to advocates, because they have lacked a compelling theory with which to rebut the powerful logic built into economic theories. In response, Fowler (1992) has applied the neopluralist theory from political science to highlight neglected values and dangers to which school choice policies may be vulnerable, especially when poorly regulated. This quality in theoretical and policy analysis is abundantly present in this book.

A third contribution Fowler makes is to show in detail how political theory and analysis can be usefully applied in practical ways by school teachers and administrators. All too often, academics are better at analyzing and lamenting problems than in offering practical suggestions for how to solve or ameliorate them. This book is a notable exception to that pattern. From the opening of the book right through to the conclusion, Fowler speaks to the concerns of educators who are caught in the increased political turbulence surrounding education and troubled by the frequent disconnect between their understanding of their domain and how it is viewed by policy makers.

For example, Fowler provides practical guidelines, advice, and vignettes to help with such questions as: How might we influence the policy agenda for education? How can we improve public knowledge of education if our state, or area within it, suffers from Swiss-cheese journalism? How should we go about lobbying legislators? What questions should we ask in appraising the likely consequences of proposed policies? How can we determine if a policy is appropriate for our school or district context? How should we go about implementing policies, including unpopular ones? How can we tell if a proposed or completed evaluation is of high quality?

A fourth contribution in this book is its extraordinarily systematic and comprehensive explanation of the state-level policy-making process. Recognizing the ever-increasing importance of state government in education policy, Fowler has provided a full and coherent presentation of information that is usually only available in piecemeal and incomplete accounts.

In sum, this is a rich and rewarding book. It is sure to be popular because it provides not only a comprehensive and insightful introduction to educational policy and politics but many valuable tools and learning exercises for those who wish to improve their skill in, as well as their understanding of, this domain. Tennessee lost an exceptional sixth-grade classroom teacher, but all educators can learn from her now.

REFERENCES

Fowler, F. (1985). Why reforms go awry. *Education Week, 10*(24): 17.

Fowler, F. (1988). The politics of school reform in Tennessee: A view from the classroom. In W. L. Boyd & C. T. Kerchner (Eds.), *The politics of excellence and choice in education.* New York: Falmer Press.

Fowler, F. (1992). American theory and French practice: A theoretical rationale for regulating school choice. *Educational Administration Quarterly, 28*(4) 452–472.

Preface

According to proverbial wisdom, necessity is the mother of invention. Proverbial wisdom is certainly correct in the case of *Policy Studies for Educational Leaders: An Introduction.* The idea for this book was born in the summer of 1990 when, new Ph.D. in hand, I was invited to teach a graduate course in education policy at the University of Tennessee–Knoxville. After discovering no suitable textbooks, I ordered a few paperbacks on current issues and put together a course packet consisting of articles on various aspects of education policy. Although my students were bright and motivated, I often felt frustrated; none had taken a college course in political science and few had been involved in the policy process at any level. I found, therefore, that I had to devote much class time to filling in the gaps in their knowledge. Often I longed for a good textbook that would provide basic information, freeing up precious class time for substantive discussions of policy issues.

That fall I began a new position at Miami University in Oxford, Ohio, where one of my responsibilities was a graduate course in education policy. As I worked with my students over the next few years, my earlier feelings were reinforced. The lack of a good, basic text hampered my teaching in various ways. Thus, the idea for this book was born. As I revised and restructured the course during those years, I also gathered materials for a future textbook, developing an organizational structure and a series of learning materials for students.

TEXT PHILOSOPHY AND FOCUS

Policy Studies for Educational Leaders: An Introduction is based on the following set of beliefs:

1. *Educational leaders need to be literate about policy and the policy process.* The time is long past (if indeed there ever was a time) when education administrators could tell themselves that "Politics and education don't mix" and sit complacently on the sidelines while others make important policy decisions for the schools. In today's rapidly changing policy environment, those who lead our schools *must* have a basic understanding of education policy and how it is made. Otherwise, they will be reactive rather than proactive; and, when they move into action, they are likely to make serious blunders.
2. *Educational leaders need both theories and practical information about education policy and policy making.* Unfortunately, many people in education believe that theory and practice are unrelated and, indeed, opposites. I reject this view. If school ad-

ministrators are truly to be reflective leaders, they need tools for thinking, deeply and critically, about education policy. Among these necessary tools are knowledge about major research findings, analytical frameworks, and important political theories. However, people who are politically inexperienced also need practical advice about how to apply this abstract information. Therefore, this book presents both the underlying theories and specific recommendations for practice.

3. *Educational leaders need to understand power and how to use it responsibly.* The underlying theory behind this book is conflict theory—the belief that policy grows out of conflict between different individuals, groups, and institutions. Since the outcome of these struggles is shaped by the balance of power among the participants, students must understand power. Conflict theory is a large theoretical house, ranging from the pluralists who focus on the dynamics of practical politics to scholars whose thinking has been influenced by Marx and Gramsci, with many stops in between. Unfortunately, education scholars in the United States tend to set up a binary opposition between the pluralists and more "critical" thinkers, focusing on either practical politics or cultural politics to the exclusion of the other. In my opinion, these approaches are neither theoretically adequate nor pedagogically sound, leading either to students who understand day-to-day politics (but ignore the more subtle play of power that shapes most social injustice) or to students who have a good grasp of how powerful cultural institutions shape consciousness (but do not know what happens in a legislature or court). My book transcends this unfortunate dichotomy by using Oxford University professor Steven Lukes' (1974) integration of pluralist and "critical" perspectives with studies of the mobilization of bias to yield a holistic theory which encompasses the many faces of power. Thus, instructors can teach their students about *both* the dynamics of everyday American power politics *and* how powerful interests use institutions and culture to perpetuate injustices based on race, gender, and class.

4. *All public policy, but especially education policy, is value laden.* In political science, one school of policy analysis seeks to conduct "value-free" analysis. In my opinion, their work is misleading because it is based on a fundamental misconception about social reality. I agree, therefore, with those political scientists who consider policy making to be inherently intertwined with values. This book reflects that belief. Not only is an entire chapter devoted to policy values and ideology, but throughout the book I raise issues of values. Because many of the conflicts in which school leaders become embroiled turn on questions of deeply held values, this emphasis lays the foundation for a good understanding of where and when struggles over values are most likely to arise.

5. *State government has become increasingly important in the last 25 years and will probably continue to be so.* In the United States, education policy is developed at four levels: federal, state, district, and school. Although this book touches on all four levels, it emphasizes the state level. Not only is this level growing in importance, but it is the least understood for several reasons: the federal focus of most civics and government courses, the split national–local focus of the media, and the patterns of practical experience that most educators develop during their careers. Therefore, filling this gap seemed essential.

TEXT ORGANIZATION

This book is divided into twelve chapters, which can be grouped in the following four categories:

1. *Introductory chapters* (Chapters 1 and 2). The first two chapters lay a general foundation for students, most of whom have never taken a basic political science course. Chapter 1 presents an overview of education policy and the policy process. Chapter 2 deals with power, presenting Lukes' theory in detail, and applying it both to day-to-day politics and the more subtle power mechanisms, which maintain inequalities based on race, class, and gender. It also provides an introduction to discursive analysis.

2. *The policy environment* (Chapters 3–5). As a social phenomenon, policy grows out of a specific socioeconomic context. Chapters 3, 4, and 5 provide background for students about the most important dimensions of this context: economics, demographics, political structures, political culture, values, and ideology.

3. *The policy process* (Chapters 6–11). Students can understand education policy—and how to influence it—only if they understand how it is developed, implemented, and assessed. Chapters 6 through 11 focus on this process, using the classical stage model. Chapter 6 introduces the major policy players, and the following chapters show them in action as policy issues are defined, moved onto the policy agenda, formulated, adopted, implemented, and evaluated.

4. *Retrospective and prospective* (Chapter 12). This chapter seeks to provide students—who should now have a much more sophisticated understanding of education policy than they did when they started the book—with an historical framework for understanding the current education reform movement.

SPECIAL FEATURES

I have tried to make this book as user friendly as possible for both students and professors. To that end, I have provided the following special features:

1. *Focus questions.* Each chapter opens with several questions that relate to the major content of the chapter. These questions serve as advance organizers for students, helping them identify the most important points as they read.

2. *Figures and tables.* The figures and tables in this book summarize important points that would be tedious in paragraph form, give a visible form to theoretical material for visual learners, and provide an easy reference for the most important principles of political action.

3. *End-of-chapter activities.* Every chapter (except Chapters 9 and 12) ends with at least four of these five types of learning activities for homework or class discussion: Questions and Activities for Discussion, a case study, a news story for analysis, a pro–con debate, and an Internet assignment. These activities can also be used as the basis for short papers.

4. *For further reading.* Each chapter, except Chapter 9, ends with a short, annotated bibliography of books and articles on the topic covered in that chapter that students and professors can use to extend and deepen the material in the chapter.

NEW TO THIS EDITION

Much has happened since I prepared the final manuscript of the first edition in 1998: the technology revolution has continued unabated, a new census has been taken, the booming 1990s economy has faltered, the United States has experienced one of the most closely contested presidential elections of its history, and terrorist attacks on New York and Washington have led to a threat of war abroad and an unprecedented state of alert at home. In education policy, both school choice and standards-based reform have flourished; and concerns about the achievement gap related to race and class have grown. Therefore, numerous changes were needed for this second edition. I will briefly describe them below.

1. *Demographic and economic information has been updated.* Chapter 3, which deals with the economic and demographic aspects of the policy environment, has been largely rewritten. It draws heavily on the 2000 census as well as economic changes resulting both from the expected downturn of the business cycle and the impact of terrorism and war.

2. *Up-to-date news stories for analysis and case studies have been provided.* All the news stories for analysis from the first edition have been replaced by new stories. Moreover, in selecting new material, I included stories that related not only to the major concepts of the chapter they followed but also to current issues such as charter schools, bilingual education, high-stakes testing, and the implementation of the No Child Left Behind Act of 2001. In addition, two new case studies also deal with contemporary issues: the teaching of Darwinian evolution and the revolt of parents against some state testing programs.

3. *The text offers more opportunities for students to learn to use the Internet as a source of information about education policy.* Given the wealth of information available on-line, it seemed important to encourage students to use the Internet to track policy. Therefore, the end-of-chapter activities now include Internet Assignments. Also, two appendices provide the URLs of major policy actors as well as instructions on locating information about policy in individual states.

4. *A glossary has been added.* At the end of the book, a brief glossary provides definitions of key terms so that students will not need to page through the text if they wish to refresh their memory about a definition.

ACKNOWLEDGMENTS

A book is a monumental and often frustrating project, one that requires much assistance and support if it is ever to reach completion. I therefore would like to acknowledge the contributions of the following people.

- Ned B. Lovell, Mississippi State University; Carla Edlefson, Ashland University; David W. Leslie, College of William and Mary; Cathy S. Jording, Georgia Southern University; Cecil F. Carter, Florida Gulf Coast University; A. Reynaldo Contreras, San Francisco State University; Austin D. Swanson, State University at Buffalo; and Tina Dawson, Antioch University Seattle, for their reviews.

- The office staff of the Educational Leadership Department at Miami University—especially Jan Clegg and Peggy Bower—who worked copying the various versions of the manuscript, preparing mailings, and taking phone calls for this project.
- My editor at Prentice Hall, Debbie Stollenwerk, and her assistant, Mary Morrill. Over the years Debbie has become a real friend, while Mary was always prompt to answer requests and questions . . . of which there were many!
- All the people in Anderson County and Nashville, Tennessee (their name is legion), who acted as my mentors when I was active in politics and gave me practical knowledge of how it is really done.
- My students at Miami University, who were eager to learn much of the material that eventually wound up in the first edition of the book and made valuable suggestions for the second.
- William Boyd, Professor of Educational Leadership at Penn State and a fellow East Tennessean, who asked me to contribute a chapter to a Politics of Education Association Yearbook when I was still a sixth-grade teacher and who has supported and assisted me on many occasions since I entered higher education.
- My late aunt, Ruth Fowler Shipe, who taught high school American history and government and whose avid and lifelong interest in the policy process was contagious.
- My sisters, Marianne and Susan Fowler, who are still politically active as a Washington lobbyist and a teacher union leader, respectively, and who have helped me keep in touch with the real world of policy making since I entered academia.
- And, finally, all those other relatives, friends, and colleagues whose support, pride, and encouragement helped me through the rough times and made sure that I finished the book.

Frances C. Fowler

THE EASIEST WAY TO ENHANCE YOUR COURSE
Proven Journals • Proven Strategies • Proven Media

www.EducatorLearningCenter.com

Merrill Education is pleased to announce a new partnership with ASCD. The result of this partnership is a joint website, www.EducatorLearningCenter.com, with recent articles and cutting-edge teaching strategies. The Educator Learning Center combines the resources of the Association for Supervision and Curriculum Development (ASCD) and Merrill Education. At www.EducatorLearningCenter.com you will find resources that will enhance your students' understanding of course topics and of current educational issues, in addition to being invaluable for further research.

How will Educator Learning Center help your students become better teachers?

- 600+ articles from the ASCD journal *Educational Leadership* discuss everyday issues faced by practicing teachers.

- Hundreds of lesson plans and teaching strategies are categorized by content area and age range.

- Excerpts from Merrill Education texts give your students insight on important topics of instructional methods, diverse populations, assessment, classroom management, technology, and refining practice.

- Case studies, classroom video, electronic tools, and computer simulations keep your students abreast of today's classrooms and current technologies.

- A direct link on the site to Research Navigator™, where your students will have access to many of the leading education journals as well as extensive content detailing the research process.

What's the cost?

A four-month subscription to Educator Learning Center is $25 but is **FREE** when used in conjunction with this text. To obtain free passcodes for your students, simply contact your local Merrill/Prentice Hall sales representative, and your representative will give you a special ISBN to give your bookstore when ordering your textbooks. To preview the value of this website to you and your students, please go to www.EducatorLearningCenter.com and click on "Demo."

Brief Contents

Contents

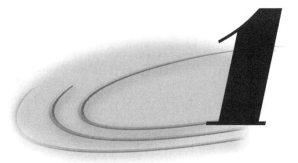

POLICY—WHAT IT IS AND WHERE IT COMES FROM

Focus Questions

Why do changes in the political and economic environment make understanding the policy process essential for today's school leaders?

How can one determine what policy a government is actually pursuing?

What roles can school leaders play in shaping and influencing education policy?

WHY STUDY POLICY?
School Leaders in Oz

"Toto, I don't think we're in Kansas anymore." A doctoral student who was taking an education policy course began one of her papers with this quotation from *The Wizard of Oz*. The student, principal of an elementary school in a large metropolitan area, had written a reflective essay about a trip that her class had taken to the state capital. This visit to the halls of power had left the students—all practicing school administrators—stunned.

The day had begun at a meeting with a state department of education official, who was supposed to brief the group on policy trends. For 50 minutes he had inundated them with facts and figures about taxes, school finance formulas, and economic growth, interspersing these statistics with complaints about how much time it took to operate a large district that the state had recently taken over. Finally, he paused and asked, "Any questions?" After a silence, another principal in the group inquired, "What about kids?" The official explained that his own background was in economics and that he had never worked in a school. This fact, he said, made it hard for him to conceptualize how education policy affects children.

After lunch, the class had an appointment with the chairman of the House Education Committee. Although the appointment had been made weeks in advance, the chairman's secretary had called just the day before to explain that the legislator's plans had changed and he would not meet with them after all. Instead, they now had an appointment with a member of his staff, who nervously explained to the administrators and their professor that he did not know much about education policy. He did, however, invite them into the office of the great man himself. Standing in this room, he praised his employer's intelligence, pointing to his bookshelves and all the books on education he had read. The educators were sobered by the fact that *The Bell Curve*—widely criticized as racist in education circles—was prominently displayed. They were even more sobered when the staffer launched into an explanation of the legislator's views on special education. "Those kids shouldn't be allowed to drag down the others," he asserted. "They should be placed in special schools where they can learn at their own rate." Only with difficulty did the special education director in the group restrain an angry response.

As the students were leaving the legislative office building, they encountered another member of the legislature in the lobby. Because he was acquainted with a member of the class, everyone stopped to talk to him for a few minutes. At first, concentrating on his words was difficult because everyone was distracted by his tie, which was covered with bright pink pigs. He later explained that he had just worn it to a meeting with a group of hog farmers who had come to the capital to lobby him. This politician talked enthusiastically about the importance of education and jubilantly announced that the General Assembly was considering a home rule bill. If passed, this law would remove almost all state regulations from school districts, leaving them "free" to plan children's education. "Are you going to abolish the state proficiency tests?" one administrator asked hopefully, referring to the regulation that the state's educators found most burdensome. The legislator looked shocked. "Oh, no, of course not! The proficiency tests are here to stay."

On the way to the car, a member of the class commented sadly, "It's amazing—we speak two entirely different languages." A colleague answered, "And yet it's *imperative* that we learn how to communicate with them."

This true story succinctly illustrates many of the tensions and frustrations that school administrators experience as they venture into the world of education policy making. Reacting by withdrawing into either resignation or fatalism is all too easy. The purpose of this book is to provide potential and practicing education leaders with a basis for alternative responses if they wish to use them. It seeks to offer them a knowledge base about education policy, including how it is made and how it can be influenced. It also seeks to sensitize them to some of the new dimensions of education leadership that are emerging as the United States moves into the twenty-first century. First, however, considering how and why the world of education policy has changed is necessary.

THE TRANSFORMATION OF THE EDUCATION POLICY ENVIRONMENT
The Way It Used to Be

If the world of education policy has changed from a relatively quiet and predictable "Kansas" to a rapidly changing and unpredictable "Oz," we need to understand the way it used to be. Until the 1980s, public schools were among the most respected institutions of U.S. society. At times, public leaders severely criticized them and offered suggestions for improvement. For example, in the late 1950s the former Soviet Union launched an artificial satellite, provoking frantic calls for better science and mathematics instruction in U.S. high schools. However, this critique and virtually all others were offered within a framework that took public education itself for granted. Few people raised questions about its fundamental legitimacy. Until the early eighties, funding for schools was more or less adequate, although this varied by district and region. At times, as in the sixties, public funding was even generous. Moreover, until the advent of the Reagan Administration, state governments delegated most of their authority over public education to local school districts without requiring them to do much to demonstrate accountability. In state legislatures, education policy was commonly developed within what was called "an iron triangle," consisting of the education committees of the legislature, the state department of education, and the major education lobbying groups. Policy changes were usually slow and incremental. When political bodies were considering new policies, all three corners of the triangle became involved in the discussion. Educators were considered experts with valuable opinions about education policy.

The New Policy Environment

In the last two decades, every aspect of this situation changed. Today, business, media, and political leaders generally consider public education to be in crisis. Many of its critics have proposed changes that would either alter it in profound ways or, over time, cause it to disappear in some areas and among some populations. Many school districts—and not just poor or urban ones—find themselves in ongoing financial emergencies. In states where school choice programs have been implemented, school leaders find themselves grappling with market pressures to which they are unaccustomed. State governments have asserted their authority over public schools by issuing a bewildering array of new policies and policy proposals. More often than not, they have not asked public school educators for input into these reforms. Instead, they have defined educators as a major part of the problem rather than as professionals qualified to offer solutions and have sought input from business leaders and think-tank researchers instead. Many public school teachers and administrators feel confused and even resentful as they cope with the resulting policy climate. Many have also become fatalistic about the new environment, perceiving it as a storm that must be passively weathered because no one can do anything about it.

Reasons for These Changes

Economic Changes. The reasons for the changed education policy environment are, of course, complex and multifaceted. However, most observers would agree that major economic changes, not only in the United States but around the world, have played an important role. World War II was followed by an unprecedented boom during which many countries experienced economic growth for close to thirty years. That period ended about 1975 and was succeeded by a period of slow to stagnant growth. During times of slow growth, citizens become increasingly reluctant to pay taxes; since the late 1970s, the United States has seen several low tax movements and tax rebellions. In such a climate, politicians are unwilling to increase taxes or even to keep public spending steady. Instead, they try to reduce spending on public services, including public education. Although an economic boom occurred during the 1990s, the "no new tax" mentality persisted. Finally, the 2001 terrorist attacks on Washington, D.C., and New York City ushered in a period during which already lean government resources have frequently been directed toward military action and domestic security rather than toward public education. The overall economic problem has been compounded in the United States by a well-documented increase in the disparity between the wealthiest portion of the population and the poorest. As the twenty-first century began, more and more children in the United States were growing up in poverty. Educating poor children well is costlier than educating those whose families have abundant or adequate resources. Thus, the schools find themselves shouldering additional burdens at a time when their own resources are declining. This fact contributes to the overall sense of crisis in education (Berliner & Biddle, 1995; Phillips, 1994; Reich, 1991; Thurow, 1992).

Demographic Trends. Another reason for the changed policy environment is demographic. In the last twenty-five years, the composition of the U.S. population has changed greatly. One demographic phenomenon of special importance is the baby boom generation, people born between 1946 and 1964. As babies, as teens, and as young adults this segment of the population had enormous impact on the nation. Now the oldest baby boomers are well into their fifties and starting to retire. Political leaders are concerned about financing their retirements as well as their health care costs. Significant funds, both private and public, will have to be invested in the aging baby boom generation over the next twenty-five years, thereby reducing the money available for schools. Moreover, older people tend to be poorly attuned to the needs of education because they have no young children. This means that political support for schools, which has been declining with the aging of the population, will probably decline still further (Rosenblatt, 1996).

Another important demographic change is the increasing diversity of the population, a trend which was apparent in both the 1990 and 2000 censuses. Because of high levels of immigration and differential birth rates, the nation is becoming more multicultural. Racial, ethnic, religious, and linguistic diversity are an important part of the context in which public schools operate and in which political decisions about them are made (Rosenblatt, 1996). This diversity means that new demands are being made on public schools. Bilingual programs, the accommodation of a wider range of religious practices, and pressures for multi-cultural curricula are just a few manifestations of the complexity resulting from diversity. Although diversity enriches society, some find it threatening. In fact, it has led some to question whether a single system of public schools can or should meet the needs of so many diverse groups. Faced with conflicting demands from different segments of the population, today some people suggest that public education be fragmented into multiple freestanding schools of choice, each specialized to meet the desires of a specific group.

Ideological Shift.   Over the last twenty-five years, a major shift in political ideas has occurred in the United States and, indeed, throughout the English-speaking world. In general, the focus of education politics has shifted from equality issues to issues relating to excellence, accountability, and choice (Boyd & Kerchner, 1988). This shift has influenced both Republicans and Democrats and affected policy not only under Reagan and both Bushes but also under Clinton. Often business leaders advance these ideas in policy debates, sometimes sounding as if they discern no differences between public schools and private firms. They criticize schools for their alleged inefficiency and insensitivity to the market—concerns that have not traditionally been the highest priorities for public educators. Moreover, for the first time in decades, traditional conservatives—such as the Religious Right—have emerged as a major force in U.S. politics. In many communities across the nation, in many state capitals, and in Washington, D.C., itself, traditional conservatives have begun to play an active role in policy development. For a variety of reasons they, too, are often critical of public education. The ideologies of both the business community and the Religious Right lead them to be skeptical of government and government initiatives. Public schools are, of course, a part of the government and are therefore automatically defined as part of the problem. As a result of these shifts in values, school leaders find themselves at the center of the attention of two groups that formerly had less to say about education.

Finally, the tone of U.S. politics has changed, becoming increasingly harsh. Lowi (1995), a political scientist at Cornell University, argues that since the 1980 presidential election U.S. politics has been "Europeanized." By this he means that it has become both more polarized and more focused on ideas. Not only are Americans advancing new ideas, but they are advancing them more aggressively and dogmatically than before. For school leaders who grew up when political discourse was more courteous, this harsh tone can be disconcerting.

Changed Roles of School Leaders

Reallocation of Authority.   To complicate matters even further during this time of rapid change, education authority has been reallocated in several ways. Because the Reagan Administration devolved, or handed down, much authority to the states—a trend reinforced by every administration since then—the federal government has less authority over education than it did in 1980. For example, the shift from categorical to block grants gave state governments more discretionary power over federal education funds than they had previously exercised.

The states, however, did not usually pass their new power on to districts and their school boards. Not only did they keep it in the state capitals, but they also took power away from local districts and made it their own. Of course, states have long had the ultimate legal authority over U.S. school systems. In 1916 in *Macqueen v. City Comm. of Port Huron* (194 Mich. 328, 160 N.W. 627), a Michigan court held that "the general policy of the state has been to retain control of its school system, to be administered throughout the state under state laws by local state agencies" (cited in Alexander & Alexander, 1985, p. 87). This Michigan ruling is consistent with the legal status of public education in all fifty states. Legally, local school districts are "state agencies." Even so, until recently most states delegated much of their authority to school boards. As long as they worked effectively with their boards, district office administrators had considerable latitude to develop education policy within school districts.

In the early 1980s, state legislatures began to take back some of their authority. Curriculum policy, for example, had traditionally been the domain of local educators. This has changed. During the 1980s, states such as Florida and Texas—in which state governments had traditionally said little or nothing about curriculum—passed basic skills curricula and statewide testing programs. In the 1990s, state standards became commonplace in many states. Even states such as New York and California, where legislatures had historically exercised some jurisdiction over curriculum, intensified their control over it. Several states have also passed "state takeover" legislation. Under such laws, school districts that are deemed "deficient" according to state criteria can be taken over and operated by state officials. New Jersey and Illinois are just two of the states in which takeovers have occurred. Finally, in the mid-1980s many education reformers started advocating site-based management. At least one state, Kentucky, has mandated it, and numerous districts in other states practice it. Site-based management moves considerable authority from the district to the building level. In the new configuration of education authority, then, the federal and district levels have lost power, and state and building levels have gained it (Fowler, 2000).

District Leadership. Not so long ago, most superintendents and other district leaders could do their jobs effectively while largely ignoring the rest of the world. They needed to understand how to work with their school board, manage district finances, select competent personnel, and build community support. Two or three times a year they visited the state capital for a legislative briefing, and once a year they attended a national conference to hear about the latest innovations. The rest of the time they tended shop at home.

The extent to which times have changed is suggested by Kowalski's (1995) study of seventeen big city superintendents. To his surprise, he found that most of the major problems that these school leaders identified were not local issues, but state and national ones. He wrote:

> Before conducting the interviews . . . I thought that the superintendents would be preoccupied with ideas that related to forcing public schools to be more competitive. Instead, what I heard

centered largely on issues that can be classified as "those essentially beyond the control of the superintendents and even their school boards." They are issues such as poverty, federal, and state funding of public education, crime, and the like. (Kowalski, 1995, p. 139)

Kowalski does not suggest what superintendents might do to address these issues. However, in her study of twelve superintendents in the Northeast, Johnson (1996) does. She argues that today, effective superintendents must understand politics at three levels: school, district, and state. She asserts that fighting for funding may well include "organizing coalitions of local leaders to petition legislators in the statehouse" (p. 156) and "challenging a finance committee's inadequate budget allocation for education" (p. 156). In her last chapter, she sketches the dimensions of the new political role of district leaders. Superintendents and their central office teams must understand how their district interfaces with "government, business, community groups, and social agencies" (p. 273). They must monitor developments in these arenas and be prepared to enter them on behalf of their districts when necessary.

Building Leadership.   Even more than district leaders, building administrators have traditionally been insulated—and isolated—from the pressures of the outside world. For the most part, they stayed within their four walls, making occasional forays to district meetings. No one expected them to follow state politics, or even the policy developments in neighboring districts. In the 1990s, however, several education reform movements began to break down this isolation. Under site-based management policies, for example, principals and assistant principals are likely to find themselves dealing directly with state policy makers. Goode (1994) studied two Kentucky high schools using site-based decision making. She found that the principals frequently had direct dealings with officials in the state capital. The principals and their councils had attended training sessions offered by the state department of education, and they had to submit their professional development plans to the state for approval, not to their school board. One of the principals had even applied for waivers from certain board policies. In order to do so, she first had to obtain rulings from the state attorney general's office. Other current reform movements that imply a need for greater sensitivity to the state policy environment on the part of building leaders include interdistrict open enrollment, charter schools, and state mandated standards. For principals, too, the days when they could close their doors and forget everything else have ended.

Public Leadership.   Public school administrators are being transformed from bureaucratic leaders into what Bryson and Crosby (1992) call "public leaders." They argue that bureaucratic leaders can rely heavily on authority and rational decision making because they work within organizations that accord them high hierarchical status. Of course, superintendents, principals, and other administrators still function bureaucratically within their school districts. Increasingly, however, they are called upon to act outside their districts and to function as leaders in networks of organizations. For school leaders, these networks often include the leaders of organizations such as the state legislature, the juvenile justice system, other school districts, local chapters of national advocacy groups, and city or state human services departments. In these networks they have no hierarchical status; rather, they must rely on such leadership tools as persuasion, coalition building, and political strategies. Effective action in such arenas requires an understanding of the broader socioeconomic context within which schools are located and an awareness of the policy environment. In short, it requires an understanding of policy issues and processes.

DEFINING *POLICY*
A Brief Definition

When one begins to explore a new field, being armed with a few definitions is usually helpful. The term *policy* derives from political science. Political science is a deeply divided field (Almond, 1990), and the various camps understand policy and related concepts in different ways. These disagreements grow out of philosophical conflicts over the nature of society, the meaning of power, and the proper role of government. The following series of definitions illustrates the range of interpretations of the term. They are ordered from the narrowest to the broadest.

1. [Public policy is] "the expressed intentions of government actors relative to a public problem and the activities related to those intentions" (Dubnick & Bardes, 1983, p. 8).

2. [Public policy is the] "outputs of a political system, usually in the form of rules, regulations, laws, ordinances, court decisions, administrative decisions, and other forms. Public policy may be perceived as a pattern of activity applied . . . consistently and repetitively. . . . [It is] a dynamic process" (Kruschke & Jackson, 1987, p. 35).

3. [Public policy is] "substantive decisions, commitments, and actions made by those who hold or affect government positions of authority, as they are interpreted by various stakeholders" (Bryson & Crosby, 1992, p. 63).

4. "A policy is sometimes the outcome of a political compromise among policy makers, none of whom had in mind quite the problem to which the argued policy is the solution. . . . And sometimes policies are not decided upon, but nevertheless 'happen'" (Lindblom, 1968, p. 4).

5. "Policy as a chain of decisions stretching from the statehouse to the classroom is a byproduct of [many] games and relationships; no one is responsible for the whole thing" (Firestone, 1989, p. 23).

6. [Public policy] "includes both official enactments of government and something as informal as 'practices.' Also, policy may be viewed as the inactions of government, not simply what the government does" (Cibulka, 1995, p. 106).

7. "Policy is clearly a matter of 'the authoritative allocation of values. . . .' [A policy] project[s] images of an ideal society" (Ball, 1990, p. 3).

In this book *policy* will be understood broadly because school leaders' involvement in the policy process tends to be multifaceted. The following short definition indicates the way the term will be used: *Public policy is the dynamic and value laden process through which a political system handles a public problem. It includes a government's expressed intentions and official enactments as well as its consistent patterns of activity and inactivity.*

In this definition, *government* includes elected and appointed public officials at the federal, state, and local levels as well as the bodies or agencies within which these officials work. Thus, school board members, school administrators, and classroom teachers in public schools are all part of government as are such individuals and groups as governors, judges, and Congress.

At this point some readers may be wondering how one can determine what a government's policy on any particular issue is. The following sections, therefore, will discuss in some detail how public policy relates to various aspects of government activity. Throughout these sections, the racial segregation policy of the United States' past will be used for illustrative purposes because it beautifully illustrates the broad range of issues involved in determining what policy a government is following.

Policy and Expressed Government Intentions—Racial Segregation

To a great extent, politics is about communication, both written and spoken. Government officials communicate frequently—through campaign speeches, televised talk show appearances, decisions reached in hearings, reports, and the Internet. In determining the overall shape of a government's approach to a particular public problem, examining this communication for clues is helpful. For example, if a European scholar had visited the United States in 1950 and sought to determine the U.S. policy on racial segregation in public schools, he would probably have looked for evidence in this body of political communication. Undoubtedly, such a scholar would have found public pronouncements made by southern leaders, who were already beginning to feel pressure from civil rights groups. Many of their statements would have clearly indicated that they were pursuing and intended to continue to pursue a policy of racial segregation in public schools. The European probably would *not* have found similar public pronouncements made by such political figures as the governors of Colorado and Massachusetts or the mayor of Columbus, Ohio. Concluding from this pattern of open expression and silence that racial segregation was a policy in the South, but not in the North, would have been wrong. During the 1970s, federal courts would find many school districts guilty of pursuing racial segregation policies, including those located in Denver, Detroit, and Columbus (Alexander & Alexander, 1998; La Morte, 1993; McCarthy & Cambron-McCabe, 1998).

Policy, Law, and Racial Segregation

Policy and Statutes.   When most people use the term *law*, they actually mean *statutes*—laws enacted by legislatures. Fifty-one legislatures are active in the United States—Congress and fifty state legislatures—and their legislation is an important clue to governmental policy. If one is seeking to determine what the policy really is, certainly one of the first sources to consult is the written law. However, law and policy are not identical. Many outdated laws are still on the books but are never enforced; some laws are purely symbolic (Edelman, 1964) and were passed to help citizens feel better about a problem but were never really intended to address it. Moreover, not every policy appears in statutes. The European scholar studying racial segregation policy would certainly have consulted the laws passed by federal and state governments. He would have found that in seventeen states and the District of Columbia segregation was mandatory and that it was optional in four other states (Alexander & Alexander, 1998; La Morte, 1993; McCarthy & Cambron-McCabe, 1998). The other twenty-nine states had no statutes in place regarding racial segregation in schools. This would not have meant, however, that they did not practice racial segregation. Ultimately, the U.S. Supreme Court would distinguish *de jure* segregation policies, based on statutes, from *de facto* segregation policies, based on official practice. It would rule that both were equally serious violations of the law.

Policy, Rules and Regulations, and Racial Segregation.   Most statutes are worded in general terms, and many of the details needed to put them into practice are not written in the statute itself. These details are usually provided by rules and regulations that government agencies develop. At the state level, the state department of education and state board of education usually exercise this responsibility. Local school boards also have the authority to develop some rules and regulations. As with statutes, these rules and regulations provide important clues as to what the policy really is. Whether the rules are narrowly or broadly written is especially important to note. Broadly worded rules give considerable flexibility to educators who are lower in the hierarchy, while narrow ones give very little flexibility. Some rules may address issues that are not covered in state or federal statutes. For example, in 1973 the U.S. Supreme Court found that the Denver School Board had an official neighborhood school policy that it had used to develop a racially segregated school system (McCarthy & Cambron-McCabe, 1998). This rule, passed by a local education agency, was an important clue to the policy that the system was really following. Chapter 8 explains the relationship between statutes and rules and regulations.

Policy, Court Decisions, and Racial Segregation.   Under the U.S. judicial system, courts have the right to review statutes in order to interpret them and to evaluate their constitutionality. Courts can also overturn earlier court decisions. This means that court decisions are part of the law; in fact, they are called *case law*. Our European scholar, researching segregation policy in 1950, would have discovered that U.S. school segregation policies had first been upheld by a Massachusetts court in the 1850s (Alexander & Alexander, 1998). This early decision had been reinforced by a related 1896 Supreme Court case, *Plessy v. Ferguson* (163 U.S. 537). In this suit, an African-American resident of Louisiana had challenged racial segregation on trains, alleging that this practice violated the equal protection clause of the Fourteenth Amendment. The court's majority had disagreed, ruling that racial segregation was constitutional as long as the facilities provided the races were "equal" (Alexander & Alexander, 1998; McCarthy & Cambron-McCabe, 1998). Later decisions applied the "separate but equal" doctrine to education. In this situation, case law was a more reliable indicator of policy than statute. It suggested that racial segregation could be legally practiced anywhere in the country. Our European scholar would have been mistaken, however, if he had concluded that the education facilities provided for children of different races were always—or even usually—equal.

Policy, Budgets, and Racial Segregation. Virtually all government bodies and agencies adopt budgets either annually or biennially. In legislatures the committees that determine the level of funding to support an education statute are different from the committees that determine its wording. In essence, two battles occur during the passage of any statute—a battle over words and a battle over dollars. Both are important clues to the seriousness with which a government is pursuing a policy. Moreover, funding levels for most education policies are reconsidered regularly and are subject to upward or downward revision. This means that, in order to determine what policy a government is pursuing, considering both the initial funding level and funding trends over time is essential. Our European scholar would have been well advised to consider budgets, financial reports, and other documents relating to education funding in his efforts to figure out the real policy on racial segregation. Financial studies that were carried out at the time clearly demonstrated that "separate but equal" education for the races was not the policy that U.S. states and school boards were pursuing. African-American children were consistently disadvantaged in resource allocation, being assigned to the oldest school buildings and provided with outdated textbooks and equipment. Careful analyses of spending trends would have suggested that the real policy was "separate and unequal" education.

Implementation, Policy, and Racial Segregation. Policies are usually developed close to the top of the political system. Presidents and governors make speeches; legislators develop statutes and pass budgets; judges issue court decisions. Policies are put into practice close to the grass roots. In education, the implementors of most policies are superintendents and their staffs, principals, and classroom teachers. Educators are not robots who mechanically carry out orders issued from above. They are human beings with minds of their own, making decisions in a specific social and cultural context that they understand better than presidents, governors, legislators, and judges. All policies are therefore mediated through the context in which they are implemented, and change in the process. These changes may take the form of minor adjustments or major transformations, but policies are *always* altered during implementation (Mazmanian & Sabatier, 1989). In determining what the real policy is, then, considering how the policy is implemented is essential. Our European researcher would have been wise to visit schools for both races to see what was happening and to talk with people there. Direct observation would probably have confirmed the inequalities suggested by the financial records. Conversations with grassroots implementors might also have provided insights into why "separate but equal" education tended to become "separate and unequal" when put into practice. Undoubtedly, the values of the implementors and their communities as well as political and economic pressures would have emerged as part of the explanation.

Segregation Policy as Governmental Action and Inaction. Sometimes the nature of the policy that is being followed becomes apparent only after an analysis of consistent patterns of government action and inaction. Our European scholar would have found it relatively easy to determine that racial segregation in public schools was the government's policy in the seventeen states with statutes mandating segregation. In such states little doubt existed, for statements of government intentions, statutes, the U.S. Supreme Court's decisions, and the allocation of education funds were all consistent, making the policy clear. The European scholar would have found determining the policy followed in northern states more difficult. There, signals were mixed. However, a study of repeated patterns of action would have made it clearer. Eventually, the U.S. Supreme Court relied on such patterns in ruling that many northern cities were practicing *de facto* segregation. For example, in *Keyes v. School District No. 1, Denver* (413 U.S. 189), the court identified several tactics that Denver had used to create a segregated school system. In addition to the neighborhood school policy mentioned earlier, the Denver school board had habitually manipulated attendance zones, selected sites for new buildings that maintained racial segregation, and used mobile classroom units to avoid integration. The result of all these actions, repeated consistently and over time, was a racially segregated system. Thus, Denver was following a policy of racial segregation in its schools and was declared in violation of federal law in 1973 (Alexander and Alexander, 1998; McCarthy & Cambron-McCabe, 1998).

Patterns of government inaction became evident after *Brown v. Board of Education of Topeka* (347 U.S. 483) declared racial segregation illegal. Although the U.S. Supreme Court's decision had become the law of the land, superseding all laws inconsistent with it, neither southern nor northern school districts rushed to dismantle segregation. Instead, they adopted patterns of inaction that, in some cases, endured for many years. Fifteen years after *Brown*, a federal district court ordered the Charlotte–Mecklenburg School District in North Carolina to create a desegregation plan (Alexander & Alexander, 1998). Ten years later other federal courts gave the Dayton and Columbus districts similar instructions (McCarthy & Cambron-McCabe, 1998). What was happening in those districts during the years after the *Brown* decision was handed down? School administrators in Charlotte–Mecklenburg, Dayton, and Columbus were certainly not unaware of the U.S. Supreme Court decision or of the possibility that their practices were violating it. Nor is it likely that legislators, governors, and judges in North Carolina and Ohio were unaware of the court's ruling or of the fact that some districts in their states continued to practice segregation. Rather, we must conclude that school officials had adopted a pattern of inaction that was tacitly supported by the inaction of their state governments. In those states—and many others—racial segregation continued to be the policy long after it had ceased to be lawful.

THE POLICY PROCESS

The policy process is the sequence of events that occurs when a political system considers different approaches to public problems, adopts one of them, tries it out, and evaluates it. Political scientists often use game metaphors to describe it. Like a game, the policy process has rules and players. Like a game, it is complex and often disorderly. Like a game, it is played in many arenas and involves the use of power. And like a game, it can have winners and losers (Firestone, 1989; Lindblom, 1968). The process is driven by policy issues (Bryson & Crosby, 1992). Therefore, the opening part of this section discusses policy issues. After that, the classical stage model of the policy process is briefly presented. Each of the stages is developed later in this book. The stage model has weaknesses because it suggests that the policy process is more orderly and also more rational than it really is (Cibulka, 1995; Lindblom, 1968). However, it does provide a helpful framework for organizing information and for investigating how policies change.

Policy Issues

Controversial Elements. A policy issue is, by definition, controversial. An issue exists only if social groups disagree about how government should approach a given problem (Coplin & O'Leary, 1981). Most education policies are not *policy issues* at all. For example, the policy goal of teaching all children to read is not an issue today. Virtually everyone in the United States—liberal and conservative, rich and poor, male and female, white, African American, and Hispanic—agrees that children need to learn how to read. Two centuries ago, however, the proposal that all children should attain literacy *was* a policy issue. At that time, most people considered reading an appropriate skill only for children from relatively affluent backgrounds. In many states, teaching slaves to read was illegal, and Native Americans were widely believed incapable of learning. Moreover, children from the large rural segment of the population—especially girls—did not usually learn to read. The goal of universal literacy ceased to be a policy issue over the next 200 years—but only after hard-fought battles in courts and state legislatures.

Public Element. Many disagreements about how children should be socialized are not policy issues, either. Policy issues are problems that the government can legitimately address. For example, psychologists disagree about the appropriateness of toy guns and war weapons for children. Some argue that such toys encourage violence, whereas others deny that allegation. However, this disagreement is not a policy issue because no government in the United States is likely to try to deal with it. In the U.S. political culture, a sharp line of demarcation exists between private problems that concern the family, and public issues that fall within the scope of government authority. Few Americans—even those who disapprove of toy weapons—believe that government policies about them would be appropriate.

Examples of Education Policy Issues.   In these early years of the twenty-first century, a large number of education policy issues are under debate. One especially controversial issue is school choice. Traditionally, school districts have had the authority to assign children to schools, usually on the basis of geographic attendance zones. Since the early 1980s, however, this practice has become an issue. Many people and interest groups argue that parents should be free to choose their child's school. They have therefore proposed such new policies as voucher plans, intradistrict and interdistrict open enrollment, and charter schools. Such policies have been adopted in many states. School choice has many opponents also. They argue that choice will weaken public education and increase the segregation of schools along race and class lines (Chubb & Moe, 1990; Cookson, 1994). Another education policy issue relates to establishing national curriculum standards. Advocates of national curriculum standards assert that they would provide clear criteria for excellence throughout the country and reduce the negative impact of mobility on children's schooling. They also argue that most other advanced industrial countries have national curricula and that because of global economic competition the United States should follow suit. Opponents of such a policy believe that it would weaken local control of education and lead to an undesirable standardization of education throughout the country. They also argue that the federal government lacks the constitutional authority to establish national curriculum standards or develop national tests to evaluate it. Both school choice and a national curriculum are policy issues because they are controversial and because they are policies that the government might adopt.

Applying the Stage Model to Standards-Based Reform

Figure 1.1 represents the classical stage model of the policy process, with minor modifications. It should be read from left to right because issue definition is the first stage in the process chronologically. The heavy arrows move from left to right, following the order of the classical model. However, lighter arrows move from right to left because sometimes a policy issue advances for a while and then moves back to an earlier stage. The diagram is shaped like a funnel because the process functions selectively; at each successive stage fewer issues or policies are involved. In the following sections, each stage of the process is briefly discussed. Throughout these sections, a single policy issue—standards-based reform—is used as an example. This discussion of standards-based reform relies heavily on books by Fuhrman (2001), Jennings (1998), and Ravitch (1995).

Issue Definition.   At any given time, every society has numerous social problems, but only a few are ever identified as public policy problems. For many rea-

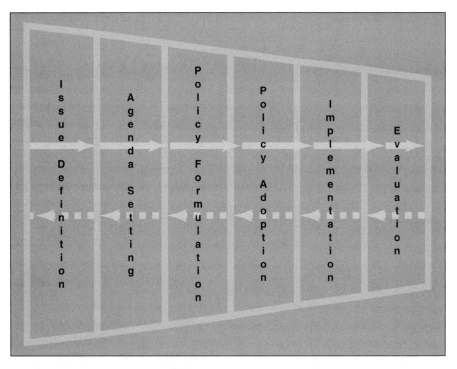

Figure 1.1 A diagram of the policy process.

sons, government never addresses most problems. Sufficient political support may not exist, for example, or the potential costs of addressing certain problems may be too high.

Standards-based reform provides a good example of a policy area that for many decades was not an issue. Although states set up public school systems and mandated school attendance during the nineteenth century, they delegated almost all of their authority to local school districts (Fowler, 2000). Throughout most of the twentieth century, they continued to let local school districts have broad latitude in the areas of curriculum and pedagogy, concentrating most of their regulatory efforts on educational inputs such as pupil–teacher ratios, teachers' qualifications, and per-pupil expenditure. However, in the mid-1970s national organizations and leaders began to express concern about performance. For example, the College Board publicly reported the fact that SAT scores had been declining since 1963. In 1981, the Southern Regional Education Board—which represented fifteen southern states—published a report called *The Need for Quality*, attacking the minimum competency reforms of the previous decade (Ravitch, 1995). However, it was the *Nation at Risk* report which most dramatically defined the quality issue in 1983. President Reagan used it as a springboard for redefining the key education issues not as access and equity, but as the need for increased excellence (Cook, 2001; Fuhrman, 2001; Ravitch, 1995).

Spearheaded by presidential rhetoric, the states launched numerous incremental reforms such as increasing graduation requirements. By the end of the decade, however, these reforms were generally perceived as inadequate. Concerns about the poor performance of American students on international tests in science and mathematics led leaders to examine the education policies of other nations. Learning that most developed countries had national content standards and tests, they began to redefine the problem of the supposedly poor quality of education in the United States as the lack of clear curriculum standards and tests to assess curriculum mastery (Ravitch, 1995). Issue definition is discussed in greater depth in Chapter 7.

Agenda Setting.   Not every problem defined as an education policy issue is acted on by a government. In order to have a chance of eventually becoming policy, an issue must be placed on the policy agenda, or "list of subjects or problems to which governmental officials, and people outside government closely associated with those officials, are paying some serious attention at any given time" (Kingdon, 1995, p. 3). The policy agenda is usually set by powerful politicians, such as presidents, governors, and legislators.

Unlike many policy issues, standards-based reform reached the national policy agenda not long after it was defined as an issue. In the mid-1980s, Secretary of Education William Bennett was a prominent, vocal spokesman for higher intellectual standards in the nation's schools. In 1987, two books which were widely read and discussed—Allan Bloom's *The Closing of the American Mind* and E. D. Hirsch, Jr.'s *Cultural Literacy*—pushed the issue into the national limelight. In the fall of 1989, President Bush and the nation's governors, who were under considerable pressure from business leaders, developed a set of national education "goals" which the president announced in his 1990 State of the Union Address. He also set up a National Education Goals Panel to monitor progress towards achieving them. Although the term used at this point was *goals* rather than *standards*, the issue was now squarely on both the state and national policy agendas (Jennings, 1998; Ravitch, 1995). Sometimes the activities of grassroots organizations influence political leaders' agendas. For example, in both Milwaukee and Cleveland the voucher issue was placed on the state policy agenda at least in part because of the efforts of grassroots African-American organizers. However, no evidence of any grassroots activity in support of standards-based reform is available. Agenda setting is also discussed in Chapter 7.

Policy Formulation.   Before a policy can be formally adopted, it must be expressed in written form. The first written text developed is usually a *bill*, a draft of a proposed statute. Most legislators in Congress and state legislatures do not write the bills they sponsor. Bills may be developed by members of their legislative staff, by lawyers retained for that purpose, or by advocacy groups who support the legislation. Often rival bills on the same subject are introduced into a legislature for consideration. Rules and regulations are written after statutes have been adopted. They, too, may pass through several drafts before becoming official. Those groups and individuals that advocate standards-based reform have cooperated nationwide to influence policy formulation. This is why, for example, a strong resemblance exists among the curriculum standards and testing programs of many states (Ravitch, 1995). Policy formulation is described in Chapter 8.

Policy Adoption.   In order for a policy to take effect, its written formulation must be officially adopted by the appropriate body. Statutes are adopted by a majority vote in Congress and state legislatures. In public education, rules and regulations are adopted by authorized officials within agencies such as the U.S. Department of Education, state departments of education, and local school districts. Some district policies, but not all, require a majority vote by a school board.

Under the first Bush Administration, two bills that endorsed standards and tests were introduced in Congress; both failed. Clinton defeated Bush in the 1992 election, but he advocated national standards and tests during his campaign. His administration tried to get Congress to pass a standards-based reform bill in 1993, but failed. However, a rewritten version of that earlier bill was passed in 1994 as the Goals 2000: Educate America Act. It set up an agency called the National Education Standards and Improvement Council to develop voluntary national standards; national tests were not included because of strong political opposition. Moreover, in 1994 the reauthorization of the Elementary and Secondary Education Act (ESEA) linked Title I funds to standards-based reform (Jennings, 1998; Ravitch, 1995). Finally, the second Bush Administration's reauthorization of ESEA, called the No Child Left Behind Act of 2001, further strengthened the policy language in support of standards and testing. Policy adoption is presented in detail in Chapter 8.

Implementation.   The passage of a statute and accompanying rules and regulations does not mean the new policy automatically goes into operation. Education policies must be implemented at the grassroots level—by district administrators, principals, and classroom teachers. These educators are not necessarily enthusiastic about new laws and rules that come down from Washington or their state capital. Therefore, the success of implementation depends upon motivating educators to implement the new policy and providing them with the necessary resources to do so. Research suggests that often new policies are either not implemented at all or are substantially modified during implementation. By 2000, forty-nine states had adopted legislation establishing curriculum standards. However, research by the Urban Institute and the Consortium for Policy Research in Education (CPRE) suggests that implementation at the district and school levels has been uneven, with some aspects of the reforms used more widely than others (DeBray, Parson, & Woodworth, 2001; Fuhrman, 2001; Hannaway & Kimball, 2001). Policy implementation is discussed in Chapter 10.

Evaluation.   Ideally, policies are evaluated in order to determine if they work the way they are supposed to. *Evaluation* is a form of applied research designed to achieve this purpose. Sometimes policies are evaluated by a research office within the government that passed the policy. Evaluations may also be conducted by outside consulting firms or by universities or think tanks that do this kind of work. Although standards-based reform is supposed to raise student achievement, its effectiveness is still unclear. A number of programs have been evaluated, generally by curriculum writers who have a vested interest in the success of their own curricula. In 2002 the National Science Foundation (NSF) commissioned a review of existing evaluations, scheduled to be released in 2003. However, these findings may also be biased since the NSF has been a major advocate of standards (Hoff, 2002, June 12). For the time being, at least, standards-based reform has not been adequately evaluated. Policy evaluation is the subject of Chapter 11.

POLICY ANALYSIS
A Brief Definition

Policy analysis has been defined as the "evaluation of alternative government policies or decisions in order to arrive at the best (or a good) policy or decision in light of given goals, constraints, and conditions" (Nagel, 1984, p. xiii). The traditional focus of policy analysis has been, as Nagel suggests, the generation of alternatives as well as the study of the effects of existing policies (Brewer & de Leon, 1983). In recent years, however, the field has expanded. Today, analysts also develop methods for implementing, evaluating, and terminating policies. Thus, their work frequently involves the study of both values and the political environment (Weimer & Vining, 1992).

A Brief History

Although government has a long history of occasionally commissioning research on policy alternatives, heavy reliance on such research—or policy analysis—is a relatively recent phenomenon. Economists began to research policy alternatives for the federal government in the early twentieth century, when science and "experts" were idealized. During the 1930s, the New Deal government made a practice of publishing some of the statistics that economists gathered. However, policy analysis did not come into its own until after World War II. During that time the U.S. Departments of State and Labor employed numerous economists to gather data, analyze them, and make recommendations based upon their findings (Nelson, 1991; Weimer & Vining, 1992).

The late 1960s saw the emergence of a large number of social issues and the passage of pioneering legislation. The federal education policies that were part of the War on Poverty stimulated the rapid growth of education policy analysis, much of it carried out by think tanks rather than the government. Analysts produced several important studies of education policy during the 1970s. For example, Congress mandated an evaluation of the Elementary and Secondary Education Act of 1965, which the National Institute of Education carried out. This study cost $15 million, and in 1978 Congress used it to amend the law. Another famous study of this period was the RAND Change Agent Study, produced by the RAND Corporation, a California think tank. It researched the results of 293 federal education projects. The findings of the Change Agent Study about policy implementation have been influential. The Carter Administration used the RAND study to develop some of its education policy proposals (Boyd, 1988).

Twenty years ago, Mitchell (1984) analyzed the entries on education policy in the Educational Resources Information Center (ERIC) between 1969 and 1981. He found that the percentage of entries relating to education policy had steadily increased during this period. ERIC published 28,000 pieces on the subject between 1975 and 1981 alone (Mitchell, 1984). Since the education reform movement began about 1983, education policy analysis has become increasingly important. Cibulka (1995) observed that policy studies in education had largely replaced the studies of education politics that were popular in the 1960s and 1970s. The growing importance of education policy analysis is suggested by the fact that in 1996 the American Educational Research Association established a new division to specialize in policy studies and the politics of education.

Objectives of Policy Analysis

The overall objective of policy analysis is to improve the quality of public policy. It is based on the well-founded premises that the policy process is not fully rational and that politicians, if left to themselves, often develop unsound policies. In contrast to political leaders, most policy analysts—usually people with doctorates who work for think tanks or universities—value a logical approach to policy issues. Through their work they hope to influence the policy process by providing information and suggesting a range of solutions to public problems. Of course, politicians are not obligated to use the results of policy analysis in developing laws even if they have commissioned an expensive study. As a result, analysts often feel frustrated. However, an indisputable strength of policy analysis is that it offers everyone who is interested in policy a variety of frameworks they can use in thinking about it.

Types of Policy Analysis

Coplin and O'Leary (1981) identify four types of policy analysis. Although many other typologies could be used to conceptualize the field (e.g., Mitchell, 1984), their scheme is useful for suggesting the range of studies that analysts conduct. The first type of policy analysis is monitoring. When researchers monitor, they systematically collect data relevant to a policy domain and to the ongoing policy process. For example, during the 1980s many states established systems for gathering education information from school districts. These data are entered in computers and allow state officials to track such phenomena as student attendance, test scores, and the percentage of children enrolled in the free lunch program. A second form of analysis is forecasting. Drawing on large data banks, policy researchers try to predict what policy issues will be important in five to ten years. For example, they may notice from their monitoring that increasing numbers of children are involved in free lunch programs and predict that child nutrition will probably be an important issue for schools in 2010. Many policy studies are evaluations. When researchers evaluate a policy or program, their objective is to provide information about how well the policy is achieving the purposes for which it was designed. Remedial and experimental education programs are often evaluated to determine if they do, indeed, help children learn better.

Coplin and O'Leary (1981) suggest that a secondary meaning of *evaluation* is studying a policy in depth to determine what values underlie it. Because ideology is becoming increasingly important in U.S. politics (Lowi, 1995), this type of evaluation is becoming common. The growing interest of policy researchers in discursive analysis—the close study of policy texts and the practices associated with them—is evidence of growing attention to values in education policy (Corson, 1995; Marshall, 2000; Yanow, 2000). Finally, policy analysts may offer prescriptions. Prescriptive policy analysis outlines the options open to policy makers and may recommend which would be most desirable.

THE SCHOOL LEADER AND POLICY STUDIES

School administrators act as hierarchical leaders within their organizations and as public leaders in the broader community. In both roles they play, or can play, a significant part in defining, developing, and implementing education policy. Although their multidimensional role is developed in detail in later chapters, understanding the general nature of that role from the outset will be helpful for readers.

Administrators as Policy Makers

Legally, school districts are agencies of the government of the state within which they are located, just as the bureau of motor vehicles and the state highway department are state agencies (Alexander & Alexander, 1998). As a result, school administrators play a major role in the development of rules and regulations. In most policy areas, the state legislature and its state education agency provide a broad framework of legislation. School boards, administrators, and classroom teachers are responsible for filling in many of the details of that framework. Their policy making takes such forms as recommending a policy revision to the school board, developing a manual of rules for classified staff, or writing a student discipline code for a school. No matter what the situation, a knowledge of policy and the policy process is helpful to administrators in their policymaking role. For example, if a principal perceives that insufficient parking is becoming an issue for her faculty, a knowledge of the policy process will suggest to her several courses of action. If the issue is still in the early stages, she may choose to participate in defining it. A knowledge of policy studies will suggest some ways to do that. If it is already clearly defined—and she agrees with the definition—she may appoint a committee to work with her to carry out an informal policy analysis and generate alternatives for discussion. An understanding of the range of policy instruments available will enable her to enter the discussion with several creative ideas and to assess alternatives suggested by others. Ultimately, her expertise should permit her and the teachers to develop a sound rule that will deal effectively with the problem.

Administrators as Implementors of Policy

Within their organizations school administrators also play a major role in implementing new policies. Whether the new policy originated at the federal, state, or local level, they will be expected to develop a plan to carry it out, motivate teachers and others to cooperate, marshal the necessary resources, and provide feedback about the process. Change is always difficult, so administrators who are responsible for implementing a new, possibly unpopular, policy find themselves in a challenging situation. Under stress, they are likely to make mistakes. Yet, much research has been done on implementation, much of it specifically on the implementation of education policy. The major mistakes that implementors make were identified long ago; so were sound approaches to organizational change. School administrators who are familiar with this literature will be well-equipped to avoid the most obvious pitfalls of implementation. They will also know some ways to reduce the stress and confusion that are inevitable components of putting any new policy in place.

Administrators as Followers of Policy Issues

School leaders of the early twenty-first century cannot restrict themselves to building and district level concerns, however. State governments are more active in education policy than ever before, and education is considered a "hot" issue at both the state and federal levels. This means that administrators who try to ignore the outside world will find themselves on the receiving end of many policy surprises. They will also begin to feel as if they have no input into many of the reforms occurring. Today, therefore, following policy issues is essential for school leaders. They need to be aware of the major changes occurring in their social and economic environment and of how those changes may eventually give rise to education policy issues. They need to know what issues are being defined in think tanks, universities, and foundations. They also need to follow the legislative process at the federal and state levels. More than ever, then, it is essential for school leaders to be professionally active and informed. Such activity is the indispensable foundation for being a knowledgeable and active participant in the policy process beyond the limits of the district.

Administrators as Influencers of Policy

In their capacity as public leaders (Bryson & Crosby, 1992), school administrators are in a position to exercise influence on the policy process at the state and federal levels. This influence can take many forms. A superintendent may call the state department of education to discuss the problems he is having implementing a program. This conversation may lead to a change in the department's rules and regulations. Or a special education supervisor may believe that a new bill in the legislature is unfair to the state's handicapped children. This belief may lead her to identify several other supervisors and leaders of parent organizations who share her views. Together they may make an appointment with the chair of the House Education Committee to discuss the issue. They may alert several professional organizations to the problem and obtain their support. These efforts may lead to the defeat of the bill or to amendments that reduce its negative impact. Or a principal may become involved in a school–university partnership that includes a number of agencies that work with children. This collaboration may make him and everyone else aware of overlaps and contradictions in the services delivered to at-risk children. After defining the issue carefully, the principal and other participants may coordinate a simultaneous approach to all their respective state agencies to inform them of the problem.

FINAL POINTS

Today's school leaders have a different role than they did in the past. In part, this new role involves exercising public leadership. School leaders who do not learn how to exercise this new role are likely to be the passive recipients of a sequence of policy surprises. Effective public leadership at the beginning of the twenty-first century requires a solid foundation of knowledge about education policy and how it is developed and changed. This book provides that foundation.

QUESTIONS AND ACTIVITIES FOR DISCUSSION

1. Develop a list of current policy issues in your state, district, or building. Situate each in a stage of the policy process.
2. What major education policy initiatives has your state government made during the last decade? How have the initiatives affected your school and district?
3. Select one of the following policy issues and describe the current status of your state's policy regarding this issue: school finance equity, school choice, the level of student achievement, or accountability for teachers and administrators. Be sure to consider not only formal laws but also funding levels and patterns of government inaction.

4. Identify and describe an instance in which school administrators you know have acted as public leaders to influence the policy process.

PRO–CON DEBATE: SHOULD POLITICS BE KEPT OUT OF EDUCATION?

YES: The education of our children is much too important to permit it to become entangled with politics. Of course, because public money funds public schools some form of government oversight must exist. Ideally this oversight should be provided by a governance body chosen through nonpartisan elections. It should have the authority to provide general policy guidelines for the schools. However, those policies should be carried out by professional educators who have considerable freedom to act without interference. After all, professionals are knowledgeable about children, curriculum, and teaching methods. They may make mistakes, but they are more likely to make decisions in the best interests of children than are politicians. Politics and education do not mix.

NO: Public schools are funded by tax money and are under the authority of state legislatures, school boards, and the courts. This means that politics *cannot* be kept out of public education. Even when education is governed by "nonpartisan" boards, political activity continues. However, it is relatively quiet and hidden, making it difficult for ordinary citizens to understand and influence it. Openness about the political nature of education is more democratic and can encourage leaders to develop governance structures and laws that facilitate healthy political activity. The idea that politics and education do not mix is an illusion.

What do YOU think?

NEWS STORY FOR ANALYSIS: *PROPOSAL FOR MORE TESTING DRAWS CRITICISM*

BALTIMORE, MD—The proposal that Maryland could expand its school testing program to more grades is drawing criticism from parents and teachers, who contend that instruction already is too focused on preparing for exams. "Teachers are up to their eyeballs in testing," said Patricia Forester, president of the Maryland State Teachers Association.

The recommendation this week for Maryland to add a new batch of testing for grades four, six, and seven was one of many suggestions from Achieve, Inc., a national nonprofit group that supports standards-based education. The group—which was commissioned by the state to study its reform efforts—is expected to influence the work of a task force appointed by the state superintendent to draw up a 10-year blueprint for public education in Maryland. Both groups recommended that Maryland develop a statewide curriculum—a proposal supported by local superintendents as well as by the state superintendent.

But for parents and teachers who contend that schools spend too much time getting third, fifth, and eighth graders ready for the spring exams, the proposal to test more grades prompted a sharp reaction. "All the schools seem to be doing is processing kids for the exams," said Chuck LaPorte, parent of a middle-school child.

In recommending that Maryland expand testing, Achieve officials said such a move would dovetail with President Bush's education plan calling for states to begin annual testing in grades three through eight. Although the House and Senate are still negotiating a final education reform bill, both chambers have passed legislation requiring annual school-wide testing. Most educators believe it will be part of the final federal plan, forcing states such as Maryland to expand their programs.

But if the state were to expand its testing program, it could become a political issue. "I've been hearing that my constituents have a lot of concerns," said Audrey Scott, potential candidate for the Republican gubernatorial nomination. "If we end up with more testing, it could very, very well become part of the next election."

(Adapted by permission of the publisher from H. Libit, "Proposal for More Testing Draws Criticism," *Baltimore Sun*, October 3, 2001, p. 1B. Copyright 2001 by the *Baltimore Sun*.)

Questions

1. What policy issues are mentioned in the article? For each, justify your opinion that it is a policy issue.
2. Situate each policy issue in a stage of the policy process.
3. Describe the policy which the State of Maryland is following.
4. List the political figures and groups mentioned in the article.

FOR FURTHER READING

Bryson, J. M., & Crosby, B. C. (1992). *Leadership for the common good: Tackling public problems in a shared power world.* **San Francisco: Jossey-Bass.**

Bryson and Crosby argue that today, managers in the public sector must assume a public leadership role. Their book includes numerous practical suggestions for dealing with issues at each stage of the policy process.

Cibulka, J. G. (1995). Policy analysis and the study of the politics of education. In J. D. Scribner & D. Layton (Eds.), *The study of educational politics.* **London: Falmer Press.**

Cibulka presents an overview of the field of education politics and policy in the mid-1990s. His discussion of new trends in education policy research is especially interesting.

Johnson, S. M. (1996). *Leading to change: The challenge of the new superintendency.* San Francisco: Jossey-Bass.

Johnson's book is based on an in-depth qualitative study of twelve northeastern superintendents, which included 312 interviews. She presents an interesting and perceptive description of how the superintendency has changed as a result of the turbulent policy environment of the late twentieth century and of how real superintendents are dealing with new challenges.

Marshall, C. (2000). Policy discourse analysis: Negotiating gender equity. *Journal of Education Policy, 15* (2), 125–156.

Marshall applies standard policy analysis procedures as well as discourse analysis to the passage and implementation of gender equity policies in Australian schools. Her article provides a good example of how a policy can be systematically analyzed.

Yanow, D. (2000). *Conducting interpretive policy analysis.* Thousand Oaks, CA: Sage Publications.

Yanow, a professor of public administration, shows how interpretive policy analysis can provide insights into the values and ideological stances of the different stakeholders in a policy environment. Of particular interest is her use of interpretive policy analysis to reveal the "architecture of policy arguments" (p. iii).

POWER AND EDUCATION POLICY

Focus Questions

What is power?

What are the major types and sources of power?

How is power used in school organizations and to shape education policy?

What ethical issues does power raise?

INTRODUCTORY COMMENTS

Power and education policy cannot be separated because "the play of power" shapes the outcome of the policy process (Lindblom, 1968, p. 28). Moreover, because power relations are institutionalized in school systems, school administrators have power through their organizational positions. They have that power in order to carry out the government's education policy as it relates to schools and school systems. In doing so, they also regularly interact with powerful individuals and groups, many of whom wish to influence or circumvent that policy. All school leaders, then, must understand power and the complex issues it raises.

DEFINING POWER

A "Contested" Concept

Power is an "essentially contested" concept (Lukes, 1974, p. 9), which means that one's understanding of it is shaped by one's theory of human nature and society, leading social scientists from different theoretical traditions to argue about its meaning. At one extreme, some utilitarians deny the very existence of power. At the other, some poststructuralists, such as Foucault, believe that power so permeates every human activity that truth itself is determined by it. Between these extremes one finds many positions.

Political scientist Robert Dahl developed one widely used definition: "A has power over B to the extent that he [sic] can get B to do something that B would not otherwise do" (Lukes, 1974, pp. 11–12). Although many people have found Dahl's definition helpful, it leaves certain points obscure: Does A have to be consciously aware of exercising power over B? Does B have to be consciously aware of A's power? Can A's exercise of power cause B not to act? Has A exercised power if B believes that what A wants is good and eagerly performs the desired action? Is it ethical to exercise power over another? The controversy over power swirls around issues such as these. In the next section a working definition of power, situated somewhere between the two extremes represented by the utilitarians and some poststructuralists, is developed for use in this book.

A Working Definition of *Power*

Despite the scholarly controversy, a working definition of power is essential in a book about education policy. The starting point for this definition is Muth's (1984) statement that power is "the ability of an actor to affect the behavior of another actor" (p. 27), a somewhat broader definition than Dahl's. The term *actor* includes both individuals—such as superintendents, governors, and teacher union presidents—and groups—such as school boards, state legislatures, and Parent–Teacher Associations (PTAs). The ability to exercise power depends on possessing appropriate resources, such as money, social status, and information. Power resources are discussed in detail later. Because power resources are limited and a "cost" is attached to using them, actors are not always willing to expend them. Thus, the ability to exercise power includes the willingness to deploy resources. Finally, behavior can be affected in many ways, using one or more general types of power. Possible effects include causing an actor to act, preventing an actor from acting, and shaping the nature of the actor's action. An actor may be conscious, unconscious, or partially conscious of the use of power (Bachrach & Baratz, 1962; Delpit, 1988).

Because power is a relationship, it always exists in a concrete social context. An actor who is relatively powerful in one context may not be in others. For example, a superintendent may be powerful in her community but have little power with the state legislature. Power relationships may be symmetrical or asymmetrical. Actors who have similar degrees of power are symmetrically related, having a "shared power" relationship (Bryson & Crosby, 1992). In symmetrical relationships, people commonly use persuasion and bargaining with economic resources. Actors with significantly different amounts of resources have an asymmetrical power relationship. Although they may use persuasion or bargaining, more powerful actors may also employ force, appeals to authority, or reward and punishment strategies to affect less powerful actors. Even in very asymmetrical relationships, however, weaker actors are rarely powerless. Various forms of resistance are available to them. For example, teachers who resent a state legislature's new testing program may find ways to sabotage it (Apple, 1985; Cherryholmes, 1988).

Power may be exercised either distributively or facilitatively (Mann, 1992). In using power distributively, one actor exercises power over the other. For instance, a superintendent may decide unilaterally that all teachers in his district must punch time clocks, proceed to have the clocks installed, and distribute a memo describing the new procedure. On the other hand, power may be exercised facilitatively to "create or sustain favorable conditions, allow[ing] subordinates to enhance their individual and collective performance" (Dunlap & Goldman, 1991, p. xx). For example, a supervisor may work facilitatively with a group of teachers to establish a computer lab, providing support in the form of information and release time.

Power, like automobiles, can be easily abused, but it is ethically neutral. Although some types of power and some power resources can never be used ethically, leaders can exercise power in an ethical manner. Ethical issues surrounding power are discussed in the final section of this chapter.

DISCOURSE AND POWER

School Administration as Talk

Language is important in school leadership. To a great extent school administration is achieved through talk: talk in meetings, talk in random hallway encounters, talk on the telephone, talk to the media, and talk on the grapevine. Research indicates that principals and superintendents spend 67% to 75% of their time talking (Gronn, 1983). This means that when school leaders exercise power or experience its pressure on their own behavior, that power is usually communicated through language. As Corson (1995) puts it: "All kinds of power are directed, mediated, or resisted through language" (p. 3).

Since about 1970 scholars in every branch of the social sciences have devoted much attention to the study of language, or discourse, in society. Because they have made more obvious the linguistic mechanisms through which people exercise power, their research provides valuable tools for exploring power in school leadership and the education policy process. Throughout this book, then, discursive exercises of power are identified and discussed.

Texts

What is discourse? According to Fairclough (1995), every instance of discourse has three aspects. The first is the text, which can consist of written, spoken, or a combination of written and spoken language. For example, when a superintendent holds his weekly meeting with the district office staff, a text is produced. That text includes everything he and the other participants said at the meeting. It also includes documents associated with the meeting, such as the agenda and written versions of committee reports. Looking at this text alone may provide important clues to power relationships in central office and the community. For example, the text may reveal that the superintendent and the business manager dominated the meeting, talking far more than anyone else. It may reveal that cost was the determining consideration in 90% of the decisions reached. The language used by participants may be full of terms borrowed from business, such as *payoff, bottom line*, and *biggest bang for the buck*. Such findings would suggest a school system dominated by a superintendent and business manager who have been influenced by the business community. One would expect district policy to reflect this influence and the values implicit in it.

Discourse Practice

The second aspect of any instance of discourse is the discourse practice that governs the production of the text. Because meetings are frequent occurrences in U.S. society, rules and traditions shape them. For example, a chairperson usually runs a meeting, determining who gains the floor, how long each issue is discussed, and how issues are resolved. Someone usually takes notes, which are later converted into minutes. Motions are usually made and seconded. Moreover, each organization has its own traditions about meetings. These traditions may include how items are placed on the agenda and how long the meeting can last. All of these formal and informal rules and traditions constitute a discourse practice (Fairclough, 1995). The discourse practice influences what can be said and done as the text is produced. In order to interpret a text accurately, one must not only have the text but understand the discourse practice that produced it. For example, in interpreting the meeting previously described, knowing how items were placed on the agenda and who appointed the committee chairs would provide important clues to power relationships.

Social Practice

The third aspect of discourse is the social practice in which both the text and the discourse practice are embedded. The superintendent and district office staff attending the meeting are part of a larger organization, a school system. If it is like most U.S. school systems, it has both a formal structure consisting of differentiated roles arranged hierarchically and an informal network of relationships and influence. Beyond the school system other relevant social practices can be found. The formal organization of most school systems reflects the Scientific Management Movement, which was popular in U.S. business circles in the early 1900s.

This movement included definitions of the appropriate roles for people at various hierarchical levels. U.S. culture also includes ideas about how men and women and people of different races should relate to each other. All of these elements—and many others—constitute the social practice in which the superintendent's meeting is situated. They, too, must be taken into account in developing a sensitive interpretation of what happened at the meeting. Of course, savvy school leaders have always understood that conversations, meetings, and official documents provide important clues to organizational power relationships and behind-the-scenes happenings. They have long conducted informal analyses of discourse in order to figure out what is really going on. However, recent research on discourse provides some useful, systematic ways to approach this task.

THE THREE-DIMENSIONAL MODEL OF POWER

Because power is a popular subject for research, many theories about it have been advanced. Lukes (1974) and Gaventa (1980) developed a three-dimensional model of power that includes all the major theories, including the Weberian theories Bendix (1960) and Wrong (1979) summarized. Table 2.1 summarizes the three dimensions of power, which are discussed in this section. Although the three dimensions of power, types of power, and power resources are presented separately, real life is more complex than textbook models. In most social settings, all three dimensions operate simultaneously, and several types of power are used.

The First Dimension of Power: Explicit Uses of Power

In Table 2.1, the first dimension of power consists of explicit exercises of power, which are often directly observable. For example, a state legislature uses first dimension power visibly when it passes a law making graduation requirements more stringent. Some exercises of first dimension power are not directly ob-

TABLE 2.1 The Three Dimensions of Power

First Dimension: Explicit Exercises of Power	Second Dimension: Mobilization of Bias	Third Dimension: Shaping of Consciousness
Mechanisms	*Mechanisms*	*Mechanisms*
Force	Customs	Communication processes
Economic dominance	Norms	Myths
Authority	Organizational structures	Symbols
Persuasion	Procedures	
	Rules of the game	
	Social usages	
	Traditions	

Note. Based on Bendix (1960), Gaventa (1980), Lukes (1974), Weber (1986), and Wrong (1979).

servable, however; nonetheless, they can be readily deduced from observable evidence. For example, in many schools, untenured teachers perform much extra work, such as chaperoning dances and sponsoring clubs. Their principals ask them to do these tasks because these teachers are in a precarious situation and are more likely to say yes than are tenured teachers. For their part, nontenured teachers know they need the principal's support to be rehired and, eventually, tenured. The principal may never explicitly point this fact out to them because she does not need to: The procedures for rehiring and obtaining tenure are spelled out in board policy and state law. Therefore, the power relationship is explicit, although not immediately observable (Gaventa, 1980; Lukes, 1974).

Types of Power. As Table 2.1 shows, four general types of power operate in the first dimension: force, economic dominance, authority, and persuasion. They should be understood as ideal types or abstract descriptions based on many concrete examples. Real-life instances of each type will include most, but not necessarily all, of the characteristics of the ideal type. Moreover, in real life, two or more types of power can be used simultaneously.

Force. Two kinds of force exist: **physical force** and **psychic force.** Exercising power through physical force involves using, or threatening to use, physical actions to impose one's will on others. Such actions include killing, injuring, or causing pain to another; restricting another's freedom; preventing another from satisfying basic biological needs; and using one's body to block another's movement. Examples of physical force in education include corporal punishment, detention halls, and in-school suspension. **Psychic force** is employed to damage another person's self-concept. Common forms include verbal or symbolic insults, nagging, malicious gossip, and negatively stereotyping an entire group. Although the use of psychic force is never ethical, it is common at all levels of education (Wrong, 1979).

Economic Dominance. According to Weber (1986) two types of power are especially important in modern societies: economic dominance and authority. **Economic dominance** involves using one's influence over the jobs, careers, or economic prosperity of others to affect their behavior. Anyone who is in a position to hire, fire, evaluate, or promote employees has access to this type of power. So do those who are most likely to be asked to write job recommendations. Another form of economic dominance is using one's influence over such working conditions as schedules, job assignments, and vacation dates to encourage people to comply with one's wishes. On a broader scale, some corporations use their economic dominance to gain tax abatements and other concessions from local governments by threatening to relocate; taking jobs with them.

Authority. **Authority** is operational when one observes "unquestioning recognition by those who are asked to obey; neither coercion nor persuasion is needed" (Arendt, 1986, p. 65). Authority depends on **legitimacy,** the belief that the person in authority has a right to special power. Students of power have identified several sorts of authority. **Patriarchal authority** is one; a more contemporary term is parental authority. Because most people grow up in families, they first experience power in their relationships with parents and other relatives. In most families, people assume that parents and other older family members have a right to exercise power over children because this right is grounded in tradition. Therefore, children usually accept it as natural. People often transfer elements of parental authority to other settings, especially in elementary schools, where children may project it onto teachers and principals (Bendix, 1960).

A second form is **legal authority,** which is conferred upon those who hold positions of responsibility within an organization. Legal authority is usually described and limited by official documents such as policy manuals and job descriptions. As long as an officeholder acts within the scope of her legal authority, other members of the organization will probably comply readily. To a great extent, the relationships among teachers, principals, and district office administrators are based on legal authority (Bendix, 1960).

Competent authority is a third form. Based on expertise, it is often the only type of power professionals use with their clients. Few people challenge the medical recommendations of their doctors or the legal advice of attorneys. Although educators have less competent authority than doctors or lawyers, many individual teachers and administrators succeed in establishing a high level of competent authority in their communities (Wrong, 1979).

Finally, some people are able to affect the behavior of others through **charismatic authority,** based on purely personal qualities. Some people, through a combination of personality, appearance, and manner, evoke spontaneous confidence and enthusiasm from others. The most striking examples of charismatic authority surface in emergency situations, and charismatic authority may evaporate as soon as the emergency ends. Educators often draw on charismatic authority for some of their effectiveness; but because this is the most unstable form of authority, relying on it heavily is unwise (Bendix, 1960).

Many writers have argued that the legitimacy of all forms of authority has declined steeply since World War II. Evidence for this "legitimation crisis" includes widespread cynicism about government and other institutions, juvenile delinquency, and increased crime rates. Educators experience the decline of their authority every day, both in education settings and beyond them. Forced by the weakening of their authority to use other forms of power, they nonetheless may feel uncomfortable exercising them.

Persuasion. The final type of power is persuasion, the overt attempt to affect the behavior of others by convincing them that the desired behavior is good. A common form of persuasion is **socialization,** which can be offered in several formats. Many organizations require new employees to participate in an induction program, whose purpose is to socialize newcomers to group norms (Wrong, 1979). In education, orientation sessions for new students and teachers serve this purpose. Many organizations that influence education policy also use socialization. For example, school board associations usually offer training programs for newly elected board members; and teachers' unions provide training conferences for local leaders.

A second form of persuasion is **rational persuasion,** in which one marshals arguments and pertinent facts in order to convince another to take a course of

TABLE 2.2 Major Power Resources

Material Resources	Social Resources	Knowledge Resources
Control over careers and working conditions Energy Money (cash or credit) Patronage Time	Access—to money, the media, the legal system Control over votes Numbers—allies or followers Official position Organization Personal impact Popularity Social status Visibility	Control over information Information Intelligence Skills Understanding how the system works Verbal ability

Note. Based on Dahl (1986), Mann (1992), Robinson (1995), and Wrong (1979).

action. Finally, **manipulative persuasion** may be used. On the surface, manipulative persuasion looks like rational persuasion; in fact, it is so intended. However, manipulative persuaders withhold important facts from the actors they are trying to affect. Most often, the hidden information relates to the persuader's true goal or to the potentially harmful impact of the suggested course of action (Wrong, 1979). For example, one reason many teachers are skeptical about implementing new programs is that they have been manipulatively persuaded to do so in the past. As with psychic force, manipulative persuasion is always unethical.

Power Resources.   Power depends upon resources (Mann, 1992). Therefore, people who wish to build a power base do so by amassing appropriate resources for the arenas in which they wish to exercise power. Table 2.2 summarizes the major power resources. Because power is cumulative, powerful people and groups usually control a wide range of resources and may deploy several simultaneously. Although these resources can be important in the first dimension of power, some operate in other dimensions as well. In the following discussion, only a few resources are described in detail.

Material resources.   Material resources, shown in the first column of Table 2.2, are essential to most exercises of power. Most important is money because its possessors can easily convert it into other resources (Dahl, 1986; Wrong, 1979). For example, a school district with a large "war chest" for a funding campaign can convert money into knowledge resources by hiring a professional campaign consultant. It can also convert money into access to the media by purchasing newspaper advertisements and television and radio spots. Using control over hiring to build and exercise power, or **patronage,** is unfortunately still an important source of power in many places (Dahl, 1986). In her study of superintendents in the Northeast, Johnson (1996) found that patronage was used frequently in about one third of the districts. **Time** is a material resource because of the relationship between time and money (Wrong, 1979). Because the majority of people spend most of each day earning a living and performing unpaid labor necessary for their household, they do not have time to build and maintain a power base. Those few people who do not have to work have a considerable advantage. Among these individuals are the independently wealthy; retired people on pensions; college students supported by their families, scholarships, or loans; and married people whose spouses earn enough to support their families. Therefore, people in these social categories often exercise disproportionate influence on public policy, including education policy.

Social resources. Even if one has abundant material resources, having social resources is important as well. People who lack significant material resources can compensate for this deficiency by building and deploying social resources. The middle column of Table 2.2 lists the major social resources. One of the most important social resources is **numbers,** or numerous allies and followers. Johnson (1996) describes one superintendent's skillful use of numbers. Soon after Dick Fitzgerald began his superintendency, the town council cut the school budget by $500,000. Fitzgerald enlisted his central office staff to go out into the school buildings to tell teachers about the problem and win their support. At their superintendent's request, the teachers packed the next meeting of the town council; the money was restored to the budget. The impact of numbers can be magnified by **effective organization.** An organization is effective when it has skillful, committed leaders; respected decision-making procedures; and a planned, systematic communications system (Mann, 1992). The Religious Right has been able to influence curriculum policy in many places because it is highly organized (Apple, 2001).

Knowledge resources. French philosopher Michel Foucault's term *power/knowledge*, which equates power and knowledge, vividly demonstrates the importance of knowledge as a source of power (Fillingham, 1993). The last column of Table 2.2 lists the most important knowledge resources. In almost any arena, people can build power by gathering pertinent **information.** Information can be of many types, including facts about relevant laws, the demographic composition of a population, the state of public opinion, and voting patterns in recent elections. Accurate information facilitates the development of realistic plans and programs. Unethical uses of information to build power include gathering "dirt" on opponents in order to smear their reputations or to blackmail them. Once an information database has been created, the issue of **control of the information** arises. Those who exercise control over information gain power because they can choose with whom they will share their knowledge and also when and how they will use it strategically (Wrong, 1979).

Discursive Power in the First Dimension. The possession of many knowledge resources can give a person considerable discursive power. In the first dimension, as in the other two, people exercise power through language, or discourse. In the first dimension, language is obviously used as an instrument of power, and the actors are usually aware of it. One frequently used discursive power technique is to produce a text designed to limit the scope of a discussion at a meeting. The person who has the authority to produce such a text—usually called an *agenda*—has at her disposition a powerful tool. At most meetings the other participants can amend the agenda, and important debate sometimes occurs around suggested amendments. Even so, people usually hesitate to propose sweeping changes in an agenda, much less suggest that it be abandoned altogether.

Nonetheless, skillful users of discourse can sabotage well-planned agendas. Waite (1995) observed a conference in which Faye, the supervisor, came armed with an agenda in the form of a checklist because she considered Bea, the teacher under supervision, "argumentative." Although Faye sought to control the discussion of Bea's teaching with her checklist, Bea successfully used other discursive techniques, finally causing the supervisor to give up all attempts to influence her. Among the teacher's discursive uses of power were: raising her voice, interrupting Faye, talking simultaneously with her, changing the subject, and getting up from the table to look out the window. Bea's most successful discursive technique was a series of innuendos suggesting that Faye was out of touch with the realities of the classroom. This anecdote is particularly interesting because it demonstrates that the person with legal authority does not always prevail when power is exercised.

The Second Dimension of Power: The Mobilization of Bias

Understanding the Second Dimension: Race.   In contrast to the first dimension, in which exercises of power are explicit, power exercised in the second dimension is implicit. Table 2.1 shows some ways of exercising power in the second dimension. In this dimension, few or none of the actors may realize that power is being exercised. Exercises of power in this dimension usually limit the meaningful participation of certain groups or restrict the issues that can be raised for debate through devices less obvious than agendas (Bachrach & Baratz, 1962; Bachrach & Botwinick, 1992). This way of exercising power is called the *mobilization of bias* (Gaventa, 1980).

An historical example will clarify the difference between the two dimensions. In the 1890s, the participation of both women and African American men in elections was limited. Although a few states had laws permitting women to vote, most did not; and the women's suffrage amendment to the U.S. Constitution had not yet been passed. Using their legal authority, Congress and most legislatures had explicitly rejected bills that would have given women the right to vote. Women's low participation in voting therefore resulted from exercises of first dimension power.

The case of African American men was different. After the Civil War, amendments to the U.S. Constitution had given them the right to vote, and they had exercised their right during Reconstruction. Their tendency not to vote in the 1890s resulted from intervening exercises of second dimension power. Instead of passing laws outlawing African American suffrage—which would have been unconstitutional—many states and local communities erected ingenious barriers to voting that disproportionately affected African Americans. For example, citizens who wanted to register to vote often had to pay a poll tax or pass a literacy test. Because higher percentages of African Americans were poor and illiterate, these rules affected them more than they affected whites. Sometimes voting places were located in the white residential districts of cities. Because African Americans found getting there difficult and felt intimidated if they did, they often decided not to vote. Thus, although the laws officially permitted African Americans to vote, other rules and practices made doing so difficult. In other words, a strong bias against their participation had been mobilized. When such rules were first established, most people understood their real purpose. However, after decades had passed, many citizens did not. Some people sincerely believed that literacy tests would ensure an informed electorate; they did not recognize them as an exercise of second dimension power.

Second Dimension Power in Education: Parental Involvement.   U.S. public education is an old institution, having been established in the first half of the nineteenth century. Organizations usually bear the marks of the beliefs and social positions of their founders, and public education is no exception. As Schattschneider (1960) points out, "Organization is itself a mobilization of bias" (p. 30). The organizational structures of public schools and the traditions, procedures, customs, and "rules of the game" associated with them, therefore, encourage the participation of some while discouraging others.

Public education was established when only white men who owned a certain amount of property had full citizens' rights; therefore, the major figures in the Common School Movement were white, middle- to upper-class men. As a result, much of the organizational bias mobilized in public education is advantageous to those who belong to one or more of these social categories and disadvantageous to those who do not. This does not mean that Horace Mann and others deliberately conspired to create an institution that would discourage participation by females, working- and lower-class people, and members of racial minority groups. Rather, they established public schools for the people who worked in schools and attended them at that time. They also established schools that reflected their beliefs and the characteristics of other large nineteenth-century organizations, such as the U.S. Army and businesses. All of these factors taken together cause the public school to mobilize bias for and against certain social groups. Other biases are inherent in public school organization as well. Because most adults were barely literate in the early 1800s, school teachers were often the most educated people in the community. Therefore, the founders of public schools did not think that building in mechanisms for broad parent or community participation was necessary. As a result, the organization of public schools also mobilizes bias in favor of professional educators and against other stakeholders.

Although Horace Mann and other early reformers did not deliberately design schools to enhance participation by educators and limit participation by others, structures and customs from the past are often perpetuated today in order to do so. For example, many educators complain about parents' lack of participation in school activities; but many parents complain just as loudly that the school sends them mixed messages about participation. Teachers and principals say that they want parents to come to school more often, but their actions often relay a different message. In the typical U.S. public school, bias is mobilized against parent participation in many ways. Educators often expect parents to participate in school activities on the school's schedule. Parents who do come to school may have to park blocks away. On a first visit, they may find locating the entrance or the principal's office difficult. When they finally find the office, it may lack a suitable waiting area. In the unlikely event that a teacher permits them to observe a class, adult-sized chairs may not be available. Finding out when the PTA or school council meetings are held, much less what is on the agenda, may be hard for parents. Procedures for electing officers for these groups may be unclear. Communication from school officials may be couched in incomprehensible "educationese." Most teachers and principals are unaware that their school mobilizes bias against parent participation. Indeed, many would be shocked at the suggestion that by maintaining the status quo they are exercising power to keep parents out. Yet, as Delpit (1988) writes, "Those with [second dimension] power are frequently least aware of—or at least willing to acknowledge—its existence" (p. 282). Many parents experience these barriers as an exercise of power and believe that educators would remove them if they sincerely desired parent participation.

The Mobilization of Bias: Race, Gender, Class.   This section presents three concrete examples of the mobilization of bias in education: bias experienced by minority children in schools, bias encountered by women who enter school administration, and bias in school-choice policies.

Mobilization of bias and minority children.   Delpit is an African-American educator who has written eloquently about the mobilization of bias against children of color in U.S. schools. Although she calls the phenomenon the *culture of power*, political scientists call it the *mobilization of bias*. She argues in a 1988 article that schools reflect the "cultural code" of the white middle class. As a result, children from that social group start school knowing the rules of the education game well. They feel comfortable in the classroom, can interpret the teacher's indirect way of expressing herself, and understand her rules. However, children from other backgrounds are disadvantaged from the beginning. At school they are expected to speak and write an unfamiliar form of English. The teacher's indirect way of expressing herself—typical of the middle class—confuses them. Their modes of presenting themselves differ from modes of self-presentation favored by the school's culture. For example, their dress may stand out as unusual, and their patterns of social interaction may differ from those of white, middle-class students.

This means that minority children face a double task at school: learning the cognitive material that is explicitly presented to them and deciphering the implicit but unfamiliar "codes" in which it is embedded. This mobilization of bias against their effective participation in the classroom often leads to frustration, alienation, and failure. Delpit (1988) suggests that teachers should explicitly teach the cultural codes of the white middle class to minority children while simultaneously teaching them to understand and treasure their own cultural heritage. In that way children can overcome some of the bias that has been mobilized against them if they wish to do so.

Bias against women in school administration.   U.S. public education was feminized early; the deaths of more than 500,000 men in the Civil War meant that women were needed to staff schools. As a result, classroom teaching was institutionalized consistently with social roles deemed appropriate for women. Because teachers often functioned as "public mothers" (Wodak, 1995), women felt comfortable in classrooms. Today, most women do not sense much mobilization of organizational bias against them as long as they remain there. In fact, male classroom teachers probably encounter it more than females.

School administration, however, has traditionally been a male-dominated field. Its rules, customs, norms, and discourse have been shaped by several generations of men. Therefore, women who become administrators soon begin to feel the mobilization of bias against them. In this respect they share the experience of women in all fields who move into management. For example, in an early book for women moving into business management, *Games Mother Never Taught You*, Harragan (1977) describes the unwritten rules of the business "game" for women. (Note that Harragan does for women exactly what Delpit recommends doing for minority schoolchildren: she makes the rules explicit.) In the first chapter she writes:

> Most women are completely unaware that once they pass through the gates [of management], they have entered an alien land with customs, traditions, security forces, and mores of its own. What's more, the natives speak a strange, oblique tongue, and the signposts are in cryptic ciphers. Although the terrain is crisscrossed with well-trodden paths, there are few visible directions to guide the unfamiliar strangers. (p. 33)

New female school administrators usually experience a similar sense of strangeness in their jobs. They feel they no longer know the rules or understand what people say to them. Colleagues often misunderstand their attempts at communication. In her study of three female superintendents who had left the superintendency, Skrla (2000) found that these women had encountered great difficulty because of the mismatch between traditional expectations for women and the demands of the superintendency. For example, one of them said:

> The passivity that we see in the general perspective for the woman is antithetical to what we would expect the role of the superintendent to be, which would be more aggressive, more assertive, more intervening. I have been told that I needed to be more assertive, speak up more—which, then when I did it, it seemed like I got slapped back down. (p. 308)

In the terms of this discussion of power, this woman was experiencing a mobilization of bias against women achieving success in the superintendency.

Bias in school choice. Since 1981 one of the most popular education reform proposals has been school choice. Although the United States has been relatively slow to embrace choice policies, the British Parliament passed legislation establishing interdistrict open enrollment in the early 1980s. A rich body of research on how school choice works over time has been developed in the United Kingdom. Between 1991 and 1994, Gewirtz, Ball, and Bowe (1995) conducted a qualitative study of school choice in London. They found that the process of choosing a school mobilizes considerable bias against working- and lower-class parents. At the most superficial level, their place of residence, access to transportation, and work schedules severely limit the number of schools they can consider seriously. At the level of discourse, these parents find the promotional materials and test results put out by schools difficult to interpret. As a result, working- and lower-class children attend "better" schools less frequently than do middle-class children. Gewirtz et al. (1995) conclude, "These parents might be described as working on the surface structure of choice, because their programmes of perception rest on . . . unfamiliarity with particular aspects of schools and schooling" (p. 47). They might also be described as encountering a massive mobilization of bias against them as they go through the choice process. The findings of this study suggest that, as choice policies become widespread in the United States, administrators will have to develop ways to help all parents make informed decisions about schools.

The Third Dimension of Power: The Shaping of Consciousness

Understanding the Shaping of Consciousness. The third column of Table 2.1 lists the mechanisms of third dimension power. In a discussion of the third dimension of power, Lukes (1974) asks, "Is not the supreme exercise of power to get another or others to have the desires you want them to have—that is, to secure their compliance by controlling their thoughts and desires?" (p. 23). All of us have been on the receiving end in this dimension of power, for all of us have undergone the acculturation that is the main business of childhood. Several social institutions are especially important in shaping consciousness. The family is the most crucial, in part because people first learn language within it. Language has long been recognized as a major shaper of consciousness, determining the basic categories of meaning that one imposes upon the world (Cherryholmes, 1988). The family also inculcates beliefs and values, and its patterns of interaction shape the child's personality structure. However, other institutions also shape consciousness. The mass media are increasingly important today, bombarding everyone with a barrage of messages, both explicit and implicit (Giroux, 1999). Schools and religious organizations also play a major role in shaping the way people see the world (Bernstein, 1996; Corson, 1995; Lemke, 1995). Questions about how consciousness is shaped and how it can be transformed preoccupy contemporary social science. A thorough discussion of this subject would go well beyond the scope of this book. However, school leaders must understand that many of the people they deal with have been either unusually empowered or unusually disempowered through the shaping of their consciousness.

Unusual Empowerment. Among the most important messages communicated by institutions that shape consciousness are messages about who should hold leading positions in society and who should be dominated by others. Some people receive a steady stream of messages suggesting that they are privileged with natural rights to positions of power and prestige. For instance, in his ethnographic study of an elite, private prep school which he called Edgewood Academy, Peshkin (2001) found that students in this school were surrounded by symbols of their importance. Although the school only had 900 students, its "pristine" and "elegant" facilities were located on a 312-acre campus. In addition, the school owned 270 acres of mountainous terrain where students engaged in "experiential education." Edgewood recruited its teachers—many of whom held Ph.D.s—in national searches, and each faculty member had a well-equipped office with a personal computer. The school's library had a staff of nine, an online catalog, and microfiche readers. Among the field trips offered was a two-week trip to Paris in March to practice French in an immersion situation. All these symbols communicated the high worth of the students. They also implicitly informed these adolescents that they were the future leaders of American society. In some instances, the students were fully conscious of the message the school was sending them. When Peshkin asked one student what Edgewood's parents thought the school could give their children, he answered very directly: "They want [us] to be on the top of the food chain. They want us to be the bosses, not the employees. . . . We are going to be the leaders" (Peshkin, 2001, p. 9).

School leaders will not find many people of this type within their school systems, either as students, employees, or parents. In their roles as public leaders in the broader community, however, they will encounter some. In working with them, keeping their socialization in mind will be helpful.

Unusual Disempowerment. At the other end of the social spectrum are people who have been unusually disempowered through the shaping of consciousness. They have grown up surrounded by messages that communicate their low status and unsuitability for leadership.

A good example is provided by Gaventa's (1980) book-length study of rural Appalachia, *Power and Powerlessness*. In the area of Kentucky and Tennessee he investigated, the people had experienced generations of exploitation. During the Civil War both armies terrorized them. Later, the lumber companies tricked them out of their land; still later the coal companies gave them menial jobs in the mines, keeping them under strict control in company towns. Local governments had sold out to the companies; and newspapers, churches, and schools praised the status quo with a united voice. The Appalachians had adapted to their powerlessness by sinking into passivity, dependence, and apathy, expressing fatalism about the future and openly stating that they were stupid. Moreover, they had internalized the views of the powerful people around them, ironically blaming themselves for their own poverty.

Gaventa worked with a group of these people to produce a film about their situation. While working on the film and seeking to get it broadcast on television, project participants emerged from their apathy. As their consciousness about their situation was raised, they developed greater self-confidence. Community leaders felt very threatened by these activities, however. Eventually, the homes of several of the people working on the film were burned—an exercise of first dimension power. In response, the people sank back into their original apathy.

Many public school leaders work in settings where they deal with people who have been disempowered to an unusual degree. When one encounters massive apathy, a natural response is to become angry and complain about the deficiencies of the population, which often amounts to blaming the victims. School leaders should consider apathy, fatalism, self-deprecation, and other signs noted by Gaventa as symptoms of a deeper problem. Reflection and a little investigation may reveal a tragic history that explains their disempowerment. Research suggests that the best way to handle such problems is to initiate projects in which the people can participate and in which they are empowered to make bona fide decisions. Through working in such projects, they gain self-confidence, skills, and knowledge. They also usually gain a more realistic understanding of their situation. In short, they gain power. Progress will probably be slow, but it can be made (Bachrach & Botwinick, 1992; Gaventa, 1980).

POWER IN EDUCATIONAL SETTINGS

The Power of Education Policy Actors

Power permeates the education system; and, although some actors are more powerful than others, all have power. Table 2.3 depicts the major types of power accessible to education actors and their most important power resources. In interpreting this chart, readers should understand that it summarizes those forms and sources of power that are most readily available to each actor. If a type of power is not listed for a given actor, that definitely does not mean that he cannot have it. Rather, it means that the actor must exert special effort to obtain it.

For example, according to the chart, school administrators have two types of power: economic dominance and legal authority. These types of power are built into the system for administrators. However, wise school leaders build their power by working to add to what the system provides them. Many administrators work to establish their competent authority, which can be done in several ways. Some people obtain a doctorate for this purpose; another approach is to stay up-to-date in professional reading and work actively in one or more professional organizations. Administrators can also establish their competent authority by clearly pointing out the educational reasons for the decisions they make. Persuasive power is important, too. Learning how to make a convincing presentation at a meeting or polishing writing skills in order to be able to draft effective news releases can enhance a school leader's power. So can making a serious effort to gain more knowledge about the community and its population. Administrators can use other types of power and obtain other resources, but they are not given; they must be achieved.

Analyzing Power Relationships

The PRINCE System. Often one must analyze the power relationships in a decision-making context. Although many leaders do this continuously and almost intuitively, a systematic framework for analysis is helpful, especially in complex

TABLE 2.3 The Power of Major Actors in Educational Settings

Actor	Types of Power	Power Resources

Governance bodies (e.g., legislatures, school boards, departments of education)	Economic dominance
	  Budget proposal
	  Budget adoption
	  Tax policy
	  Withholding funds
	
	Legal authority
	  Adoption of laws, rules, policies
	  Court decisions
		Access to money
		Control over information
		Information
		Official positions
		Organization

School administrators	Economic dominance Legal authority	Control over careers and working conditions Control over information Information Official positions Patronage Visibility

Teachers	Economic dominance
	  Work stoppages
	  Work slowdowns
	  Tenure (job protection)
	Legal authority
	  Control over classroom
		Control over information about classroom activities
		Numbers
		Official positions
		Organization

Support staff	Economic dominance
	  Work stoppages
	  Work slowdowns
		Numbers
		Organization

Students	Force Physical (i.e., threat of disruption, actual disruption, fights) Psychic (i.e., heckling, verbal insults)	Numbers
Parents	Persuasion	Numbers Organization
Public	Economic dominance (e.g., voting on funding issues) Legal authority (e.g., voting in school elections)	Numbers Organization

Actors	Issue Position	×	Power	×	Priority	=	Total Support by Actor
	−3−0 −+3		1−3		1−3		
For							
Educational community	+3	×	2	×	3	×	18
City government	+2	×	3	×	1	×	6
Ministerial association	+3	×	1	×	2	×	6
Realtors	+1	×	3	×	2	×	6
Total							+36
Against							
Representative Blake	−1	×	2	×	1	×	−2
Chamber of Commerce	−1	×	3	×	1	×	−3
Golden Agers Club	−3	×	2	×	3	×	−18
Tax Rebellion Movement	−3	×	2	×	3	×	−18
Total							−41

Figure 2.1 Analyzing power relationships. A modified PRINCE system issue: Pass a bond issue.
Note: Based on forms in W. D. Coplin and M. K. O'Leary, *Basic Policy Studies Skills,* 3rd edition, Croton-on-Hudson, NY: Policy Studies Associates, 1998.

situations. One such framework is the PRINCE system of power analysis, which appears in Figure 2.1. This is a modified version of a system which Coplin and O'Leary (1981; 1998) developed for political science students; its name, PRINCE, is an allusion to Machiavelli's classic political handbook, *The Prince.* The analytical chart has been completed for a local policy question with which most readers will be familiar: passing a bond issue.

Issue Statements. Because power is relational and is never exercised in a social vacuum, the first step in the analysis is defining the issue, which should be as specific as possible. Coplin and O'Leary (1981) recommend beginning the statement of the issue with an active verb. Here are two contrasting pairs of appropriate and inappropriate issue statements:

Pass a bond issue to build a middle school next year.

not

More funding for schools.

and

Defeat H.B. 128 to limit choice of textbooks.

not

Keep legislature out of textbook selection.

Identifying Actors. After the issue has been carefully defined, one should list the actors who are interested in the issue or who may become interested. The actors can be individuals, such as the governor; informal groups, such as parents of schoolchildren; or formal organizations, such as the state affiliate of the National School Boards Association. In developing this list of actors, one should include:

- actors who have legal authority regarding the issue;
- actors who are powerful enough to block a decision;
- actors who will be significantly affected by any policy change; and
- actors whose cooperation will be essential in implementing any proposed policy change.

Coplin and O'Leary (1981) recommend limiting the number of actors to no more than 10. This means that grouping actors is sometimes necessary. In Figure 2.1, for example, the education community is a group. Only actors who have the same economic interests and who agree on the issue should be grouped together. If the members of the education community disagreed over the bond issue, then listing them as a single actor would not be appropriate. In developing a list of actors, the goal is not to produce a perfect description; rather, it is to come up with "a configuration of actors that taken together constitute a reasonable picture of the overall power distribution" (Coplin & O'Leary, 1981, p. 161). Much reflection and input from others are necessary to achieve this objective.

Identifying Positions. After developing the list of actors, one should estimate the position of each on the issue. Positions range from strongly opposed (−3) to strongly supportive (+3). A neutral or undecided position is scored 0. Scores of −3 or +3 should be restricted to actors whose positions are so strong that they are unlikely to change. Scores of −1 and −2 or +1 and +2 indicate softer positions. Next, these scores and the actors should be entered in the chart, listing supporters, opponents, and neutral actors together.

Assessing Power. The power of each actor regarding this issue is estimated next. Using the discussion of types and sources of power presented earlier, the analyst should determine each actor's level of power and assign it a number from 1 (low) to 3 (high). The analyst must remember that power is relational and contextual. In Figure 2.1, for example, the area's representative in the state legislature has been rated only 2. That is because, although he has considerable influence locally, his influence is indirect and mediated through local officials and groups. If the issue were a bill under consideration in the statehouse committee he chairs, his power would be rated 3.

Assessing Priority. Finally, the priority of the issue for each actor must be assessed. Because each actor has limited power resources and priorities for using them, any actor may decide not to deploy resources for a particular issue, even if it holds a strong position. In Figure 2.1, the city government is relatively supportive of the bond issue but unlikely to become actively involved in the campaign.

Interpreting. Next, each actor's scores are multiplied together, yielding a total score. Then, scores for all supporters, all opponents, and all neutral actors are added. The relative scores of the groups indicate the most likely outcome unless the balance of power changes. The major value of the PRINCE exercise is not that it predicts the future but that it suggests strategies for altering an unfavorable balance of power. Studying such an analysis, supporters of the bond issue should recognize several things to do to shift the balance of power. They could build the power of the education community. They could seek to persuade the realtors to support them more strongly and city government to change its priorities. They could try to move the Chamber of Commerce into a position of support. Obviously, expending resources on the Golden Agers Club and the Tax Rebellion Movement would be pointless. However, neutralizing Representative Blake might be possible by persuading him not to take sides publicly. By pursuing several of these strategies, supporters of the bond issue might alter the balance of power enough to affect the outcome of the referendum.

Building Power

Opening Comments. Achieving a policy goal often requires building power. People build power by obtaining more, or different, power resources. They also build power by obtaining access to new types of power. Ways to build power in education will be illustrated by a fictional story; a running analysis of power-building techniques appears in brackets.

"Building Power for Kids." Dr. Dolores Hernandez, superintendent of a suburban district in a southwestern state, got angry when she read the February issue of the newsletter published by the superintendents' association. A bill requiring second and fifth graders to take basic skills proficiency tests had been introduced in the General Assembly. [Hernandez builds power by gathering knowledge.] "We test these kids to death," she muttered. She supported accountability and high performance, but the state already required tests in the first, third, and sixth grades. "Enough already," she muttered.

Dolores called the man who represented the district in the legislature. Four busy signals, two holds, and three secretaries later, she reached a legislative staffer said to specialize in education issues. She registered her concern with this individual, who replied: "I'll leave a note in the representative's box." [Her call signals possible lost votes to the representative and his staff.]

Over the next two weeks, Dolores also contacted lobbyists at the superintendents' and school board association's headquarters. She gained the support of four other superintendents. The elementary teachers in her district seemed apathetic, but the teachers' union president agreed with her. [Dolores builds power by gaining numbers; some of her new allies have better access resources than she does.] This handful of people generated several letters and phone calls to members of the legislature. In early April, a phone message from one of the lobbyists came through: "The bill has been defeated in committee. They'll probably get their ducks in a row and try again next year."

"I don't have time to fight this fight," Dolores thought as she drove home late that evening. But the next day she asked the central office supervisor who handled government relations, a retired social studies teacher, and an active parent to spearhead a committee to get their own ducks in a row. She selected the retired teacher and the parent—a woman whose husband's income permitted her to be a full-time mother—because she knew they would have lots of time to devote to the project. [She increases her numbers and adds to her time and knowledge resources.]

The committee considered establishing a special organization called something like Spare Our Kids but decided instead to work through existing organizations. Before school ended, they had gained a sympathetic hearing from the associations representing superintendents, principals, and school boards as well as the two teachers' unions. The state chapter of the PTA and the International Reading Association (IRA) were also supportive. Several of these organizations were considering amending their legislative agendas to include opposition to additional basic-skills tests. [The power of numbers is magnified through effective organization. These organizations also have wealth, knowledge, and access resources to contribute to the cause.]

During the summer the state PTA developed a flyer against excessive testing, which cited research about the stress caused by tests. [Knowledge has been gained and is deployed.] Attaching a price tag to testing all the state's second and fifth graders, the flyer suggested that more testing "would be a waste of taxpayers' dollars." [The child-centered discourse is preserved, but a new, cost-conscious discourse is added. This broadening of the discourse increases the persuasiveness of the argument.]

Meanwhile, Dolores had told her committee about how much difficulty she had contacting their representative. Soon the committee members had tales of their own to add to hers. Everyone agreed that people who tried to contact anyone in the legislature or find out what was going on in the statehouse wasted a lot of time and energy jumping through hoops. Several committee members wrote letters to legislators complaining about this problem. They also sent three letters to the editor of the nearest city newspaper. The last letter ran under the heading "Do They Really Want to Hear From Voters?" [The mobilization of bias against effective participation in state politics is explicitly identified and made public.] In September, the local representative revamped his system for handling phone calls and letters.

Dolores was also concerned about the apathy of the elementary teachers in her district. She realized that most were women who might have grown up believing the myth that "women do not belong in politics." Moreover, the district had previously had several authoritarian elementary principals who ruled "their teachers" like benign dictators. She felt these old ideas and behavior patterns needed to change, so she pushed the committee to actively recruit some elementary teachers. She was delighted when several agreed to participate and began to develop more confidence in their leadership potential. [A disempowered group is identified and becomes active. Numbers and knowledge resources are increased.] As the opening of the next session of the legislature approached, Dolores did not know what the future held. She did know, however, that the opponents of pointless testing "had their ducks in a row." She thought they had done their best to protect the state's children from time-wasting tests.

ETHICAL ISSUES SURROUNDING POWER

The Dangers of Power

"Power tends to corrupt and absolute power corrupts absolutely," wrote Lord Acton about a century ago (Tripp, 1970, p. 713). Acton belongs to a long tradition of thinkers who have expressed moral reservations about power. Under the Roman Empire, Jesus said: "You know that among the gentiles the rulers lord it over them, and great men make their authority felt. Among you this is not to happen" (Matt. 20:25–26, *New Jerusalem Bible*). Sixteen centuries later, the English philosopher Thomas Hobbes argued that human beings have "a perpetual and restless desire of power after power, that ceaseth only in death" (Hobbes, 1958, p. 86). In the twentieth century, German sociologist Max Weber wrote about politicians who "enjoy the naked possession of the power [they] exert" (Gerth & Mills, 1946, p. 84).

Such doubts have led many to conclude that all exercises of power are unethical by nature. Writing specifically about power in education, Burbules (1986) asserts:

> Power is a seductive, even addictive tonic, and anyone who takes it, ostensibly for a limited time and for a limited purpose, invariably finds it easier and easier to justify retaining and exercising it beyond these limits. . . . Educators have been notably susceptible to this temptation. (p. 105)

Burbules's solution to the ethical problem posed by power is to refuse to exercise it. On the surface this conclusion appears high-minded, but deeper reflection suggests that it does not resolve the ethical dilemma surrounding power after all. If every person with moral reservations about power refused to exercise it, power would not cease to exist. Rather, it would be exercised only by those people who lack moral reservations about it. The result would be more abuses of power than exist today, and those who refused to exercise power on moral grounds would be partially responsible. Thus, the refusal to exercise power because of its corrupting potential is itself an unethical exercise of power.

Another answer to the dilemma posed by power is to exercise it consciously—that is, with awareness of its corrupting potential and of one's own susceptibility. Peck (1978), a psychotherapist, advocates this course of action, writing: "Awareness . . . comes slowly, piece by piece, and each piece must be worked for by the patient effort of study and observation of everything, including [one's self]" (p. 285). This means that school leaders should consider power a useful but potentially dangerous tool, similar to an automobile. Just as one should never drive thoughtlessly, so leaders should never fall into the habit of exercising power without thinking about what they are doing. The next two sections offer guidance for thinking about using power.

Power as Means and End

Wrong (1979) identifies four purposes for which power can be used and discusses the ethical implications of each. His major points are summarized here.

Power as Individual Means. An individual may exercise power to pursue an individual goal. For example, for financial reasons a superintendent near retirement may want to finish his career in the district that currently employs him. In order to enhance his job security, he may build personal power within the district. Exercising power to achieve a personal goal is not necessarily unethical. Even so, over time the temptation will be strong to sacrifice the good of the district to the personal goal. In order to behave ethically, the superintendent will have to monitor his behavior closely to make sure that pursuing his personal goal is always consistent with district goals.

Power as Individual End. An individual may exercise power solely because of the sense of importance she experiences as she does so. For example, a principal may enjoy demonstrating her power over parents, teachers, students, and staff by making unilateral decisions and suddenly reversing them without explanation. Such a use of power as an end in itself is always unethical.

Power as Means for a Group. An individual may exercise power to advance the goals of a group. For example, a secondary supervisor may use her power to obtain funds to purchase lab equipment for the chemistry teachers. Assuming that the group's goals are ethical, this use of power is the least susceptible to abuse.

Power as End for a Group. A group leader may exercise power to enhance his group's power solely because the group enjoys being influential. For example, the president of a teachers' union may engage in numerous activities to build the union's power. He does so because he and other leaders enjoy packing board meetings, walking out of bargaining sessions, and threatening strikes. This behavior feeds their sense of self-importance. Exercising power for such a purpose is unethical.

Using Discursive Power Ethically

Discourse, especially speech, has always been an important instrument of power for school leaders. With the introduction of site-based management in many districts, it is more important than ever. Like other power resources, discourse can be used both ethically and unethically.

Robinson (1995) provides valuable guidelines for exercising discursive power ethically, suggesting that people must adhere to three values in responsible discourse:

- *Respect.* The more powerful actors must understand that the less powerful ones have the same basic rights that they do. The less powerful actors must be given the opportunity to suggest issues for the agenda, speak in discussions, and question positions taken by the more powerful actors.
- *Commitment to valid information.* All participants in the discourse should be willing to change their opinions in response to new and valid information.

- *Freedom of choice.* Less powerful actors should be genuinely free to take positions or choose courses of action without fear of negative repercussions.

Robinson (1995) believes that people find acting consistently with these values difficult because they lack the necessary skills. People must know how to be open about their intentions and how to place their opinions under public scrutiny. Moreover, leaders need to be able to facilitate open discussions and group decision making. Several facilitative skills are important, including:

- the ability to listen well;
- the ability to invite contributions from others;
- open, receptive body language;
- the ability to test and revise ideas; and
- the ability to guide a group toward closure.

To illustrate her points, Robinson (1995) describes a school council meeting that she observed. The topic of discussion was adopting a school uniform, a subject that had previously been discussed at length. The principal, Tony, who chaired the meeting, was receptive to everyone's opinion, and many people participated. However, Tony was unwilling (or unable) to facilitate the meaningful discussion of different suggestions or to guide the group toward closure. As a result, after a second entire meeting had been devoted to the uniform issue, faculty felt frustrated. One of them later told Robinson that although Tony tended to listen to everyone's opinion in meetings, he later made decisions unilaterally. Robinson concludes that both excluding voices and failing to lead a group to a sound decision are abuses of discursive power.

Using power ethically requires considerable maturity, self-awareness, and effort. Yet, school leaders must make the effort if they wish to avoid becoming victims of power's insidious lure. Only by exercising power thoughtfully and with deep respect for others can education leaders build healthy, humane organizations.

FINAL POINTS

Power permeates education systems and the policies that shape them. Much of that power is wielded by individual employees of the system, acting in their capacity as government officials. Their power ultimately rests on their institution and the policies and traditions behind it, not on their personal characteristics. Traditionally, much of the power wielded by educational institutions has been authority—a type of power that society considers right and legitimate. However, authority rests on legitimacy, and legitimacy is easily lost. As the twenty-first century begins, the legitimacy of all authority—including educational authority—is in crisis. When their authority is weakened, educators have to learn to use other types of power, and understanding the power relations in their policy environment becomes more important than ever. Developing an understanding of power is therefore crucial for education leaders.

QUESTIONS AND ACTIVITIES FOR DISCUSSION

1. List the types of power to which your educational position entitles you and the major power resources at your disposal. How could you make more effective use of your power? What ethical challenges have you encountered because of your power?

2. Call your representative in the state legislature and request some information from the office. Keep a list of everything that happens, starting with locating the representative's phone number. Analyze the bias mobilized against public participation in legislative policy making.

3. What evidence suggests that some people in your district have been disempowered through the shaping of their consciousness? How does their disempowerment affect district education policy?

4. Do a PRINCE analysis of a current issue in your district or state. How could the less powerful stakeholders build their power?

CASE STUDY

SATANISM AND WITCHCRAFT IN THE SCHOOLS

Bob Mathews is the superintendent of a school district that includes a small city and the surrounding rural area. The district is about thirty miles from a large metropolis; but recently many former city dwellers have purchased houses in two new subdivisions. About ten days ago Bob received a phone call from a man who identified himself as Clyde Ruggles. Saying that he had some concerns about the language arts books used in the district, Ruggles requested an opportunity to address the school board at its next meeting. Because Ruggles spoke with a "country" accent and made several grammatical errors, Bob thought, "Just a harmless crackpot." He agreed to place him on the agenda and forgot about him.

At last night's school board meeting, Bob was astonished to see that every seat in the meeting room was occupied. Many in the crowd were wearing red, white, and blue buttons that read, "Save our children from the devil." Some were holding up professional-looking signs containing the same words. As he made his way through the crowd, someone shoved a leaflet into his hand and a flashbulb went off. Looking around, Bob recognized several reporters in the audience.

Because Bob had placed Ruggles first on the agenda, Ruggles strode to the microphone right after the Pledge of Allegiance and read a brilliantly written speech to the school board. In it he claimed that the language arts series used by the system taught Satanism, magic, and witchcraft. After citing several examples, Ruggles concluded: "This school district systematically teaches our children a heathen religion: Satanism. Under the Establishment Clause of the First Amendment of the U.S. Constitution, this practice is illegal. I therefore request that the school board immediately stop using this textbook series." The room rang with thunderous applause.

Then Ed Zabriski, one of the board members, said, "I move that we stop using this series." After considerable hesitation, Jay Bullock seconded the motion, and the audience applauded again. The motion failed, 3–2, on a roll call vote. Then, in a voice not much above a whisper, Dr. Dale Attali said, "I move we adjourn to the superintendent's office to discuss personnel matters in an executive session." This motion passed, 3–2. Bob did not know if this motion was legal or not, but he did not care. He, the board members, and the treasurer hurriedly left the room to calls of "Cowards! Cowards!" In his office Bob learned that Zabriski strongly supported Ruggles and his group. Bullock, on the other hand, had supported the motion because many voters from his district were present. Attali and the other two board members, both from the new subdivisions, were appalled by Ruggles's ideas.

The next morning Bob attended a Kiwanis pancake breakfast before meeting with the city manager. When he reached his office at 10:00 A.M., he found a stack of telephone messages on the desk. They included: (1) "Jane Cohen, president of the REA called. Several English teachers have contacted her, concerned about censorship after last night." (Eighty-five percent of the teachers belong to the union, which has been bargaining for twenty years.) (2) "Harold Brook of Realtors Association—concerned about declining home sales in new subdivision if 'kooks' take over." (3) "Jasper Powers, pastor of the Four Square Solid Bible Gospel Temple called. Concerned about Satanism in our schools." (This church has 800 members, mostly from working-class families.) (4) "George P. Trotwood, president of First Home Fidelity Bank called—wants to know what in h— is going on around here? Have you lost control?" (5) Every elementary principal had left a message to the effect that several students were refusing to participate in reading class. (6) "Robert Bachfeld, pastor of the Holy Light Tabernacle, wants an appointment to discuss the curriculum with you." (This church has about 600 members.) (7) "Tammy Brouillette, Channel 7 News Reporter, wants to interview you about Satanism."

QUESTIONS

1. Do a PRINCE analysis of power relationships in this district.
2. Apparently, Bob Mathews has based his behavior on a faulty analysis of power relationships. Describe his apparent analysis. In your opinion, why did he make these mistakes?
3. In what ways do the second and third dimensions of power probably operate in this district?
4. Develop a plan that Bob Mathews and the majority on the board could use to alter power relationships so that this conflict can be resolved in a positive, ethical manner.

NEWS STORY FOR ANALYSIS TEACHERS' CLAIMS ON CHARTER PLAN CONTRADICTED

Buffalo, NY—The claims of the Buffalo Teachers Federation that School 18's charter school proposal would wipe out tenure and seniority for teachers was undercut Thursday by a New York City school official who said teachers automatically retained those protections when conversion charters were established there. State education officials said there is no reason similar arrangements couldn't be made in Buffalo if school administrators and the BTF approached the issue cooperatively. And Board of Education President Paul G. Buchanan said any plan at School 18 would fully retain those protections for teachers. But BTF President Philip Rumore continued to insist Thursday that the proposal to convert School 18 into a charter school would automatically strip teachers of seniority and tenure. "There are no ifs, ands or buts," Rumore said. "Those are not things that can be worked out. It's precluded by law."

Buffalo's School 18, a West Side elementary school with low test scores and an overwhelmingly minority enrollment, had been planning for months to transform itself into a charter school that would employ multi-age classrooms and build instruction around community service projects. The school's teaching staff initially voted overwhelmingly to support the conversion, but then reversed itself in a second vote taken after Rumore claimed they could lose tenure protection and possibly their pensions. Principal Gary R. Stillman put the charter school planning on hold indefinitely after the second vote. A majority vote of the school's parents would be needed for the change to take place, along with approval from the Board of Education and the state. When a handful of New York City public schools became the first conversion charters in the state several years ago, teachers fully retained their tenure and seniority protections, a New York City School official said Thursday. That was not by special arrangement, she said, but simply by law.

Buchanan said that would also be the case in Buffalo. "What the BTF has done is stop the process, even though those are the things we would have worked on," he said. "That doesn't really bode well for any kind of reform." Rumore said his opposition to the School 18 proposal remains firm. "I don't see any reason to support it," he said. Rumore said traditional public schools can institute the same reforms as charter schools. "I don't really think charter schools serve any purpose but to undermine the Buffalo Public Schools," he said.

(Adapted by permission of the publisher from P. Simon, "Teachers' claims on charter plan contradicted," *Buffalo News*, January 4, 2002, p. C1. Copyright 2002 by the *Buffalo News*.)

Questions

1. List all actors mentioned in the article. Identify the types of power they hold and the resources on which each depends.

2. Identify the ethical issues related to power in this article. Be prepared to discuss them.

3. Assuming that each actor is trying to maintain or gain power, explain the differing positions that each takes in the article.

FOR FURTHER READING

Delpit, L. D. (1988). The silenced dialogue: Power and pedagogy in educating other people's children. *Harvard Educational Review*, 58, 280–298.

Delpit describes "the culture of power" that children of color encounter in public schools and suggests ways to reduce its negative effect.

Dunlap, D. M., & Goldman, P. (1991). Rethinking power in schools. *Educational Administration Quarterly*, 27, 5–29.

Dunlap and Goldman argue that in educational settings power can and should be used facilitatively. They provide some examples of the facilitative use of power.

Gaventa, J. (1980). *Power and powerlessness*. Urbana, IL: University of Illinois Press.

Gaventa's award-winning book poignantly describes disempowered people in a valley in Appalachia. His sensitive portrayal of their past and present promotes understanding of why some people seem unable to help themselves.

Robinson, V. M. J. (1995). The identification and evaluation of power in discourse. In D. Corson (Ed.), *Discourse and power in educational organizations*. Cresskill, NJ: Hampton Press.

Robinson insists that power can be used ethically and deplores the lack of materials discussing the responsible use of power in education. Her description of a school meeting raises interesting issues about using power both to give voice to others and to facilitate group decision making.

Wrong, D. H. (1979). *Power*. New York: Harper & Row.

Wrong's book provides a good overview of the major theories about first dimension power and sensitive discussions of some of the ethical issues surrounding power.

THE ECONOMY AND DEMOGRAPHICS

Focus Questions

What is the business cycle?

How does the business cycle affect spending on education?

According to the 2000 Census, how is the U.S. population changing?

What are the implications of these demographic changes for education policy?

WHY ANALYZE THE POLICY ENVIRONMENT?

Defining Policy Environment

Every public policy—including every education policy—is a response to a specific social setting that includes a wide range of phenomena studied by the social sciences: economic forces, demographic trends, ideological belief systems, deeply held values, the structure and traditions of the political system, and the culture of the broader society. Although these phenomena change over time, most of them also reveal historical continuity. The complex social dimensions of a specific place at a particular time constitute its policy environment.

Policy and Its Social Context

In Greek mythology, Zeus, the king of the gods, suffered from a severe headache one day. As he agonized in pain, his head split open and a new goddess emerged. Athena, as she was called, was already fully grown and appeared to have no mother; she was dressed in a complete set of armor and ready for battle. Since that time, Athena has provided a useful symbol for ideas or social forces that suddenly appear, full-blown, as if from nowhere. Public policies—including education policies—are not like the goddess Athena! They do not suddenly emerge from nowhere, taking everyone by surprise. Public policies are responses to the complex dynamics of a specific social setting. Although shifts in policy are not fully predictable, people who are knowledgeable about a policy environment are usually not taken completely by surprise. Their understanding of broad social trends prepares them for certain types of change.

As public leaders, school administrators need to be keenly attuned to their social context and how it is changing (Bryson & Crosby, 1992). Such knowledge permits them to get ready to respond intelligently to relatively predictable changes in policy. For example, a superintendent who knows that the economy is sliding into a recession realizes that tax revenues will drop and that, as a result, school boards, state legislatures, and Congress will probably lose interest in expensive education programs. These bodies may also be strongly motivated to increase accountability for education expenditures. If the superintendent understands this, she may be able to modify district plans to suit the changing economic climate.

Another reason for understanding the policy environment is that such knowledge can help school leaders avoid wasting time, energy, and resources as educational Don Quixotes tilting at policy windmills. Some school leaders, unaware of a changed environment, continue to push for policy changes that have become unrealistic. For example, a curriculum supervisor who has been working with the state department of education to get funds for a professional development program may think he does not have time to follow the news. Unaware of economic indicators that a recession is looming, he may plough ahead with his project, not realizing that developing alternative strategies for this changing policy environment would be wise. If the legislature cuts the department's budget, eliminating the money he had hoped to obtain, he may be caught by surprise, even perceiving this legislative action as sudden. Caught off-guard without a contingency plan, he may feel he has wasted many months of hard work. Sensitivity to the changing policy environment makes avoiding such disappointments easier.

Finally, understanding the relationship between the social environment and education policy helps school leaders conceptualize the broad direction of education policy. Human beings need to make sense out of their experience, especially in periods of rapid change. School leaders who have developed an intellectual framework to use in thinking about policy issues are equipped to interpret the flow of policy change; the policy world no longer seems like Oz to them. Such understanding builds their confidence in their own ability to act constructively as public leaders in a changing world.

THE ECONOMIC ENVIRONMENT

Importance of the Economy

Two of the most important aspects of the policy environment are the structure of the economic system and the current economic climate. In fact, some thinkers believe that ultimately, the economy is the only aspect of the social environment that matters and that all other social phenomena are determined by it. Although this book does not take this extreme position, it does assume that the economic environment is important. In trying to understand why a policy has been proposed or what its real purpose is, one should always consider the economic dimension of the social environment first. Although the economy does not determine public policy, it does establish important parameters within which policy must be adopted and implemented. The next section provides a brief overview of the economic history of the United States and permits readers to situate the discussion of economic issues that follows within a meaningful intellectual framework.

Overview of U.S. Economic History

The Early Days.   The British colonies that became the United States and the early republic that succeeded them did not have a capitalistic economic system. Based on an agrarian economy of small farms, the early U.S. economy still bore traces of Europe's feudal past, particularly in institutions such as slavery and indentured servitude. Market forces were severely constrained by government regulation of prices and other aspects of the economy (Galbraith, 1994).

The Emergence of Capitalism.   During the last decades of the eighteenth century, the Industrial Revolution began in the British Isles, gradually spreading to North America and the European continent. Capitalism was born with the Industrial Revolution, causing not only major economic changes but also the development of new ideas about economics. One of the most important economic thinkers of this period was Adam Smith (1723–1790), who published his masterpiece, *The Wealth of Nations*, in 1776. In it Smith argued that human beings have a natural desire to pursue their own economic self-interest. Government should not interfere with natural human tendencies, but permit them full play. In the resulting free-market economy, both self-interest and broader social purposes will be served, for although each person "intends only his [sic] own gain, . . . he is . . . led by an invisible hand to promote an end which was no part of his intention" (Smith, 1976 [1776], p. 456). Smith's invisible-hand theory and other ideas were used to justify the relatively unregulated development of industrial society in the nineteenth century (Buchholz, 1989).

Problems Develop.   Industrial development in an atmosphere of relative economic freedom led to the development of great wealth and unprecedented standards of living. It also led to serious problems in the United States and elsewhere.

Urban slums, huge inequalities between the rich and poor, and consumer fraud were major issues by the 1890s. Another issue was the wild swings of industrial economies between periods of rapid economic growth and periods of sudden economic "crashes" leading to joblessness, hunger, and social unrest. In this country a few reforms were put in place in the early 1900s, but they were insufficient to prevent the onset of the Great Depression in 1929 (Galbraith, 1994).

The New Deal and Its Aftermath. Many U.S. economists interpreted the Great Depression as proof that capitalism did not work well without considerable government intervention. Franklin Roosevelt's New Deal Administration accepted this interpretation and as a result adopted much activist economic legislation. By 1940 or so, the necessity for government intervention in the economy had become economic orthodoxy in the United States. The result was a long period during which the federal government pursued policies that regulated the economy in order to minimize the risk of another major depression. These policies were generally effective because, although many economic slowdowns or recessions have occurred since 1933, no major depression has happened. The New Deal culminated in twenty-eight years of unprecedented economic growth, stretching from 1945 to 1973. This does not necessarily mean that government economic policy caused the growth, although some economists support that interpretation. Other economists argue that the long period of prosperity was caused by factors such as World War II, the rebuilding of Europe and Japan, and the Baby Boom (Galbraith, 1994; Hamrin, 1988).

Economic Troubles Reappear. By 1973, the postwar boom was clearly ending. In all developed countries, economic growth slowed and an array of puzzling problems appeared. Both inflation and unemployment rates were high, although, according to prevailing economic theory, this should not happen. The rate of productivity growth declined, and wages stagnated. Table 3.1 shows unemployment rates by decade for the four decades immediately after World War II; Table 3.2 shows changes in the consumer price index (CPI), an indicator of inflation, during the same period. In both tables, the strength of the economy between 1950 and 1969 and its problems during the 1970s and 1980s are apparent. Why political leaders of the 1980s and early 1990s were concerned about the U.S. economy is easy to understand.

TABLE 3.1 U.S. Unemployment Rates, Averaged by Decade, 1950–1990

Decade	Average Rate
1950s	4.5%
1960s	4.8%
1970s	6.2%
1980s	8.4%

Note. Based on Plotkin and Scheuerman (1994), p. 44.

TABLE 3.2 Increases in U.S. Consumer Price Index by Decade, 1950–1990

Decade	Percent Change
1950s	20.7%
1960s	23.9%
1970s	87.1%
1980s	33.3%

Note. Based on Plotkin and Scheuerman (1994), p. 52.

In part, these problems were caused by the actions of the Oil Producing and Exporting Countries (OPEC), which raised oil prices in the early 1970s. However, as the 1970s wore on, it became clear that other, deeper problems were also causing economic growth to slow. Many economists began to question the theories that led to New Deal policies and to advance new theories or revive old ones (Baily & Okun, 1982; Hamrin, 1988; Thurow, 1996).

Reaganomics. One of the new theories was called supply-side economics; in many ways this "new" theory was a revival of traditional, pre-New-Deal economics. In fact, workers in the Reagan Administration who advocated supply-side economics wore ties adorned with pictures of Adam Smith (Buchholz, 1989). Supply-side economics recommends pursuing a four-part economic policy: (1) indexing taxes to inflation; (2) reducing taxes; (3) reducing government expenditures; and (4) deregulation (Bartlett, 1981). After the Reagan Administration adopted supply-side economics in the early 1980s, this economic policy was nicknamed Reaganomics. In many respects Reaganomics succeeded. As Table 3.2 demonstrates, during the 1980s inflation was reduced, many jobs were created, and taxes were cut. As early as the fall of 1983, however, some economists started warning about the rising federal deficit (see, e.g., Summers, 1984). By 1990, concern about the deficit was widespread, and it was not limited to economists. In the 1992 presidential campaign both Democrat Bill Clinton and Independent Ross Perot made the deficit an issue, promising to reduce it if elected. The Republican Congress elected in 1994 also ran on a deficit reduction platform. By the late 1990s, the deficit had been greatly reduced; but political leaders, fearful of driving it up again, were still unwilling to support lavish government programs.

The Long Expansion of the 1990s. To a great extent, George Bush, Sr., lost his 1992 bid for the presidency because the recession of 1990–91 caused voters to perceive him as an ineffective leader of the U.S. economy. Bill Clinton's campaign team seized upon the economy as its major issue, going so far as to display a sign in their campaign headquarters that read, "It's the economy, stupid." In actual fact, the economy had bottomed out in March 1991; and the longest economic expansion in U.S. history had begun before Clinton took office. It was to last until the spring of 2001, shortly after George Bush, Jr., took office. During this period, the gross domestic product grew about 4% a year, unemployment fell to 4.1% by 1999, and inflation dropped to its lowest level since the early 1960s.

The value of the stock market tripled. To a certain degree, this flourishing economy resulted from the policies of the Clinton Administration; for example, economists believe that its deficit reduction plan positively impacted economic expansion. Many experts have also attributed this strong economy to decisions made by Federal Reserve Board Chairman Alan Greenspan, who raised and lowered interest rates to keep the system from either overheating or slipping into recession. However, Clinton and Greenspan also reaped the benefits of some of their predecessors' policies. Moreover, they were lucky; although the steep declines in the prices of oil and computer equipment that occurred during the 1990s did not result from public policy, they contributed significantly to the prosperity of the period. All was not rosy during the 1990s, however. The trade deficit reached unprecedented levels in 1998, and wealth became increasingly concentrated in the top 1% of the population (Blank, 2000; Brouwer, 1998; Hatch & Clinton, 2000; Penner, Sawhill, & Taylor, 2000).

Conclusions. This brief overview suggests several general conclusions of importance to those interested in education policy. The first is that economic systems are not stable; they change over the short term, the intermediate term, and the long term. The short-term changes of the business cycle are discussed in the next section. Major changes in the direction of general economic policy such as the New Deal or Reaganomics occur less frequently. Economic upheavals such as the Industrial Revolution happen only occasionally in history. A second conclusion is that although economic changes are somewhat predictable, economics is not an exact science like chemistry. Economists adhere to different schools of thought and hold conflicting theories about why economic phenomena occur. Moreover, no simple formula exists for eliminating unemployment, reducing inflation, or achieving prosperity. Finally, economics is closely intertwined with politics. Ultimately, most economic decisions have political implications, which is why economics cannot be ignored in the study of any area of public policy, including education policy.

Short-Term Economic Changes

Business Cycles. Business cycles are a structural feature of capitalistic economies, resulting from the fact that most economic decisions are made by private businesses rather than by governments. A business cycle consists of two parts: an expansion and a recession. During an expansion production rises, more jobs are available, and business profits increase; prices are likely to rise more quickly than usual, too. The earliest phase of an expansion, which occurs right after the end of a recession, is called a recovery. The high point of an expansion is termed its peak. After the expansion peaks, production, profits, and employment begin to fall. This part of the business cycle is called a recession. Its lowest point is the trough. If an economic contraction becomes extremely severe, it is labelled a depression. In the United States the last depression occurred in the 1930s.

Figure 3.1 provides a graphic example of how the business cycle consists of alternating periods of growth and contraction. It illustrates the business cycles in

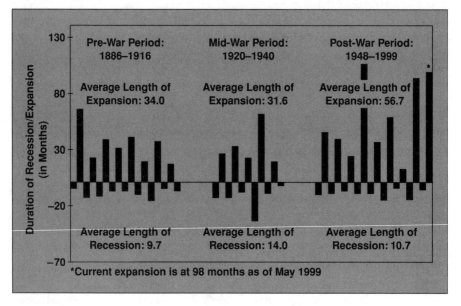

Figure 3.1 Length of business cycle recessions and expansions, 1886–1999.
Note. Graph from *Updating America's Social Contract,* by R. G. Penner, I. V. Sawhill, and T. Taylor, 2000, p. 68. Reprinted by permission of W. W. Norton & Co., New York.

the United States for most of a 113-year period, 1886 to 1999. The figure was prepared in 1999; the last expansion shown lasted until the spring of 2001, when a recession began.

In the economic history of the United States, thirty-two complete business cycles had occurred through 2001. Expansions usually last about four times longer than recessions. The longest expansion lasted ten years, running from 1991 to 2001; the second longest lasted eight years, from 1961 to 1969. The longest recession lasted six years, from 1873 to 1879. As Figure 3.1 suggests, since World War II, expansions have become considerably longer and recessions considerably shorter than previously. Neither the length of the phases of a business cycle nor its peak and trough are predictable. However, the recurrent pattern of the cycles is. "Business cycles are as intrinsic to capitalism as earthquakes are to the earth's geology," writes Massachusetts Institute of Technology (MIT) economist Thurow (1996, p. 211).

Economic Indicators. Economists use various statistics, known as indicators, to track the general trends of the economy. The most important is probably the gross national product (GNP), a measure of a country's total economic output. When adjusted for inflation, this indicator is called the real GNP; real GNP figures for two or more consecutive years can be compared. The unemployment rate, which is the percentage of residents older than age 16 who want to work but lack jobs, is another important indicator. A third is the Consumer Price Index

(CPI), a general measure of the prices of goods and services prepared regularly by the U.S. Bureau of Labor Statistics. It suggests what the inflation rate is doing. The Misery Index is calculated by adding the unemployment rate to the inflation rate; it provides a rough way of predicting the outcome of presidential elections. Almost always, if the Misery Index has declined within the twelve months before an election, the candidate of the incumbent party will win; if it has increased, the other party will win. Other indicators of the economy's direction include: (1) sales of durable goods such as furniture, cars, and major appliances; (2) consumer installment credit; (3) business investment in plant and equipment; and (4) new housing starts (Frumkin, 1987; 1994).

In general, an economic expansion is indicated by such signs as strong growth in the real GNP, a decline in the unemployment rate, and important increases in the sales of durable goods, consumer installment credit, new housing starts, and business investments. A recession is indicated by the opposite signals. The CPI increases during both expansions and recessions; however, it increases more slowly during recessions (Frumkin, 1987; 1994).

Monitoring Business Cycles.   Education leaders must be aware of where the economy is in the business cycle; they can use many methods to maintain such awareness. Most daily newspapers include a business section that covers both national and regional economic news. Major metropolitan newspapers periodically publish a summary of indicators for their area. Cable and commercial television channels as well as some radio stations broadcast shows about business. Online services such as America Online also offer up-to-date business and economic news, as do many Internet sites. Today, following economic trends is easier than ever.

Tracking the local economy in informal ways is also wise because national and regional trends do not always predict local economic situations. Alert school leaders know where new subdivisions are being built in their districts and how much the houses cost. They notice how many shoppers are at the mall on weekends and are aware of business closures and neighborhoods full of "for sale" signs. In thinking about the economic environment, they consider information that they have gathered both from the media and from observation. Figure 3.2 provides a set of questions for analyzing the economic environment.

Long-Term Economic Trends

Slow Growth.   Unfortunately, relatively slow growth has been a characteristic of the world economy since the early 1970s; and experts have no reason to believe that this trend will reverse itself in the foreseeable future. In the United States, the absolute growth of the economy from year to year, as measured by increases in the per capita GNP, has declined since the 1950s and 1960s; so has the growth of productivity, as measured by increases in the GNP per employed worker. During the long expansion of the 1990s, the growth rate in the United States improved significantly; nonetheless, it was just average when compared to the entire post-World-War II period (Penner, Sawhill, & Taylor, 2000). Most mainstream

Which of these is rising? Falling?

- Real GNP (over the last two years)
- Unemployment
- Misery Index
- New housing starts
- Sales of durable goods
- Business investment

What is the current inflation rate?

From local observation, what is happening?

- Are businesses moving in or leaving?
- Are any businesses expanding?
- Are shopping areas busy or relatively deserted?
- Are new houses being built?
- Are sales of existing houses moving well or slowly?
- Are restaurants and recreational facilities doing a lot of business?

Figure 3.2 Analyzing the economic environment.

economists expect, therefore, that growth will eventually slow to the pre-1990s level. For example, Penner, Sawhill, and Taylor (2000) warn that this will probably happen, cautioning: "When making public policy, it's typically wiser to avoid assuming that fundamental changes have occurred, and instead wait for them to be demonstrated" (p. 70). As a result of concerns like theirs, worries about slowed economic growth continue to shadow the economic policy environment, making politicians much more cautious about spending money than they were 30 or 40 years ago.

From Manufacturing to Service and Information. For well in excess of one hundred years, heavy industry provided the driving force of the U.S. economy, with U.S. factories producing cars, machinery, steel, and chemicals for domestic use and export. However, by 1980 the industrial sector was clearly in decline. Factories were beginning to lay off large numbers of workers; eventually, many closed altogether. A poll conducted by the *New York Times* in the mid-1990s found that since 1980, 72% of the respondents had either been laid off themselves or had seen a member of their household or close circle of friends and relatives laid off (*New York Times*, 1996). Nor have factory workers been the only ones to lose their jobs; by the early 1990s people in white-collar and middle-management jobs were being caught in massive "downsizings" as well. Although several causes for these layoffs have been identified, a major one is the transformation of the U.S. economy into one based primarily on service and information rather than on manufacturing. The statistics are rather staggering. According to United Nations' figures, between 1980 and 1993 alone, 6.2% of U.S. manufacturing jobs were lost while the number of jobs in financial and insurance services grew by 55% and the positions in the hospitality industry (largely hotels and restaurants) went up 22.7% (Reif et al., 1997). Although many of these new jobs—such as hotel maids and kitchen workers—were low paying, others—such as financial planners—commanded respectable salaries.

The development of new technologies, such as robotics, computers, and electronic telecommunications is also transforming both manufacturing and service industries. Undoubtedly, these new technologies offer unparalleled opportunities to human individuals and societies, but the transition from an industrial economic base to a service and information base can be difficult. For example, in an information economy a few highly skilled knowledge workers may tend to prosper, but many other types of workers tend to flounder, especially if they lack technological skills. As Reif et al. (1997) put it: "Job creation in the United States is skewing along educational and high-skill lines. The 'middle ground' may be losing way, especially in traditional manufacturing. The fastest growing employment sectors in services are now educationally based—in high . . . technology sectors . . ." (pp. 2–3). Although some people have predicted that virtually all jobs will be eliminated by the new technologies of the Information Age, avoiding specific predictions is more prudent. We can, however, safely suggest that as the Information Age unfolds, virtually every aspect of the U.S. economy will change. These changes will probably present everyone "with the challenge to rethink the way we work, play, communicate, consume, invest, and yes, even think" (Hamrin, 1988, p. 21).

Globalization.   Another major long-term trend of the U.S. economy is globalization, meaning that increasingly our economy is not independent but rather part of a larger, worldwide economic system. Many causes for this trend have been identified; however, the most important ones are probably technological. Because of advances in computer science and telecommunications, information, money, and processed data can move thousands of miles in seconds. As a result, "for the first time in human history, anything can be made anywhere and sold everywhere" (Thurow, 1996, p. 115). This means that businesses—which are more and more likely to be parts of large multinational corporations—can move their factories and offices to places where labor is cheap, taxes are low, and regulation is minimal. This also means that national governments have lost much of their power to influence their own economies through national economic policies. By providing them with stiff international competition, globalization has forced many businesses to restructure, merge, or even go bankrupt. The collapse of the former Soviet Union and its eastern European satellites in the early 1990s further accelerated the globalization process (Galbraith, 1994; Thurow, 1996).

Heavy Debt.   In the United States, increasing indebtedness, both public and private, has been a trend since the 1970s. A major indicator of public indebtedness, the soaring federal budget deficit, was much in the news during the late 1980s and early 1990s. It grew from about half a trillion dollars in 1975 to more than four trillion in 1992, an eightfold increase in fewer than 20 years (Perot, 1993). It increased under every president during that period, but growth was most rapid after 1982. By 1985 the United States was the world's largest debtor nation; and by the early 1990s, 14.4% of the federal budget was being used to pay interest on the national debt (Hamrin, 1988; Perot, 1993). Under Clinton, the federal budget deficit declined substantially and was eventually replaced by surpluses. However, the terrorist attacks of September 11, 2001, led to greatly increased spending on domestic security as well as to military action in Afghanistan. As a result, the federal government moved once more into deficit spending.

Although business leaders and private citizens relish criticizing the federal government's spendthrift habits, their stance can best be described as the pot calling the kettle black. Both corporate and personal indebtedness have also soared since the 1970s. For example, levels of consumer loans and personal mortgage debt nearly tripled between 1976 and 1985. To a great extent this growth was fueled by the rapid expansion of the use of bank credit cards. During the 1980s, millions of U.S. families became overextended financially and the rate of personal bankruptcy increased dramatically. Private indebtedness continued to accelerate during the 1990s, with credit card debt an increasingly important dimension of the phenomenon. Toward the end of the decade, 63% of households with incomes of $50,000 to $100,000 owed on credit cards. Of course, with debt come finance costs; so, not surprisingly, by the late 1990s, 18% of Americans' disposable income was going to pay for debt service. Perhaps the most alarming trend is the tendency for young adults to begin their first jobs with thousands of dollars of credit card debt in addition to large student loans to pay off. By 2000, a third of all college students owned four or more credit cards, and the average student's consumer debt was $2,748. In that year people under twenty-five filed 7% of the bankruptcies in the United States (Haddad, 2001; Hamrin, 1988; Schor, 1998).

Inflation.   Since the end of World War II, the United States has experienced what some economists call "endemic inflation"—persistent, ongoing price increases that cannot be completely controlled (Heilbroner, 1985). In fact, since 1945, the CPI has increased in all years but two. It was relatively low until the 1970s when it exceeded 10% in some years; under Reagan's supply-side economics it dropped again. During the 1990s, the inflation rate averaged about 3% although by the very end of the decade it was running between 1 and 2% (Blank, 2000; Hamrin, 1988; Makin, 1996, 1997). Although high inflation weakens an economy and disturbs citizens, a certain amount of inflation is helpful to debtors. They can pay off their loans in dollars that are cheaper than the dollars they borrowed. However, even a relatively low inflation rate makes financial planning difficult.

Growing Gap Between Rich and Poor.   One of the most troubling trends of the U.S. economy is the increasing difference in income between the top 20% of the population and the bottom 80%. This trend is well documented and has provoked concerned commentary from conservatives such as Kevin Phillips (1994), liberals such as Lester Thurow (1996), and independents such as Ross Perot (1993). It began in 1968 and has accelerated with the passage of time, caused by a complex set of factors. First of all, the top 20% of the population is doing better than ever; they are well-educated, highly skilled workers who can command

TABLE 3.3 Share of Aggregate Income Received by Each Fifth and Top 5% of Families, 1950–97

Year	Shares of aggregate income					
	Lowest fifth	**Second fifth**	**Third fifth**	**Fourth fifth**	**Highest fifth**	**Top 5 percent**
1997	4.2	9.9	15.7	23.0	47.2	20.7
1995	4.4	10.1	15.8	23.2	46.5	20.0
1990	4.6	10.8	16.6	23.8	44.3	17.4
1985	4.8	11.0	16.9	24.3	43.1	16.1
1980	5.3	11.6	17.6	24.4	41.1	14.6
1975	5.6	11.9	17.7	24.2	40.7	14.9
1970	5.4	12.2	17.6	23.8	40.9	15.6
1965	5.2	12.2	17.8	23.9	40.9	15.5
1960	4.8	12.2	17.8	24.0	41.3	15.9
1955	4.8	12.3	17.8	23.7	41.3	16.4
1950	4.5	12.0	17.4	23.4	42.7	17.3

Note. From *Updating America's Social Contract,* by R. G. Penner, I. V. Sawhill, and T. Taylor, 2000, p. 91. Reprinted by permission of W. W. Norton & Co., New York.

good salaries in the emerging information economy. On the other hand, the lower 80% is less skilled and is therefore doing less well; in fact, the less skilled a worker is, the more difficulty he or she has earning a decent wage. Table 3.3 shows how the distribution of wealth among the five quintiles (or fifths) of the U.S. population and the wealthiest 5% changed between 1950 and 1997. The table clearly shows that both the richest 5% and the richest 20% of the population have become richer while everyone else has experienced a decline in their share of the national wealth. Younger workers have been especially hard hit by this change in the distribution of wealth; in the 1990s almost one third of American men aged twenty-five to thirty-four did not earn enough to keep a family of four above the poverty line. An especially distressing aspect of this problem is its impact on children. Between 1974 and 1994, the child poverty rate in the United States increased by 49%. Although it dropped slightly during the long expansion of the 1990s, it still hovers around 20%—by far the highest rate among industrialized nations (Brouwer, 1998; Penner, Sawhill, & Taylor, 2000; Phillips, 1994; Thurow, 1996).

DEMOGRAPHICS AND THE POLICY ENVIRONMENT

The Importance of Demographics

Those who wish to understand education policy must pay as much attention to demographics as they pay to the economy. *Demography* is the scientific study of the characteristics of human populations and how they change over time. The closely related term *demographics* refers to the characteristics of a specific population, such as U.S. residents or U.S. schoolchildren (*The American Heritage Dictionary of the English Language*, 1992). Demographers record and analyze information about the size of a specific population, its growth patterns, age distribution, and vital statistics.

Like the economy, the demographic context can create severe constraints for education policy. After World War II, for example, the U.S. birthrate soared. Suddenly, school systems accustomed to demographic stability because of the Great Depression and World War II faced the challenge of educating unusually large numbers of children. They had little choice: most of the available resources had to be channeled into constructing school buildings, hiring additional staff, and equipping new classrooms. A declining school enrollment presents a different set of challenges, and an aging population creates special pressures for schools. School leaders must be aware of broad demographic trends not only in the nation, but also in their own geographical area because, as demographer Harold Hodgkinson (2000/2001) puts it: *"Nothing is distributed evenly across the United States* [emphasis in the original]. Not race, not religion, not age, not fertility, not wealth, and certainly not access to higher education" (p. 6). Figure 3.3 provides a set of questions for analyzing the demographic environment.

Long-Term Demographic Trends

An Aging Population With a "Mini Baby Boom."   In the United States, as in most developed countries, the population is aging: the average age is increasing, and higher and higher percentages of the population are found in older age groups. This phenomenon is partly the result of better health care and nutrition; in wealthy countries people often enjoy 80 years or more of active, productive living. Another reason is the presence of the baby boom generation—people born between 1946 and 1964. The oldest members of this unusually large age cohort of 75,000,000 people are now in their late 50s, pushing the median age of the

---

Which of these is rising? Falling? Remaining stable?

- The percentage of people older than 50?
- The percentage of people between ages 5 and 18?
- The percentage of high-income families?
- The percentage of low-income families?
- The percentage of minority population?
- The percentage of white population?
- The percentage of people whose native language is English?
- The total population?

What is happening to rural, urban, and suburban populations?

What is happening to family composition and lifestyle?

Figure 3.3 Analyzing the demographic environment.

---

general population higher and higher. Based on the 2000 census, demographers predict a major shift in age distribution over the next 30 years, with a massive increase in the percentage of the population over the age of 50. Meanwhile, the percentage of the population which is school age will decline (It's all relative, 2000; Morrison, 2001).

However, the absolute *number* of school-age children will *not* decline. Rather, the U.S. Department of Education predicts that it will increase through 2005, dip slightly between 2005 and 2010, and then expand rapidly through 2020. This growth will result from what is called the "baby boom echo" caused by the youngest boomers, many of whom had their children late, and the growing families of new immigrants, most of whom are young and have a higher birth rate than the native-born population. The growth will not, however, be evenly distributed across the country. Metropolitan areas will grow more rapidly than rural and small-town ones, and some states will see huge growth while others will actually see their school-age population decline. As Figure 3.4 shows, most of this growth will occur in the West and South (It's all relative, 2000; Morrison, 2001; Olson, 2000; U.S. Department of Education, 1999).

Immigration and Migration. We live in a period of enormous population movement. The United States and several other nations receive hundreds of thousands of immigrants each year, many of them from Third World countries. During the 1990s, the estimated number of legal and illegal immigrants into the United States was 820,000 annually. As a result, the percentage of the population which is foreign-born is similar to the percentage in the early 1900s when millions of Europeans immigrated to the United States. However, the immigrants of the late twentieth and early twenty-first centuries do not usually come from Europe, but from Latin America and Asia; the three countries which have contributed the most to this growth are Mexico, the Philippines, and Vietnam. A great deal of internal migration has occurred as well. States in the South, West, and Southwest have been drawing large numbers of

Alaska	Maryland
Arizona	New Jersey
California	New Mexico
Colorado	Oregon
Florida	Texas
Georgia	Utah
Hawaii	Virginia
Idaho	Washington
Kansas	Wyoming

Note. Based on data from the U.S. Census Bureau, *Series A: Population Projections by Age for 1995 to 2025.*

Figure 3.4 States whose school-age populations will grow, 2000–2015.

people away from states in the Northeast, Midwest, and North-Central states for almost 35 years. This internal migration, combined with the arrival of many new immigrants in the West and South has contributed to the uneven growth patterns shown in Table 3.4 (Growth spurts, 2000; Largest foreign-born populations in the U.S., 2000; Mixed needs of immigrants pose challenges for schools, 2000; The immigration wave, 2000).

Suburbanization.   Another internal population shift that has been occurring for decades is suburbanization. The rural population has been in decline for a long time; but, as the twenty-first century begins, the urban population is also dwindling. City dwellers are not, however, fleeing to the country but rather settling in the suburban belts that girdle large cities. Nevertheless, suburbs are no longer the sheltered havens from the pressures of modern life they once were. Most large cities are surrounded by at least three rings of suburbs: (1) older suburbs that sprang up between 1920 and 1945; (2) the suburbs of the post-World War II era; and (3) newer suburbs, often many miles from the inner city. The older suburbs have taken on many of the characteristics of the inner city. Not surprisingly, then, for twenty-five years child poverty has increased most rapidly in suburban areas, growing by 76%. By the mid-1990s, 14% of suburban children were living below the poverty line (Cohen, 1994; DeWitt, 1994; Hodginkson, 2000/2001; Olson, 2000; Roberts, 1993).

Increasing Diversity.   Because of both immigration and differential birth rates, the U.S. population is becoming more diverse ethnically, linguistically, and religiously. The fastest-growing ethnic groups are Hispanics and Asians/Pacific Islanders. The 2000 census found that 35.2% of U.S. schoolchildren belong to a minority group; for the first time, Hispanic children outnumbered African American ones. In addition, the number of Americans who consider themselves bi- or multiracial is growing. People like golfer Tiger Woods—who is Asian, Black, Caucasian, and Native American—are becoming increasingly common. Table 3.4 compares the current ethnic composition of the school-age population with the anticipated composition of this population in 2020. Because immigration levels vary considerably among states, some areas have experienced the challenges of greater cultural diversity for years. For example, in 1990 40% of the children enrolled in the public schools of New York City belonged to racial minority groups. In the same year 31.4% of public school pupils in California were Hispanic, 11% were Asian, and 8.9% were African American. Until recently, in fact, five states (California, Florida, Illinois, New York, and Texas) received most new immigrants, so the impact of this new diversity was geographically restricted. Today, however, this wave of immigration is fanning out into other areas which are less experienced in dealing with it. For example, in North Carolina the number of students with limited English proficiency grew by 440% between 1990 and 1997; the corresponding figures for Alabama and Kentucky are 429% and 208% respectively. Peter Morrison (2001), a demographer with RAND, concludes:

TABLE 3.4 The Ethnic Composition of the School-Age Population in 2000 and 2020

Ethnic Group	2000	2020 (projected)
White, non-Hispanic	64.8%	55.6%
Hispanic	15.3%	22.9%
Black, non-Hispanic	14.8%	14.2%
Asian/Pacific Islander	4.1%	6.3%
Native American	1.0%	1.0%

Note. Based on data from the U.S. Census Bureau, *Series A: Population Projections by Age, Sex, Race, and Hispanic Origin for 1999 to 2100.*

California is on the verge of becoming the first state in which everyone is a minority (mathematically speaking). The United States as a whole is gradually advancing toward that future, unsure what it will be like to live in a nation in which no single racial or ethnic group predominates. (p. 40)

With ethnic diversity come other kinds of diversity. In many schools, linguistic diversity is a daily reality, with most pupils speaking Spanish or an Asian language more fluently than English. Religious diversity is also growing. The old formula "Protestant–Catholic–Jew" is remote from the reality of classrooms in which many children come from Moslem, Buddhist, or Hindu traditions. And the challenges of ethnic, cultural, linguistic, and religious diversity are spreading as the new immigrants and their children migrate out of the states which originally welcomed them (Archer, 1996; Henry, 1990; Newton, 1992; Roberts, 1993; Rosenblatt, 1996).

Changing Family Life. Changes in the U.S. family provided much fuel for political fires in the 1980s and 1990s. Although the demographic statistics do not fully support politicians' rhetoric about family values, they are troubling. Between 1980 and 1990, births to unwed mothers increased by 76%; most of this increase was caused by an increase in births to unmarried white women, and many of these mothers were in their 20s and 30s rather than in their teens. Although the teen pregnancy rate dropped significantly during the 1990s, the 2000 census reported that less than a quarter of U.S. households consist of a married couple with school-age children, a slight decline since 1990. Moreover, the percentage of households made up of unmarried mothers with children under 18 has grown slightly. In 1994, 24% of children in the United States lived in fatherless homes, four times as many as in 1950. Because such children are more likely to be poor, to drop out of school, to be placed in foster care, to commit crimes or felonies, and to become teenaged parents than children with a father in the home, this trend has raised widespread concern. A related fact recently documented by the Urban Institute is that approximately 4,000,000 children between the ages of 6 and 12 are unsupervised by adults for part of the day (Jacobson, 2000; Outtz, 1994; Trotter, 2001; Vobejda, 1995).

Even those children who are growing up in two-parent households do not experience the idyllic lifestyle frequently depicted in the television situation comedies of the 1960s and 1970s. Because their parents and older siblings often hold down one or two jobs outside the home and because commuting time has increased, children receive less attention at home than previously. Mother usually is not standing at the door when they arrive home from school, milk and cookies in hand, ready to assist with homework. As Figure 3.5 suggests, she probably has a full-time paid job; and, if she is typical, she spends a total of 65 hours a week working at her job for pay and in her home without it. Nor is Dad as available to take children to the park or to lead a Boy Scout troop as he used to be. In a study of working hours in the United States, Schor (1992) found that between 1973 and 1991 men increased their work time by 98 hours a year while their commuting time increased by 23 hours a week. Almost one third of the fathers of preteen children worked 50 hours a week or more on their jobs. Even older brothers and sisters have less time to spend with young children since teenage employment has also soared; and Grandmother is also likely to work outside the home (Schor, 1992; Trotter, 2001).

Conclusions. The U.S. population and its lifestyle are changing rapidly. As a result, today's children are growing up in a world that differs substantially from the world in which school administrators—even relatively young ones—grew up. Moreover, this world is one that changes very quickly. The experience of the children of 1990 was somewhat different from the experience of their younger siblings in 2000. The experience of 2010 will differ from that of 2000. In thinking about the demographic policy environment, school leaders are truly dealing with a moving target. Those who do not stay abreast of these changes risk creating the impression that they are hopelessly out of date. For example, school leaders commonly hear long discourses on parent-involvement policies that never acknowledge that parents have less time to be involved in school activities than they did 20, or even 10 years ago. Such discourses create understandable skepticism in those who hear them. Certainly, the increase in working hours and commuting time does not mean that parent-involvement programs should be dropped. However, parent-involvement programs that fail to take this into account are likely to encounter serious problems. Wise school leaders read newspaper and magazine articles about changing demographics with keen interest, asking themselves: What does this mean for children? For schools and teachers? For districts and administrators? What policy changes are needed in order to better deal with this trend?

IMPLICATIONS FOR EDUCATION POLICY

Implications of the Business Cycle

Because tax revenues expand and contract with the business cycle, that cycle has important implications for the level of funding that is likely to be available for

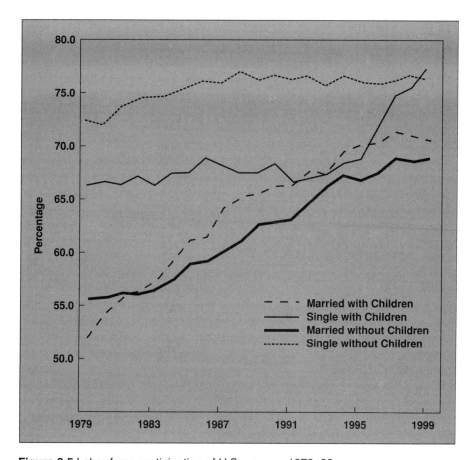

Figure 3.5 Labor force participation of U.S. women, 1979–99.
Note. From "Strong Employment, Low Inflation: How Has the U.S. Economy Done So Well?" *Canadian Public Policy XXVI* (Supplementary issue), by R. M. Blank, 2000, p. S182. Reprinted by permission of *Canadian Public Policy,* Guelph, Ontario.

public education. Guthrie and Koppich (1987) analyzed the political economy underlying each of four national education reforms: (1) the passage of the National Defense Education Act under President Eisenhower in 1958; (2) the passage of the Elementary and Secondary Education Act during President Johnson's War on Poverty in 1965; (3) the passage of Public Law 94–142, the Education for All Handicapped Children Act, in 1975; and (4) the education excellence movement of the 1980s. They compared these four reform periods in relation to nine variables of the political and economic environment, finding that only two of the variables were consistent across all four cases. The first was that all four reform periods were sparked by a catalyst such as the launching of Sputnik or the release of a commission report. The second was that "an upbeat economy undergird[ed] enactment or initiation of all four reform efforts" (p. 37). They concluded: "It may well be that economic buoyancy is a precondition of widespread change" (p. 38).

This finding has both reactive and proactive implications for school leaders. The reactive implication is that, although "economic buoyancy" does not always stimulate reforms in education, reform periods almost always occur against the backdrop of a strong economy. Thus, whenever the national, state, or local economy enters a strong expansion, school leaders should anticipate that proposals for major changes in education policy may be made. During such periods keeping abreast of what is happening in Washington, in the major think tanks, and in professional publications is especially important. However, school leaders should not sit passively by, watching new policy proposals unfold. Leaders who wish to work for changes in education policy should lay the groundwork for such changes during relatively slow economic times and try to catch the groundswell of the next expansion as they start to push publicly for reform. With more public resources available and an upbeat mood in the air, they will find persuading others to support their proposed policy change easier. Even more important, if their timing is right, they will not only have a better chance of getting the policy change adopted, but may also have sufficient funding for the early years of implementation. Working with the business cycle is always easier than working against it.

Implications of Long-Range Trends

The Economic/Demographic Scenario. Policy makers and policy scholars are fully aware of the economic and demographic data discussed above and have been for a long time. For example, in their introduction to the first *Politics of Education Association Yearbook*, Boyd and Kerchner (1988) wrote of "the serious implications of current social and demographic trends in the United States" (p. 2). To a considerable degree, concern about these trends has driven U.S. education policy since the early 1980s.

The demographic trends suggest that the task of public schools is going to become increasingly difficult. First of all, about one out of every five schoolchildren is growing up in poverty with all its associated problems: poor nutrition, inadequate health care, transience, and stress. Moreover, many children—and not just poor ones—have special social and educational needs. These needs might include bilingual or English-as-a-second-language programs; activities to introduce their parents to the expectations of U.S. schools; academic curricula that include more coverage of Asia, Africa, and Latin America; before- and after-school programs; tutors to help with homework; remediation; and mentoring. Finally, discipline problems and violence in school have increased and are likely to continue to do so. The probable needs of today's and tomorrow's schoolchildren are such that public education will need far more money in the near future than it receives today.

However, the economic and demographic trends together suggest that raising more money will not be easy and that raising as much as was raised in the recent past may even be impossible. For complex reasons including slower economic growth, stagnating wages, the aging of the population, the threat of unemployment, and heavy consumer debt, Americans have become averse to tax increases—and even to maintaining the current level of taxation. So-called tax revolts were common in the late 1970s; as a result many states passed tax and expenditure limitation laws that are still on the books. Experts see no signs that these will be lifted soon; in fact, such limitations are likely to be made more restrictive. Moreover, increased concerns about terrorism and military actions to counter it have diverted public funds that might have gone to education under different circumstances. Another problem is that growing proportions of the population have no school-age children. Of course, most senior citizens fall in this category; and the tendencies to marry late, start a family late, or decide not to have children at all further increase the percentage of childless households. These economic and demographic trends interact, intensifying opposition to paying taxes to support schools. Figure 3.6 contains a letter to the editor written by a citizen of a midwestern state, vividly expressing this opposition. Finally, although few people admit it openly, the changing social, racial, ethnic, religious, socioeconomic, and linguistic composition of the school-age population probably makes identifying with today's children and feeling any responsibility for their education or general welfare hard for some Americans.

"Do More with Less"

Two broad reactions can be found to the implications of long-term economic and demographic trends. One can be described as the "Do more with less"

TO THE EDITOR: The article, "Schools 1 for 3 on levies" [Aug. 7], said that the superintendent of the Maple Hills school district was disappointed that the "neighborhood did not support the schools." I was one of those "disappointments."

If I have my information correct, the Maple Hills school levy would have cost my spouse and me $540 a year based on what we feel our home is worth. My spouse and I have no children and we both work. This year my spouse will make what she made in 1994 and I will make about one half of what I made in 1994. This is all due to the "extensive job opportunities and high-paying positions" that all the newspapers write about.

Someone with a $100,000 home and five kids pays $180 a year for the tax levy. Someone with a more expensive home and no kids pays $540. Where is the logic to this formula?

My neighbor told me that my home value went down when I informed him how I voted. If this type of taxation continues, someone else will own this house.

Tom Drysdale
Maple Hills

Figure 3.6 Why he won't vote for more school taxes.
Note. Adapted from a letter to the editor at the *Cincinnati Enquirer,* August 14, 1996, p. A15. The names of the letter writer and school district have been changed to protect their privacy.

philosophy. Those who hold this position believe that public schools already receive more money than they need; the real problem is that educators waste it. This position was espoused by Reagan's second secretary of education, William Bennett, who stated in a February 1988 speech: "Money doesn't cure school problems" (Baker, 1991, p. 628). His opinions were based largely on studies conducted by economist Hanushek (1989, 1994), who has analyzed dozens of studies of the relationship between educational expenditure and student achievement, concluding that: "There is no consistent relationship between the resources applied to schools and student performance" (Hanushek, 1994, p. 464). He argues that the incentive structure in education needs to be changed, not the amount of money available.

Many of the reforms of the 1980s and 1990s can be understood as attempts to alter the incentive structure in order to encourage more effective educational practices. For example, in the early days of the excellence in education movement, graduation requirements were increased and statewide testing programs were initiated or revised. Other popular policy proposals during this period included merit pay for teachers and career ladders. Many states also began to gather detailed education performance statistics and use them to publish "report cards" for school districts and individual schools, making them available to parents and the general public.

More recently, the desire to change the incentive structure in education has led to numerous school-choice proposals, including magnet schools, intradistrict open enrollment, interdistrict open enrollment, and vouchers. The common thread linking these policies is competition; many proponents of school choice believe that if schools have to compete for students (and money), their staffs will be motivated to improve their programs. Inadequate schools will either get better or go out of business. Moreover, competition will force educators to use their resources more efficiently than they do now (Chubb & Moe, 1990). Ultimately, schools will both be better and cost less.

"Do a Lot More with a Little More"

Others are willing to provide more money for schools, but only if it is used in certain ways. Representative of this school of thought is policy scholar Clune (1994a, 1994b). Starting with the assumption that educational "productivity" is too low, he argues both for a funding level that would promote "high minimum outcomes" for all children and for curricular and structural changes to support such outcomes. Additional funding would be "targeted": low-performing districts— whether poor or not—would be eligible for extra financial support, but only if they used it to implement specific improvement plans (Clune 1994a, 1994b). Proposed and actual education policies that reflect ideas similar to Clune's include: (1) standards-based reform; (2) authentic assessment; (3) school-linked services; (4) curricula that emphasize higher order thinking skills; and (5) professional development to support new curricula and pedagogies. Indeed, the No Child Left Behind Act of 2001 provides an excellent example of this approach.

Many people who hold this position are also interested in improved education for at-risk children. Three nationally known and well-researched programs for elementary schools that serve such children are Slavin's Success for All Schools, Comer's School Development Program, and Levin's Accelerated Schools. In an article that beautifully reveals the mentality of those who advocate carefully targeted spending, King (1994) analyzes the costs of these three programs. Concluding that Slavin's program is the most expensive and Levin's the least, she recommends that school districts carefully assess the comparative costs and requirements of the programs before adopting one of them. Because much contemporary school finance research focuses on the education production function—or how best to allocate funds to raise student achievement—most new education policies with considerable funding attached will probably impose both program and performance requirements.

Reading Between the Lines

Most readers have undoubtedly been struck that many of the economic and demographic issues discussed in this chapter are politically charged. As a result, policy makers do not always make fully explicit their rationales for adopting policies that touch on these areas. For example, openly advocating a reduction in teachers' salaries would be tantamount to political suicide in most states. However, legislatures sometimes quietly reduce teachers' hourly pay by increasing their work load without providing additional clerical support. In effect, some of the testing programs of the 1980s did exactly this. Similarly, parents would rise up in anger at the suggestion that they assume a greater share of the costs of transporting their children to school. Yet, this is one hidden effect of some school choice proposals. Figure 3.7 contains questions to use in assessing some of the hidden implications of actual or proposed education policies.

HOW ABOUT LARGE NEW INVESTMENTS IN SCHOOLS?

Theoretically, a third possible policy response to the current economic and demographic environment would be to make massive new investments in schools to help them meet the unprecedented challenges that they face. No major U.S. political leaders have seriously advocated this alternative. In fact, many policy makers argue that, given the economic and demographic situation, this alternative is out of the question. However, cross-national comparisons suggest that it is not. France, for example, has a more elderly population than the United States, has received numerous Third World immigrants in recent years, has a relatively high percentage of poor people, has a heavier tax burden than the United States, and has experienced severe economic problems since 1973. Yet, in 1985 the French government adopted a policy of massive investment in secondary education to be phased in between 1985 and 2000. This policy was pursued by governments of different political parties and enjoyed widespread public support. As a result, between 1985 and 1989, French senior high school enrollments increased by 7.4% *every year* (Husen, Tuijnman, & Halls, 1992).

- What are the financial implications of this policy?
- Will it cost the same as, more than, or less than alternative policies?
- Will anyone gain financially from the policy? If so, who?
- Will anyone lose financially because of this policy? If so, who?
- Will this policy shift costs—as measured in money, materials, or time—from government to parents, teachers, administrators, or others?
- Will this policy shift costs from one level of government to another?
- Could this policy be used to cut costs in ways not intended by its advocates?
- How will this policy affect the affluent, the middle class, and the poor?
- Will this policy encourage more diversity, less diversity, or leave the current degree of diversity unchanged? (Consider racial, ethnic, religious, linguistic, and social class diversity as well as handicapping conditions.)
- Will this policy support family life? If so, how? If not, why not?

Figure 3.7 Ten questions to help in reading between the lines of education policies.

The French example, as well as other international examples that could be cited, clearly demonstrates that economic and demographic trends alone do not determine education policy. These trends have to be interpreted by human beings, and in each society human beings interpret them by means of deeply held beliefs and values shaped by their culture. Moreover, education policies have to be developed and implemented within a political system. These aspects of the policy environment also influence education policies. They are explored in the next two chapters.

QUESTIONS AND ACTIVITIES FOR DISCUSSION

1. Using a daily newspaper, find several indicators of the health of the economy. What are the implications of your findings for education policy?

2. In class, brainstorm ideas for gaining senior citizens' support for public schools.

3. Identify a major problem of at-risk children in your geographic area and suggest a policy for dealing with it.

4. Write a letter to the editor in response to the letter in Figure 3.6.

5. Using the questions in Figure 3.7, determine some of the unmentioned objectives that occasionally lie behind the adoption of these education policies: inclusion, site-based management, and vouchers.

INTERNET ASSIGNMENT

Use a search engine or search directory to locate the Web page of the U.S. Census Bureau. Then locate data about your state and county. How do demographic and economic trends in your area compare to those of your state as a whole? To the nation as a whole?

PRO–CON DEBATE: **SHOULD THE SCHOOLS TEACH ALL CHILDREN A CORE CURRICULUM?**

Yes: Today, more than ever, children in all U.S. public schools must be exposed to the same core curriculum. This curriculum should include the basic skills of reading, writing, and mathematics as well as exposure to the cultural heritage of the United States and its European antecedents. Two reasons exist for adopting such a curriculum. First, U.S. schools have historically been common schools because all children could attend them and also because they provided all children with a common experience. In a nation as diverse as ours, continuing this tradition is essential. How else can we develop in children the understanding that we are all part of the same culture and should be loyal to other Americans? Second, our society has become extremely mobile. A core curriculum would make life easier for children who move from school to school and from district to district without falling behind.

No: The genius of the United States has always been its diversity. We have citizens whose ancestors came from many continents, and we also have many fine local traditions of education. Honoring this rich tradition by adapting the curriculum to the needs of the specific children who will use it is important. In some places this will mean including much material about the African American experience; in others it will mean an emphasis on our European roots; in still others it may mean delving into the history of the labor movement. Each school, each ethnic group, and each community should have the freedom to develop a curriculum tailor-made for the needs of its children. Let a thousand flowers bloom!

What do YOU think?

NEWS STORY FOR ANALYSIS: **THE PRESSURE IS ON THE FEDERAL GOVERNMENT TO PAY MORE FOR SPECIAL EDUCATION**

San Antonio, TX—As a presidential commission picks apart the nation's special education system Monday in Houston, few cities could be affected more by its findings than San Antonio. In the 2000–2001 school year, 15% of Bexar County students qualified for special education services. That compares with 12% of students statewide and 10% in other urban centers such as Houston and Dallas.

Special education serves children who have disabilities and medical conditions that interfere with their ability to learn. San Antonio's figures are high, officials say, because of things like high mobility, a military system that brings in families from all over the world to be near top-notch medical facilities, and the reputations of its school districts. But they also admit some students in special education shouldn't be there.

The pressure is on the federal government to pick up more of the cost of special education. In 1976, when the first law was passed, Congress promised to pay 40% of the bill, but the federal government now pays only 15%. But first, Republicans have pledged to seek reform in the system and they have zeroed in on minority students being put in special education when they simply need extra help with school work.

Some Bexar County districts are already tackling the problem by first dealing with other issues that affect learning, such as limited English skills, cultural differences in learning styles, or not being read to often as a young child. In the Somerset School District, for example, officials have boosted their bilingual education program. Somerset has seen its special ed numbers drop from 17% of enrollment in 1999–2000 to 15% last year.

Several districts, including Somerset, look at how they assess students so no one is automatically shifted into special ed when there is a problem. "It's a paradigm shift from special education being the first thing to fix a problem to the last," said Michelle Harmon, Judson School District's special education director. "Being disabled is very different from being a slow learner," Harmon said. "We should be more aggressive, because of the diversity of the population, about understanding cultural difference."

(Adapted by permission of the publisher from S. K. Hughes, "Special Education: The Pressure Is on the Federal Government to Pick Up More of the Cost of Special Education," *San Antonio Express-News*, February 24, 2002, p. 1B. Copyright 2002 by the *San Antonio Express-News*.)

Questions

1. What aspects of the economic environment in 2002 may have led school districts to pressure the federal government to pay more for special education?
2. Why do you think that the federal government has not kept its promise to pay 40% of the cost of special education?
3. Given the demographics of San Antonio, Texas, why do you think that school officials have placed minority children who don't speak English and come from other cultures in special education?
4. What kinds of policies would be more effective in dealing with these children than special education placements?

FOR FURTHER READING

Brouwer, S. (1998). *Sharing the pie*. New York: Henry Holt and Company.
Writing from a liberal perspective, Brouwer describes the U.S. economy at the end of the twentieth century, emphasizing the disparities between the rich and the poor. After discussing corporate dominance, deficit spending, and the privatization movement, he suggests how the "economic pie" could be shared more equitably.

Buchholz, T. G. (1989). *New ideas from dead economists.* **New York: New American Library.**

Written from a conservative perspective, this book explains the ideas of important economists of the past and tells how they are important today. It provides a readable introduction to some of the conservative economic concepts that have shaped public policy in the United States since 1980.

Galbraith, J. K. (1994). *A journey through economic time.* **Boston: Houghton Mifflin.**

Born in 1908, Harvard economist Galbraith observed a great deal of economic history firsthand. In this book, he recounts the economic history of the United States, emphasizing those portions he experienced. Galbraith served in the Roosevelt Administration and advised Kennedy, providing a liberal counterbalance for Buchholz.

Hodgkinson, H. (2000/2001). Educational demographics: What teachers should know. *Educational Leadership 58 (4),* **pp. 6–11.**

Hodgkinson, a demographer with the Institute for Educational Leadership, summarizes the major demographic trends revealed by the 2000 census and discusses their significance for public education. One of his major points is that different sections of the country are experiencing very different types of change.

Morrison, P. A. (2001). *A demographic perspective on our nation's future.* **Santa Monica, CA: RAND.**

Morrison draws on recent demographic data to paint a troubling picture of our nation's future. Along with increasing racial and ethnic diversity, he foresees an increasing gap between the haves and have-nots and suggests issues with which Americans must deal if they are to avoid significant social unrest in the future.

THE POLITICAL SYSTEM AND POLITICAL CULTURE

Focus Questions

What are the distinctive characteristics of the U.S. political system?

How can school leaders work most effectively within this system?

What is political culture?

Why should school leaders take into account the political culture of the geographical area in which they work?

THE IMPORTANCE OF THE LESS OBVIOUS

The importance of economic conditions and the demographic situation is relatively apparent. However, other aspects of the education policy environment are considerably less obvious to casual observers and may even seem insignificant at first glance. This chapter deals with two of these less obvious factors: the political system and political culture.

The United States has a distinctive **political system** that was devised in the late eighteenth century by men who had a good knowledge of political theory but few contemporary working models available for study. Although many Americans idealize the system of separated powers that the Founding Fathers developed, some political scientists believe that, as the first modern attempt at representative government, it is clumsier than the parliamentary system that evolved in Great Britain during the nineteenth century. Indeed, today most democratic countries use the parliamentary system because it is widely considered more efficient and responsive than our system (Coulter, 1991). Be that as it may, the United States is unlikely to change its political system. This means that school leaders must understand this system's strengths and limitations in order to work intelligently within it. The first portion of this chapter, therefore, deals with the U.S. political system, describing how it constrains and shapes education policy and suggesting ways education leaders can function effectively within it.

Even less obvious than the political system is **political culture.** Daniel Elazar (1994), well known for his research on U.S. political culture, defines political culture as "the particular pattern of orientation to political action in which [a] political system is embedded" (p. 109). He has identified three basic political cultures in the United States: individualistic, moralistic, and traditionalistic. Although on paper the formal political systems of the 50 states resemble each other greatly, in practice those structures operate somewhat differently in each of the three political cultures. This means that a school leader who moves from Pennsylvania (which has an individualistic culture) to Tennessee (which is traditionalistic) will need to relearn many principles of practical politics in order to work well in the new setting. These issues are discussed in the second part of this chapter.

THE U.S. POLITICAL SYSTEM

Federalism

Federalism Defined. The fundamental characteristic of the U.S. political system is that it has a **federal structure.** The best way to define *federalism* is to contrast it with **unitary government,** the other major modern political structure. Under a unitary system, only one government in the country can exercise sovereign power by taking such actions as passing laws and levying taxes; this is the national government, headquartered in the country's capital. Local governing bodies exist, but they are subordinate to the national government that created them and can also overrule, or even abolish, them. Three major countries that use a unitary political structure are France, Japan, and the United Kingdom. Unitary governments also exist in the United States; the relationship between the 50 state governments and their respective local governments is unitary (Coulter, 1991; Isaak, 1987).

In contrast, under a **federal system** several governments share sovereign powers among themselves; and the national government cannot abolish the subsidiary governments. In the United States, for example, the states actually founded the national government; and the federal constitution clearly delineates which sovereign powers belong to the states and which to the federal government. The federal government does not have the authority to overrule state governments when they are acting within their area of sovereignty, nor can it abolish them (Coulter, 1991; Hanson, 1996; Isaak, 1987). Federalism is often used by countries that have strong regional traditions. The young United States, for instance, consisted of 13 former British Colonies with distinctive histories and cultures. Two centuries later, regional traditions are still strong, a fact school leaders should always bear in mind, especially if they are "transplants" to the region in which they work.

History of U.S. Federalism.   The relationship between the federal and state governments is not fixed and unchanging, but dynamic. During the more than two centuries since the signing of the Declaration of Independence, U.S. federalism has gone through several distinctive phases. Because the founding fathers were suspicious of centralized political power, they established an extremely weak federal system under the Articles of Confederation. This structure was so glaringly inadequate that after just a few years the current Constitution was written and ratified, establishing a stronger federal government. However, the new Constitution was controversial from the start; several major leaders, including Thomas Jefferson, had serious reservations about it. For decades the amount of power appropriate for the federal government was a central issue in national politics. Indeed, one major party called itself the Federalists because strengthening the national government was one of its major objectives. The early arguments over federalism culminated in the Civil War, when the Southern states exercised what they considered their sovereign right to secede from the Union. The Northern victory in that war meant that the weakest interpretation of federalism was seriously discredited (Bowman & Kearney, 1986; Cohen & Spillane, 1993). However, other weak interpretations still flourish today alongside stronger ones.

   During the 64 years between the end of the Civil War and the beginning of the Great Depression, the federal government enjoyed a new legitimacy that it used to promote the construction of the railroads, the settlement of the West, and the conquest of numerous Native American tribes. Even so, it was relatively weak by contemporary standards; it did not even begin to levy an income tax until 1916. The Great Depression, followed by World War II, led to an enormous increase in federal power. The economic collapse of 1929 caused bank failures as well as business and personal bankruptcies across the nation, leading to widespread unemployment. Because these economic problems were of such magnitude that state and local governments were unable to address them effectively, the federal government stepped in, assuming an enhanced role in economic and labor policy. This tendency to strengthen federal power at the expense of state and local governments was further accelerated by another crisis, World War II. For more than 20 years after the end of the war, Washington played an activist role, taking the lead in such areas as civil rights and urban policy. The tide began to turn in 1968, with the election of Richard Nixon to the White House. His successors, Gerald Ford and Jimmy Carter, also sought to alter the federal relationship by empowering the states. However, under Ronald Reagan, elected president in 1980, the shift in the balance of power between the states and the federal government accelerated (Bowman & Kearney, 1986; Gray, 1996; Lewis & Maruna, 1996; Nathan, 1993; Van Horn, 1993).

Federalism Today.   In his 1982 State of the Union address, Ronald Reagan called for a "New Federalism," which involved giving the states more power in several policy areas and more discretion over the use of federal funds (Bowman & Kearney, 1986; Mazzoni, 1995). Because education is a major function of state government, the New Federalism had a great impact on education policy. At the most tangible level, it meant decreased federal funding. In 1978, just before the beginning of the Reagan Administration, the federal government provided 8.1% of all money for U.S. schools; under Reagan this percentage dropped to 6%, a decline of more than 25% (Sroufe, 1995). Moreover, under Reagan, the federal government streamlined the administration of education funds by consolidating 37 programs into a single block grant entitled Elementary and Secondary Education. Under this new approach, federal guidelines for spending education funds were relaxed, empowering state governments to make decisions about the direction of education policy in several new areas (Kaplan & O'Brien, 1991). The overall effect of the New Federalism was to reduce the relative importance of the federal government in education policy making while increasing the relative importance of the states.

However, Reagan's New Federalism was not the only factor that led to increased state power over education policy. Starting in the early 1960s, several changes had strengthened state governments, giving them more capacity for exercising political leadership. *Baker v. Carr*, a 1962 U.S. Supreme Court decision, was an important first step in this process. By affirming the one person–one vote principle, it required the reapportionment of state legislative districts, making state legislatures more representative of the general population. As these bodies became more representative, they also began to attract young, well-educated people. This new breed of state officials worked hard during the 1970s and 1980s to professionalize state government; today, therefore, most states have more efficient and modern governments than they had 30 years ago. The professionalization of state government occurred simultaneously with the growth of intergovernmental lobbies such as the National Governors' Association (NGA) and the National Conference of State Legislatures (NCSL). Such organizations facilitate communication among state officials and provide a forum in which information about policy can be disseminated and discussed.

As a result of these changes in state government, state leaders were able to spearhead the national education reform movement, which began in 1983. Although the federal government played an important role—notably by sponsoring the 1983 commission report *A Nation at Risk*—governors such as Lamar Alexander and Bill Clinton worked through the NGA to push steadily for the reform of public education. In many states their efforts led to the adoption of such policies as increased graduation requirements, proficiency tests, career ladders, and school choice. Such an intense and coordinated level of activity in education policy on the part of state governments was unprecedented in U.S. history (Bowman & Kearney, 1986; Mazzoni, 1995; Nathan, 1993).

Historically, states have delegated much of their authority over education policy to local school districts. However, since about 1980 this traditional allocation of power has progressively shifted. The major reason is that local government is often in crisis. Economic stagnation and the widespread adoption of tax and expenditure limitations during the 1970s have reduced tax revenues, and many local governments find continuing to provide high-quality public services difficult. This crisis is particularly severe in large cities, where the loss of tax revenues, deterioration of infrastructure and housing stock, and growing impoverishment of the population combine to create problems so overwhelming that few municipal governments have the capacity to address them. However, the crisis has also hit other areas hard; many small-town and rural communities that were self-sufficient a generation ago find themselves struggling today.

As one type of local government, school districts represent an important dimension of this crisis. Indeed, some big city school districts have collapsed under the weight of financial and social problems; many rural districts are in ongoing bankruptcy. In a crisis of such proportions, state governments have been obliged to take unprecedented steps. In some cases state departments of education have taken over the daily administration of floundering school districts. In far more instances, they have provided emergency loans or assigned state consultants to work with troubled districts. But, of course, when one government gives resources to another, it also expects to have some say about how those resources are used. As a result, state governments are playing a more active role than ever in spelling out how districts should educate children and in monitoring their activities (Bowman & Kearney, 1986; Mazzoni, 1995).

Separation of Powers

Another important characteristic of U.S. government is that it is based on the *separation of powers* rather than on a structure of fused powers. Ever fearful of powerful government, the Founding Fathers constitutionally delegated the executive, legislative, and judicial functions of government to separate branches that could check or restrain each other. Moreover, although the states were free to adopt any form of republican government they pleased, all 50 wrote constitutions that separated government functions into three branches. This pattern is also imitated to a certain degree at the local level. For example, school boards and superintendents sometimes work at cross purposes because of a formal or informal separation of powers. The Founding Fathers thus succeeded admirably in establishing a "political system . . . designed to frustrate central power" (Cohen & Spillane, 1993, p. 38). However, they also raised an interesting question for the public leaders who must work within the system: How does one build coalitions across the system in order to bring about needed change? Cohen and Spillane (1993) observe that the greatest challenge in developing education policy in the United States is "bridging vast political chasms artfully designed to frustrate central power" (p. 43).

Fragmentation of Governance

Fragmentation of Local Government.   Public leadership in the United States is further complicated by **fragmentation,** both the fragmentation of local government and the proliferation of governance structures. Units of local government

```
Counties
Municipalities
Towns
Townships
Special Districts
```

Figure 4.1 Five types of local government.
Note. Based on Bowman and Kearney (1986).

are established by law in the state in which they are located, and usually their powers and responsibilities are spelled out in either a charter or a special act of the legislature. Figure 4.1 lists the five types of local government. Most U.S. school districts are **special districts,** which are governed by an elected **school board.** Other types of special districts include park districts, water districts, and sewer districts; they, too, are often governed by elected or appointed boards. Although some states do not use all five types of local government, many do. As a result, school leaders must deal not only with the different branches of government at the state and federal levels, but also with numerous local governments whose geographic borders may overlap those of the school district and whose officials may perceive the school district as a competitor rather than an ally (Bowman & Kearney, 1986; Fuhrman, 1993; Hanson, 1996).

The relationship between a school system and local government can take one of two general forms: independence or dependence. Ninety-two percent of U.S. school districts are independent. This means they are completely autonomous in relationship to other local governments; in particular, it means they are financially autonomous, or **fiscally independent.** They have the power to levy school taxes within a regulatory framework established by their state legislature. The school board of an independent district also develops its own budget and is not required to submit it to any other unit of local government for approval. Although fiscal independence has some advantages, it also has drawbacks. One of the most important is that an independent school district lacks a natural ally at the local level. Leaders in independent districts must work especially hard to build positive relationships with other units of local government; not infrequently they find themselves alone when the time comes to increase school taxes (Bowman and Kearney, 1986).

Only 8% of school districts are dependent; however, this pattern is more important than the percentages suggest because many of the largest districts in the nation are dependent. In five states (Alaska, Hawaii, Maryland, North Carolina, and Virginia), all school districts are dependent; in 13 other states many districts are dependent. **Fiscal dependence** is especially common in the South. A fiscally-dependent school district is actually an education agency operated by a unit of local government, usually a city or county. Its school board does not have the power either to raise taxes or to approve its own budget; instead, it depends on the controlling government unit to do so. Although this approach has obvious drawbacks, it also has one great advantage: the school system has a natural ally among local governments. For example, if the Virginia House of Delegates is considering legislation that would negatively affect the Fairfax County schools, leaders of the school system will probably work side by side with Fairfax County leaders to try to blunt this effort (Bowman & Kearney, 1986).

Fragmentation Through Separate Structures   A second aspect of the fragmentation of U.S. school governance is the splitting of responsibility among various official or semiofficial boards and agencies. In part, this fragmentation can be attributed to the reforms put in place during the Progressive Movement of the early 1900s. In an attempt to depoliticize school governance, Progressive reformers established separate boards, especially at the state level. State boards of education, for instance, are largely a legacy of the Progressive period. However, scholars have also identified a more general tendency in the United States to establish separate governance structures, both in education and in other policy domains. What happens is that leaders, working within an already fragmented system, become frustrated with its unresponsiveness, so they establish new structures. For a while the new structures are relatively responsive; as time passes, however, they too become unresponsive. The result is a proliferation of boards, agencies, and commissions. In education these structures often cluster around specific policy areas or professional interests. For example, a variety of structures have arisen around P.L. 94-142 (the Education for All Handicapped Children Act), around the compensatory programs established by the Elementary and Secondary Education Act of 1965, and around vocational education and high school athletics. Moreover, in the United States several areas of education policy, which in most countries would be departments of a ministry of education, have been turned over to private agencies. Probably the most important of these areas is evaluation. A large percentage of the tests used to make major decisions about students and teachers is developed by private organizations such as the Educational Testing Service (ETS). Another area of evaluation that has been largely given over to private groups is school and district accreditation (Cohen & Spillane, 1993; Fuhrman, 1993; Iannaccone & Lutz, 1995).

Focus on Elections

Another unusual characteristic of our political system is its focus on elections rather than on governing, a phenomenon that has been nicknamed "the permanent campaign" (Fuhrman, 1993, p. 9). This preoccupation with elections results from two structural factors. First, U.S. elections occur at fixed time intervals established by law. No matter how high a president's or state legislator's public approval ratings are with the public, he must run for reelection when the fixed election date comes around. In contrast, under the parliamentary system of government, most elected officials serve as long as their party has public support and is able to govern effectively. Elections are held when a "crisis of confidence" occurs. Although parliamentary systems can experience periods of instability during which several short-lived governments replace each other in rapid succession, they do focus attention on maintaining public support and governing well rather than on elections. The U.S. system, however, encourages everyone—politicians, the mass media, and the general public—to concentrate on elections and campaigns. Another structural factor that focuses attention on elections is short terms of office. Members of Congress and of the lower house in most state legislatures have two-year terms; quite literally, they are always campaigning for office. Governors, who usually serve four-year terms, and U.S. senators, who serve six, feel somewhat less electoral pressure. Judges—some of whom are appointed for long terms and some of whom are elected in low-key, infrequent elections—feel the least electoral pressure (Coulter, 1991; Fuhrman, 1993).

Judicial Review

A final characteristic of the U.S. political system is that courts have the power of **judicial review,** meaning that they can declare legislation unconstitutional. Although most democratic countries have procedures for evaluating the constitutionality of legislation, because of their power of judicial review, courts in the United States are unusually influential in the policy-making process. In fact, the U.S. Supreme Court has been called the most powerful court in the world (Isaak, 1987). Nor should the power of the fifty state court systems be overlooked. "State supreme courts are policy makers of considerable and wide-ranging importance," insists political scientist Lawrence Baum (1993, p. 149), identifying education policy as a domain in which state courts are particularly active. Indeed, in many states, education interest groups consider the court system and the state legislature alternative routes for reaching policy goals. State courts have played an especially important role in school finance policy, having declared the finance systems of several states unconstitutional. Frequently, legislators are more than willing to let judges make unpopular decisions, for in their ever-recurring electoral campaigns they can blame the black-robed justices. Because judges are subject to less electoral pressure than legislators, they are often willing to take some political heat for them (Baum, 1993).

IMPLICATIONS OF THE POLITICAL SYSTEM FOR SCHOOL LEADERS

Competition Among Governance Bodies

Nature of the Competition.   Dutch sociologist Geert Hofstede (1987) conducted a cross-cultural study of organizational behavior in IBM offices in 67 countries, finding that Americans prefer an organizational structure that he described metaphorically as a "village market." In a village market, numerous vendors compete for customers and sales by shouting loudly, bargaining to make attractive deals, and inventing creative ways to display their goods. The structure of the U.S. political system establishes a sort of "village market" among the various components of government, leading to competition among the three levels (federal, state, and local), the three branches (executive, legislative, and judicial), the many local governments, and various quasi-independent governance bodies.

These political entities primarily compete for two things: resources and power. One major resource for which competition is especially keen is, of course, money, which may take the form of a generous line in a budget proposal, a grant, or approval of a tax increase. Nevertheless, readers should remember that other resources can spark competition. Agencies and branches of the government frequently jockey for desirable perquisites such as office space in a prestigious or convenient location, new equipment, and skilled personnel. Power is the second major stake in this competition. Governance bodies and government agencies often struggle with each other for jurisdiction over specific policy areas or for the right to representation on a board or committee. Sometimes policy decisions that make little sense from a purely rational perspective make a great deal of sense when interpreted as the outcome of a competition among a set of specific government actors striving for resources and power.

Identifying and Monitoring Competitors. Clear-headed thinking by school leaders thus depends on accurately identifying actual and potential competitors. One way to identify them is to ask, "If our district (or school) wanted a budget increase (or to submit a grant proposal, or to hold a referendum to raise school taxes), what government bodies or officials might openly or covertly oppose us?" Figure 4.2 lists possible competitors who should be considered in developing a detailed answer to this question.

Simply identifying one's competitors is not enough, however, monitoring them is also important. One way to do this is to regularly read local newspapers,

City governments
County governments
Fire departments
Health departments
Human services departments
Infrastructure (roads, bridges, sewers)
Institutions of higher education
Justice system
Museums
Other school districts
Other schools
Park systems
Police departments
Prisons
Public hospitals
Public libraries
Recreation programs
Senior citizen programs

Figure 4.2 Government entities that often compete with public schools.

including weeklies, because they are often the only media outlets that consistently cover local government. In reading newspapers as part of a monitoring effort, school leaders should be sure to pay particular attention to reports of local government meetings and to public notices that announce upcoming bids for construction projects because these items frequently contain important information about competitors' goals. Another way to monitor competitors is to establish a good network of local contacts and maintain positive relations with them. Developing friendships in the community and participating in organizations such as Kiwanis, Rotary, and Soroptimist are good ways to ensure that one is involved in "grapevine" communication. Sometimes information is available through these channels weeks or months before it is discussed in a public meeting or becomes the subject of a newspaper article. School leaders' general goal should be a sensitive awareness of all the local demands on public resources most likely to be made in the near future. Such an awareness can facilitate their intelligent planning in a number of areas and help them avoid mistakes. For example, a superintendent who knows the city police department is cooperating with police departments throughout the region to lobby the legislature for funds to purchase new computer equipment may decide this is not the best time to lobby for increased spending on school libraries. Instead, she may conclude that her district's energies would be better applied to writing a grant proposal to a private corporation to obtain financial support.

Multiple Veto Points

The complex, multi-tiered structure of the U.S. political system creates numerous sites in which a policy proposal can be sidetracked or defeated. As a result, moving an idea from the proposal stage to the official policy stage can take years. For a proposal to be introduced several times before it finally passes a major legislative committee is not unusual; indeed, the large majority of bills introduced in a U.S. legislature not only never become laws, but they are never even voted on by the full legislature. They "die" in one of the many committees through which they must pass (Ohio State University [OSU], 1991). Outside the formal legislative process, various additional veto points exist. Strong opposition to a proposed policy change by a powerful interest group or by the agency that will have to implement it can slow down the process as much as any legislative committee can. Similarly, opposition by a teachers' union or an accrediting association can also throw up roadblocks. As a result, school leaders who wish to influence education policy must be persistent and must also build a broad strategic base of support for their ideas. They should not expect that they as individuals or the professional groups in which they are active will be able to influence policy in a short time. They should anticipate a process that will take several years (OSU, 1991). Usually, policy makers must be educated, support among key policy actors must be built, and negotiations with other stakeholders must take place. In the United States, policy changes are the outcome of patient, long-term efforts and broad-based coalitions. Leaders who want quick results or who like to play "Lone Ranger," shunning all alliances, are unlikely to succeed.

TABLE 4.1 Offices and Election Dates	
Offices	**Date of Next Election**
U.S. Representative	
U.S. Senator #1	
U.S. Senator #2	
Governor	
State Representative	
State Senator	
Chair, House Education Committee (State)	
Chair, Senate Education Committee (State)	
Mayor	
City Council Members	
County Executive	
County Commission Members	
Tax Assessor	

Timing Policy Concerns with Elections

Given the tendency of the U.S. political system to focus on elections, school leaders must be closely attuned to the electoral cycle. First, they need to know precisely when all the elections that could affect them will occur at the federal, state, and local levels. Table 4.1 provides a sample chart that can be used to organize this information for easy reference. Second, school leaders need to know the electoral status of every public official with whom they interact. They must know, however, more than just when he will next stand for election. With elected leaders, questions such as how long they have already served, party affiliation, margin of victory in the last election, and the probability of seeking reelection are also important. In states with term limits, knowing how many years or terms politicians have left to serve is also essential. Table 4.2 provides a sample chart for organizing such information.

Selecting the Time and the People.   Both research and years of practical experience suggest that timing is often the key to successfully influencing policy. The electoral cycle is an important aspect of this timing (Kingdon, 1995). As a rule of thumb, the closer a politician is to an election, the less likely she is to support a policy change that would require increasing taxes. Conversely, the most propitious time for advocating such a change is immediately after an election. Similarly, most politicians shy away from supporting controversial policy issues right before an election; those whose position in their district is shaky are generally unwilling to support such issues at any time. Therefore, school leaders who wish to bring about a policy change that is likely to provoke opposition from a segment of the electorate should reflect carefully before asking elected officials for support. Most likely to take a strong stance on a controversial issue is a politician who has been in office for a long time, has a comfortable margin of victory in her

TABLE 4.2 Key Information on Electoral Status of Officials				
Officials	**Years in Office**	**Party Affiliation**	**Last Margin of Victory**	**Likely to Run Again?**
U.S. Representative				
U.S. Senator #1				
U.S. Senator #2				
Governor				
State Representative				
State Senator				
Chair, House Education Committee (State)				
Chair, Senate Education Committee (State)				
Mayor				
City Council Members				
County Executive				
County Commission Members				
Tax Assessor				

district, and does not face reelection in the near future. Another type of politician who may be willing to take chances is one who either cannot run for reelection or does not intend to do so. However, the temporary status of such "lame ducks" limits their power and effectiveness. Although a lame duck may be the right person to approach for a vote in a key committee, he would probably make a poor sponsor of legislation.

Political party affiliation is another variable to consider in timing policy activity. Democratic politicians and legislatures controlled by the Democratic Party are more likely to support increased spending on public education than are Republicans. Thus, school leaders should consider the presence of Democrats in office an opportunity to work for policy changes with significant price tags attached. On the other hand, Republicans are usually more sympathetic to management, including school management, than are Democrats. School leaders should therefore consider the presence of Republicans in office an opportunity to work for policy changes that enhance their own power, such as changes in the tenure and collective bargaining laws.

Windows of Opportunity. John Kingdon (1995) has found that success in influencing policy often depends on recognizing the opening of a "window of opportunity," or a period during which both politicians and the public will be especially receptive to a specific policy idea. Because policy windows open suddenly and do not remain open long, moving quickly when one opens is essential. One predictable policy window is related to the electoral cycle; whenever a change in administration occurs, an opportunity to seek innovative policy changes occurs. This is because a new administration wants to make a name for itself by initiating reforms that will be popular with the public. Moreover, in future reelection campaigns, members of the administration will be able to mention these reforms in their list of accomplishments. Politically alert school leaders are aware of impending changes in administration, especially at the state level. Because most governors serve four-year terms and can be reelected once, such a change usually occurs every eight years. Well before such an election, school leaders—working through their professional organizations and other networks—should begin to discuss needed education policy changes that might appeal to a new administration. Through their legislative liaisons, professional organizations can then bring these ideas to the attention of potential candidates. Although such policy proposals should not be controversial, they can require additional expenditures; new administrations are especially likely to reallocate public funds. Examples of education policy changes brought about by new administrations include: teacher testing, career ladders, preschool programs, and school-to-work initiatives.

Network and Coalition Building

Because of the fragmentation of U.S. educational governance, effectiveness in the policy realm requires building both networks and coalitions. As Kaplan and Usdan (1992) observe:

> To function largely in isolation—which has been the norm in some sectors of education, is to volunteer for obscurity—even extinction. . . . Finding and making common cause with people and groups of similar purpose and vision and so rising above the professional roles and governmental jurisdictions is a necessity. (p. 672)

In thinking about building networks and coalitions, education leaders will find Bryson and Crosby's (1992) concepts of **forums** and **arenas** helpful.

A **forum** is a venue in which ideas are presented, discussed, and debated. As a result of such exchanges, people may change their minds, find that their beliefs are stronger than they thought, or learn that those beliefs are more widely shared than they ever imagined. Issue definition, the earliest stage of the policy process, occurs in a wide range of forums, including think tanks, scholarly journals, radio talk shows, professional organizations, and online bulletin boards and chat rooms. People who do not participate in forums where policy issues important to them are discussed are excluded from an important phase of the policy process—some would say the most important phase.

Arenas are venues in which decisions about policies are made. Rules, laws, and various procedures are established in them. Arenas are far more restricted domains of activity than are forums. Examples of arenas include state legislatures, school boards, the board of directors of a corporation, and the executive committee of a labor union. Forums and arenas are connected with each other because the people who make decisions in arenas also participate in numerous forums.

Building Relationships With Education Professionals. The fragmentation of education in the United States into 15,000 school districts in 50 states means that education leaders must deliberately develop ways to establish and maintain relationships with other professionals in their field. In Bryson and Crosby's (1992) terms they must find (and sometimes create) forums in which the educational ideas and problems that concern them can be discussed. At the state level—and sometimes at the local level as well—professional organizations often provide such forums for discussion. Indeed, this is one of their major functions. After carefully considering the professional organizations that she is entitled to join, each school leader should select a few with which to affiliate, and at least one or two in which to become truly active.

Leaders can participate at several levels in the forums offered by these organizations. Simply reading a professional magazine regularly is an easy way to participate in a forum. A higher level of participation involves attending conferences, workshops, and dinners. An even higher level encompasses presenting at conferences or organizing workshops. The highest level of involvement is assuming a formal leadership role in the organization. At every level of activity, members have opportunities to participate in forums where policy issues are discussed and clarified. As an outgrowth of such discussions, many organizations take official policy positions, which their lobbyists then communicate to politicians. Active members help determine what these official positions will be.

Often, however, forums in which educators can discuss ideas do not exist at the local or regional level. Therefore, in order to address local or regional policy issues effectively, education leaders may need to create a forum first, which can take many forms. In some places, all the high school principals in the county meet for lunch once a month. The superintendents in the southeastern corner of the state may golf together regularly. Sometimes people establish formal councils, roundtables, or task forces. Often, broader forums develop out of more limited ones. For example, in many states the rather informal forums established by superintendents have evolved into statewide forums used to discuss school finance issues. In some states—Ohio and Tennessee are just two examples—such forums eventually led to organizations that retained legal counsel in order to challenge the constitutionality of school finance systems. In such cases, the close link between forums and arenas becomes clear.

Building Relationships With Other Government Agencies. Unfortunately, the relationship between local government agencies tends to be a competitive one, more often marked by the determination to "protect turf" than by a desire to cooperate in serving the public (Garvin & Young, 1994). As a result, agency programs often overlap and duplicate each other, wasting precious resources. For more than a decade, both federal and state governments have encouraged local agencies, including school districts, to work together more collaboratively. For example, in 1988 New Jersey initiated a School-Based Youth Services Program at every school site, which must offer several social and educational services (First, Curcio, & Young, 1994). Pressure to collaborate will most likely continue; additionally, if resources remain meager, officials in public service agencies will increasingly understand the rationale for cooperating rather than competing.

However, launching and sustaining collaborative efforts are notoriously difficult, in part because of the absence of appropriate forums and arenas at the local level. New Orleans provides an illuminating example of how one can go about overcoming this problem by first creating a forum. Convinced of the importance of linking schools with social services, the mayor worked with the University of New Orleans to call a summit conference in 1991. They invited a wide range of participants, including representatives of the public and Catholic school systems, the police department, parent organizations, area universities, the city health department, and the juvenile justice system. At the summit conference, representatives of these agencies began to communicate with each other for the first time. The conference led to a joint grant proposal by the University of New Orleans, the Orleans Parish Public School System, and the mayor's office for financial support for collaborative efforts. Participants believed that one person had to take the first step and provide leadership for the effort, saying: "These groups have been willing to cooperate because someone took the initiative and talked to them about the possibilities of collaboration. . . . Someone has to step forward and begin the dialogue" (Garvin & Young, 1994, p. 100).

Of course, many efforts at local coalition building are less ambitious than the New Orleans Summit Conference. The possibilities for establishing local forums in which representatives of several government agencies can interact are endless and include activities such as monthly luncheons with a speaker, an ongoing discussion group, an annual conference, and a newsletter. Whatever form a local forum takes, at least one forum should exist in which education leaders can communicate with people from other public agencies. A long history of communication and interaction will facilitate networking and the development of eventual coalitions if leaders need them in order to collaborate or seek policy change.

POLITICAL CULTURE

Defining *Political Culture*

In order to understand what a **political culture** is, one should first have a general understanding of what a **culture** is. Sociologist Geert Hofstede (1987) defines *culture* this way:

> [It] is the collective programming of the mind which distinguishes the members of one group or society from another. . . . Culture is reflected in the meanings people attach to various aspects of life; their way of looking at the world and their role in

it; in their values . . . Culture . . . becomes crystallized in the institutions and tangible products of a society. . . . (pp. 401–402)

A more informal, but also useful, definition was offered by a business executive, speaking of organizational culture: "the way we do things around here" (Deal & Kennedy, 1982, p. 4). A **political culture**, then, is a collective way of thinking about politics that includes beliefs about the political process, its proper goals, and appropriate behavior for politicians. Over time, political culture becomes crystallized in institutions such as the campaign fund raiser, the party machine, and the town meeting; over time, such political "products" as campaign speeches, laws, and education policies increasingly reflect it. A political culture is not the same as a **political system**, which consists of a set of formal structures and constitutional laws; the first part of this chapter described the U.S. political system. Even if two groups of people have political systems that appear identical on paper, they will play the political game differently within those identical structures if their political cultures differ.

Political scientists identify three basic political cultures in the United States: the traditionalistic, the moralistic, and the individualistic. Although each of these cultures is associated with particular geographic areas, they are of roughly equal importance in national politics. Moreover, in several states educational leaders can best understand many political conflicts as confrontations between parts of the state with different political cultures. In the following sections, the three cultures are briefly described; they are arranged in chronological order according to their appearance in the United States.

Traditionalistic Political Culture

As readers can see from Figure 4.3 and Table 4.3, traditionalistic political culture is dominant in the South and in regions of the country where southerners originally settled. One major characteristic of this culture is ambivalence toward the market and unrestrained commercial enterprise. It is no coincidence, for example, that the first major American critique of capitalism was produced by a southern politician, John C. Calhoun, whose analysis of the social ills produced by industrialization anticipated some of Karl Marx's ideas. A second major characteristic of traditionalistic political culture is the belief that an established elite should provide political leadership. Although the exact nature of this elite can vary—it may consist of the local "good ole boys" in one place and of a group of highly educated patricians in another—membership in it is achieved through family or other social ties. The overriding political goal is maintaining the established order or, if it must change because of changing circumstances, bringing about the transition with minimal disruption.

In traditionalistic political cultures, government is seen as a positive force in society—as long as it restricts its activity to maintaining the status quo. Active participation in politics is considered a privilege that should be restricted to the members of the elite and those whom they invite to become involved. Political parties and political ideology are unimportant; typically, traditionalist areas have

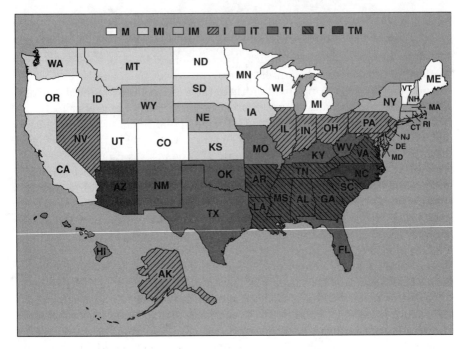

Figure 4.3 Map showing predominant political cultures, by state.
Note. From *American Federalism: A View from the States,* 3rd ed., by Daniel J. Elazar. Copyright © 1984 by Harper & Row, Publishers, Inc. Reprinted by permission of Pearson Education, Inc.

TABLE 4.3 The Predominant Political Cultures of the 50 States

Traditionalistic	Moralistic	Individualistic
Alabama	California	Alaska
Arizona	Colorado	Connecticut
Arkansas	Idaho	Delaware
Florida	Iowa	Hawaii
Georgia	Kansas	Illinois
Kentucky	Maine	Indiana
Louisiana	Michigan	Maryland
Mississippi	Minnesota	Massachusetts
New Mexico	Montana	Missouri
North Carolina	New Hampshire	Nebraska
Oklahoma	North Dakota	Nevada
South Carolina	Oregon	New Jersey
Tennessee	South Dakota	New York
Texas	Utah	Ohio
Virginia	Vermont	Pennsylvania
West Virginia	Washington	Rhode Island
	Wisconsin	Wyoming

Note. Based on Elazar (1984), p. 136.

a one-party system, and major issues are fought out between factions of the dominant party. On the other hand, kinship, social connections, and personal relationships are extremely important. In this culture, politicians are expected to have and steadily maintain a wide-ranging network of personal relationships. Although the traditionalistic political culture is not as likely to become corrupt as is the individualistic culture, domination by corrupt elites is sometimes a problem in traditionalistic areas.

Traditionalistic political culture brings several strengths to U.S. politics. Its skepticism about unrestrained commercial activity sometimes causes its representatives to raise important questions, and its concern for continuity provides needed balance in a rapidly changing society. Moreover, elite political systems occasionally produce courageous, even brilliant, leaders who probably would never succeed in politics in the other two cultures. Senators William Fulbright of Arkansas, Estes Kefauver of Tennessee, and Sam Ervin of North Carolina come readily to mind. Because their power was rooted in a base comprising kinship and other social ties, they were sometimes able to take unpopular stands, secure in the knowledge that they would be reelected anyway. Obviously, the traditionalistic political culture also has major weaknesses. Its resistance to change has been a major factor in perpetuating racism, and its elitism discourages widespread political participation, including high voter turnout (Elazar, 1994).

Moralistic Political Culture

As readers can see from Figure 4.3 and Table 4.3, the moralistic political culture is dominant in New England and in areas where New Englanders originally settled. It is also dominant in areas that received large numbers of Scandinavian immigrants in the nineteenth century, such as Minnesota and Wisconsin. Members of this culture believe politics is (or should be) "a public activity centered on some notion of the public good and properly devoted to the advancement of the public interest" (Elazar, 1994, p. 232). Because they see government positively, as an important way to improve life for everyone, people in a moralistic political culture favor an activist government that initiates new programs when necessary. They also believe participation in politics should be as widespread as possible; the New England town meeting is typical of the participative institutions this culture tends to produce. Ideas and issues are important in this culture, and its members often debate them with great intensity. Unlike representatives of the other two cultures, members of the moralistic culture view government bureaucracies and civil service systems positively because they believe that they encourage the fair and impartial implementation of government policies. Clean government is of great importance in this culture, and political corruption is seen as a shocking betrayal of public trust.

Historically, the moralistic political culture has been the source of most of the "clean government reforms" in U.S. society, such as laws requiring the publication of campaign finance records or forbidding nepotism (the hiring of relatives in government jobs). The moralistic belief in widespread political participation has also had a positive impact on U.S. government, leading to such institutions as citizens' advisory councils and public debates of important issues. Sometimes, however, members of the moralistic political culture become overly rigid in their beliefs or veer toward fanaticism. Representatives of the other two cultures often perceive them as too idealistic and out of touch with the realities of practical politics (Elazar, 1994).

Individualistic Political Culture

The individualistic political culture developed in Middle Atlantic states such as Pennsylvania and New Jersey; settlers from this area spread it westward. Moreover, in the twentieth century its influence spread into southern New England, changing the flavor of politics in Massachusetts, Rhode Island, and Connecticut. In the individualistic culture, politics is understood as a type of marketplace in which the government should serve utilitarian—primarily economic—purposes. Members of this culture believe government should keep to a strict minimum its intervention in "private" spheres such as business, the family, and churches; however, they do want it to provide the framework needed to keep the economy working efficiently. In this culture, politics is seen as a business like any other; individuals enter it in order to advance themselves socially and financially. The political process is based on an exchange of favors that exists within a system of mutual obligation. For example, in exchange for a large campaign contribution from a corporation, a state representative may vote against a law that the corporation opposes. Or, at the local level, a city councilman may help the son of a loyal party worker get a job teaching in the city schools. The party machine—based on a complex system of mutual obligations and strong party loyalty—is an institution typical of this culture. Issues, ideas, and ideology are unimportant in it, as is tradition. Loyalty and strict respect for the system of mutual obligation are what really count. At its best, politics in this culture operates in a smooth, efficient, and businesslike manner; at its worst, it becomes corrupt. The individualistic culture is more susceptible to corruption than are the other two cultures, which is perhaps why people in the individualistic culture frequently consider political activity morally questionable or "dirty."

The individualistic political culture has made important contributions to the nation as a whole. In particular, its emphasis on smooth, efficient, businesslike government has had a national impact, as has its preference for nonideological politics. However, it is vulnerable to the criticism that its practitioners have no principles and believe that everything is for sale to the highest bidder (Elazar, 1994). Several of the political developments of recent years, including the rise of the Religious Right, John McCain's 2000 presidential campaign, and the resurgence of the old Populist Movement on the left can be understood in part as a rejection of individualistic politics by people from the traditionalistic and moralistic cultures.

Political Culture and Education Policy

In the late 1980s, Marshall, Mitchell, and Wirt (1989) conducted a cross-state comparative study of education policy making, using a cultural framework for their analysis. One portion of their research specifically explored the impact of political culture on both policy makers and education policy. Indeed, they selected the six states for their study to include two states with a predominantly traditionalistic culture (Arizona and West Virginia), two with a predominantly moralistic culture (California and Wisconsin), and two with a predominantly individualistic culture (Illinois and Pennsylvania). Marshall et al. (1989) made two major findings with regard to political culture and education policy. First, they discovered that powerful national policy movements can overwhelm the importance of political culture in state level policy making. For example, the impact of national movements in such policy areas as school desegregation, compensatory and bilingual education, and special education was apparent in all six states, regardless of their political cultures. At the time of their study, national reform movements were focusing on school finance reform and personnel reforms. Marshall et al. (1989) found that these rather transitory national trends had also taken precedence over the states' political cultures, even though they were considerably less powerful than the movements for desegregation, compensatory and bilingual education, and special education.

Their second major finding, however, was that in the absence of a national movement, policy differences related to political culture do emerge. For example, policy makers in the traditionalistic states reported that their legislatures were considering reforms in areas such as student testing, stronger student discipline, and weakening the power of education professionals. All these changes are consistent with the traditionalistic desire to maintain elite power and protect the status quo. In contrast, the moralistic states reported they were interested in policies that would target funds for special needs children, establish long-range planning for the development of school facilities, and strengthen state education agencies. These interests reflect both the moralistic concern for the common good and their confidence in activist government. Finally, the individualistic states favored an incremental, piecemeal approach to school facilities and often used cost-saving arguments to support their preferred policy changes. These positions are consistent with their perception of politics as a marketplace. Thus, political culture seems to be an important variable in education policy making at the state level, but it is limited and constrained by the national education policy agenda.

Implications for School Administrators

Suggestions for Identifying Political Cultures.   Because school leadership involves considerable interaction with local and state politicians, education leaders will find reflecting upon the political culture in which they work and also upon their own cultural assumptions helpful. Figure 4.4 provides a framework for such reflection. In using this framework, however, leaders should be careful not to approach these issues in a simplistic manner.

Recognizing that the traditionalistic, moralistic, and individualistic political cultures are examples of what social scientists call *ideal types* is important. An ideal type is an abstract description of a social phenomenon that depicts that phenomenon in a simple, purified form. Although ideal types provide useful frameworks

For each of the following categories, "yes" answers suggest the presence of a given culture; the more "yes" answers in each category, the more dominant the culture is.

Traditionalistic Political Culture

Is political participation viewed as a privilege for an elite few?
Do most political leaders belong to an elite group based on kinship or social ties?
Are government bureaucracy and civil service systems viewed negatively?
Are most political conflicts played out within a single dominant party?
Is government's major role seen as maintaining the existing status quo?

Moralistic Political Culture

Is widespread political participation valued?
Are issues and principles important, especially in political conflicts?
Are government bureaucracy and civil service systems viewed positively, as a way to have impartial government?
Do two parties exist with different ideological platforms, supplemented by occasional third party activity?
Is government's major role seen as advancing the common good?

Individualistic Political Culture

Is politics viewed as a "dirty" marketplace best left to a few professionals?
Do two political parties exist that are businesslike organizations, characterized by a high level of cohesiveness and competition between themselves?
Is remembering one's political debts and paying them off in an appropriate manner important?
Are government bureaucracy and civil service systems viewed ambivalently—efficient but too restrictive of the system of mutual favors?
Is government's major role seen as favoring economic development?

Figure 4.4 A framework for reflection on the dominant political culture(s).

for analyzing concrete situations, they are less complex than the real world, in which phenomena overlap and mingle with each other. For example, although in every state a dominant political culture can be identified, elements of the other cultures are often present as well. In Illinois, the individualistic pattern is most important; however, many communities along the Wisconsin border are moralistic, whereas people in the southernmost tip of the state tend to be traditionalistic. Similarly, California—basically a moralistic state—has strong individualistic elements in the San Francisco Bay and Los Angeles areas and traditionalistic tendencies around San Diego. Thus, assuming that because political scientists have assigned one's state a particular label, the other cultures are totally absent from it would be a mistake. Particularly in metropolitan centers, where people are highly mobile and well traveled, a rich mix of political cultures is often found. Moreover, some evidence suggests that well-educated people, no matter where they live or originally came from, tend to accept the values of the moralistic political culture (Elazar, 1994). As a result, university towns and other communities with a high percentage of college-educated people are likely to contain strong moralistic elements regardless of their geographic location. This means that school leaders who are trying to determine the political culture in which they work should not jump to conclusions but instead carefully observe the political behavior around them before attaching labels to it. They may conclude that two or even three of the cultures are present in their area, and they may actually be able to distinguish community groups or individuals on the basis of their political culture.

Leading in a Traditionalistic Setting. Men and women selected to serve as school leaders in traditionalistic settings are usually people who are acceptable to the local elite either because they are already part of the established order or because they come from a similar environment elsewhere. Even so, leaders in traditionalistic places are not always as traditionalistic as the local elite; their education, reading, and travel have often caused them to develop new ideas about education that differ considerably from the views of the local establishment. As a result, even "down home boys" and "girls from next door" may encounter problems if they do not carefully think through their situation.

This reflection should include three major components. First, in a traditionalistic setting, identifying the members of the local elite is essential. Although they probably will not be openly active in school affairs, they will be interested in them and will have close associates who are active. To a great extent, success in the traditionalistic setting depends upon gaining and keeping the support of this group. In addition, school leaders who work in a traditionalistic area must recognize that personal contacts and social ties provide the basis for political effectiveness in this environment and must invest their energies accordingly, paying special attention to the ruling elite and its close allies. Leaders should never spring unexpected policy surprises on the elite; rather, they should use their social network to prepare for change, laying a foundation through many conversations, offhand comments, articles in newsletters, and other channels. Finally, school leaders in a traditionalistic setting should make a point of finding out what the local education traditions are; and, when arguing for needed changes, they should draw on these traditions to justify them. For example, a superintendent who wants to improve the computer education program of her school system should not make the mistake of arguing primarily that such a change will cause graduates to be more productive workers in the local economy (an individualistic argument) or that it will contribute to the development of a more enlightened citizenry (a moralistic argument). Rather, her major arguments for the proposed change should relate it to successful past changes in the school district and to other local traditions.

Leading in a Moralistic Setting. In a moralistic environment, school leaders usually have the advantage that citizens consider education an important contribution to the common good and are inclined to support it. However, people who are part of this culture also expect to be very involved in government, including school government. A major challenge for school leaders in this environment is providing numerous opportunities for local citizens—and not just parents—to provide input on school policies and practices. Advisory councils, citizen task forces, and town meeting style debates of issues are popular in this culture; leaders should take care to develop them if they do not already exist and to use them frequently if they do. Leaders must also open channels of communication and keep them open, using frequent newsletters, an annual report, a series of articles in the local paper, and other communication devices. Thorough reports of official meetings and understandable copies of school and district budgets should be readily available for public perusal. In a moralistic setting few secrets should exist; most school activities and problems should be well publicized and openly discussed. The development of—or even the appearance of—a ruling clique that makes decisions behind closed doors should be avoided at all costs. Avoiding any hint of favoritism or scandal is also important because in this culture both government impartiality and government honesty are highly valued. Finally, in a moralistic setting, school leaders should clearly identify themselves with certain education principles and ideals; they should also be prepared to defend their ideas with principled arguments as well as with facts and figures. Neither a pragmatic orientation nor appeals to tradition work as well in this culture as do good ideas that can be supported in an ethically convincing way.

Leading in an Individualistic Setting. School administrators who find themselves in leadership roles in a predominantly individualistic political culture should bear in mind that people in this culture tend to have a pragmatic, economic orientation. One of the leader's highest priorities should therefore be running a smooth, efficient, and businesslike operation that offers area taxpayers a good value for their tax dollars. In this environment, school leaders would also do well to develop strong relationships with local business leaders and with local business organizations such as the Chamber of Commerce and Jaycees. Although school–business partnerships can be an effective device for building community support in any setting, they are especially appropriate in an individualistic environment. In developing long-range plans for education, leaders should be sure to consider the needs of the local economy and the job market. Although rationales for change could—and indeed should—include noneconomic arguments, economic arguments should always be included as well. Moreover, having a clear concept of the potential financial costs of any proposed change is essential. Finally, remembering that people in the individualistic culture consider politics a "dirty" business, education leaders in this environment should keep a low profile when they engage in political activity or meet with well-known political figures. In fact, in all their dealings with politicians, educational leaders should bear in mind that the individualistic political system operates on the basis of mutual obligation and the exchange of favors. Although at times requesting a favor may be necessary, school leaders should be careful who they ask and should give serious thought to the nature of the favors they may be asked in return. In particular, they should bear in mind that, of the three political cultures, the individualistic culture is the most prone to corruption. Indeed, in some individualistic settings school leaders would be wise to hold themselves somewhat aloof from local politics, justifying their stance with the old saw, "Politics and education don't mix," if necessary.

FINAL POINTS

In order to be effective as public leaders, education administrators must understand both the political structure and the political culture within which they work. The political environment in the United States is a complex one, filled with many potential pitfalls for the unwary. Even so, it offers many opportunities for those who possess a sensitive understanding of it. School leaders should always strive, therefore, to work with the system rather than against it.

QUESTIONS AND ACTIVITIES FOR DISCUSSION

1. What evidence have you seen in your state of the weakening of local power over education policy? Of the increase in state power?
2. Identify a policy change that would be beneficial to your school system and estimate its probable cost. Then develop a list of all other agencies, offices, departments, and programs at the state and local levels whose support would be helpful if you were to try to bring about this change.
3. Use the information in Table 4.3 to develop a chart that summarizes key information about elected political leaders for your area. What are the implications of your chart for education policy at this time?
4. Use Figure 4.3 to analyze your own political beliefs and attitudes. Then use it to analyze the political culture of the area in which you work professionally. What conclusions can you draw from these analyses?

INTERNET ASSIGNMENT

Find the Web sites for three state departments of education, one in a state with a traditionalistic political culture, one in a state with a moralistic political culture, and one in a state with an individualistic political culture. Do you find any differences which could be attributed to differences in political culture? Seek to explain your findings.

PRO-CON DEBATE   SHOULD SCHOOL BOARDS BE ABOLISHED?

YES: The school board was a wonderful institution for nineteenth-century America. It was appropriate at a time when only a few rudiments of the "three R's" were necessary for most children and when teachers themselves were not well educated. In an age of global competition, however, school boards are an anachronism. Most states do not even require that school board members be literate, much less knowledgeable about education. Putting more and more accountability measures in place for teachers and administrators while still giving the ultimate control of the school system to people who mean well but know very little about the learning process no longer makes sense. Nor does it make sense to raise the standards for teacher and administrator training and then put professional educators under the supervision of a lay school board. Can you imagine what our health care system would be like if doctors had to follow the policy dictates of elected "medical boards"? It is time to modernize our governance system by eliminating the old-fashioned school board!

NO: The school board is one of the last bastions of democracy in the United States. It also is an important way of building community support for public schools. Electing school board members gives people an interest in their school system and in their local community. It also provides a way for them to express their views on one of the most important functions of government—providing education for children and youth. Moreover, elected school boards help prevent education from becoming the preserve of a few professional experts. The education of our children is every citizen's concern because it shapes the future of our whole society. Therefore, everyone should have a chance to participate in the governing of the school system by electing people to school boards. Abolishing school boards would be a disastrous step for us to take; it would remove education from public control and cause many citizens to lose all interest in it. Ultimately, this could mean considerable financial loss for our public schools.

What do YOU think?

NEWS STORY FOR ANALYSIS **LYNN SCHOOL COULD LOSE CHARTER**

Lynn, MA—The Lynn Community Charter School could become the first in the state to lose its charter because of poor academic achievement, the State Department of Education said. State Education Commissioner David Driscoll will recommend to the Board of Education that the school's charter be revoked, because it has not fulfilled its promise to deliver high academic achievement since it opened in 1997.

Specifically, the state said the school has consistently performed below the average of the state and Lynn public schools on the MCAS exam, a requirement for high school graduation in Massachusetts. Scores on the California Achievement Tests, a national test that measures student performance in math and reading in grades 1 through 8, also were substandard. If the board approves Driscoll's recommendation, the school would close in June. Lynn Community Charter School would be the first in the state to close because of academic concerns.

School officials acknowledge the 2001 MCAS scores did not improve significantly. Still, they defended the school's academic performance and plan to appeal Driscoll's recommendation by requesting a hearing before state education officials, they said. Herb Fox, chairman of the board of directors at the school said, "It appears that Commissioner Driscoll and I have different views on our weaknesses. We can overcome our weakness. Every organization has strengths and weaknesses. We should be given a chance to prove ourselves."

It might be an uphill battle. A state evaluation of the school, conducted over a three-day period in November, found the school failed to satisfy three key questions that determine whether a school's charter can be renewed: Is its academic program a success? Is it a viable organization? Is it faithful to the terms of its charter? The report followed a tumultuous year for the Lynn Community Charter School. Conflict between the board and administration resulted in the resignation in August of the school's founder and executive director, Lisa Drake. Since then, the K-8 school has been operating without an executive director, with Amy Marx, a four-year staff member, solely at the helm.

Although the state report also cited lack of stability in the school administration and on the board of trustees, officials say progress is being made on both fronts. In the last year, the school hired a director of operations and a director of development to work on fund raising. The board of directors also is recruiting new members. Although the 12-member board now has five voting members, including four parents, a search is on for new members who can bring strength and commitment to the board.

For their part, parents and students said they plan to fight for their school. A grassroots campaign is already underway, with calls being made and e-mails sent to Driscoll and the Board of Education. Plans also are being made for parents and students to attend the board meetings. "Each and every parent has to take action," said Micheal Brown, a parent of four children at the school. "Without us, nothing will get done." Students, too, said they're prepared to fight for their school. Some have already started a petition drive.

(Adapted by permission of the publisher from K. McCabe, "Lynn School Could Lose Charter; Test Scores Cited; Revocation Sought," *The Boston Globe*, January 20, 2002, p. 1. Copyright 2002 by *The Boston Globe*.)

Questions

1. What is the predominant political culture of the state in which the Lynn Community Charter School is located?
2. Briefly summarize the major characteristics of this political culture.
3. In what ways does the behavior of the people and groups mentioned in the article reflect this culture?
4. How might a similar situation be handled differently in areas with other political cultures?

FOR FURTHER READING

Benham, M. K. P., & Heck, R. H. (1994). Political culture and policy in a state-controlled educational system: The case of educational politics in Hawai'i. *Educational Administration Quarterly, 30*, 419–450.

As the only U.S. state with a single, centralized school district, Hawaii makes an interesting case study in politics and school governance. Applying

Marshall et al.'s (1989) concept of political culture to Hawaii's history of education policy making, the authors conclude that efficiency has always been a central goal in state policy and that the policy process has always been dominated by an elite.

Cohen, D. K., & Spillane, J. P. (1993). **Policy and practice: The relations between governance and instruction. In S. H. Fuhrman (Ed.),** *Designing coherent education policy.* **San Francisco: Jossey-Bass.**

Cohen and Spillane vividly describe the fragmented U.S. system of school governance and discuss the various ways that people interested in education policy making have used to try to overcome it. This chapter provides a good overview of some of the most important education policy networks.

Fuhrman, S. H. (1993). **The politics of coherence. In S. H. Fuhrman (Ed.),** *Designing coherent education policy.* **San Francisco: Jossey-Bass.**

One of the greatest challenges in U.S. education policy making is learning to work within a remarkably complex governance system. Fuhrman analyzes the major characteristics of this system, including fragmentation, emphasis on elections, policy overload, and overspecialization. She also describes recent efforts to overcome fragmentation.

Iannaccone, L., & Lutz, F. W. (1995). **The crucible of democracy: The local arena. In J. D. Scribner & D. Layton (Eds.),** *The study of educational politics.* **Washington, DC: Falmer Press.**

In their discussion of policy making at the local level, the authors include a perceptive analysis of current trends toward reducing local power. They also discuss the legacy of the municipal reform movement of the early 1900s and its long-term effects on school politics.

Marshall, C., Mitchell, D., & Wirt, F. (1989). *Culture and education policy in the American states.* **New York: Falmer Press.**

This is the only full-length work that applies the concepts of political culture to education policy making. The findings regarding political culture and the discussion of the culture of state legislatures make this book a valuable source of information on the deep background of education policy.

VALUES AND IDEOLOGY

Focus Questions

What values shape education policy?

How do these values relate to the major U.S. political ideologies?

How can education leaders identify the values and ideological positions behind policies and policy proposals?

In an increasingly ideological policy environment, how can education leaders act both effectively and democratically?

THE IMPORTANCE OF IDEAS

An aspect of the policy environment as intangible as political culture is ideas: those values and thought systems located, not in the outer world, but in human minds. Because for generations politics in the United States was generally considered nonideological, or unconcerned with ideas, early policy analysts advocated the "value-free" analysis of public policies. In part, this mind-set was a product of the individualistic political culture that dominated mainstream U.S. politics for several decades. In part, too, it resulted from a widespread consensus around a few central ideas and values that had grown out of the Great Depression and World War II experiences of the 1930s and 1940s. Seen from an international perspective, this U.S. consensus was always ideological because it was based on values such as individualism, limited government intervention in society, and the free (although regulated) market. Since the early 1980s, however, this consensus has eroded—primarily because of the resurgence of conservatism. Although today's conservatives value individualism at least as much as the supporters of the earlier ideological consensus did, many advocate severely restricting government power to regulate the economy. Some of them also support increased government power over moral behavior. This growing conservative influence, conflicting with the older belief system, has thrown into sharp relief the ideological and value conflicts that were latent earlier. In the early twenty-first century, politics in the United States can no longer accurately be described as nonideological, nor is it any longer realistic to ignore values when studying policy (Boyd, 1984; Lowi, 1995). As a result, today's school leaders need a general understanding of the political ideas that swirl around them in order to think intelligently about education policy.

"Ideas operate as the proximate driving force in American politics, in particular in domestic affairs and consequently in the politics of education at every level of American government," insists Iannaccone (1988). Ideas, beliefs, and values are important for at least two reasons. First, they shape the way people define policy problems. For example, one of the most fundamental American ideas is individualism, a high value placed on "independence and self-reliance above all else" (Bellah, Madsen, Sullivan, Swidler, & Tipton, 1996, p. viii). Americans' individualistic orientation encourages them to understand problems in terms of personal rather than social responsibility. Faced with evidence that many parents struggle to find adequate day care for their preschoolers, Americans are more likely to define the problem as "too many working mothers" rather than as "inadequate social support for young families." Second, ideas, beliefs, and values constrain people's ability to perceive possible solutions to policy problems. Having defined the child-care problem at the individual level, most Americans are more likely to see possible solutions such as a public relations campaign encouraging mothers to stay home with their children or a tax break for private businesses that provide day care for their employees. They are less likely to perceive possible solutions such as government-operated nursery schools or government subsidies to families to make staying home with young children easier for parents—policy solutions that are in effect in several western democracies. Even if they did perceive such solutions, U.S. politicians would probably not support them. In their research on policy making at the state level, Marshall et al. (1989) found that policy makers will not consider ideas "that diverge from the prevailing dominant values" (p. 42) because advocating such ideas makes them sound "irrelevant." Due to the importance of ideas in the development and implementation of education policy, no policy or policy proposal can be fully understood without considering the values and ideological system that undergird it. In thinking about education policy, therefore, school leaders must ask questions such as: What values led people to propose this policy? Are any value conflicts inherent in it? What assumptions about society, government, and economics lie behind it? With what broader ideological position is this policy consistent?

BASIC VALUES IN U.S. POLITICS

Self-Interest and Other Values

Starting in the 1950s, utilitarian social theories derived from economics began to dominate political science in the United States. According to utilitarian philosophy, all human behavior is determined by **self-interest;** therefore, the only values operative in the policy environment are those that directly advance the interests of particular individuals or groups (Fowler, 1995b). In the last ten or fifteen years, however, many political scientists have challenged the utilitarian position, producing research evidence in support of their contention that other values also shape political behavior (e.g., Jackson & Kingdon, 1992; Kelman, 1988; McDonnell, 1991). This book takes a position consistent with this newer research and also with the Weberian tradition in social theory, which insists that human behavior is shaped by *both* self-interest and other values such as commitments to ideological, philosophical, or religious principles. Weber used a railroad metaphor to compare the relationship between self-interest and other values, describing self-interest as the fuel that made the engine's operation possible and the other values as the switchmen who decided on which tracks the train would actually run (Schroeder, 1992). This means that, in analyzing the values that undergird an education policy or policy proposal, one must always consider issues of self-interest. Nevertheless, one must also always move beyond mere self-interest to consider other values, as well as the general belief systems of the advocates of the policy. Only in this manner can the underlying ideas behind a policy be accurately determined.

Self-Interest Values

Economic.   Many people are motivated almost entirely by their own **economic interests** or by the economic interests of a group with which they identify. Moreover, very few people act without considering how their behavior will affect their economic situation. Therefore, one of the first steps in the analysis of any education policy or policy proposal should be to ask: Who benefits economically from this policy? Who is economically penalized by it? The beneficiary may be an individual; a broad class of individuals, such as businesspeople; or an organized group, such as a teachers' union. The economic benefit may be obvious (e.g., tax breaks for businesses, salary increases for teachers). Sometimes, however, the benefits are not immediately clear; a complex piece of special education legislation may financially benefit lawyers by establishing an ambiguous legal situation that increases their business. Similarly, who suffers economically from a policy may be immediately clear or may require considerable reflection in order to identify those who are penalized. Figure 5.1 summarizes some of the more common economic benefits related to education policy; the most common economic penalties are the reverse of these benefits.

Power.   Individuals and groups also often act to increase their power. Therefore, additional questions that should always be asked early in the analysis of an

```
Salary increases
Increases in fringe benefits—leaves, insurance,
    retirement, etc.
Tax reductions or waivers
Increased demand for one's services
Increased number of jobs in a department or field
Shifts of costs from one institution to another
Increases in available materials, clerical aid, etc.
```

Figure 5.1 Types of economic benefits.

```
A new legal right
Representation in a decision-making group
Veto power over decisions
Access to information
Access to channels of communication
The right to serve long or indefinite terms
Authority to advise decision makers
An extension of one's jurisdiction
An increase in job security
```

Figure 5.2 Types of power benefits.

education policy or policy proposal are: Who will gain power as a result of this policy? Who will lose power? Answering these questions often requires considerable thought because power plays are frequently well hidden beneath seemingly neutral policies or cloaked in high-flown rhetoric. Figure 5.2 summarizes some major policy devices for increasing power; again, the loss of any of these privileges constitutes a loss of power.

General Social Values

General social values pervade a society and are held by virtually all people, regardless of their ideological, philosophical, or religious commitments. Often members of the society see these values as so self-evident that they do not even try to explain or justify them.

Order.   Coplin and O'Leary (1981) consider **order** an overarching value of such central importance that it is a high priority in every society—developed and developing, democratic and nondemocratic, Eastern and Western. The reason is clear: Human beings want and need to live in an environment in which they are relatively safe from physical harm and in which their property is relatively secure. Few places are more frightening than those in which social order has broken down; therefore, most governments will go to great lengths to prevent such an occurrence. The United States is no exception; crime, terrorism, war, and other threats to order always rank high on the public policy agenda. Because broader social problems spill over into the schools, order is also a major education policy concern. During the late 1990s, a series of school shootings, such as those at Columbine High School in Colorado and Paducah, Kentucky, dramatized for the general public the possibility that violent deaths could occur at school. Of course, violent deaths have not occurred in many schools, but other types of violence happen in them regularly, from bullying on the playground to fights in hallways. In 1995, problems of this type led parents in Nashua, New Hampshire, to form an organization called Citizens for Discipline in Schools, which lobbies for stricter discipline policies. Within little more than a year, sixteen chapters had been formed in New Hampshire, and parents in three other states had expressed interest, suggesting the level of public concern about order in schools (Portner, 1996a). Explicitly or implicitly, the high value that most Americans—including practicing educators—place on orderly schools is always an important influence on education policy.

Individualism. "Individualism lies at the very core of American culture," wrote Bellah et al. (1996) in their modern classic, *Habits of the Heart*. The findings of Dutch sociologist Hofstede (1987) are consistent with this assertion: In a study of IBM employees in sixty-seven countries, Hofstede found that Americans were the most individualistic. Valuing **individualism** means both tending to consider the single person and her needs before those of the group and emphasizing self-reliance. Bellah and his co-authors describe two forms of U.S. individualism. **Utilitarian individualism** refers to the belief that people can—and should—take the initiative to advance their own economic success even at the expense of other worthwhile pursuits such as family life, friendship, and community involvement. **Expressive individualism** is in many ways a reaction against this emphasis on one's economic interests; expressive individualists stress the "deeper cultivation of the self" (p. 33) and the freedom to express that self and its feelings with minimal restraint from social conventions. The quintessential American utilitarian individualist is the self-made man, Benjamin Franklin; while poet Walt Whitman, author of *Song of Myself*, represents expressive individualism.

U.S. education policy reflects the underlying individualism of the culture and tends to swing between the utilitarian and expressive forms of the value. The very structure of the system, with its thousands of small local school districts, is an expression of individualism; and resistance by Americans to policies such as national standards, curriculum, and examinations can be understood as a desire for individualistic rather than group-oriented policies. The current emphasis on the pragmatic purposes of education and the tendency to reject subjects such as music and art as "frills" are consistent with the utilitarian orientation. Periodically, however, expressive individualism resurges. For example, in the 1960s and early 1970s, many U.S. school districts established open-space schools and expanded the number of high school electives. These policy approaches—designed to encourage children's self-actualization—were largely abandoned during the more utilitarian 1980s. Whether utilitarian or expressive, individualism is a major value underlying U.S. education policy. Although strong rational arguments can be advanced for a more group-oriented—or "systemic"—approach to education policy, the deeply ingrained individualism of U.S. culture makes the adoption and implementation of such policies difficult.

Democratic Values

The great rallying cry of the French Revolution of 1789 was "Liberty, Fraternity, Equality!" Political scientists agree that this slogan provides a succinct summary of the values essential in a society that wishes to have a democratic government. Each of these three values is, however, multifaceted and can be defined in several ways. Many of the value conflicts in democratic countries and in their education policies center around these values—around what they mean and how they can best be achieved, protected, or expanded.

Liberty.   **Liberty**—sometimes also called *freedom, independence,* or *choice*—is a fundamental principle of democracy, and these words resonate deeply in the hearts of most people. The U.S. Bill of Rights guarantees several basic freedoms essential to the operation of our form of government, including the freedoms of speech, the press, conscience, and association (Rawls, 1971). The U.S. Constitution also implicitly grants citizens the freedom to own property and to engage in commercial activity. Although the freedom to lead one's private life without interference is not guaranteed by the literal wording of the Constitution, twentieth-century courts developed a body of case law defining various privacy rights, which constitute a general freedom to select one's lifestyle. Included among these freedoms are the rights to marry (or not marry), to have children, to make major decisions about the upbringing of one's children, and to protect one's privacy.

These freedoms do not exist in splendid isolation from each other, however; political philosopher Rawls (1971) argues in *A Theory of Justice* that "liberty is a certain structure of institutions, a certain system of public rules defining rights and duties" (p. 202). This means that no freedom is unrestricted; each freedom has limits, and all the freedoms must constantly be balanced against each other in law and custom. As the popular saying goes, "Your freedom to swing your arm ends where my nose begins."

Liberty is a major education policy value. During the 1960s and 1970s, for example, a series of court decisions clearly stated that students and teachers do not lose their political freedoms when they enter a school building. As U.S. citizens, they have the constitutional right to speak out, to form organizations, and to assemble peacefully. Students' and teachers' civil liberties are not unlimited, however; they can be asserted at school only insofar as their exercise does not disrupt the learning process or infringe upon the freedom of other people. Thus, students do not have the freedom to run around the room while the teacher explains a lesson; and a teacher's religious freedom does not include the right to proselytize students. Since the early 1980s, many people have advocated the adoption of school-choice policies, arguing that such policies are an inherent aspect of parents' freedom to raise their children and also of freedom of conscience (Viteritti, 1999). This freedom, too, has limitations. No parents are free to

How does this policy affect the political freedoms (speech, press, association, assembly) of teachers?

How does this policy affect the political freedoms (speech, press, association, assembly) of students?

How does this policy affect the range of choices open to parents?

How does this policy affect the range of choices open to students?

How does this policy affect the freedom of thought in areas such as access to knowledge, encouragement of open debate, and presentation of a range of ideas in school?

How does this policy affect the religious freedom of students? of faculty?

How does this policy affect the autonomy of the faculty as a decision-making group?

Is the policy justified with discourse that includes words such as *free, freedom, choice, independence, autonomy,* and *liberty?*

Figure 5.3 Questions to ask in evaluating the freedom issues in a policy.

choose to raise their children in illiteracy or to send them to a school in which they are abused physically or emotionally. Figure 5.3 provides some questions to use in evaluating the aspects of an education policy that relate to freedom.

Equality.   The second central democratic value is **equality;** the Declaration of Independence reads in part: ". . . all men are created equal. . . . " Of course, this statement does not mean that all human beings have equal intelligence, physical strength, power, wealth, or other attributes people value. Rather, it means that all people are equally human and are therefore entitled to an equal standing before the law and to an equal opportunity to live their lives in a way not too remote from the norms of their society. Democracy depends on a certain degree of social equality because extreme variations in wealth and power lead to distrust and also to social conflict. Not coincidentally, medieval Europe and nineteenth-century India were not governed democratically—the enormous social inequalities that characterized both societies made democracy impossible.

Equality—sometimes called *equity* or *social justice*—has several meanings. **Political equality** is the equal right to participate in the political system, whereas **economic equality** means equal wealth. Neither is an absolute; both political equality and economic equality are relative terms. Countries and historical periods are often systematically compared in order to determine the relative degree to which they have achieved both forms of equality. In such a study of equality, Verba and Orren (1985) found that the United States is politically rather egalitarian because, compared to citizens of other developed countries, Americans have great access to participation in the political system. The United States compares less favorably on measures of economic equality, however; of all developed countries, it has the largest gap between rich and poor.

Equality can also be analyzed in terms of **equality of opportunity** and **equality of results.** Equal opportunity exists when everyone has a similar chance to get a good education or find a decent job, regardless of race, sex, handicapping condition, age, or national origin. Where equal opportunity really exists, unequal results are caused largely by factors under the control of the individual such as effort and extra study. Most Americans strongly believe in equal opportunity. Equality of results exists when the range from high to low is relatively narrow. For example, when the range between the 75th and 25th scores on a standardized mathematics tests is small, rough equality of educational results has occurred. Or, when the difference between the salaries of an average worker and an average CEO is relatively small, equality of income results has occurred. This form of equality cannot be achieved by permitting children to compete freely in school or by allowing the market to determine salaries; it requires some form of intervention. Relatively equal mathematics scores might be achieved by providing special tutoring programs for weaker students; relatively equal salaries could be achieved by legislating minimums and maximums for wages. Although many democratic countries use such policies to increase equality of results, the United States generally does not. According to Verba and Orren (1985), the major reason is that most Americans dislike the concept of equality of results because it is inconsistent with the ideal of individual achievement.

Equal opportunity has always been a major value in U.S. education policy. "Equality of educational opportunity has appeared as a normative goal of education policy in the United States since the beginning of the republic," writes Verstegen (1994, p. 366). In the nineteenth century the pursuit of educational equality took the form of providing every child with access to a public elementary school; in the early twentieth century this ideal was expanded to include secondary education. As the twentieth century progressed, education policies were adopted to improve the access of minority children, girls, and the handicapped to various portions of the school program. In the last decades of the century, the struggle for equality expanded to include greater financial equality between school districts; in several states, courts struck down the finance system on the grounds that it was inherently unequal. Although education in the United States has made progress toward greater equality, the battle is far from over, and experts can safely predict that it will continue well into the twenty-first century (Verstegen, 1994). Figure 5.4 provides some questions to use in identifying the implications of an education policy for equality.

Fraternity.   The third democratic value is often called *fraternity*, but a more accurate translation of the French word *fraternité* is *brotherhood*. An alternative term used in the political discourse of many countries today is *solidarity*, and in the United States the concept is increasingly subsumed under the term *social capital* (Putnam, 2000). **Fraternity** means the ability to perceive other members of one's society as brothers and sisters, to have a sense of responsibility for them, and to feel that in difficult times one can turn to them for help. People develop feelings of fraternity through social interactions in relatively small groups such as the family; the classroom; the church, synagogue, or mosque; local chapters of political parties and labor unions; civic organizations; athletic clubs; and the like. In *Bowling Alone*, Putnam (2000) analyzed a rich database of sociological information which spanned the last century, concluding that civic and social involvement

Does the rhetoric surrounding the policy or policy proposal include words such as *fair, just, justice, equal, equality,* or *level playing field?*

Is *equality* understood as equality of opportunity or as equality of outcome?

Will this policy advance political equality by facilitating participation in the school or in the broader society?

Will this policy advance economic equality by preparing a broader range of young people to participate effectively in the workplace?

How will this policy affect members of racial minorities?

How will this policy affect girls and women (both students and employees)?

How will this policy affect families with low incomes?

How will this policy affect children and parents from working-class backgrounds?

How will this policy affect people (students, parents, and employees) with disabilities?

How will this policy affect people whose native language is not English?

How will this policy affect members of religious minority groups?

Figure 5.4 Questions to ask in evaluating the equality issues raised by a policy.

peaked in the 1960s and has been in decline since. Organizations of all types, including the PTA, Veterans of Foreign Wars, NAACP, and local groups like bowling leagues and bridge clubs have experienced dramatic decreases in both membership and participation. Similarly, voter turnout is down, and people express less trust in their neighbors and in government than they did forty years ago. His analysis suggested that one major cause of this phenomenon is the gradual dying off of the "long civic generation" which was born between 1900 and 1940 and which developed norms of solidarity during two world wars and a severe depression. Another major cause is heavy use of television and other electronic media for entertainment; two-career families and longer commuting time have been lesser contributing factors. Putnam suggested in his book that a major national crisis might reverse this trend; therefore, after the September 2001 terrorist attacks on New York City and Washington, D.C., he surveyed 500 Americans to see if their values and behavior had changed since the attacks. He found that trust in neighbors and the government had increased dramatically, and several other indicators of social involvement such as giving blood and attending political meetings had increased somewhat. He suggested that "a window of opportunity has opened for a sort of civic renewal that occurs only once or twice a century" (Putnam, 2002, p. 22). However, he expressed concern that the United States might not take advantage of this opportunity to build community.

Fraternity has traditionally been a central goal of U.S. education policy, however; the nineteenth-century Common School Movement advocated that everyone attend public elementary schools in order to promote a sense of common identity among Americans (Spring, 1994). More recently, the movements for racial integration and the inclusion of the handicapped in regular schools—although most often justified on the basis of equality arguments—have also been

Does the discourse supporting this policy include terms such as *brotherhood, group, solidarity, belonging,* or *community*?

Does this policy make developing social relationships in an ongoing, relatively small group easier for students?

Does this policy make developing social relationships in an ongoing, relatively small group easier for teachers and other employees?

Does this policy make factual information about different social groups widely available?

Does this policy support the development of clubs and other social organizations?

Does this policy protect or provide the time and space necessary for face-to-face social interaction?

Does this policy encourage people from different social groups (racial, religious, age, class, gender, disability) to interact in relatively small groups and facilitate their doing so?

Figure 5.5 Questions to ask in evaluating the fraternity issues raised by a policy.

understood as ways to promote positive social interactions and feelings of brotherhood among children who might otherwise never meet. Especially at a time when fraternity is being weakened by several broad social trends, evaluating education policies to determine to what extent they foster brotherhood—and to what extent they weaken it—is important. Figure 5.5 provides some questions to use in evaluating the aspects of an education policy that relate to fraternity.

Economic Values

Like most developed countries, the United States has a democratic political system and a capitalistic economic system; a different set of values undergirds each. In some ways these values reinforce each other. For example, the democratic value of freedom is especially compatible with some of the central values of capitalism. Even so, the combination of democratic and capitalistic values in life in the United States occasionally leads to interesting value conflicts. During some historical periods democratic values are emphasized more than capitalistic ones, and during others the situation is reversed. Some of the major conflicts between democratic values and capitalistic ones are discussed later in this chapter.

Efficiency. Because making a profit is the central purpose of capitalistic enterprises, efficiency is always an important value in a capitalistic society. In its most fundamental sense, **efficiency** means obtaining the best possible return on an expenditure or investment. Closely related terms are *cost-effectiveness* and *output maximization* (Boyd, 1984; Fowler, 1995b). An education system is efficient when it achieves high levels of student learning with relatively low expenditures.

Education policy experts agree that efficiency is one of the most important of the values driving U.S. education policy (Boyd, 1984; Guthrie, Garms, & Pierce, 1988; Iannaccone, 1988; Kahne, 1996; Swanson, 1989). At every level, policy makers are extremely concerned about the costs of education and about whether various policies are worth the financial outlays they entail. As a result, they frequently complain about the inefficiency of schools and develop policies designed to achieve higher levels of efficiency. In finance and budgeting, this search for efficiency can take forms such as strategic planning and zero-based budgeting. In other policy areas, the drive for efficiency often means accountability measures such as state proficiency tests, the allocation of funding for districts on the basis of student test performance, and merit pay for teachers. Requiring schools and districts to gather statistics on indicators such as student attendance, teacher attendance, and pupil-teacher ratios and then to report them to the state government is another measure designed to improve efficiency. A popular slogan reflecting an emphasis on efficiency is: "You must do more with less." Figure 5.6 provides some questions to use in evaluating the aspects of an education policy that relate to efficiency.

Economic Growth. An underlying assumption of every capitalistic economy is that the economy should expand; therefore, economic growth in and of itself is a major policy value. This growth can be achieved in three interrelated ways: by increasing production, stimulating domestic consumption, and expanding foreign trade. Education contributes to economic growth in various ways. First—and most important—is the fact that a modern economy requires a highly skilled workforce. Rudimentary literacy and numeracy are necessary even for most unskilled jobs; and many jobs necessitate advanced knowledge such as computer skills, the ability to read and write at sophisticated levels, and specialized mathematical knowledge. Seen from an historical perspective or from the perspective of contemporary developing countries, our educational requirements are enormous. A major task of the school system, then, is to guarantee the perpetuation of an educated workforce; otherwise, production will eventually drop and economic growth will slow.

However, education contributes to economic growth in other ways as well. Schools are expensive enterprises that purchase large numbers of products: building materials, books, computers, buses, and so on. Moreover, the millions

---

Does the discourse supporting the policy include terms adopted from business discourse such as *effectiveness, cost–benefit analysis, accountability, output maximization,* or *performance?*

Does this policy cost less than the previous policy (policies) that it replaced?

Does this policy include close monitoring of "inputs" such as direct costs, instructional time, and materials?

Does this policy include close monitoring of "outputs" such as student achievement, student or teacher attendance, college scholarships awarded, or jobs attained by graduates?

Does this policy encourage competition among students, teachers, schools, or school districts as a way to improve performance?

Figure 5.6 Questions to ask in evaluating the efficiency issues raised by a policy.

---

of children and young people who attend schools are already the consumers of many products and constitute the adult consumers of the future. Recently the privatization of many school services as well as the privatization of school management in some places has also contributed to making education an area of economic growth. All these trends mean that schools aid economic growth both by purchasing products and by providing a setting in which children can be encouraged to become willing consumers of the many products marketed to them.

Economic growth is therefore an important value behind many education policies, whether this fact is made explicit or remains implicit. For example, many of the policies proposed during the education reform movement of the 1980s were justified in terms of how they would contribute to economic growth. The high productivity of Japan and a few European countries was praised in the U.S. press, and their school systems were given much of the credit for their economic success. Experts suggested that U.S. schools needed to improve so the country's economy could continue to grow and compete against these foreign powerhouses. During the same period, other policies that were advocated and adopted were designed to exploit schools in order to stimulate consumption. For example, soft drink machines and advertisements appeared in many schools; Channel One, a television news program with commercials aimed at teenagers, became part of many school programs; and computer manufacturers became deeply involved in campaigns for education policies promoting computer literacy. Economic growth has remained a major policy value since then. In her content analysis of articles by four major thinkers associated with the Clinton Administration, Fowler (1995b) found that economic growth was the value they wrote about most. And in 2002, President Bush argued that a better educational system would stimulate economic growth and pull the country out of recession. Figure 5.7 provides some questions to use in evaluating the aspects of an education policy that relate to economic growth.

Quality.   **Quality** is a policy value that is frequently invoked in public rhetoric such as speeches and commission reports; often the closely related terms *excellence* and *high standards* are used instead. However, quality is not necessarily

---

Does the discourse supporting the policy include references to the need for economic growth and more jobs at the local, state, or national levels?
Does this policy require major purchases of new materials or equipment?
Does this policy include provisions for training students for relatively specific jobs in one or more growth industries?
Does this policy provide businesses with new access to young consumers, using the school as a site for various forms of marketing or advertising?

Figure 5.7 Questions to ask in evaluating the economic growth issues raised by a policy.

an economic value (Gewirtz, 2000). In *Reframing Education Policy*, Kahne (1996) argues that U.S. education policy debates are almost always framed in the terms of either a utilitarian or a rights-based philosophy. Drawing on other major philosophies, he demonstrates how changing the philosophical framework of education policy discussions also changes one's definition of many values. For example, proponents of a humanistic philosophy that emphasizes self-actualization would define a quality education as one that stimulates creativity and autonomous learning. However, because the utilitarian philosophy that has been in ascendance since the early 1980s defines quality in economic terms and draws on business concepts of quality such as Total Quality Management (TQM) (Gewirtz, 2000), it is listed among the economic values in this chapter.

Discussions of quality entered the popular business literature in the 1980s as Americans discovered that workers in several other countries—most notably Japan and Germany—were manufacturing products of higher quality than Americans were. Much of the public debate focused on the automobile industry. Since Americans had figured out that Japanese cars required fewer repairs than American ones, they were—not surprisingly—purchasing more and more Japanese automobiles, making Toyota and Honda common makes on U.S. highways (Halberstam, 1986). Before long, popular writers and politicians made a connection between the "shoddy" products of U.S. industry and the allegedly low quality of education in the United States. The argument ran that U.S. schools emphasized a lowest common intellectual denominator through basic-skills curricula, "dumbed-down" textbooks, and multiple-choice tests. As a result, young people in the United States were not being challenged to think critically or engage in difficult problem solving. Later, when they entered the workplace, they were unable to make high-quality products or provide high-quality services. In contemporary political discourse, then, a concern about the quality of education usually takes the form of seeking higher, more intellectually demanding standards in schools. Policy proposals such as including essay questions on state proficiency tests, introducing portfolio assessment, developing curricula that stress critical thinking, and requiring more study of advanced mathematics reflect a concern for educational quality. Figure 5.8 provides some questions to use in evaluating the aspects of an education policy that relate to quality.

VALUES INTERACTING WITH EACH OTHER

Cyclical Shifts in Dominant Values

A high percentage of Americans support all the values discussed thus far. Who is against "more choice," "social justice," "cost-effective management," or "order and safety"? Virtually no one! Americans differ not in whether they believe in these values, but in how they prioritize them. The way people prioritize the major values is crucially important; in the real world of limited choices and resource

Does the discourse supporting the policy include such terms as *standards, world-class, excellence, quality control, total quality management,* or *high performance?*

Does the policy include measures to raise the cognitive or conceptual level of the curriculum?

Does the policy include measures to raise the cognitive level of assessment procedures, requiring more essay questions, performance testing, and problem solving?

Does the policy include measures designed to raise standards in areas such as Carnegie units required for graduation, number of instructional hours required, or level of education required of teachers?

Figure 5.8 Questions to ask in evaluating the quality issues raised by a policy.

constraints, one cannot pursue all the values at the same time. Rather, policy advocates must emphasize a few central values, ignoring or at least downplaying the others. Because all the values cannot be simultaneously pursued with equal vigor, the set of dominant values behind education policy changes cyclically over time (Boyd, 1984; Boyd & Kerchner, 1987; Iannaccone, 1988). The history of education in the United States beautifully illustrates this shifting emphasis. Speaking in general terms, U.S. education policy tends to alternate between a focus on achieving more equality and an equally strong focus on advancing the economic values. The most recent period of emphasis on equality occurred between 1945 and 1980. The United States emerged from World War II as one of two superpowers and as a major player on the international stage, yet one aspect of U.S. life was painfully embarrassing—the segregation of African Americans in every social domain, including public education. When urging other nations to adopt democratic constitutions or protect human rights, Americans lacked credibility because their own record was so poor. In the postwar years, then, powerful reasons existed for abolishing the most obvious forms of segregation; and public schools and universities were among the easiest institutions to influence. As a result, during this period, members of racial minorities as well as women and handicapped individuals made important advances.

Perhaps in part as a reaction against the gains made by members of racial minorities, women, and the handicapped, the pendulum began to swing in the other direction in the late 1970s. Under the leadership of business and conservative politicians, a new educational discourse developed. It stressed one of the democratic values—freedom, interpreted primarily as choice among alternatives—and all three economic values (Carl, 1994; Fowler, 1992). The eventual result was an education reform movement generally considered to have begun in 1983 with the publication of *A Nation at Risk.* Arguing that public schools had failed, business and political leaders called for a wide-ranging package of reforms including school choice, proficiency testing, merit pay for teachers, a national curriculum and tests, and up-to-date technology. Words and phrases such as *choice for parents, educational freedom, accountability, world-class schools, more bang for the buck,* and *greater productivity* studded their discourse (Carl, 1994; Fowler, 1992). How long this emphasis on economic values and freedom will continue is impossible to predict; however, history suggests that eventually the pendulum will swing back toward equality again.

Important Value Conflicts

The Search for Balance. "The political problem of mankind is to combine three things: Economic Efficiency, Social Justice, and Individual Liberty," wrote British economist John Maynard Keynes in 1925 (as cited in Kuttner, 1984, p.1). Although many policy scholars would argue that more than "three things" should be combined in public policy, most would agree with Keynes that the art of developing good policy involves finding a good equilibrium among competing values. As suggested earlier, the democratic values sometimes conflict with the economic ones. In a broader sense, any value when pursued to an extreme will conflict with other values (Boyd, 1984). A central goal of enlightened education policy making is therefore to establish a **balance** among the most important values so none is seriously compromised. In contrast, fanatics and ideologues often pursue one or two values with such single-minded zeal that their policies endanger or negate other important values. Although any of the values discussed here can conflict with the others, this chapter focuses on the conflicts associated with the two values currently in ascendance: freedom and efficiency.

Conflicts Involving Freedom. **Freedom** never exists in a vacuum. As philosopher John Rawls (1971) argues, an unrestricted freedom always conflicts with other freedoms. Therefore, freedom is most truly enhanced when all the freedoms are intelligently balanced against each other in order to protect all. His argument can be extended to assert that, ultimately, any unrestricted freedom compromises all the other values. This is probably most obvious with the value **order.** If laws and social custom did not set limits on human behavior and enforce those limits when necessary, social order would completely break down, a fact brutally apparent in situations where governments have collapsed or are incapable of meaningful intervention, such as in war zones, during riots, and after major natural disasters. Although such extreme situations rarely occur in education, conflicts between freedom and order occur frequently. In the 1960s and 1970s, for example, such conflicts sometimes developed during the implementation of policies designed to introduce the open pedagogy of the British infant school in the United States. The emphasis on the freedom of children to choose their own activities sometimes led to classrooms that some observers deemed chaotic. Teachers and parents quickly reasserted the importance of order; in some schools, they actually erected walls, turning large "open classrooms" into smaller spaces where they believed maintaining order would be easier.

Unrestricted **freedom** also conflicts with **efficiency.** Freedom by its very nature requires choices, options, and the means to permit people to follow several paths; yet variety is more costly than a single, one-size-fits-all program. For example, a curriculum policy that reflects Americans' love for freedom is the high-school elective system. Americans build large high schools offering a wide range of courses, allowing students to select among many course offerings and programs. Such a curriculum involves many extra costs. Some large high schools develop and print booklets describing all the choices; guidance counselors must spend much time explaining different options; some specialized courses have low enrollments; teachers spend time developing new courses. Because of these and other costs, many high schools have had to restrict their course offerings. In some cases, when schools did not voluntarily impose limits, cost-conscious school boards and state legislatures have done so.

Freedom can also conflict with **quality.** The fact that everyone is free to do his own thing does not mean that all those things will conform to high standards. Indeed, the very idea of a standard of excellence runs counter to the value that Bellah et al.'s (1996) expressive individualists place on the freedom to develop one's "authentic self" through spontaneous, creative endeavor. As soon as a high standard is recognized and rewarded, many people will abandon their freedom of expression in order to compete for the rewards offered for "excellence." The result may be a desirable increase in quality, but it will be achieved at some cost to freedom. In the debate over national standards, the latent conflict between quality and freedom often emerges in sharp relief. For example, in 1993 the Commission on Educational Excellence for Connecticut, charged by the legislature to develop a world-class school system, recommended a set of new academic goals to be used in reforming public schools. In the angry controversy that ensued, opponents charged that the standards would "enforce homogeneity among students" (Frahm, 1994, p. 158). The reform plan eventually died, freedom winning out over excellence.

Finally, an inherent tension exists between **freedom** and **equality.** Because people do in fact differ with regard to traits such as intelligence, motivation, energy, physical strength, and unscrupulousness, unrestricted competition among them will lead to unequal outcomes. As good elementary teachers know, if they do not make some rules about sharing toys and playground equipment, the same children will play with the most desirable items day after day, leading to a festering sense of resentment among the others. On a broader scale, unrestricted freedom for individuals to compete for wealth and power leads to a society in which a few people are very wealthy whereas most live in poverty. As suggested earlier, this situation is not compatible with political democracy. Because it is also incompatible with long-term social stability, most societies—democratic or not—seek to prevent the development of great social inequalities. On the other hand, when equality is imposed by law, as in the former Soviet Union, the almost complete lack of freedom that results can lead to a loss of motivation and low morale. The goal in sound public policy, then, is not to pursue either freedom or equality to an extreme, but to seek a judicious balance between the two.

Conflicts Involving Efficiency. When zealously pursued for whatever reason, **efficiency**—the attempt to keep costs low and productivity high—is likely to come into conflict with all the other values. A central question in the social sciences concerns the relationship between efficiency and **equality;** it "is the contested terrain of several disciplines" (Kuttner, 1984, p. 3). The dominant school of economics argues that limiting social equality is necessary in order to promote the efficiency of the economic system. This position, supported by conservatives such as Milton Friedman (1962), as well as by moderate liberals such as Arthur Okun (1975), is based on several assumptions about the way markets operate. One is that if the market is permitted to operate with minimal government regulation, people will receive economic rewards in proportion to how hard and how well they work. As a result, they will have an incentive to do their best—to exert a serious effort, to produce the best quality of which they are capable, and to work as efficiently as they know how. One side effect of this operation of the market is that some people will achieve more than others, and inequality will inevitably result. However, this inequality is necessary for workers to remain motivated and for the system to function at a high level of efficiency. Okun (1975) calls this conflict between efficiency and equality "the big trade-off." Advocates of this position are critical of the welfare state and other social programs that try to reduce the unequal results of market competition. In education policy, Friedman (1962) and others support introducing more market mechanisms into public education in order to increase its efficiency. They have been leaders in the movement to adopt school-choice policies such as charter schools and vouchers (Cookson, 1994).

Although they represent a minority opinion in the United States, other thinkers such as Kuttner (1984) and Thurow (1985) have attacked the notion that an inherent trade-off exists between efficiency and equality. On the contrary, they argue that over the long run a relatively high degree of social equality promotes efficiency and is a major prerequisite for productivity growth. In their view, great economic inequality creates resentment, undermining worker commitment and willingness to produce high-quality work. In support of this argument, they cite the productivity of Japan and Germany, two countries with a much higher degree of economic equality than the United States.

The pursuit of **efficiency** can also undercut **quality.** No matter how one defines a high-quality education—as high academic standards, as encouraging the natural unfolding of the child's personality, or as developing democratic citizenship—relentless pressures for efficiency will most likely undercut it because education is expensive. Upholding academic standards requires up-to-date teaching materials, well-educated teachers, relatively small classes, and much teacher preparation time. Similarly, educational programs for developing well-rounded children or well-informed citizens require the facilities, personnel, and materials to achieve these goals. Pressures to cut expenditures lead to reductions in all these areas, often causing such increased workloads for teachers and administrators that they change their goal from achieving quality to meeting minimum standards. Many of the policy battles in local school districts and state legislatures revolve around this value conflict, with professional educators upholding some vision of quality and policy makers seeking to bring public budgets under control.

Finally, an overemphasis on efficiency can also weaken **fraternity.** Building relationships, developing a strong organization, and establishing a collegial atmosphere in a school all require time, and, as the saying goes, time is money. Or at least it is in the United States. Thirty-five years ago, anthropologist Edward T. Hall (1966) found in cross-cultural studies of attitudes toward time that, compared to Europeans, Americans schedule time very tightly, do not schedule much free time, and allow little time for the cultivation of relationships. Recent studies show that the growth in the number of single parent households and two-career families has increased the time pressures on Americans (Jacobs & Gerson, 2000); therefore, Hall's findings are probably more relevant today than they were in 1966. Although he did not speculate about the reasons for these differences between Americans and Europeans, generations of concern about efficiency have probably led Americans to consider time spent building relationships with colleagues a waste of money. Yet, good communication and teamwork in schools and districts do not develop in a vacuum—they flourish in an environment where fraternity is valued enough to provide time for it.

IDEOLOGY

Defining Ideology

Most people do not accept a hodgepodge of unrelated ideas and beliefs; usually their major ideas about society, politics, and economics are organized into a structured but simplistic set of ideas called an *ideology*. Alan Isaak (1987) defines *ideology* as "a fairly coherent set of values and beliefs about the way the social, economic, and political systems should be organized and operated and recommendations about how these values and beliefs should be put into effect" (p. 133). Although all ideologies are based on several core assumptions about human nature and the nature of the universe, these ideas remain implicit. Adherents of the ideology take them for granted, perceiving them as common sense (Susser, 1995). Ideologies do, however, provide an analysis of the current social situation, a vision of the ideal society, and a plan for bringing society closer to this ideal (Iannaccone, 1988). All ideologies contain at least a few shreds of truth, and some offer their adherents a relatively sophisticated world view, but no ideology is completely consistent with reality. Nonetheless, the adherents of an ideology accept its major tenets without question and react emotionally rather than rationally when someone challenges them (Iannaccone, 1988; Susser, 1995). In modern societies, ideologies are widely disseminated through the school system, the mass media, and advertising; therefore, most people's thinking is at least partially ideological. People who reach full intellectual maturity may continue to accept some elements of the most prevalent ideologies; however, they have also subjected their beliefs to rational analysis and are willing to change them if presented with compelling evidence. Their belief systems are more accurately described as *political philosophies* than as *ideologies*. Because U.S. education policy is more ideologically driven than it used to be, school leaders need to have a general understanding of the ideological positions that they are likely to encounter.

MAJOR U.S. IDEOLOGIES

Conservatism

The Divided House of Conservatism. Although several types of conservatism exist, two were dominant in the United States as the twenty-first century began: **business conservatism** and **religious conservatism.** Together, believers in these two ideologies constitute the core of the modern Republican Party. Their open quarrels—which became prominent in the national media during the presidential campaign of 1996 and when Senator Jeffords resigned from the party in 2001—reflect the basic contradictions between their ideologies, contradictions that led political scientist Lowi (1995) to predict the eventual fall of U.S. conservatism in *The End of the Republican Era.* The nature of their conflict over what matters most in life is suggested by religious conservative James Dobson's (1995) comments in a fund-raising letter: "Americans care about more than money. Character, values and morality are now very important to them" (p. 2). He was aiming this criticism at his business conservative allies in the Republican Party as much as at the Democrats, who had used the slogan, "It's the economy, stupid" in their 1992 campaign. As of this writing, the two groups are living under an uneasy truce, but how long the truce will last is unclear.

Business Conservatism. Once regarded as a discredited economic theory that had caused the Great Depression of 1929, **business conservatism** experienced a renaissance in the last 25 years of the twentieth century. During the 1980s President Reagan and Prime Minister Thatcher of the United Kingdom based both their public discourse and their official policies on the core beliefs of business conservatism, contributing to the renewed legitimacy of this ideology (Apple, 2001; Bellah et al., 1996; Lowi, 1995; Spring, 1997).

Business conservatives believe human beings are motivated purely by self-interest, especially their own economic interests, and that the achievement of material well-being is the central goal of society. In their view, if people can pursue their individual interests by competing freely in the marketplace, the economy will flourish because the market's "invisible hand" will regulate the process naturally. No need exists for government interference in economic matters; in fact, such interference is detrimental. Business conservatives interpret current global economic problems as the natural result of the misguided policies of the welfare state. As solutions to the problems, they advocate numerous policy measures, all of which would reduce the government's influence over the economy: tax reductions, deregulation, privatization, eliminating or reforming welfare programs, abolishing many government agencies, and expanding "market discipline" into previously protected domains of society. The result of following these prescriptions would, in their view, be a prosperous society in which individuals and businesses would operate freely, pursuing their own interests with minimal government regulation. In their discourse and policy proposals, business conservatives emphasize two values: efficiency and freedom. They believe the free operation of the market produces a high level of economic efficiency. They define *freedom* as economic freedom, the liberty to compete in business and make consumer choices. They say little about the political freedoms (Carl, 1994; Lowi, 1995; Susser, 1995).

Business conservatives have a well-thought-out education policy agenda consistent with their ideology. They have been leaders in the push for higher standards, more accountability in schools, merit pay, and proficiency testing—all policies designed to improve the economy. They also advocate policies that would turn education into a competitive market, such as vouchers, charter schools, monetary awards and publicity for high-achieving schools, and deregulation. Although they also say the U.S. Department of Education (USDOE) should be abolished, their failure to abolish it during the twelve years of the Reagan and first Bush Administrations suggests that their commitment to this policy proposal is not strong (Carl, 1994; Susser, 1995).

Religious Conservatism.   The last quarter of the twentieth century saw a resurgence of religious fundamentalism in many parts of the world. Examples that come readily to mind include the Moslem fundamentalists who have restored the ancient principles of the Koran in several Middle Eastern countries as well as the growing power of Jewish fundamentalists in Israel. In the United States, one manifestation of this trend is the increasing influence of the Religious Right—a largely Protestant expression of the fundamentalist mentality (Boyd, Lugg, & Zahorchak, 1996). Like all orthodox Christians, adherents of the Religious Right believe that human beings, although created in the image of a good God, are sinners who often fall short of God's will. Also like all orthodox Christians they believe Christians should make moral decisions based on religious teachings. However, the leaders of the Christian Right leave classical Christian doctrine behind and move into the realm of ideology when they depict the United States as a once-Christian nation that has fallen into moral chaos because it has rebelled against God and traditional Christian values. In their view, the solution to this problem is for Christians to wage a "cultural war" against the forces of moral corruption, thereby winning the country back to God. In order to prevail in this battle, Christians must work through the political system to restore traditional values—especially traditional family values—to American life, imposing them by law if need be. The value that religious conservatives most emphasize is order, understood as moral order in the traditional Protestant, American sense (Apple, 2001; Lowi, 1995; Spring, 1997).

The Religious Right has advanced its education policy agenda with some success. Like its conservative business allies, it supports school choice and wishes to abolish the USDOE. However, its rationale for these policies is different; it supports both as a way to strengthen parents' right to raise their children without interference. Moreover, adherents advocate the passage of a federal Parental Rights Act to give parents more power vis à vis the government, including schools. They support an amendment to the U.S. Constitution that would make school prayer constitutional and oppose most sex and drug education programs on the grounds that they are inconsistent with Christian family values. Moreover, adherents are against all school policies or programs that seem to reflect the relativistic values of "secular humanism" or undercut parental power, including some psychological testing and multicultural education (Boyd et al., 1996; Burron, 1994; Christian Coalition, 1995; Zitterkopf, 1994).

Liberalism

Another Divided House. **Liberalism** is the dominant ideology of the modern Democratic Party. Because two major variants of liberalism—New Politics Liberalism and Neoliberalism—are dominant, many conflicts within that party play out between these two ideologies. However, the two wings of the Democratic Party share a broader consensus than do the two wings of the Republican Party and disagree less intensely; therefore, their battles are reported by the popular media less often.

New Politics Liberalism. The **new politics liberals** seized control of the Democratic Party between 1968, when Eugene McCarthy lost his bid for the Democratic presidential nomination, and 1972, when George McGovern's bid for the same position succeeded. The new politics liberals were mostly affluent young white men whose political activism had been sparked by the civil rights and anti-war movements of their student days. After the Democratic defeat in 1968, they became leading figures on the commissions that rewrote the rules governing the Democratic Party, especially those rules related to the selection of convention delegates. Those rewritten rules required "affirmative steps to overcome past discrimination" (Shafer, 1983, p. 541) by party leaders against party members based on "race, color, creed . . . , national origin . . . , age or sex" (p. 541). The new procedures facilitated McGovern's selection as the Democratic presidential candidate in 1972 and also inaugurated a new type of politics— "race-and-gender identity politics" (Lind, 1996, p. 60) in the Democratic Party. This new politics was further institutionalized within the party in 1982 when the Democratic National Committee established "official caucuses" for "women, blacks, Hispanics, Asians, gays, liberals, and business/professionals" (p. 30). New politics liberals tend to believe that many, perhaps most, of the problems in U.S. society result from a history of discrimination and oppression based on factors beyond individual control. These problems can be overcome by making it easier for members of oppressed groups to receive a good education, obtain good jobs, and in general enjoy the good things the United States has to offer. The major values of new politics liberals are equality and fraternity, understood as solidarity within an oppressed group. In education policy, new politics liberals advocate equal access to quality education for all children, regardless of race, gender, sexual orientation, or handicap. They also support affirmative action in hiring, multicultural education, and programs that promote sensitivity to diversity issues (Davis, 1974; Lind, 1996; Shafer, 1983).

Neoliberalism. The **neoliberal** wing of the Democratic Party consists of party members who have serious doubts about new politics liberalism as well as its

---

predecessor, New Deal liberalism. They believe that race-and-gender identity politics has alienated working-class citizens and largely ignored growing economic inequality in the United States. Nonetheless, neoliberals do not wish to restore New Deal liberalism, even though they believe that the New Deal and Great Society programs were appropriate for their times. They consider such policies poorly adapted to the problems of today, however. Like both new politics and New Deal liberals, they accept the basic soundness of capitalism, believe government has an important role to play in a modern society, and are deeply concerned about equality issues. Neoliberals differ from the opposing wing of their party about the best way to bring about greater equality in U.S. society. They are skeptical of many entitlement programs, especially those designed to give special help to disadvantaged groups, feeling that they address symptoms rather than causes. To them, the basic problems are a slow growth economy and growing disunity in the United States. In a content analysis of articles and books by four leading Neoliberal thinkers, Fowler (1995b) found that they most emphasized the values of economic growth and fraternity. They understood progress toward realizing these values as the key to achieving greater equality, or equity, in U.S. society. With the election of Bill Clinton to the presidency in 1992, the United States had for the first time an administration strongly influenced by neoliberal thought. Clinton and his secretary of education put forth an education policy agenda consistent with neoliberal beliefs. Neoliberals advocate programs of national and community service for young people as one way to strengthen their sense of brotherhood. They are also interested in improved vocational and technical education as a way to stimulate economic growth. Their support for national curriculum standards and assessments reflects both their desire to improve education in order to spur the economy and their commitment to policies that build a sense of national unity (Fowler, 1995b; Lind, 1996; Peters, 1983).

OTHER IDEOLOGIES

Extremist Ideologies in the United States

Extremist movements of both the Left and Right have a long history in the United States. However, experts on extremism agree that currently right-wing extremism is more widespread and influential than the left-wing variety. Usually, extremist ideologies are not directly involved in mainstream policy making; however, they often exercise considerable influence in the background. For example, policy makers who live in areas where extremist groups are active may take care not to advocate policies that might provoke them, leading to public demonstrations of their power or to civil disorder. Moreover, in such areas a few policy makers are likely to have covert connections with extremist organizations. Therefore, education leaders need to be aware of extremist activity in their state and of its possible influence on education policy.

Left-Wing Extremism.   **Left-wing extremists** feel deeply alienated from the social mainstream and oppose many of its major institutions. They are especially likely to blame social ills on large corporations, the military, modern technology, or the institution of private property. Their most typical solution is to withdraw from society to establish an ideal or utopian community, which they hope will serve as a shining example for everyone else. In this community—often called a commune—property is usually shared; few hierarchical relationships exist, and everyone works together to provide the material necessities of life. A contemporary example is the Left Green Network (Sargent, 1995). Their major political values are equality and fraternity. Although left-wing extremists are often pacifists, sometimes they are violent. In the 1960s and 1970s, such left-wing groups as the Weathermen and the Symbionese Liberation Front engaged in violent behavior: bombing buildings, kidnapping hostages, and robbing banks. Their usual targets were persons or institutions connected with large corporations, especially those involved in the military-industrial complex. The extreme Left tends to be suspicious of public education, seeing it as a major instrument of government and corporate propaganda. Insofar as it has an agenda for public schools, it supports "free" schools that impose minimal restraints on children and teachers (Rothman & Lichter, 1982; Sargent, 1995).

Right-Wing Extremism.   Like the extremists on the Left, those on the Right feel deeply alienated from the social mainstream and oppose many of its major institutions. Unlike the Left, they are likely to blame social problems on racial, religious, or ethnic minority groups, often believing that these groups are conspiring to destroy the way of life they hold dear. Many contemporary extremist groups are also very antigovernment, going so far as refusing to pay their taxes or respond to a court summons. **Right-wing extremists** advocate solving the problems they have identified by restricting the rights of the offending minority groups, eliminating or severely controlling immigration, and reducing the power of the government or overthrowing it. Their broad purpose is often to maintain or restore a mythical white Christian nation that, in their opinion, is threatened by "alien" conspirators supported by the government. Their major political values are order—interpreted as adherence to the norms of their mythical tradition—and a version of fraternity that is limited to their own group. The extreme Right is likely to support violent action to achieve its aims; indeed, right-wing groups are often paramilitary organizations. Timothy McVeigh, who bombed the Federal Building in Oklahoma City in 1995 and was executed six years later, had ties with right-wing extremist groups. One of the oldest right-wing extremist organizations is the Ku Klux Klan. In the last two decades the Klan has been joined on the Right by a variety of similar groups; among them are the Aryan Nation, the Posse Comitatus, and various militias. Because public schools are agencies run by the hated government and have been a major force for racial integration, right-wing extremists are usually hostile toward them (Abanes, 1996; Sargent, 1995).

Ideologies in Other Countries

The study of the ideologies of other countries is fascinating, but one that far exceeds the scope of this book. However, for the sake of comparison, the major ideologies of the countries with which Americans are most likely to have contact are briefly presented. **Social democracy** and **Christian democracy** are the dominant ideologies of Western Europe and several Latin American countries.

Social Democracy. The **social democrats** are the most moderate contemporary descendants of nineteenth-century socialism. As early as 1875, some German socialist leaders began to point out that many of Marx's predictions about capitalism were not coming true and suggested that elements of his economic analysis were probably wrong. Therefore, they eventually developed **reformist socialism.** Like all socialists, social democrats believe the root cause of most contemporary social problems is capitalism. They do not, however, want to overthrow it through a revolution; rather, they hope to transform it from within by implementing a series of strategic reforms over a long period of time. One set of reforms is political. Major social democratic goals include both a fully democratic political system and full workplace democracy based on strong trade unions and representative councils in firms and factories. Another set of desired reforms is economic: the nationalization of some key industries, proportional income taxes, inheritance taxes, economic planning, full employment, and a welfare state. Social democrats are supportive of public education, advocating policies such as extending compulsory education, abolishing tracking and ability grouping, and providing students with free books and materials. Equality and fraternity—understood as national solidarity—are the key values for social democrats, but they also advocate economic growth. Social democracy has been a major force in Scandinavia, Germany, and Austria and has exercised considerable influence in the United Kingdom, Japan, France, and Canada. Indeed, the United States is the only major developed country that has never had a strong social democratic party (Miller, 1987; Przeworski, 1993; Robertson, 1985).

Christian Democracy. In the early 1900s, **Christian democracy** emerged in Europe as a reaction against the monarchist stance of the Roman Catholic Church between 1600 and 1900. Its founders were Catholic intellectuals who wished to develop a "third way": a political program that would be progressive but not socialistic, and modern but not procapitalist. Like the social democrats, Christian democrats have serious reservations about capitalism, but their concerns grow out of the Judaeo-Christian religious tradition rather than Marxist teachings. For example, they object to business conservatism on the grounds that it is based on a cynical view of human nature, attributes quasi-divine qualities to the market, and encourages immoral behavior such as consumerism and the pursuit of self-interest. They believe that democratic leaders should seek to build a humane and just society in which everyone's basic needs are met, yet people are free to develop their full potential without undue interference from either government or employers. Therefore, they advocate full political democracy, a mixed economy, a moderate welfare state, and participative governance structures in both the private and public sectors. They are usually anti-Communist but are often willing to cooperate with social democrats to pursue desirable social goals. Their major values are fraternity and equality, understood as social justice. Since 1900 the Christian democratic movement has been progressively secularized; today many parties have dropped the word Christian from their name and welcome as members Protestants, Jews, Moslems, and sympathetic unbelievers. Instead of drawing solely on religious traditions, they are also inspired by a broad range of humanistic and humanitarian thinking. Although Christian democrats generally support public schools, they also advocate the right of religious organizations to operate private schools and to offer religious instruction in public ones. Countries with important Christian democratic movements include France, Germany, Italy, Chile, Venezuela, and El Salvador (Fleet, 1993; Robertson, 1985; Shafritz, Williams, & Calinger, 1993).

SCHOOL LEADERS CAUGHT IN IDEOLOGICAL CROSSFIRE

Schools as Contested Terrain

During the last twenty years, the public schools have become a major site of ideological conflict; increasingly, principals, superintendents, and other school leaders find themselves in the middle of heated disputes which appear to have erupted out of nowhere and to turn on points that seem (to people from other ideological camps) to be nonissues. More often than not, such quarrels are fundamentally ideological and can be understood only within an ideological or philosophical framework.

In a 1994 article significantly entitled "Politics in the Nation's Schools: The Battle for the Principalship," English describes the conflicting agendas of two groups that he believes seek to control U.S. schools. The "agenda of the Right" is a business conservative agenda, calling for the transformation of public education into a competitive market in which school leaders would become marketing experts. Because business conservatives want to deregulate public education through policies such as privatization and charter schools, they have little sympathy for school administrators, whom they perceive as inefficient bureaucrats who are a central part of the problem. In curriculum policy they favor programs that prepare students for the workplace and focus on the values of Western civilization. In contrast is the "agenda of the Left," a new politics liberal agenda calling for egalitarian, participatively governed schools in which principals would play a minimal role. Like business conservatives, new politics liberals hate bureaucracy. Unlike conservatives, however, they are deeply concerned about equality issues—especially as they relate to race, gender, and sexual orientation—and they decry the school system's tendency to reproduce the economic system through a "hidden curriculum" that confers advantages on those who are already privileged. They are likely to support a multicultural curriculum that is locally developed and to oppose curricula, tests, or standards developed at the state or national levels. English sees educators caught between these two groups and cautions, "This is not a 'nice-nice' game. It is in every respect a battleground" (p. 24).

Although English does not discuss the ideological agenda of the Religious Right, some would argue that it is at least as important in public education as the other two agendas. Indeed, because the Religious Right tends to focus its efforts at the local level more than do the business conservatives and new politics liberals—who more often seek to influence education policy at the state level—local school leaders are more likely to encounter ideological conflicts with the Religious Right on what they consider their home territory. Detwiler (1993/1994) describes the ideological struggle that erupted when two Michigan districts voted to participate in a systemic reform initiative that emphasized critical thinking skills. School leaders unexpectedly encountered opposition from parents who believed the reform projects involved New Age religion, secular humanism, and witchcraft among other things. In both districts, school leaders were caught off-guard. Although one of the districts successfully built public support for continued involvement in the project, the other could not do so and quickly abandoned its reform efforts. In addition to leading direct opposition against local policy changes, the Religious Right maintains steady attacks on public education that reach citizens' homes through direct-mail fund-raising campaigns. In a study of ideological mailings in which public education figured prominently, Harrington-Lueker (1994) found that the Christian Coalition and an offshoot, the American Center for Law and Justice, were two of the most aggressive mailers. They sought to raise money for causes such as organized school prayer by mailing hundreds of thousands of inflammatory fund-raising letters full of charges similar to this one: public schools are now places "where condoms are given to young children, homosexuality is legitimized, prayers are banned, and traditional morality is mocked" (a Christian Coalition fund-raising letter, as cited in Harrington-Lueker, 1994, p. 38). School leaders must realize they have numerous constituents who regularly receive such letters, and that some (but by no means all) have been influenced by them. Among the local curriculum policy issues especially likely to ignite ideological conflicts with the Religious Right are anti-drug programs, self-esteem programs, the teaching of evolution, values clarification, forbidding prayer or Bible study in school, and sex education (Spring, 1997).

School leaders, then, need to know what types of ideological conflicts they are likely to encounter and how to deal with them effectively. Moreover, although developing genuine empathy for people who hold ideological views different from their own is important, having the courage to take a stand for the integrity of the school program and its governance processes is also crucial.

Dealing Effectively with Ideological Conflicts

Assessing Your Own Ideological Stance. The indispensable precondition for effective action during an ideological conflict is recognition of your own ideological position. Otherwise, you will see your own beliefs as self-evidently true and find understanding differing perspectives impossible. Therefore, this section contains three activities designed to raise your consciousness of where you stand.

You should engage in these activities reflectively and, ideally, in written form. If you write them out, later you will be able to return to your responses for further reflection and, perhaps, elaboration.

First Activity. The section of this chapter entitled "General Social Values" discusses eight values: order, individualism, liberty, equality, fraternity, efficiency, economic growth, and quality. Rank these eight values to reflect their relative importance to you with the value most important to you first and the least important value last. Now, consider the values that you ranked first through fourth as a group. If equality is in this group, you probably have leanings toward liberalism. If both equality and fraternity appear, those leanings are probably strong; you may even be close to one of the two foreign ideologies described. On the other hand, a group containing two or more of the economic values suggests leanings toward business conservatism, especially if liberty or individualism or both also appear. Most religious conservatives are likely to include order in their top four values; they may also include fraternity (understood as community), or liberty (understood as religious freedom), or both.

Second Activity. Briefly answer these three questions:

1. In your opinion, what is the major cause of current social, economic, and political problems in the United States?

2. How would an ideal society differ from contemporary U.S. society?

3. Which two or three public policy changes would do most to move U.S. society toward this ideal?

Now, carefully compare your responses to the positions of the eight ideologies described in this chapter. You will probably find your answers are similar to the positions of one or two of the ideologies. You should not feel concerned if you are unable to identify clearly with a single ideology. The descriptions offered in this chapter are what social scientists call *ideal types*: abstract, simplified versions of a more complex and ambiguous reality. Thus, in real life people often hold mixed positions. Usually those positions belong to the same broad ideological camp, however. For example, a person who is basically a business conservative may share some of the views of religious conservatives. This is why both kinds of conservatives have been able to work together in the Republican Party.

Third Activity. Imagine that during a presidential campaign you hear eight candidates speak, each of whom espouses a different platform similar to one of the eight ideologies described here. Now, reread the eight descriptions, seeing them as political platforms. For which two candidates would you be most likely to vote? least likely? Did you find yourself getting angry or disgusted as you reread some of the platforms? If so, which ones provoked this response?

The two platforms for which you would vote are probably close to your own ideological position. Now ask yourself: Which portions of these platforms most appealed to me? What facts could I mention in support of the validity of those portions? What portions of these platforms do you consider "self-evident," "a part of nature," or "what everyone with common sense believes"? Any ideas you accept on the basis of few or no facts or consider self-evident point toward areas of your thinking that are especially ideological.

Now, make a list of the following: the two platforms for which you would be least likely to vote plus all of the platforms that contained ideas that angered or disgusted you. For which of your negative reactions could you produce facts, including well-documented examples from history, to support your feelings? Eliminate the platforms containing them from your list. The remaining ideologies are ones that you probably have special difficulty understanding or relating to.

An Ounce of Prevention.   Although no one can totally prevent the eruption of ideological conflicts, school leaders can do several things to minimize the likelihood of one occurring or at least to make sure they are on solid ground in that event. Most local conflicts over ideology relate to one of two things: curriculum policy or religious issues. Ensuring that all formal policies and procedures in these two areas are clear and consistent with current legal opinion is therefore essential for schools and school districts. Moreover, curriculum adoption policies—including the adoption of supplementary materials by classroom teachers—should provide opportunities for the general public or parents to provide input. Periodically, an attorney should review all these policies and recommend needed changes.

However, merely having sound policies on the books is never enough; steps must also be taken to increase the likelihood that they will be followed. School leaders should make brief copies of the guidelines available to building administrators and classroom teachers and provide in-service education about these issues regularly. Moreover, school leaders should deal quickly and effectively with policy violations. At one time, administrators could afford to ignore the high-school biology teacher who mocked the creation account in Genesis or the fifth-grade teacher who entertained her pupils with a dramatic account of the séance in which she had recently participated. Those days are over. Today such irresponsible teacher behavior could land a whole school district in a prolonged and costly conflict; therefore, school leaders must clearly state what is acceptable and what is unacceptable. At the same time, however, they should urge teachers to continue to teach modern biology and to use literary classics such as "Hansel and Gretel," *The Canterbury Tales,* and *Romeo and Juliet* (all of which have been challenged in recent years). They should also be prepared—and prepare their teachers—to offer a well-thought-out rationale for teaching such material to anyone who asks. Today, public school educators walk a fine line between course content and attitudes that needlessly offend some students on the one hand, and their professional responsibility to provide an intellectually sound curriculum on the other. This line is fine indeed—but leaders must know where it lies and communicate its location clearly to teachers.

Recognizing an Ideological Conflict.   Recognizing an ideological conflict is not always easy. However, school leaders should be on the alert for three indications that an ideological disagreement is at the root of a conflict. The first is the emotional intensity surrounding the issue. Ideological beliefs are deeply held; because they are closely related to people's ideas about human nature and the universe, they structure the way people perceive reality (Paris & Reynolds, 1983). As a result, when these beliefs are challenged—directly or indirectly—people become distressed. Ideological beliefs are often held as fervently as religious ones—indeed, ideological and religious beliefs are often intertwined—and during an ideological argument people sometimes feel as if everything they believe is under attack.

A second sign to look for is faulty communication patterns. Often, people are unable to respond cogently to statements made from an ideological perspective different from their own. They may completely misinterpret another person's meaning or ignore views with which they do not agree. Or they may respond by calling the people who hold the other ideological position names such as "communist" or "religious nut." They may even express astonishment at the ideas being expressed, making statements such as: "I can't believe you said that," or "No intelligent person could really believe that!" People involved in an ideological conflict often feel as if those on the other side are not really listening and that everything they say is falling on deaf ears.

A final sign that an argument is basically ideological is that the participants make "strenuous efforts . . . to explain away the inconsistencies, incongruences, and practical failings" of their ideology (Paris & Reynolds, 1983, p. 209). A case study by Ray and Mickelson (1990) provides an excellent example of this phenomenon in education. They studied a business-education task force's attempts to reach agreement on a reform for the local school system. The business representatives—ardent advocates of business conservatism—strongly believed that public schools were turning out inferior graduates and that area employers were dissatisfied with the local labor force. They had not reached this conclusion from their personal experience in the region, however; rather, they had absorbed it while attending national business conferences and reading articles in the national business press about the "education crisis." As developed in these forums, the "crisis in educational quality" was an integral part of a larger ideological attempt to explain economic problems in the United States. The business representatives on the task force set out to bolster their arguments for reform by surveying local employers. Neither the 11% response rate to the survey nor the fact that only 50% of the employers who responded expressed dissatisfaction with their workers supported their ideological position. Eventually, however, they nevertheless developed a complex explanation for their survey results that was obviously false but that was consistent with their ideology. They never abandoned the idea that a large majority of local employers were dissatisfied with the quality of the workforce, even though the results of their own survey raised serious doubts about this belief. Whenever school leaders notice similar behavior or other signs of ideological conflict they should ask themselves: Is this basically an ideological argument? What ideologies are involved?

Obtaining Information About an Ideological Issue.   As soon as school leaders realize they are dealing with an ideological conflict, they should begin seeking information about the underlying ideological position. The obvious starting point is their opponents in the conflict. Two or three of the apparent leaders should be invited to meet in a relaxed atmosphere to discuss their grievances with a few selected school leaders. If possible, at least one of the school leaders should feel some sympathy (if not total agreement) with the opposing view. In such a discussion, really listening and trying to determine the major outlines of the ideology and the most significant areas of conflict are important. Identifying possible points of compromise is also important. In many instances such a discussion is heartening because school leaders may realize that the gulf between them is not as wide as they had originally feared. In all instances, giving challengers a chance to speak and listening to them attentively communicates the fundamental respect for others without which no solutions can be reached.

Obtaining information from other sources is also wise, however. Usually, such conflicts are not isolated occurrences; often they have already surfaced in other places not far away. The state affiliates of the school boards' association and administrator groups should be able to provide information about other schools or districts where similar conflicts have occurred. Talking to school administrators in those places may be helpful. The information gathered may provide valuable insights into the issue and suggest the best way to deal with it.

Opening Up the Democratic Process.   When facing an angry group with loud voices and strong opinions, leaders easily make one of two mistakes. The first is to capitulate to the dissatisfied group. Such a unilateral surrender has nothing to do with democracy because small dissident groups usually represent the views of a tiny but vocal minority of the general population. Moreover, collapse in the face of opposition sets a dangerous precedent, encouraging numerous dissatisfied groups to cause an uproar and exert some pressure, hoping for a collapse favorable to their interests. A second undemocratic response is to circle the wagons and stonewall the opposition, hoping that it will just go away. This reaction will probably cause dissatisfaction to spread as more and more people reach the conclusion that the school leadership is unresponsive.

The best response in an ideological conflict is to open up the democratic process. In his 1993/1994 article, "A Tale of Two School Districts," Detwiler tells how the Adrian School District in Michigan did precisely this when faced with a conservative religious group that stridently opposed the district's participation in a systemic reform project. Unfortunately, Adrian had not entered the reform process in a democratic fashion; top administrators had unilaterally decided to become part of the reform initiative without involving teachers, parents, or the general public. However, once an ideological conflict broke out, district leaders did respond democratically.

First, Superintendent Al Meloy determined the numerical strength of his opposition. When he discovered they were less than 8% of community residents, he communicated this fact to the board and the public, supporting his claim with careful documentation. Next, a concerned citizen allied with the district leadership, wrote a series of four articles about the challenging group for an area newspaper. These factual articles explained the group's ideology and linked them and their materials to the national organizations with which they were connected. The author did not deny the group's right to challenge the reform project through the political process; of course, it had that right, and he expressed deep respect for it. However, entering the political process *does* mean "enter[ing] into the arena of public discussion and democratic debate" (Detwiler, 1993/1994, p. 27). Everyone who becomes involved in politics and policy making should expect to see their ideas studied, analyzed, and assessed in public and private debate. The articles gave the public an opportunity to do just this, and it began to feel increasingly skeptical about the ideas of the challenging group and its connections with national organizations.

Next, the Adrian district broadened the base of participation in the democratic process. Administrators, school board members, and many teachers held meetings with church and community organizations; they also held open houses in each school building in the district where they displayed examples of the new curriculum. As a result, the community united behind the school district and its new project. In Adrian, opening up the democratic process led to stronger community support, defusing the ideological conflict.

FINAL POINTS

At one time, education leaders could ignore questions of value and leave ideology out of consideration. That time has ended; as policy making in the United States becomes more and more ideological and value laden, the dimension of ideas becomes an increasingly important dimension of the policy environment. School leaders who overlook or underestimate the significance of this dimension will find themselves in a poor position to deal with ideological conflicts when they arise or to understand why particular policies are proposed. As the third millennium begins, the intangible and invisible domain of ideas is more important than ever in U.S. education policy.

QUESTIONS AND ACTIVITIES FOR DISCUSSION

1. In class, share the results of your assessments of your own ideologies. Which ideologies are represented in the class? Which are most common? Are any missing? How do you explain the general ideological complexion of the class?
2. Attend a school board or faculty meeting and try to identify all the policy values to which participants refer. Which values were mentioned most frequently? Least? Not at all? How do you explain the policy values of this group?
3. Clip an editorial on education or a letter to the editor about education from a newspaper. Analyze its policy values and ideology. Then write a brief response to it.
4. Describe any ideological conflicts in education with which you are familiar. How did the conflict unfold? Why?

INTERNET ASSIGNMENT

Using a search engine, locate the Web sites of the Heritage Foundation and the Economic Policy Institute. Analyze these Web sites in order to answer the following questions for each: What policy values are most important to this organization? Which of the ideologies discussed in this chapter is closest to its ideological position?

THE KANSAS BOARD OF EDUCATION TAKES ON DARWIN

In 1999, the Kansas Board of Education was scheduled to adopt new statewide standards for teaching science. It had appointed a 27-member committee of experts on K–12 science education to develop and recommend a new set of standards for its consideration. However, the document which this group produced included numerous references to both Darwin's theory of evolution and the "Big Bang" theory of the origin of the universe. From the perspective of the board, one of the most controversial sentences in this text was: "Evolution by natural selection is a broad, unifying theoretical framework in biology" (Hoff, 1999, p. 3).

Although Republicans dominated the board, they were split into two factions. The moderate group had no objections to the proposed new standards, but the conservatives did because they considered them anti-religious. After three months of an acrimonious debate which was widely reported in the state's news media, the board voted 6–4 to adopt an amended version of the standards recommended by its own committee. The board had stripped most of the references to evolution and theories about the origin of the universe from the science standards.

No local district had to stop teaching evolution and other controversial science topics since the new standards were optional. Nonetheless, the board's decision unleashed a storm of controversy. Outside Kansas, both Stephen Jay Gould, a professor of geology at Harvard and New York University, and Bill Nye at PBS attacked the board's stance. Groups which criticized the new standards included the American Jewish Congress, the American Chemical Society, and the National Center for Science Education. The *Wall Street Journal* and *USA Today* reported extensively on the board's action.

Inside Kansas, this incident stirred up the longstanding rivalry between the moderate and religious conservative wings of the Republican Party. Complaining that the state board's action had made Kansas the laughingstock of the nation, the Republican speaker of the house advocated restructuring the board while the Republican governor exploited the situation to reduce the religious conservatives' power in his party.

In the fall of 2000, four of the six board members who had voted to amend the standards were up for reelection. Although Kansas state board of education elections are usually low-key and candidates spend about $500 on their campaigns, in 2000 the board candidates raised thousands of dollars and their campaigns were well covered by both state and national media. The religious conservatives defined the issue as local control, arguing that their faction was true to the conservative legacy of Ronald Reagan. In contrast, the moderates insisted that the board had lowered the quality of education in Kansas and made the state look backward. Shortly before the August Republican Primary, ABC devoted an entire *Nightline* program to the issue; on that program an ABC reporter stated that a British company had decided not to locate in Kansas because of the brouhaha over teaching evolution. Just before election day the Republican lieutenant-governor publicly confirmed that the social conservatives' stand had indeed cost Kansas business.

In the primary election, moderate Republicans won three of the four races; they went on to win the November election as well. Early in 2001 the new board reversed the old one, reinstating evolution in the science standards.

(Based on: Bowman, 2000; Hanna, 2000; Hoff, 1999a, 1999b, 1999c; Keller & Coles, 1999; McLean, 2000; Miles, 2000; Problem Is Politics, 1999).

QUESTIONS

1. Identify and contrast the political values of the two factions of the Republican Party in Kansas.
2. Identify and contrast the ideological stances of these two groups.
3. Analyze the role the media played in the downfall of the religious conservatives in Kansas.
4. Describe any similar ideological struggles with which you are familiar.

NEWS STORY FOR ANALYSIS: *NO CUTTING SEATTLE'S SUMMER SCHOOL*

Seattle, WA—Seattle Public Schools Superintendent Joseph Olchefske, bracing for a budget shortfall this year and next, plans deep cuts in central office and services. A planned expansion of the district's summer-school session may be one of the victims. Bad idea. The School Board recently adopted academic improvement goals that are far more aggressive than the state's. To make good on those goals, the only tinkering to summer school should be an expansion. The school budget crisis is real. The district faces a budget shortfall of a few million this year and $10 million next year. But the district appears to be overreacting to what is a relatively small problem, making a 2-percent cut from an overall budget of $435 million.

Olchefske says he will not touch classroom services to get that 2 percent, though the pledge takes 60 percent of the budget off the table. Good. But Olchefske has not made the same pledge to protect indirect classroom services such as curriculum specialists, support staff and summer school. Last spring, fewer than 30 percent of seventh graders passed the Washington Assessment of Student Learning math test. For that appalling figure to change, money for classroom services, both direct and indirect, must stay.

Olchefske has proposed a buy-back strategy in which schools would be given money to purchase services from central administration. Schools could buy curriculum and professional development, instructional technology development, counseling and psychological support and facilities upkeep, all in amounts tailored to their individual school. This demand-driven strategy could create significant savings and streamline services. It won't help the immediate fiscal crisis the district faces caused by several factors, including declining state revenue, increased cost of new teacher contracts and higher expenses associated with the district's new headquarters.

Olchefske is right, he has problems, but reducing the number of students who can get into summer school will create more.

(Adapted by permission of the publisher from "No Cutting Seattle's Summer School," an editorial from the *Seattle Times*, January 26, 2002, p. B5. Copyright 2002 by the *Seattle Times*.)

Questions

1. What are the major political values of the editor who wrote this editorial?
2. How would you situate the editor ideologically? Why?
3. Describe the value conflict that seems to underlie this editorial.
4. Describe an education policy issue in your district or state that turns on a similar conflict.

FOR FURTHER READING

Browder, L. H., Jr. (1998). The religious right, the secular left, and their shared dilemma: The public school. *International Journal of Educational Reform,* 7 (4), 309–318.

   Browder describes the ideological positions of religious conservatives and new politics liberals, drawing on several seminal works in the field. He then discusses their contrasting views of the mission of public schools.

English, F. W. (1994). Politics in the nation's schools: The battle for the principalship. *NASSP Bulletin,* 78(558), 18–25.

   According to English, the U.S. school principalship is currently the site of an ideological battle between the Right and the Left. He provides useful information about typical education policy agendas of these two ideological positions.

Gewirtz, S. (2000). Bring the politics back in: A critical analysis of quality discourses in education. *British Journal of Educational Studies,* 48, 352–370.

   The author analyzes the educational discourse of Tony Blair's Labour Party in the United Kingdom, finding that although it seems to focus on quality, it defines quality in very narrow economic terms. This phenomenon is also evident in the United States.

Kahne, J. (1996). *Reframing educational policy.* New York: Teachers College Press.

   The author argues that U.S. education policy is shaped primarily by utilitarian and rights-based philosophies. After developing in detail the major concepts of each philosophy, he describes how education policy might change if education policy discourse were broadened to include other perspectives. The book offers a good introduction to some of the major values and ideological positions that shape—and could potentially shape—U.S. education policy.

Moen, M. C. (1993). The preacher versus the teacher. *Thought & Action,* IX(1), 125–143.

   With considerable sympathy for the Christian Right, Moen describes the origins of the movement, its education policy agenda, and the network of organizations that cooperate to advance it. The article provides a good— and relatively objective—overview of the movement.

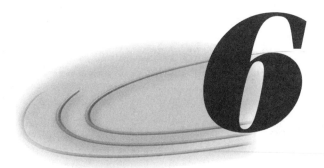

THE MAJOR EDUCATION POLICY ACTORS

Focus Questions

Who are the major participants in the policy process at the state level?

Which ones wield the most influence?

How can education leaders identify the major players in their own states and obtain information about them?

How can education leaders follow state level education policy making?

THE *DRAMATIS PERSONAE* OF THE POLICY DRAMA

Before exploring the policy process itself, identifying those who are actively involved in it is important. In policy discourse, these individuals and groups are called **policy actors.** Collectively, they comprise the *dramatis personae*, or cast of characters, who play major and minor roles in the ongoing drama of policy development, adoption, and implementation. Although policy actors exist at the federal, state, and local levels, this chapter emphasizes state level actors for two reasons. First, education is a domain that is implicitly reserved to the states by the Tenth Amendment of the U.S. Constitution. Although for generations states delegated much power over education to local governments, over the last 25 years the states have taken back much of their constitutional authority over education

---

policy (Mazzoni, 1993). This means that in education, state policy actors are now considerably more important than either federal or local ones. Second, because both political science textbooks and the mass media emphasize policy making at the federal level, the state level is often poorly known and understood. Especially in a book designed for education leaders such as this one, redressing this imbalance is important.

Because the purpose of this chapter is to identify and introduce the major education policy actors, their activities are not presented in detail here. Rather, their roles are briefly described so readers can develop a general sense of who they are and what they do. In the next five chapters—which present the stages of the policy process in some depth—these actors' patterns of behavior and interaction will become clearer. Table 6.1 and Figure 6.1 are referred to throughout the chapter. They summarize the findings of two studies of the relative influence of education policy actors. Table 6.1 is based on the research of Marshall et al. (1989), who, in the mid-1980s, studied the education policy process in six states:

TABLE 6.1 Ranking of Education Policy Actors' Influence in Six States

Rank	Policy Actor	Mean Score
1	Individual legislators	5.85
2	Legislature as a whole	5.73
3	Chief state school officer	5.21
4	Education interest groups combined	5.14
5	Teachers' organizations	5.10
6	Governor and executive staff	4.88
7	Legislative staff	4.66
8	State board of education	4.51
9	School boards' association	4.18
10	Administrators' association	4.00
11	Courts	3.92
12	Federal government	3.89
13	Noneducator groups	3.87
14	Lay groups	3.10
15	Education research organizations	2.66

Note. Based on C. Marshall, D. Mitchell, and F. Wirt, 1989, *Culture and Education Policy in the American States,* p. 18. New York: Falmer Press. Used by permission.

Teachers' unions
State departments of education
School boards' associations
Administrators' associations
Parent-Teacher Association (PTA)

Figure 6.1 The most influential education groups at the state level.[*]
Note. Based on "Questionable Clout," *Education Week,* September 28, 1994, p. 30.
[*]Groups are listed in rank order from most to least influential.

Arizona, California, Illinois, Pennsylvania, West Virginia, and Wisconsin. As part of their project, they asked 135 state policy actors to assign each of 15 individuals or groups a score from one (lowest) to seven (highest), reflecting their importance to education policy in their own state. Figure 6.1 is based on a 1994 study by *Education Week*. Staff researchers telephoned governors' offices and state legislative education committees in 46 states (four did not respond), asking them to rank the influence of six types of education groups. Note that in this study only education groups were included (Questionable Clout, 1994). Therefore, the two studies are not fully comparable.

This chapter is divided into three broad sections. In the first, the major government actors, elected and appointed officials of the three branches of government, are presented. Next, the nongovernment actors are described. These include interest groups, policy planning organizations, and the media. Although these policy actors usually keep a low profile, often they are as important as the more visible government actors. The last section includes practical suggestions for identifying the important government and nongovernment policy actors in a specific setting and obtaining information about them.

GOVERNMENT ACTORS

The Legislative Branch

The Legislature: Function and Structure. Fifty-one legislatures exist in the United States: the U.S. Congress and the 50 state legislatures. All of them bear a strong resemblance to each other because they exercise similar functions and are organized in similar ways. A major function of every legislature is, of course, the development and passage of statutes, one type of law. However, legislatures play other roles as well. For example, before developing bills, legislatures often hold hearings where experts provide testimony on public issues. Periodically, legislatures also review existing laws to determine if they should be continued, amended, or repealed. A major legislative function is approving the government's budget. Occasionally, legislatures establish task forces or appoint commissions to which they delegate the responsibility for studying a policy issue. They may also establish a special committee to oversee the implementation of a new piece of legislation. Finally, legislatures sometimes exercise an investigatory function (McCarthy, Langdon, & Olson, 1993). Appendix A gives the addresses of the Web sites of the U.S. House and Senate while Appendix B tells how to find similar information for a given state.

The U.S. Congress and 49 of the state legislatures are bicameral; they have two chambers or houses. The single exception is Nebraska, which has a unicameral legislature that, unlike the other legislatures, is nonpartisan. In all the bicameral bodies, the smaller chamber is called the **Senate.** Senates tend to be rather sedate, in part because senators usually serve relatively long terms and can afford to move slowly. According to a 1993 study of state legislatures, 14% of state senators were full-time legislators, 27% were business people, 23%

were lawyers, 17% were professionals other than lawyers, and the remainder worked at other occupations. The most common name for the larger chamber of a legislature is **House of Representatives;** other names used include *Assembly, General Assembly,* and *House of Delegates.* In contrast to senates, houses tend to be colorful, lively, and partisan. Moreover, because most house members serve two-year terms, they are always running for reelection. In 1993, 15% of state representatives worked as full-time legislators, 29% were in business, 19% were lawyers, 19% were professionals other than lawyers, and the remainder worked at other occupations (Patterson, 1996). A 1997 study revealed that 21% of state legislators were women while 8% of all state legislators were African Americans. More than 67% of Hispanic legislators worked in one of just five states—California, Florida, New Mexico, New York, or Texas (Hamm & Moncrief, 1999).

Both senates and houses have officers. The most important officer in a state senate is usually called the **President;** in 28 states the lieutenant governor serves as the president of the senate by virtue of his office. In the other states, the president is a senator who is either elected by the senate or appointed by another official and then confirmed by the senate. The top officer in the house is the **Speaker.** Speakers are elected by the members of the house in an election which is often fierce and filled with conflict because the Speaker wields great power. Usually the Speaker is a veteran leader of the party that holds a majority of the seats in the house. Other important legislative officers include the majority leader, minority leader, and whip in each chamber (Patterson, 1996).

Both Congress and state legislatures have numerous **committees** that accomplish most of the actual work of the legislature. Each chamber has a committee to handle proposed legislation in each specific policy domain. Typical committees in a state legislature deal with areas such as highways, prisons, welfare, education, and the justice system. Each chamber also has a committee that determines the level at which new laws will be funded; this committee may be called the *Ways and Means Committee, Appropriations Committee, Finance Committee,* or something similar. The legislative leaders control committee appointments; each party has appointees on every committee, but the majority party usually holds the majority of the votes on all of them (Patterson, 1996).

Finally, in most state legislatures each political party has a **caucus,** which consists of all the legislators affiliated with the party, regardless of the chamber in which they serve. The caucuses are important because they develop the policy agenda that the party pursues in the legislature. Although some caucuses are led by chairpersons who play no other major role in the legislature, in others one of the legislative officers also chairs the party caucus (Patterson, 1996).

Legislative Staff. State senators and representatives are relatively visible: their names and pictures appear in newspapers and they make frequent public appearances. Much less visible—but almost as important in the policy process—are the men and women who staff their offices. State legislators have not always had staffs. In fact, throughout most of U.S. history, state legislatures have been amateurish bodies dominated by a group of each state's leading "good ole boys," who were better known for living it up during their brief visits to the state capital than for effective governing. Because state legislatures lacked the resources necessary to function well in the modern world, nothing more could be expected of them. For example, as recently as the early 1960s, the only staff serving the 240 members of the Massachusetts House were five typists working in a secretarial pool. Because the representatives did not have offices in the state capital, they were forced to conduct official business wherever they could find an empty spot—perhaps on a couch in the lobby or in a cafeteria across the street from the capital. Their mail and other messages were placed in a set of pigeonholes similar to those found in some college dormitories (Bowman & Kearney, 1986). Massachusetts was not unusual; this was the norm across the country.

Today, most state legislatures have modern office buildings and staffs. What happened? First, in 1962 the U.S. Supreme Court handed down the *Baker v. Carr* one-man–one-vote decision. This ruling forced states to redraw the electoral districts for their legislatures, weakening the power of rural areas and leading to more representative legislatures. Second, in the early 1970s groups such as the Citizens' Conference on State Legislatures recommended reforms to make state legislatures more modern and efficient. Among the recommended reforms were larger staffs and sufficient office space and equipment for those staffs to do a good job. Third, President Reagan's New Federalism gave the states more responsibility for initiating and implementing policy. As a result of these occurrences, state legislatures have become more professionalized. Increasingly, state level lawmakers receive fair compensation for performing their legislative tasks, work full-time at their legislative jobs, and receive the resources needed to hire competent staffs. However, state legislatures differ considerably in the extent of their professionalization (Bowman & Kearney, 1986; Davey, 1995; Hamm & Moncrief, 1999). Table 6.2 divides the states into three groups based on their legislature's degree of professionalization. The criteria used to determine the degree of professionalization are (1) the number of full-time legislators, (2) the salaries paid to legislators, and (3) the size of the legislative staff (Hamm & Moncrief, 1999).

State legislators normally use three types of staff members. **Clerical staff** perform the tasks involved in running any office: answering telephones, word processing letters and other documents, preparing mailings, and maintaining calendars. Although sometimes these workers are young and poorly paid, a legislator's clerical staff often wields considerable power. In particular, they control access to the legislator or to her **professional staff members.** The latter are, as their name suggests, people with professional expertise who help with the substantive aspects of legislative work. Usually they have college degrees in fields such as political science, sociology, or law. They perform tasks such as screening and filtering the volumes of printed material that reach a legislative office and summarizing its important elements for the lawmaker. They also do much of the routine casework with constituents, such as writing letters and making phone calls to help a mayor from the district obtain a grant to repair a bridge, or meeting with a citizens' group that opposes the construction of a new prison in their

TABLE 6.2 The Degree of Professionalization of the State Legislatures

Highly Professionalized	Partially Professionalized	Largely Unprofessionalized
California	Alabama	Arkansas
Illinois	Alaska	Georgia
Massachusetts	Arizona	Idaho
Michigan	Colorado	Indiana
New Jersey	Connecticut	Maine
New York	Delaware	Montana
Ohio	Florida	Nevada
Pennsylvania	Hawaii	New Hampshire
Wisconsin	Iowa	New Mexico
	Kansas	North Dakota
	Kentucky	Rhode Island
	Louisiana	South Dakota
	Maryland	Utah
	Minnesota	Vermont
	Mississippi	West Virginia
	Missouri	Wyoming
	Nebraska	
	North Carolina	
	Oklahoma	
	Oregon	
	South Carolina	
	Tennessee	
	Texas	
	Virginia	
	Washington	

Note. Based on Patterson (1996).

community. In addition, professional staff members review and analyze budgets for busy legislators and prepare succinct reports on major issues for them. Education leaders should not underestimate the power and influence of the professional legislative staff. "Legislative staffs have a major effect on policy making because of their proximity to the legislators and the centers of legislative power and because of their key role in processing and providing the information legislators require," states Patterson (1996, p. 194). Finally, in addition to the clerical and professional staff members who work in their own office, lawmakers usually have access to a **centralized staff agency** that provides services for the entire legislature. Often called a *legislative reference service* or a *legislative research bureau*, this agency performs specialized work such as drafting sample bills, researching legal questions, and providing the background of previous attempts to pass a law. Although staff workers in these agencies are even less visible than office staff, they too are in a position to exercise considerable influence on the policy process (Bowman & Kearney, 1986; Patterson, 1996; Weaver & Geske, 1995).

Important Legislative Actors. As Table 6.1 shows, Marshall et al. (1989) found that although the legislature as a whole was quite influential in relation to education policy, individual legislators were even more so. In fact, they emerged as the most important actors in the process overall. Usually the most influential individual legislators are members of an **education committee,** with the committee chair likely to be especially important. Every state legislature has at least one education committee. Four states—Nebraska, Connecticut, Maine, and Massachusetts—have only one. Thirty states have two education committees—one in the House and one in the Senate. Sixteen states have three or four education committees; the third and fourth committees are either joint committees (including both Senate and House members) or special committees for higher education. Regardless of the number of committees or their names, the members of those committees have great influence on state education policy because education committees exercise several important functions. These include developing education laws, reviewing existing legislation, and holding hearings on education policy issues (McCarthy et al., 1993). Because education is a major item in every state budget, the members of the finance committee—again, especially the chair—are also influential. A powerful speaker is another individual legislator who may have enormous impact on what kind of education policies are developed. Although legislative staff members ranked far below the legislature in influence, note that in Table 6.1 they ranked higher than many people would expect. Indeed, they scored higher than the state board of education (SBE), school boards' and administrators' associations, and the federal government. The Marshall et al. (1989) study supports the importance of legislative staff in shaping education policy and suggests that overlooking them is a serious mistake.

The Executive Branch

Governors. Although Marshall et al. (1989) found that governors have considerably less influence on education policy than the legislature, their influence is nonetheless substantial. Activist governors who place education high on their policy agendas can have a great impact not only within their own states but also nationally. Prominent examples in the last 15 years include former Governor Bill Clinton of Arkansas and former Governor George W. Bush of Texas.

The power of the governor's office varies considerably among states. Although as a general rule the strongest governors are found in the Northeast and the weakest in the South, notable exceptions exist. Tennessee, for example, has a strong governor and New Hampshire a weak one (Bowman & Kearney, 1986). A governor's power is a function of several factors. The first of these is institutional power—the authority granted the governor by the state constitution and other state laws. The strongest governors are elected to serve a four-year term and can be reelected at least once, have the power to appoint numerous state officials, have considerable control over the state budget, and can veto legislation of which they disapprove. Several other factors can enhance gubernatorial power. A governor elected by a landslide or by a comfortable majority is more powerful than one who just barely won an election or succeeded to office because of a death or a resignation. Governors with much previous experience in state government have an advantage over those who are new to state politics. A governor who belongs to the most powerful political party in the state has an advantage over a governor from a minority party. Finally, a governor with an appealing personal style and strong presence is more powerful than one who is drab and lackluster (Beyle, 2001).

Governors often act as "issue catalysts" in state policy making. An activist governor selects key issues, publicizes them in his speeches, and leads the public and the legislature to focus on them. Increasingly, education policy is one of governors' favorite issue areas. In part, this interest results from the activities of the **National Governors' Association** (NGA). Headquartered in Washington, D.C., it had 94 staff members in 2002 and operated research, lobbying, and state service branches. The first of its research studies focused on public education. Its Center for Best Practices provides information and assistance to governors who wish to develop and implement new policies; one of its five areas of interest is education policy. As an example, in 2002 the Center was providing help to states as they implemented the federal No Child Left Behind Act. The NGA provides an important forum where governors can discuss education and exchange ideas about possible policy initiatives. It also serves as a clearinghouse for governors and their staffs, providing information about policy in various states (Beyle, 2001; *National Governors Association Online*, n.d.). The importance of the NGA's influence on governors' education reform agendas is well documented. For example, Edlefson (1994)—who served as the education specialist on Ohio Governor Celeste's staff in the late 1980s—identified it as the major influence on his reform proposals. Similarly, Kaplan and O'Brien (1991) described the impact of attending three NGA annual meetings on Governor Janklow of South Dakota, and Mazzoni (1995) indicated that the NGA was one of several organizations active in Minnesota during its reforms.

State Boards of Education.   Although **State Boards of Education** (SBEs) exercise both quasi-legislative and quasi-judicial functions, they also have an important administrative role and are appointed by the governor in two thirds of the states. Therefore, they have been included in the executive branch.

SBEs first became a part of U.S. school governance in the early 1800s. By 1900, 28 states had them; today, only Wisconsin lacks one. SBEs are second only to legislatures in exercising direct authority over education policy at the state level. The typical SBE has nine or eleven appointed members, most of whom are not professional educators. With few exceptions, SBEs are responsible only for K–12 and vocational education; a board of regents usually exercises similar functions for public higher education. Within a legal framework developed by the legislature, SBEs make education policy in areas other than school finance. Their most important policy tasks include (1) either developing, approving, or developing and approving the rules and regulations used in implementing education laws enacted by the legislature; (2) developing certification requirements for

K–12 teachers and administrators; (3) approving and monitoring educational assessment programs, including state tests; (4) deciding on minimum high-school graduation requirements; and (5) determining accreditation standards. In addition, SBEs often serve as the final step in the appeals process for administrative redress cases that have arisen in K–12 school systems (Madsen, 1994; McCarthy et al., 1993).

As Table 6.1 shows, Marshall et al. (1989) found that SBEs were not among the most influential policy actors in the states studied. One reason for their relative lack of activism is that often SBEs do not have enough resources or staff of their own to act independently of the chief state school officer (CSSO), the state department of education (SDE), and the legislative education committees. Occasionally, however, when granted such resources they do become more active in influencing education policy. A case in point is Tennessee, where governance reforms in the mid-1980s stimulated the SBE and its chair to become important players in Nashville (Fowler, 1987).

Chief State School Officers.   Since 1900, all U.S. states have had a **chief state school officer** (CSSO), a public official charged with the supervision of public education. The CSSO is often called the *superintendent of public instruction,* the *state superintendent of schools,* or the *commissioner of education.* Most CSSOs are professional educators with several years of administrative experience. CSSOs are appointed in 35 of the states—most often by the SBE—but in nine states they are appointed by the governor. In the other 15 states, the CSSO is popularly elected. The method used for selecting the CSSO reveals a lot about a state's education policy system. CSSOs appointed by the governor are more likely than others to accept the governor's policy agenda and work to advance it. Although they usually have a good working relationship with the governor and his office, they may or may not work effectively with the legislature and usually hesitate to resist the governor or take independent initiatives. On the other hand, a CSSO appointed by an SBE will probably act independently and may even challenge or resist the governor or the legislature on occasion. Most independent are the few CSSOs who are still popularly elected. However, because they have no built-in connection to any other individual or governing body, they may be so isolated in the state capital that they can accomplish little.

In a broad sense, the CSSO's job is the general supervision of all public schools in the state. In discharging this responsibility, she heads and is assisted by the SDE, which is discussed later. Effective CSSOs can have a great impact on education policy; Marshall et al. (1989) found that they ranked just below the legislature in importance. As McCarthy et al. (1993) explain: "By preparing legislation, setting the department's agenda, and controlling information provided by the SDE, the CSSO can influence what issues are considered by the state legislature and the SBE" (p. 19).

State Departments of Education.   One of the most important education policy actors in any state is the **state department of education** (SDE), sometimes called the *state education agency.* Although the SDE does not appear explicitly in Table 6.1,

---

Marshall et al. (1989) combined it with the CSSO in their study. This means that, working with the CSSO as head, it ranks immediately below the legislature in influence. In Figure 6.1, where the SDE is considered merely an "education group," it ranks second—immediately after the teachers' unions. Both studies concur that the SDE is one of the most important actors in the state education policy process.

The SDE is a state bureaucracy headed by the CSSO and headquartered in the state capital, often right downtown near all the legislative and other offices. Although many SDE employees are professional educators, others are not; people with training in fields such as finance, accounting, political science, and economics are often employed by SDEs. Much of the influence of the SDE on education policy grows out of its legally defined role. While new legislation is under consideration, SDE legislative liaisons provide the education committees with data and with their assessments of the probable impact of a proposed policy. After the passage of a new law, it develops the detailed rules and regulations to use during implementation. As the new law goes into effect, the SDE provides assistance to districts and oversees and monitors their degree of compliance. Of course, the SDE is not a neutral machine at the service of the legislature and the CSSO. It is staffed by human beings who have their own perspectives on education policy and may or may not agree with new directives. An SDE may ignore or block legislation, or it may opt to dilute it by the way it writes the rules to accompany it. It may monitor district compliance aggressively, loosely, or not at all (Madsen, 1994; Pipho, 1990).

In her book *Educational Reform at the State Level*, Madsen (1994) recounts the fascinating tale of how the unnamed SDE in which she worked for three years essentially blocked the implementation of the Excellence in Education Act (EEA), which its legislature had passed in 1986. This SDE apparently did not resist for ideological reasons but rather because the legislature failed to provide it with enough resources to implement the reforms, thereby overwhelming SDE employees with work. Madsen's story underlines the key importance of the SDE in the policy process. She concludes several years later: "Today in this state, the EEA, so promising at the outset, is almost nonexistent" (p. 166). Such is the potential power of an unsupportive SDE.

The Judicial Branch

Just as the U.S. Supreme Court and the lower federal courts play an important policy making role, so do the 50 **state court systems.** Two types of state court systems exist: two-tiered systems and three-tiered systems. The eleven states with two-tiered systems—trial courts and a supreme court—are either sparsely populated or small in area. The systems of the other 39 states include an intermediate appellate court that hands down the final decision in most cases, thereby lightening the supreme court's workload. At the trial court level, evidence is presented and cases are argued in a courtroom, often before juries. Higher courts take cases only on appeal from lower courts and base their decisions not on factual evidence, but on the correctness of the legal procedures followed in the trial court and the soundness of the judge's legal interpretation. If the judges of a higher court find that insufficient factual evidence was presented, they send the case back to the trial court, or remand it. At all levels of state court systems, judges are former lawyers. Procedures for selecting judges vary among states; they can be either appointed or elected. Even if they are elected, however, state judges usually keep a very low public profile; in fact, they have been described as the "least visible" state officials (Beyle, 2001; Jacob, 1996).

Despite their low profile, **judges** are political figures who can exercise considerable influence over education policy. Ultimately, judges interpret the statutes enacted by legislatures and can overturn them. Assuming that judges are somehow isolated from the broader policy process and therefore "above" it is a serious mistake. Both groups and individuals with definite policy agendas often seek to influence the courts. One way to do so is to quietly support the election or appointment of judges favorable to one's cause. Another way is to pay the legal expenses of plaintiffs whose cases are relevant to a specific policy issue. For example, at the federal level the National Association for the Advancement of Colored People (NAACP) financially supported the parents who brought suit against the Topeka Board of Education in the 1950s, ultimately leading to the U.S. Supreme Court decision that outlawed racial segregation in schools. Similar support is frequently provided at the state level, too. In addition, interested groups can file *amicus curiae* (friend of the court) briefs presenting their position on a key case. These briefs then become part of the official record. In short, the courts are an important policy arena (Jacob, 1996). Since the 1970s, state courts have played a major role in shaping school finance policy by either upholding or overturning those school finance systems that have been challenged by dissatisfied plaintiffs. Often the plaintiffs in these cases have been school administrators in districts with financial troubles—an excellent example of education leaders working together to influence policy through the state court systems.

Local Government Actors

This book focuses on state education policy processes and, therefore, on policy actors at the state level. Nonetheless, local officials play a role in this process. Thus, this section describes that role. Its purpose is *not* to provide an exhaustive discussion of the functions of local boards of education or superintendents, but rather to suggest their roles in the broad sweep of state policy processes.

Local Boards of Education. **Local school boards** play an important role in 49 states; Hawaii is the lone exception. Legally, local boards are agencies of state government; their make-up, how they are selected, and what powers they may exercise are spelled out in state law. Historically, boards of education have played a central role in education policy making, for state governments traditionally delegated most of their constitutional authority over education to them. However, since the mid-1960s states have increasingly reclaimed that power and asserted their dominance by engaging in policy making in such areas as setting state curriculum standards, requiring students to pass state tests; and, in many states, gathering data on district performance and publishing it in the form of "state report cards" (Fowler, 2000; Kowalski, 1999).

Nonetheless, boards still play an important role in the policy process in most states. First, they typically develop policies suited to their district within a broader policy framework developed by the legislature or SDE. For example, state law may require public schools to be in session for a minimum of 180 days. Local school boards usually have the authority to determine if their district will exceed the minimum and, if so, by how much. They also may determine the dates when school will begin and end as well as when vacations during the academic year will occur. A second important school board task is the implementation of state-mandated policies. In recent years, for instance, many state legislatures have passed laws establishing state testing programs. Local school boards cannot choose whether or not their students will take these tests. However, they can decide how much emphasis will be placed on preparing students for them, if special curriculum materials will be purchased to strengthen instruction in areas covered by the tests, and what type of remedial programs will be offered to students who fail tests. Local boards of education can greatly influence the success or failure of state policies by the way they implement them.

Superintendents. As the chief executive officers of local school districts, almost all **superintendents** are appointed by school boards. A survey conducted by Cooper, Fusarelli, and Corella (2000) determined that 64.2% of current superintendents have doctorates and slightly more than two-thirds of them are in their 50s. Only 12.2% are female; although this survey did not ask for the respondents' race or ethnic background, other sources indicate that the percentage of superintendents who are African American, Hispanic, or Asian is extremely low (Kowalski, 1999). A central theme in contemporary books about the superintendency is the crisis surrounding this role. The average age of superintendents is higher than it used to be; turnover, especially in urban districts, is rapid; and the number of applicants for openings is down (Brunner & Björk, 2001; Cooper, Fusarelli, & Corella, 2000).

Many causes for this crisis have been identified, but one is certainly increased pressure from state governments to implement mandates which are often unfunded and to participate in accountability systems. According to Carter and Cunningham (1997), two decades of state initiated reforms have pushed superintendents into subordinate roles and caused them to feel powerless. These authors argue that implementing state policies is a major task for today's superintendents. However, they also argue that more and more superintendents are becoming active in the state-level policy-making process and seeking to give state officials advice about policy development and evaluation. They say: "As superintendents become dissatisfied with the barrage of shifting state and federal mandates that have drained their resources, they find themselves actively involved in trying to influence and shape those mandates. . . . " (p. 66). Thus, increasingly superintendents not only implement state policies, but they try—both as individuals and through their professional organizations—to offer substantive input throughout the policy-making process.

NONGOVERNMENTAL POLICY ACTORS

Interest Groups: What They Are and What They Do

An **interest group** is "an association of individuals or organizations, usually formally organized, that attempts to influence public policy" (Thomas & Hrebenar, 1996, p. 123). Both the number of interest groups and the intensity of their activities have grown in recent decades; more and more of their attention is focused at the state level. In a series of three studies conducted in 1987, 1992, and 1993, political scientists Thomas and Hrebenar identified the types of groups most active in the fifty states. Figure 6.2 summarizes their findings. Interest groups usually retain one or more lobbyists, who operate under the euphemistic title *legislative liaison*. Despite their somewhat shady public image, most lobbyists are honest, personable individuals whose jobs consist primarily of (1) establishing the relationships that facilitate their access to governmental policy actors and (2) providing these actors with information about their organization's key issues. Lobbyists' major source of power is their specialized knowledge about a specific policy area. Most of their efforts are aimed at legislators and at officials in the

---

Businesses

Business and trade associations
Health-care corporations
Hospital associations
Individual corporations
Manufacturers

Government Groups

Local government units
Public higher education

Senior Citizens' Groups

Unions
Public employees' unions
Teachers' unions
Other unions

Figure 6.2 Most active interest groups at the state level.
Note. Based on Thomas and Hrebenar, 1996.

state agencies relevant to their issues. Sometimes such agencies are so powerfully influenced by lobbyists that they become subservient to the industry they are supposed to be regulating. Such agencies are said to have been "captured" (Elling, 1996; Thomas & Hrebenar, 1996).

Education Interest Groups

Although the levels of their activity and effectiveness vary, the same set of education interest groups can be found in most states. The literature agrees that the **teachers' unions** are by far the most powerful education interest groups. This fact emerged in both the Marshall et al. (1989) and *Education Week* studies (Questionable Clout, 1994). Political science researchers agree. Indeed, because they found that in 43 states, teachers' unions ranked at the highest level of effectiveness, Thomas and Hrebenar (1996) considered teachers' unions the most powerful group at the state level period. The larger of the two unions is the National Education Association (NEA) with 2.7 million members, 50 state affiliates and thousands of local chapters. Indeed, the NEA is the largest union in the United States and is a force to be reckoned with in nearly every state (About NEA, 2002). The smaller union, the American Federation of Teachers (AFT), has a million members. Concentrated primarily in large metropolitan areas and affiliated with the American Federation of Labor–Congress of Industrial Organizations (AFL–CIO), the AFT has historically been the NEA's strong rival. Nonetheless, in recent years the two organizations have drawn closer; NEA members rejected a proposed merger in 1999, but the two groups collaborate extensively (Archer, 2001, July).

The other education groups are significantly weaker than the two unions, largely because of their smaller size. The National School Boards Association (NSBA) with about 100,000 members and the American Association of School Administrators (AASA) with about 15,000 members usually maintain a visible presence in the state capitals (Toch, 1996). As for the Parent–Teacher Association (PTA), its 6.5 million members in 26,000 local chapters in all 50 states should give it considerable strength (About National PTA, 2002). However, its disparate membership—parents, administrators, teachers, and students—often cannot reach consensus on a policy agenda (Questionable Clout, 1994; Toch, 1996). Appendix A provides the addresses of the Web sites of nine national education interest groups.

In 1967 Iannaccone developed a typology of state educational governance patterns, which attempted to describe and organize the ways in which these interest groups can interact; in 1984 McGivney revised it. The typology consists of four "stages" through which a state's education establishment can evolve. In Stage I, **Disparate Structure,** education interest groups are unimportant; rather, school districts represent their own interests in the state capital. At Stage II, **Monolithic Structure,** statewide interest groups become more important than the local districts in state education policy making. With the SDE acting as a coordinating agency, an education alliance that typically consists of the NEA, NSBA, and PTA affiliates, as well as one or two administrator groups, seeks to attain its policy goals. However, when a state reaches Stage III, **Competitive Structure,** this consensus breaks down; the passage of a collective bargaining law is often the precipitating factor. Statewide education interest groups are still important and active, but instead of cooperating they compete—often in an atmosphere of great distrust. In 1984 McGivney did not believe that any U.S. state (with the possible exception of Hawaii) had reached State IV, **Statewide Bureaucratized,** but he argued that it exists in Europe. At this stage, collaboration begins again, and it is formalized by the establishment of a state-level umbrella organization that coordinates the activities of all the education interest groups (McGivney, 1984). Although somewhat dated, this typology provides a useful tool for conceptualizing the different ways in which a state's education interest groups may interact.

Noneducation Interest Groups

The interest groups that represent business—often collectively called the **business lobby**—are among the most influential policy actors in every state capital. Indeed, Thomas and Hrebenar (1999) ranked business as the most influential interest group at the state level, closely followed by teachers' unions. In a 1991 study of 40 states, Grady (1991) found several types of business groups active in state politics including: (1) trade associations, which represent a specific economic sector such as banking or agriculture; (2) chambers of commerce; (3) manufacturing associations; and (4) business roundtables, often affiliated with the national Business Roundtable. The exact composition of the business lobby varies among states; in some states the Farm Bureau is a powerful player, in others service industries or heavy manufacturing is important. Regardless of the type of business, however, Grady found they all agreed on one policy goal: keeping taxes low. Because public schools are a major beneficiary of state tax dollars, this means that the education and business lobbies often find themselves on opposite sides of policy issues in state legislatures. In recent years, business has developed a keen interest in education policy that extends far beyond reducing its cost. For example, in a study of trends in state politics, Mazzoni (1995) found business leaders and organizations increasingly involved in state-level education reforms. He identified the Business Roundtable, National Association of Manufacturers, U.S. Chamber of Commerce, and National Alliance of Business as especially important.

While no other general type of interest group is as influential as business, others may wield considerable clout in certain states or in relationship to particular issues. Especially worthy of mention are **ethnic-** and **religious-based interest groups.** Ethnically oriented groups such as the NAACP and La Raza—which represent the interests of African Americans and Hispanics respectively—do not lobby on most education issues but may become intensely involved regarding a few policy controversies that touch them closely. Obviously, both are usually concerned about any policy proposal that could increase segregation or that relates to teaching about their racial group in the schools. In addition, Hispanics have a special interest in bilingual education. Similarly, religious interest groups such as the Catholic Bishops' Conference, the Christian Coalition, and the Anti-Defamation League tend to mobilize only when certain key issues are under consideration. Moreover, in recent years, **single-issue ideological groups** such as anti-abortion organizations have grown in influence in many states (Thomas & Hrebenar, 1999). In order to avoid unpleasant surprises, education leaders must be aware of those groups in the state that are likely to surface—often with a great show of force—when particular issues are at stake. Appendix A provides the addresses of the Web sites of eight general interest groups and six business groups.

Policy Networks

Increasingly, groups interested in education policy are becoming part of large, loose national organizations called policy networks, which coordinate a wide range of efforts to influence policy. The most important education policy network is probably the **Education Commission of the States** (ECS), founded in 1966 by the National Governors' Conference. First proposed by Harvard president James Bryant Conant, on its Web site the ECS describes itself as "an interstate compact created . . . to improve public education by facilitating the exchange of information, ideas and experiences among state policymakers and education leaders" (Education Commission of the States, 2002). Forty-nine states, the District of Columbia, and three territories belong to the ECS, which is based in Denver and funded by the government and private foundations. As a nonpartisan clearinghouse, it is an important source of information on education policy for government officials.

Other policy networks are active in state policy arenas as well. For example, the **National Alliance of Business,** which describes itself on its Web site as "the business voice on excellence in education" plays a leading role in the efforts of large corporations to influence both K–12 and higher education policy. Its 5,000 members include companies, CEOs, top business executives, educators, and state and local political leaders. Its eight-item agenda for K–12 education includes "standards and assessment," "quality management using Baldrige Criteria," and "competition in public education." Through its publications, conferences, and lobbying it exercises considerable influence on education policy (*National Alliance of Business*, 2002). Several national policy networks for children's issues, such as the Children's Defense Fund and the New Coalition for America's Children, often become involved in education policy issues as well. Policy networks are increasingly important actors in the development of education policy at both the state and national levels (Kaplan & Usdan, 1992).

Policy Planning Organizations

Think Tanks Defined.   Even less visible to the general public than the courts are the **policy planning organizations.** Popularly called think tanks, they emerged in the early twentieth century and greatly expanded in number and activity during the period immediately following World War II. Although some are connected with the government, most are not and thus depend on foundations, corporations, and individuals for financial support. Officially, think tanks gather empirical data about public policy issues and then communicate those findings to governments (Weiss, 1992). However, as they do so, they play a crucial role in defining policy issues. In the process of deciding what problems to study, selecting sources of information about them, and summarizing the results of their research, the staffs of think tanks quietly determine which social problems will be considered public policy issues and how those issues will be conceptualized, both by policy makers and by the general public. Think tanks are arguably the most important actors in the policy process; as political scientist Schattschneider (1960) insisted decades ago, "The definition of the alternatives is the supreme instrument of power" (p. 68).

Think Tanks and Policy Entrepreneurs. In addition to publishing books and holding conferences, think tanks sometimes disseminate their ideas by sponsoring the activities of **policy entrepreneurs.** These individuals are outspoken advocates of a specific policy proposal—such as vouchers or site-based management—who invest much time, energy, and money in working to bring about the policy changes they desire. They tirelessly speak up on its behalf and lobby for it, often playing a key role when a fleeting opportunity presents itself to turn their pet idea into legislation. Policy entrepreneurs do not always work for think tanks—they may also be government employees, politicians, or academics (Kingdon, 1995). However, entrepreneurs funded by think tanks play an important role in education policy innovations. In a study of 38 states whose legislatures considered adopting school choice policies between 1987 and 1992, Mintrom (1997) found that the presence of active policy entrepreneurs in a state significantly increased the likelihood that a school choice policy would be approved. He concluded:

> Policy entrepreneurs play an important role in articulating innovative ideas onto government agendas. They work hard at developing close ties with people through whom they can realize their policy goals and they seek to develop convincing arguments for selling their policy ideas. (p. 765)

The Web addresses of several important think tanks and policy research institutes are included in Appendix A.

The Media

Their Policy Role. The **mass media**—including print and broadcast media, wire services, online services, and the Internet—not only report on policy issues and some stages of the policy process, but are also important actors in it. A newspaper story, radio or television program, or information offered by an online service should never be considered a neutral presentation of mere facts. All result from an important process of selection and recontextualization that reflects, consciously or unconsciously, a stance on questions such as what constitutes real news and the meaning of that news. Because the media must screen, select, and recontextualize information, they inevitably play a major role in the policy process. Although they can potentially have an impact at several stages of that process, they are most important in **agenda setting:** the process by which issues move onto the short list of public problems to which policy makers devote serious consideration.

Editors decide what topics will receive attention in the media, thereby setting the **media agenda.** Often, such media attention leads the general public and political figures to become so concerned about a problem that they insist it be addressed. In such cases, the issue has moved from the media agenda to the **policy agenda** (Mead, 1994). Of course, this procedure is far from automatic. The media may persistently cover a topic that stimulates little interest among the general public and politicians. Or, the public may respond to it with great interest whereas policy makers prefer to continue to ignore the situation, perhaps because it appears too complex to solve quickly. Although most people first become aware of issues through television and radio coverage, the broadcast media are less important policy actors than the wire services and newspapers. Indeed, the wire services and newspapers largely set the agenda for television and radio (Beyle, 2001). To a great extent, they also set it for the online services and the Internet.

The Organization of the Media. The four major **wire services** (Associated Press, United Press International, Reuters, and Agence France Presse) are organized internationally, providing news stories, background information, and pictures to media outlets around the world (Fenby, 1986). **Television channels** and the **online services** are usually organized at the national level and therefore focus on national news. Although **newspapers** are increasingly part of large national or international syndicates, they tend to focus on national news (provided by the wire services) and local news (provided by their own reporters). Radio also has a dual focus: national and local. Media outlets are rarely organized at the *state* level.

This aspect of the structure of the U.S. mass media leads to what Doris Graber (1994) calls *Swiss cheese journalism:* news coverage that omits numerous important public events and issues. Many of the holes in the cheese relate to state-level policy making, including education policy making. This journalistic inadequacy is intensified by the fact that the U.S. media are also organized around markets that have nothing to do with political units. Thad Beyle (2001) identifies three types of state media market structures. In the first, some states are overpowered by the media markets of large metropolitan areas outside the state. For example, New Jersey is dominated by the New York City and Philadelphia media; West Virginia is split by three outside markets—Cincinnati, Pittsburgh, and Washington, D.C. In such states finding good coverage of events in the state capital can be extremely difficult. A second possibility is fragmentation into several large markets within the state. California, Florida, New York, North Carolina, and Texas are some states that conform to this pattern. In these places, some coverage of state politics is provided, but none of the markets (except the one including the state capital) offers thorough reporting of it. Finally, some states are dominated by the media market of one large city in the state, such as Denver, Atlanta, and Boston. In this situation, state capital affairs will probably be amply reported *if* the dominant city is also the state capital! Where this is not the case, state politics may take a back seat to the politics of the dominant metropolitan area.

The structure of the U.S. media means that people who are interested in education policy and policy making may discover that finding out about state level politics, even in their own states, is difficult. Some ways to solve this problem are suggested in the last section of this chapter.

IDENTIFYING AND LEARNING ABOUT POLICY ACTORS

Overall Approach

Effective interaction with policy actors requires knowing who they are, where they can be reached, and who should be contacted about specific issues. This means that school leaders should have a thorough, up-to-date listing of all the key players in their state. Yet, school leaders are extremely busy people and become busier every year. The same is true for their staffs, to whom the development of such a list might be delegated. Moreover, because resources are limited, few can afford to travel widely to search for information or to make numerous long-distance telephone calls. Therefore, the following principles should be followed in developing the list:

1. Where possible, existing lists should be used in developing one's own comprehensive directory of policy actors.

2. The least expensive methods of obtaining information should be tried first.

3. As it is developed, the list should be put into a form readily accessible and easily updated. The ideal format is a computer file that can be easily modified and printed out.

In developing the lists of suggestions in the following sections, the author sought to follow the first two of these principles. Recommendations are therefore organized from the closest, cheapest sources, to the most distant and possibly expensive. However, in some settings switching the order of the recommendations in order to follow the general principles may be advisable.

Locating Elected Government Officials

Tables 6.3 and 6.4 list elected officials at the federal and state levels who should be identified and the information one should gather about them. Facts about these policy actors are relatively easy to find; therefore, this process should not be particularly onerous. Places to look for information include:

1. *The district office.* Possibly it maintains a current list or has a slightly out-of-date one that could be revised.

TABLE 6.3 Federal Officials to Identify and Information Needed

Officials	Information Needed
Representative Both Senators	Address Phone number e-mail address Fax number Web page, if any Party affiliation Length of tenure in office Year of next reelection campaign Margin of victory in last election Known positions on education Does the official serve on an education or finance committee?

TABLE 6.4 Elected State Officials to Identify and Information Needed

Officials	Information Needed
Governor Senator(s) for school district Representative(s) for school district Speaker of the House President of the Senate Chair of House Education Committee Chair of Senate Education Committee	Address Phone number e-mail address Fax number Web page, if any Party affiliation Length of tenure in office Year of next reelection campaign Margin of victory in last election Known positions on education

2. *The telephone book.* The introductory section may list area politicians with their addresses and phone numbers. It may also provide phone numbers for the state capitol building or statehouse. Additional information is probably available in the white or business pages under the headings "U.S. Government" and "[Name of State], State of."

3. *The public library.* In the reference section one can find various directories to state government. A librarian may also be able to suggest additional sources on CD-ROM, in vertical files, and so forth.

4. *The Internet.* People with access to the Internet can use a search engine such as InfoSeek or a search directory such as Yahoo to locate information.

5. *The League of Women Voters.* The league produces and disseminates factual information about area politicians.

6. *Politicians' offices.* Upon request, most offices will provide citizens with information about the politician's record and policy positions.

7. *Newspapers.* Around election time most papers carry information on candidates; moreover, when the legislature convenes—usually in January—many carry special features on state government. Back issues of local newspapers should be available on microfilm in the local library; Lexis-Nexis indexes major newspapers in every state, and provides an electronic version of the text. It is accessible through many university Web sites.

Identifying Appointed Officials and Groups

These policy actors are less visible than elected officials; nonetheless, finding them should not be difficult. Table 6.5 provides a framework for organizing information about them. The following sources are recommended:

1. *The SDE directory.* Most state departments of education publish a directory or handbook for administrators in the state; it may also be available online. Generally, it includes information on the SDE itself, the CSSO, and the SBE. It may also list major education interest groups with their addresses and phone numbers.

2. *The telephone book for the state capital.* A copy should be in the local library, in either book, microfiche, or electronic form. Sections to consult include government listings in the introduction, the state government listings in the white or business pages, and listings of "Associations" in the yellow pages.

3. *Organizational headquarters.* Upon request, most interest groups will gladly provide flyers and brochures that provide facts about their group and its policy positions. Most also maintain Web sites and can be found by searching for their name in AltaVista or Excite.

TABLE 6.5 Appointed State Officials to Identify and Information Needed	
Officials	**Information Needed**
Chief State School Officer*	Address
Members of State Board of Education*	Phone number
	e-mail address
	Fax number
	Web page, if any
	Party affiliation, where applicable
	Length of tenure in office
	Who appointed the official
	Year term expires
	Known positions on education

*Elected in a few states—use Table 6.4 in those cases.

Identifying Policy Planning and Related Organizations

Because these groups maintain a low public profile, they are the hardest to find. However, checking the sources recommended here over a year or two should facilitate the identification of most of the groups—including national organizations—active in the state. Tables 6.6 and 6.7 help organize information about these groups.

1. *Recent policy reports.* Policy planning groups develop and disseminate reports on issues that interest them; foundations sponsor research and summaries of it. The documents they issue commonly list those who participated in the project as well as the funders. Because school leaders frequently receive such reports in the mail or at professional meetings, copies are probably available in the district.

2. *Newspapers.* Most papers occasionally publish feature articles on innovative school programs in their area; sometimes these articles reveal information about the foundations and other groups that are backing the project.

3. *Education Week.* This national weekly devoted to education carries articles about think tank and foundation reports, as well as the requests for proposals

TABLE 6.6 Groups to Identify and Information Needed

Groups	Information Needed
State administrator associations	Address
State business roundtable	Phone number
State chamber of commerce	e-mail address
State department of education	Fax number
State Parent–Teacher Association	Web page, if any
State school board association	Name of current head
State teachers' unions	Name(s) of publication(s)
Other influential groups in state	Number of members or employees
	Known positions on education

TABLE 6.7 Policy Planning and Related Organizations to Identify and Information Needed

Groups and Individuals	Information Needed
Active state or national policy research organizations	Address
	Phone number
Active state or national foundations	e-mail address
University-based policy research centers	Fax number
	Web page, if any
Foundation-supported policy entrepreneurs	Party connections
	Ideological tendencies
	Funding sources
	Known positions on education

put out by such groups. This information can be helpful in identifying the organizations that advocate for specific education policies and that may be behind similar policy movements in a given state.

4. *Internet.* Once the name of a policy planning group has been identified, further information can be obtained by searching the Internet.

COUNTERACTING "SWISS-CHEESE JOURNALISM"

School leaders who wish to follow state education policy making should first assess the quality of the coverage by media outlets in their geographic area. A good time to conduct such an assessment is when the legislature is in session. Coverage should be monitored for several weeks because some newspapers provide only periodic summaries of legislation enacted and the votes of local lawmakers. Assessing the coverage of any newspapers published in the state capital and of any prestige newspapers published in the state, such as the *New York Times*, the *Philadelphia Inquirer*, and the *Los Angeles Times* is also important. If some of these provide excellent coverage, their Web versions should be consulted regularly.

If newspaper coverage is inadequate—and this is more often the case than not—the school leader should identify the interest groups that publish newsletters containing legislative updates when the legislature is in session. Most likely to do so are the NSBA state affiliate and the NEA and AFT state affiliates. School leaders may ask to be placed on these groups' mailing lists, or they may be able to locate a local member willing to pass on her copy.

School leaders should also identify all the legislative hot lines associated with education in the state. These are recorded updates of the status of pertinent bills and can be accessed by dialing a toll-free number. Again, education interest groups based in the state capital are most likely to maintain these. Sometimes the statehouse also has one that provides general information about committee meetings and scheduled hearings. Finally, virtually all groups now have Web pages. Valuable information about their activities in relationship to policy initiatives is often available there.

Swiss cheese journalism is truly an anachronism in a period of increasing activity at the state level of the federal system. Nonetheless, those who want to follow state education policy making can do so if they identify and systematically use alternative sources of information. For now, we can hope the day will soon come when the media will recognize the importance of state government and provide more thorough coverage of it.

QUESTIONS AND ACTIVITIES FOR DISCUSSION

1. In your opinion, is the professionalization of state legislatures a positive trend or not? Be prepared to support your position.

2. Find out how the SBE and CSSO are selected in your state. To which of the models discussed in this chapter does your state conform, if any? How does this governance structure affect the relationships among the governor, the SBE, and the CSSO?

3. Identify the most important education and business interest groups in your state. How do they interact with each other?

4. Analyze and evaluate the coverage of state politics in a daily newspaper available in your area.

INTERNET ASSIGNMENT

Find the Web sites of your governor and legislature as well as the Web sites of three interest groups active there. Identify the educational issues that are important to each. Are different issues important to different policy actors? Explain any differences and similarities that you found.

NEWS STORY FOR ANALYSIS **THE POLITICS OF EDUCATION: CTA PICKS A FIGHT**

Sacramento, CA—"Children aren't widgets and a classroom is not an assembly line."

Those fighting words poured out of radios across the state this spring as the California Teachers Association launched Sacramento's biggest education battle of the year. Their bill, AB 2160, would grant unprecedented authority to teachers and their union by including textbook choices, curriculum design and even school maintenance decisions in the collective bargaining negotiations that are now limited mostly to wages and benefits. Teachers say the bill is a reaction to many of the recent education reforms that have been popular with politicians but have increased the accountability and the burden on classroom teachers. If lawmakers set academic goals, teachers say, then they want to choose the tools to achieve those goals.

Even before its first hearing, the bill triggered controversy and a high-stakes political showdown. It split the education community, with school administrators saying the process of negotiating wages is often too adversarial for constructive decision-making about books and curriculum. Several have branded the bill a "power grab" by the union.

The bill also threatens to split the Democratic Party. Some party members, including Governor Gray Davis, have expressed concern about the merits of the plan. But the pressure to support it is considerable because the teachers' union is the second largest contributor to the Democratic Party and two of the co-authors of the bill are Assembly Speaker Herb Wesson and Assemblywoman Virginia Strom-Martin, Chair of the Assembly Education Committee. With the speaker's critical backing, the bill is likely to succeed in the Senate.

But the biggest political drama is the fact that some consider the bill a direct challenge to Davis, who has received substantial contributions from the union but has opposed it on some key education reforms. If the bill reaches his desk, it would be politically difficult and embarrassing for the governor to veto an education bill in an election year. The governor met with CTA president Wayne

Johnson for three hours in April to talk about the bill, attention not bestowed on many bills or interest groups.

Opponents of the CTA bill say it is "ludicrous" for Johnson to deny the union's political manipulation, as he has recently done. "The CTA is a master at pressure and opportunistic tactics," said Scott Plotkin, executive director of the California School Boards Association. "They timed it well." "One of the difficulties is that a lot of members of the Legislature support unions," said Laura Jeffries, lobbyist for the Association of California School Administrators. "And they are being told this is a way for teachers to get more of a voice." "I wonder if the teachers aren't shooting at the wrong target," said the statewide school board association president, Dan Walden. "The problem is the Legislature. Maybe it's time we put our heads together for a collaborative effort."

(Adapted by permission of the publisher from L. Gledhill, "The Politics of Education: CTA Picks a Fight," *California Journal*, May 1, 2002, p. 8. Copyright 2002 by the *California Journal*.)

Questions

1. Identify all the policy actors in this article and categorize them, using headings from this chapter.

2. Analyze the sources of power of the CTA, the Association of California School Administrators, and the California School Boards Association. Which is most powerful and why?

3. Based on the first sentence of this article, what do you think is the prevailing ideology of those members of the California Assembly who have passed accountability measures?

4. Discuss the challenges which the leaders of California's "education establishment" would face if they were to try to act on Dan Walden's suggestion.

CASE STUDY

"STOP THE BULLIES!" THE POLITICS OF ACCOUNTABILITY

In 1987, the Ohio General Assembly passed H.B. 231, adopting learning outcomes in mathematics, reading, writing, and citizenship; these outcomes then became the basis of Ohio's first proficiency test, a ninth-grade test that students had to pass in order to graduate, starting in 1993. As the years passed, the legislature expanded its testing program, adding fourth, sixth, and twelfth-grade tests and including a science section. Increasingly, instruction in Ohio's schools focused on preparing students to take the tests. Educators were not happy about this narrowing of the curriculum, and among themselves they questioned the tests' validity. However, they made few attempts to get this policy changed; for they thought the legislature would interpret such efforts as opposition to accountability.

In 1997, the General Assembly unveiled an even more rigorous version of its accountability system. With S.B. 55 it established a district report card system, based almost entirely on test scores. These report cards were to be released to the media each year so that taxpayers could see how effective (or ineffective) their public schools were. S.B. 55 also included a "Fourth Grade Guarantee" which required fourth-grade children who failed the reading section of their tests to be retained, starting in 2001, unless they had an Individualized Education Plan (IEP) or the principal and teacher waived the requirement.

Among themselves, Ohio educators joked sarcastically that soon the fourth-grade population would explode and elementary schools would need to expand their parking lots to accommodate all the teenaged students who would be driving to fourth grade. But the state's parents were not amused, especially when it was revealed that about 42% of fourth graders regularly failed the reading test. Mary O'Brien and Teri Zeigler, mothers in an affluent Columbus suburb, formed a grassroots movement called "Stop Ohio Proficiency Tests," adopting the slogan, "Stop the Bullies!" The "bullies" were the state's legislators. Over a period of several months, they wrote numerous letters to newspaper editors, appeared on television, gave testimony before the State Board of Education, and held noisy demonstrations on the lawn of the state capitol.

Ohio's political leaders responded quickly. Governor Taft appointed a Commission for Student Success to study the issue and make recommendations in December 2000. Although he urged his fellow Republicans in the legislature to wait for the commission report, several of them introduced bills to amend the policy during the fall of 2000.

Meanwhile, educators began to speak out, too. The Ohio Education Association sponsored 33 public forums across the state to discuss problems with the tests. Administrators and their organizations began publicly to criticize both the tests and the district report cards. For example, Joyce Bowersock, an assistant superintendent, complained: "We're punishing 9-year-olds because they're not reading where . . . legislators think they should be reading. I think that's ridiculous." Superintendent David McWilliams said, "I am frustrated with the comparisons between school districts. Districts represent different communities." And John Stanford of the Ohio School Boards Association observed that the publication of district report cards hurt some districts' reputations and made it hard for them to pass tax referenda.

In December, the governor's commission recommended reducing the number of tests. In 2001, the General Assembly accepted that recommendation and also greatly weakened the Fourth Grade Guarantee.

(Based on *About Us*, n.d.; Clark, December 16, 2000; Ebbing, September 6, 2000; *History of Ohio Proficiency Tests*, n.d.; Hunt, Tortora, & Mrozowski, September 3, 2000; *OEA Online News*, n.d.; Sidoti, September 5, 2000; Welsh-Huggins, September 5, 2000; Welsh-Huggins, November 30, 2000).

QUESTIONS

1. Identify all the policy actors in this case study and categorize them, using headings from this chapter.

2. Were the state's educators wise to delay their attack against this accountability system until the parents revolted? Why or why not?

3. Why were the parents so successful in getting the policy changed?

4. Discuss Superintendent McWilliams's statement.

FOR FURTHER READING

Bowman, A. O'M., & Kearney, R. C. (1986). *The resurgence of the states.* Englewood Cliffs, NJ: Prentice Hall.

The authors document the shift of power toward the states that began during the presidency of Richard Nixon. They explain the reasons for this change, providing examples of how governorships, legislatures, court systems, and local governments have been affected.

Edlefson, C. (1994). The substance and politics of education reform: A view from a governor's office. *Planning and Changing, 25*(1/2), 41–55.

Edlefson, who was the educational specialist on Ohio Governor Celeste's staff in the late 1980s, gives the inside story of how Celeste set the agenda for education reform. Her article provides a rare glimpse of the usually hidden workings of the governor's office.

Gray, V., Hanson, R. L., & Jacob, H. (Eds.). (1999). *Politics in the American states.* **7th ed. Washington, D.C.: Congressional Quarterly Press.**

This edited book is the standard political science overview of state politics. Its valuable chapters summarize recent developments and new research in every branch of state government and in special policy areas—an indispensable source on politics at the state level.

Madsen, J. (1994). *Educational reform at the state level.* **Bristol, PA: Falmer Press.**

As a low-ranking administrator in an SDE, Madsen had the opportunity to observe how the agency put up roadblocks during the implementation of the state legislature's education reform act. She provides an interesting—and passionately felt—description of the power of a state agency.

Mazzoni, T. L. (1995). State policymaking and school reform: Influences and influentials. In J. D. Scribner and D. Layton (Eds.), *The study of educational politics.* **London: Falmer Press.**

Drawing on a wide database, Mazzoni synthesizes recent developments in state education policy making. His book chapter provides a valuable overview of contemporary trends in education policy at this level.

SETTING THE STAGE AND GETTING ON IT: ISSUE DEFINITION AND AGENDA SETTING

Focus Questions

How are policy issues defined?

Why is the definition of an issue important?

What is a policy agenda and how do policy issues get on it?

How can education leaders follow and influence these stages of the policy process?

PERCEPTION AND REALITY IN THE POLICY PROCESS

In an amusing story from his own high school days, scientist Benno Muller-Hill (1988) provides an example of how human perceptions of reality are shaped by others. As part of one of Muller-Hill's high school science classes, the teacher set up a telescope on the school grounds and asked his students to line up to look through it; they were supposed to observe one of the planets and its moons. The first student announced that he could not see the planet; however, after the teacher showed him how to adjust the focus, he stated that he could see it clearly.

After him, several other students looked through the instrument and said they could see the planet and its moons. But the boy just ahead of Muller-Hill in line loudly insisted that he saw nothing. The exasperated teacher looked through the telescope himself, and a strange expression came over his face. He had forgotten to remove the cover from the lens! Not a single one of the students had really seen the planet and its moons. For our purposes, whether the students pretended to see the planet and its moons in order to avoid embarrassment (and a poor grade) or whether they actually thought some speck of dust or glint of light on the lens was the planet is irrelevant. The point is that we human beings have a powerful desire to perceive the reality we think we should perceive. Breaking free of a definition of reality that those around us accept and expect us to accept also is extremely difficult for us.

This tendency is especially important in the first two stages of the policy process: issue definition and agenda setting. If a policy issue is not well defined, it will not be perceived as important. If it is not perceived as important by a large number of people, it will never attract enough attention to reach the policy agenda. If it never reaches the policy agenda, it will certainly never become formal policy. Important as they are, these two stages of the policy process are relatively unfamiliar to the general public, including school leaders. In part, this is because they occur quietly and out of the glare of media attention. In part, too, it is because high school government classes and even many college courses in political science overlook them entirely, focusing instead on the more visible stages of policy formulation and adoption. Yet issue definition and agenda setting are arguably the most important steps in the entire policy process, irreversibly influencing what happens next.

Education leaders who are unaware of these two stages of the policy process often feel blindsided by education policy proposals and changes. To them, new policy ideas seemingly emerge from nowhere and move rapidly into the legislatures or the courts, drawing on a surprising level of support. They often feel that somehow professional educators have been left out of the loop and that no one cares about their ideas or experience. Leaders who wish to be ahead of the game rather than always trying to figure out what the game is need to understand these first stages, know how to follow them, and have the skill to influence them.

Chapter 7, then, describes the issue-definition and agenda-setting phases of the policy process. The final section of this chapter presents ways that school leaders can monitor and influence these processes.

ISSUE DEFINITION: SETTING THE STAGE

Defining *Issue Definition*

Defining a policy issue is a political process that involves transforming a **problem** into an **issue** that the government can address. It is a discursive process, occurring through both written and spoken communication. It also involves developing an attractive image of the issue and associating appealing symbols with it in order to attract public support. Intelligent definition of an issue can increase the likelihood of political support, reduce the likelihood of opposition, and shape the policy debate. It sets the stage for the more visible phases of the process to follow (Anderson, 1984; Baumgartner & Jones, 1993; Rochefort & Cobb, 1994).

In thinking about issue definition, distinguishing **problems** from **policy issues** is important (Best, 1989; Stone, 1989). The world is full of problems—difficult situations that render life unpleasant and inconvenient. All educators know that schools abound with problems: school buses sometimes break down, teachers often feel out of sorts, and children's minds are more often filled with fantasies derived from television than with reflections on their lessons. Yet, for the most part educators accept these problems either as an inevitable part of school life or as minor daily annoyances. They do not usually see them as issues requiring government action.

Figure 7.1 lists five common problems in schools. Most educators would agree that these are problems, but they probably feel no urgency about dealing with them. In Figure 7.2, however, each of the five problems has been transformed into a policy issue. Unlike the problems, the issues are controversial; they imply an interpretation of the problem, a set of values, and an understanding of the proper role of government. Leaders should understand that any problem can yield several policy issues. Figure 7.3 lists five of the many issues that could be derived from the second problem noted in Figure 7.1—that of motivating students. During the issue-definition stage, several competing understandings of a single problem are often under discussion simultaneously. Ultimately, however, only two or three will be accepted as valid definitions of the problem; the "winners" will prevail primarily because of the skill with which their supporters define them.

---

1. Many teachers and principals suffer from low morale.
2. Students are often hard to motivate.
3. Many children change schools during the school year because their families move.
4. Children who spend a lot of time watching television and playing computer games may find school boring.
5. Educational resources are often used unwisely.

Figure 7.1 Five common problems in schools.

---

1. Because low morale results from a lack of control over major professional decisions, teachers and principals ought to be empowered through site-based decision making.
2. If students had to maintain a C or higher average in order to obtain a driver's license, their motivation in school would increase.
3. Parents with school-age children should be legally prohibited from moving outside their school attendance zone during the school year.
4. Only educational and motivational media should be available to children younger than 18.
5. If schools had to compete with each other for students, they would use their resources more wisely.

Figure 7.2 Five policy issues based on the problems in Figure 7.1.

---

1. If students had to maintain a C or higher average in order to obtain a driver's license, their motivation would increase.
2. If corporal punishment were restored in U.S. schools, we would see a dramatic increase in student motivation.
3. National standards and assessments would motivate students to work harder in school.
4. If teachers taught a curriculum that was more relevant to students and used more hands-on learning activities, motivation problems would decrease.
5. If schools were small enough that students could know their teachers and classmates better, students would be more motivated.

Figure 7.3 Five policy issues regarding student motivation.

The Education Policy Planning and Research Community

Its Nature and Structure. Although issue definition is an intellectual process and therefore occurs within human minds, minds are found in bodies that must be located somewhere. This means that issue definition has to occur in specific places at identifiable times. In the United States almost all education policy issues are defined within a loosely linked set of institutions that some call the **education policy planning and research community** (EPPRC). Some aspects of agenda setting also occur there. Although these institutions play an important role in the policy process, their public visibility is low. Fred Burke (1990), former commissioner of education in Rhode Island and New Jersey, describes this network's issue-definition process as a "para-private" one that is "peculiarly informal, private, diffuse, episodic, and from a public policy point of view, unaccountable" (p. 11). Among the participants, he identifies the U.S. Department of Education (USDOE), nonprofit foundations, professors and administrators at a few leading universities, teachers' unions, education associations and umbrella organizations, and textbook publishers.

Figure 7.4 depicts the EPPRC and relates it to government and the media. In this diagram, foundations, universities, policy planning groups (think tanks), and the USDOE constitute the core of the EPPRC. Although more than 20,000 foundations, approximately 1,000 policy planning organizations, and many universities are located in the United States, not all of them are important in education policy development (Nielsen, 1985; Weiss, 1992). Many specialize in other policy areas such as defense or agriculture; many more are not involved in policy development at all. Only a few are major players in education. Figure 7.5 lists eleven foundations that have been especially interested in education; Figure 7.6 lists eight think tanks known for their work in education policy; and Figure 7.7 lists five major universities that work in this area. These five universities form the Consortium for Policy Research in Education (CPRE). Although other foundations, think tanks, and universities participate in education policy development, these 24 institutions are unusually important. Most of their names will be familiar to school leaders.

These 24 institutions are by no means monolithic, and they do not all agree with each other. Most foundations and think tanks have an ideological orientation. For example, the Economic Policy Institute is extremely liberal, while the Carnegie Corporation, RAND Corporation, and the Committee for Economic

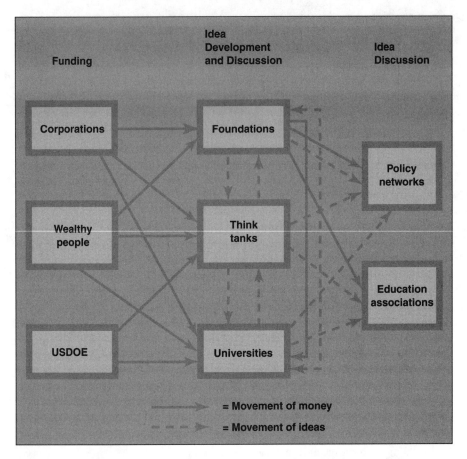

Figure 7.4 The education policy planning and research community.
Note. This diagram is loosely based on *Who's Running America?* 6/e by Dye, Thomas R., © 1995. Adapted by permission of Prentice Hall, Inc., Upper Saddle River, NJ.

Annie Casey Foundation
Carnegie Corporation
Danforth Foundation
Dewitt Wallace–Reader's Digest Fund
Ford Foundation
Kellogg Foundation
Lilly Endowment
MacArthur Foundation
Pew Charitable Trusts
Rockefeller Foundation
Spencer Foundation

Figure 7.5 Some foundations that sponsor educational policy research and initiatives.

```
American Enterprise Institute
Brookings Institution
Committee for Economic Development
Economic Policy Institute
Heritage Foundation
Hudson Institute
Manhattan Institute
RAND Corporation
```

Figure 7.6 Some policy research organizations (think tanks) that study educational policy.

```
Harvard University
Stanford University
University of Michigan
University of Pennsylvania
University of Wisconsin–Madison
```

Figure 7.7 University members of the Consortium for Policy Research in Education (CPRE).

Development are liberal. In contrast, the American Enterprise Institute, the Hudson Institute, and the Manhattan Institute are well known for conservative research and publications. The Heritage Foundation is to the right of most the groups listed here, although it is by no means the most conservative U.S. think tank (Lagemann, 1989; McGann, 1995; Nielsen, 1985; Peschek, 1987). This means that, far from cooperating in some type of conspiracy, these organizations actually compete fiercely with each other to have their definitions of education problems accepted by other participants in the issue-definition process.

Funding the EPPRC. Like all organizations, participants in the EPPRC require substantial financial support to keep their programs going. Their funding comes from three major sources: corporations, wealthy individuals, and the government (especially the USDOE). Many think tanks receive much of their financial support from foundations—but ultimately most foundation money comes from either corporations or wealthy people.

Money can be given to these institutions in several ways. Corporations and wealthy individuals sometimes give outright donations. When the Heritage Foundation was founded in 1973, a wealthy businessman—Joseph Coors of Colorado—provided much of its original funding. Other donors included Richard Mellon Scaife (another wealthy man), the Olin Foundation, and several corporations (Peschek, 1987). Another common way to give money is to contribute to an institution's endowment fund. Because endowment moneys are invested and only their income is available for spending, they provide a stable source of revenue. The Brookings Institution, one of the oldest think tanks in the United States, is heavily endowed; much of its original endowment was provided by steel magnate

Andrew Carnegie (McGann, 1995). Many universities are also heavily endowed; Harvard, Princeton, and Yale top the list (Dye, 1995).

Another way to provide money for these institutions is to make grants to them. Grants, of course, are competitive. When the federal government or a foundation plans to give money through a grant program, it first issues a request for proposals (RFP). The RFP usually includes a description of what kind of project is eligible to receive grant money and guidelines for writing the proposal. Institutions and individuals submit their proposals, and a few are selected for funding. Much of the education research conducted by both universities and think tanks is funded this way. CPRE, for example, was founded in 1985 with a five-year grant from the Office of Educational Research and Improvement (OERI), a division of the USDOE. It also receives grant money from several foundations, including the Carnegie Corporation and the Pew Charitable Trusts (CPRE, n.d.).

Sometimes funding comes in the form of contracts. The RAND Corporation, a California-based think tank, provides a good example. Under federal government contracts, it conducted many of the evaluations of federal education programs in the 1960s and 1970s. Commissioned books and research involve a special kind of contract. The Carnegie Corporation has commissioned many books on education policy, including Christopher Jencks's *Inequality* and James B. Conant's *Shaping Educational Policy* (Lagemann, 1989). Of course, most institutions involved in developing policy ideas receive funding from several sources and in several forms. The Brookings Institution is heavily endowed but also depends on foundations for support (Smith, 1991). The RAND Corporation—which has an annual budget of approximately $100 million—receives financial support from its endowment fund but also from the government and foundations (Weiss, 1992). Universities, too, receive support from several funding streams: government grants and contracts, gifts from corporations and wealthy individuals, and foundation moneys as well as student tuition and (in some cases) taxes. For all these institutions, obtaining a steady supply of sufficient funding is a constant challenge.

Developing and Discussing New Ideas. The EPPRC provides multiple forums in which new policy ideas can be developed, discussed, and then disseminated to policy planning groups, the media, and policy makers (McGann, 1995). Think tanks and research-oriented universities are the sites of most of this intellectual activity. Think tanks employ researchers and writers who work together to pursue a research and publishing agenda developed by the organization's leadership. In research-oriented universities, professors are hired with the understanding that their job includes scholarship: conducting research and then making presentations, writing articles, and publishing books based on it. In a world where knowledge is an increasingly crucial source of power, producing new knowledge is important. The United States is fortunate to have a network of think tanks and universities that produces much of the new knowledge in the world.

New Ideas From Research.   One important source of new ideas is research. Researchers employed by think tanks and universities conduct three broad types of research: **basic, applied,** and **integrative. Basic research** is the most theoretical and (some would say) the least practical. Yet, as basic researchers point out, much research that was originally pursued for purely intellectual reasons has had important practical applications. One area of basic research that has had considerable impact on education policy is learning theory, an aspect of psychology. For much of the twentieth century, the psychological theory behaviorism dominated. University researchers such as B. F. Skinner taught rats to negotiate mazes and press levers for food pellet rewards, demonstrating that some learning is based on a stimulus–response reaction and that rewards and punishments can improve it. Under the influence of this basic research, curriculum policy changed. Schools in the United States adopted "behavioral objectives" and encouraged teachers to use reward systems to manage their classrooms (Ravitch, 1995). In the last three decades, however, learning theory has changed considerably, again largely because of basic research. Cognitive psychology, today's dominant theory, emphasizes the social nature of learning and the fact that human beings "construct" their own knowledge as they learn. It also suggests that both children and adults learn better by solving open-ended problems with several possible answers than by memorizing facts. Cognitive theory, too, has had considerable impact on curriculum policy; portfolio assessment and the return of essay-type examinations reflect this influence (Ravitch, 1995).

Applied research tests theory in real-life settings. Whereas a basic researcher usually works in a carefully controlled laboratory-like environment, an applied researcher may study a school or a classroom to see if a curriculum based on cognitive theory leads to improved learning. A special type of applied research is **evaluation research,** which seeks to assess how well a new education policy or program is working. Although both universities and think tanks enter into contracts to conduct evaluation research, several of the most influential evaluation studies have been done by think tanks. Probably the most famous were the RAND Corporation's evaluations of several federal education programs during the 1970s (Williams & Palmatier, 1992). The findings of evaluation research sometimes lead to major policy changes.

Finally, **integrative research** draws on a wide range of past research studies on a single topic, integrating them into a single work that seeks to describe what the research as a whole says. Examples of integrative research include textbooks, literature reviews, and general overviews of a subject. Diane Ravitch (1995), working under the auspices of the Brookings Institution, wrote *National Standards in American Education: A Citizen's Guide.* In it she provides a history of curriculum and testing in the United States, a history of the development of the movement for national standards, and a description of the political conflicts surrounding national standards. As the title of her book suggests, it offers a useful overview of the subject for a broad audience.

Although basic, applied, and integrative research provide some new policy ideas, assuming that policy makers immediately accept researchers' findings and translate them into policy or that they accept all the ideas scholars develop would be naive. On the contrary, policy researchers often lament that policy makers are uninterested in their work and resist applying it. However, studies of policy development over long periods of time—a decade or more—indicate that some research findings do ultimately change people's understanding of policy problems and thus influence policy development (Sabatier & Jenkins-Smith, 1993).

New Ideas From Ideology. Ideology shapes issue definition at least as much as research does. Most think tanks and foundations adhere to a specific ideological position, and so do many university policy researchers. Their ideology influences their issue definition work in at least two ways. First, their basic beliefs predispose them to analyze policy problems in some ways rather than in others (Sabatier & Jenkins-Smith, 1993). For example, both conservatives and liberals are concerned about low school achievement among schoolchildren, but they understand this problem differently. Conservatives are more likely to view low school achievement as the result of individualistic factors, such as broken families and inadequate efforts by both children and their teachers. Therefore, conservative solutions often encourage a return to traditional values and basic education. Because conservatives distrust activist government, they are also more likely to select a policy delivery system based on the market or privatization. Some form of school choice, private tutoring, or economic incentives for parents to stay together would occur to them as ways to solve this problem. In contrast, liberals would define the problem as one caused primarily by the larger society rather than by individual families, children, and teachers. Typical liberal solutions would include improved nutrition for poor children, remedial programs for the schools that serve them, and job training for parents. Because liberals favor active government intervention in social problems, they feel comfortable with these approaches even though they expand government and increase public spending.

Second, ideology helps determine the type of research that is done and the questions that guide it. Foundations award grant money to researchers and writers whose proposed projects are consistent with their own ideological positions. Similarly, most think tanks employ people who share their views. Not surprisingly, then, much research and writing is done on those topics that are at the center of current ideological controversy. Not coincidentally, in recent years several conservative foundations have funded private voucher programs and sponsored research on them. Also not coincidentally, the liberal Carnegie Corporation and Economic Policy Institute have provided financial support for scholars who have reservations about school choice. As groups that oppose conservative definitions of education issues, they have good reason to gather evidence to use to challenge them (Sabatier & Jenkins-Smith, 1993). Thus, the research and writing the EPPRC produces as it defines policy issues should never be uncritically accepted as purely scientific or impartial. Although some of it conforms to high standards of scholarship, it varies in quality. And all of it must be considered the product of a political process in which ideology plays an important role.

Forums for Discussion. Universities and think tanks do more than pay the salaries of researchers and writers, however. They provide a work environment that not only supports research and writing but also stimulates it. Scholars have access to superb libraries, state-of-the-art computer facilities, clerical support, and research assistants. They normally have travel budgets that permit them to attend professional conferences and visit other scholars in their field. Universities and think tanks also sponsor workshops and symposia in order to give them a chance to hear stimulating speakers.

Especially in think tanks, but also in many research universities, a considerable effort is made to maintain a stimulating intellectual environment in which new ideas can be discussed, refined, or explored. "Food is essential to a successful think tank," argues Patrick Ford (1992, p. 35) as he describes the breakfasts, luncheons, and dinners that the American Enterprise Institute sponsors to encourage policy scholars to congregate and talk about their work. And Diane Ravitch (1995), who had previously worked at Columbia University, describes her experience working at the Brookings Institution in these glowing terms:

> Brookings is the most pleasant and productive environment in which I have ever worked. Casual conversations—over the lunch table, at the water cooler, or in the frequent luncheon seminars—were invariably stimulating. The facilities, including the library and the computer services, are state of the art. . . . There are no strictures, formal or informal, on what may be said, written, or argued. (p. x)

In such environments, researchers, scholars, writers, and other members of the EPPRC have the opportunity to discuss social problems, develop new ideas for solving them, and define them through thought and conversation.

Disseminating New Ideas.   Of course, foundations, think tanks, and universities have little interest in merely stimulating thinkers to talk among themselves; they reward them for disseminating their new knowledge. Ideas can be communicated in several ways. The publication of printed materials is one of them. Both professors and think-tank researchers write articles and books in which they make new ideas widely available. Think tanks typically produce several other types of written documents as well, including research reports, policy briefs, and newsletters. Several think-tank scholars also write newspaper columns. Many think tanks also make their publications or other texts available on their Web sites.

Ideas can be spread through the spoken word as well. University professors, foundation representatives, and think-tank researchers often present talks at professional conferences, appear as members of symposium panels, and, when invited, testify before committees of Congress and state legislatures. In addition, they often sponsor events at which new ideas are orally presented to an audience. CPRE sponsors education policy workshops (funded by the Danforth Foundation) for state and local policy makers. The Heritage Foundation sponsors frequent lectures on and debates about policy issues at its Washington, D.C., headquarters (Peschek, 1987). The Education Commission of the States (ECS)—a nonpartisan policy network that serves state governments by acting as a clearinghouse for education policy ideas—holds an annual meeting at which scholars and others present ideas to an audience consisting largely of state officials from across the nation. Many people consider this ECS meeting "the most useful in education" (Kaplan & Usdan, 1992, p. 671) for sharing and discussing new policy ideas.

Finally, ideas are often spread as scholars move from one institution to another—a frequent occurrence within the EPPRC. For example, conservative scholar Diane Ravitch was a professor at Columbia University's Teachers' College for many years; she then served as assistant secretary for OERI under the first Bush Administration. After Bush's defeat in the 1992 presidential election, she was invited to join the Brookings Institution (Ravitch, 1995). Liberal scholar Marshall Smith—a major leader in the movement for standards-based reform—has made even more professional moves. After graduating from Harvard University's School of Education, he held several education positions in the Carter Administration. After Reagan became president in 1981, Smith moved to Wisconsin, where he directed the Wisconsin Center for Education Research. Five years later, he became the dean of the School of Education at Stanford University. During his years at Stanford, Smith was involved with CPRE; he also had close connections with the National Science Foundation. In 1993, he moved back into government, becoming an undersecretary in the USDOE (Vinovskis, 1996). These examples illustrate the close ties between government and the EPPRC. People move back and forth in a fluid fashion, taking their interpretations of society's problems and their solutions with them. As they move from one institution to another, their ideas spread.

The Spread of a Policy Idea: Site-based Management. The development and spread of site-based management (SBM) provides a good example of how the EPPRC works. In the early 1990s, Ogawa (1994) analyzed articles, conference presentations, and printed materials from several national education organizations in an attempt to trace the development of the SBM movement. He also interviewed 32 people. He traced the basic SBM idea back to a group of individuals who had worked at the National Institute of Education in the 1970s, several of whom had ties to Harvard University. They had seen SBM as a way to improve education in the United States by professionalizing teaching. The late Al Shanker, then president of the American Federation of Teachers (AFT), had been intrigued by the idea and had persuaded three AFT locals to negotiate SBM into their contracts in the early 1980s.

In 1985, the president of the ECS suggested to the president of the Carnegie Corporation that the foundation should become involved in studying linkages between education and the economy. As part of this project, the Carnegie president established the Carnegie Forum on Education and the Economy, which in turn established the Task Force on Teaching as a Profession. This task force conducted a study of teaching, publishing its findings in a 1986 report entitled *A Nation Prepared*. In the same year, the National Governors' Association (NGA) published a report called *Time for Results*. Both reports proposed SBM as a way to professionalize teaching, and both cited the three AFT locals who had negotiated SBM as positive examples.

Next, the Carnegie Forum established a speakers' bureau that provided speakers to present the report to teachers' unions, education organizations, and business groups. It also arranged for local newspapers and television stations to cover these speeches. Ogawa found that these 1986 events constituted a "watershed period" for the movement. After 1986, national education organizations such as the American Association of School Administrators (AASA), the National Association of Secondary School Principals (NASSP), the National Association of Elementary School Principals (NAESP), and both teachers' unions began to hold SBM workshops. In 1988, the NGA used a Carnegie Corporation grant to fund a conference on SBM. By 1990, articles on SBM were appearing frequently in both scholarly and practitioner journals. Most of the authors were connected with CPRE, one of whose members is Harvard. Ogawa (1994) concluded that there is "an unofficial policy environment, one in which entrepreneurs shape and advance policy initiatives" (p. 545). This "unofficial policy environment" is, of course, what this book calls the EPPRC.

Elements of Skillful Issue Definition.   Several factors influence which policy definitions succeed in moving onto an agenda, but the skill with which the issue has been defined is probably the most important. In the next sections, the elements of good issue definition are described. Throughout this discussion, most of the examples will be based on a current policy issue—school choice.

Claims.   Claims must be made about a problem in order to transform it into a policy issue. A claim is an assertion that grows out of a broader interpretation of the problem, its nature, and its causes. At least one of the claims made about a problem should indicate what has caused it (Best, 1989a, 1989b). For example, the fifth issue in Figure 7.2, "If schools had to compete with each other for students, they would use their resources more wisely," implies two claims: (1) schools do not use their resources as efficiently as they might, and (2) a lack of competition among schools causes inefficiency.

Evidence.   Descriptive material should be presented as evidence to support at least some of the most important claims made about a problem. The best forms of evidence are dramatic anecdotes, atrocity stories, and statistics—especially big statistics drawn from official sources (Baumann, 1989; Best, 1989c). For example, claims about the outrageous wastefulness of schools could be supported with a vivid description of the Mercedes Benz a school district allegedly provides for its superintendent and with numbers drawn from a major government report on the small percentage of school funds that actually reaches the classroom.

Solution.   A good issue definition includes a realistic solution for the problem it has identified and described. A realistic solution is both politically feasible and financially affordable (Portz, 1994). Various forms of school choice have been suggested as ways to introduce more competition into education and encourage greater student achievement and more careful use of funds. Given the current prevalence of conservative ideas and the public's resistance to tax increases, the school-choice solution has broad appeal.

Discourse. A good issue definition is expressed in powerful language that links the issue to deeply held values, hopes, fears, and aspirations. Emotional words and expressions, including assertions that the issue has a bearing on key national priorities such as military security and economic growth can further strengthen a definition. So can the use of metaphors to describe the problem—especially metaphors drawn from medicine, family, warfare, or athletics (Cobb & Elder, 1972; Placier, 1996). Among the reasons for the appeal of school choice to many people is the fact that it lends itself to athletic metaphors of competition and can easily be linked to the American values of freedom and individualism.

Broad Appeal. A skillfully defined issue is potentially appealing to a wide audience. Issues have broad appeal when they are relatively vague rather than narrowly specific, important to a high percentage of citizens, significant for the future as well as the present, and defined in laymen's terms rather than in technical jargon (Baumann, 1989; Cobb & Elder, 1972). In relation to these requirements, the school-choice issue does not fare as well as it does in relationship to the other criteria. It is a specific issue, primarily important to the parents of school children—a demographic group that has been declining in relative size for several decades. Such terms and phrases as *voucher, interdistrict open enrollment,* and *charter school* have a technical ring to them. This is probably part of the explanation for the relatively slow progress of the school-choice movement over the last forty years.

Constraints on Issue Definition. Although any problem can provide the basis for defining numerous policy issues, some definitions are more likely than others. Ideas, values, and ideologies are extraordinarily important in issue definition; they shape and restrict the interpretations that people are able—or willing—to give problems, as well as the solutions they are willing to offer. Interpretations and solutions that are immediately obvious to people in one society do not even occur to people in another . . . and vice versa. In the United States, for example, major government intervention in what is considered the private sphere—businesses, churches, families, voluntary organizations and the like—are rarely considered. In Figure 7.2, the third policy issue ("Parents with school-age children should be legally prohibited from moving outside their school attendance zone during the school year") and the fourth issue ("Only educational and motivational media should be available to children younger than 18") would be unthinkable issue definitions in the contemporary United States and in most other democratic countries. They imply a level of government control over private life that most citizens of those countries would find intolerable. Yet, in many totalitarian states today and during certain historical periods in the United States and Western Europe, such issue definitions would be possible.

Another constraint on issue definition in the United States is constitutionality. A large body of case law developed by federal and state courts over more than two centuries has caused some policy areas to resemble unpredictable minefields.

As a result, many people hesitate to define issues in certain ways because they fear that policies growing out of such definitions will be ruled unconstitutional. Issue areas of this sort in education include religious activity in schools, race, gender, and censorship.

Finally, issue definition is often constrained by the cyclical movement of popular values and policy mechanisms. In the 1930s, the most popular approach to solving a policy problem was to establish a large government bureaucracy to deal with it by developing regulations. In the 1980s and 1990s, issue definitions that offered more bureaucracy or government regulation as a solution were likely to be dismissed out of hand. This fact discouraged many people from proposing a wide range of conceivable, but unpopular, issue definitions. Instead, they were likely to propose definitions that interpreted problems as the result of excessive bureaucracy and to suggest solutions such as deregulation, privatization, or market incentives.

THE POLICY AGENDA

No matter how brilliantly an issue has been defined within the EPPRC and no matter how much research university professors can produce in support of policy change, it may go nowhere, remaining the topic of heated debate in the ivory tower, but never attracting the interest of a politician. In order to have a chance to become an actual policy, an issue must reach the **policy agenda,** and this occurs neither automatically nor easily. In this section, *policy agenda* is defined and different types of policy agendas are described. Problems involved in getting on the agenda (and staying there) will be discussed before this section concludes with some discussion of **nondecisions.**

Defining *Policy Agenda*

A **policy agenda** comprises all those issues under serious discussion in relation to a specific policy domain. In the broadest sense, the education policy agenda includes all issues under discussion at professional conferences, in education journals, among well-informed educators, in the mass media, among the general public, and among government officials (Kingdon, 1995). However, political scientists distinguish several types of policy agendas. Often an issue will appear on one or two agendas, but not all. If an issue is ever to become official policy, it must eventually reach the **governmental policy agenda.**

Types of Policy Agendas

The Systemic Agenda. The **systemic policy agenda** is broad, consisting of all the issues people outside government are currently discussing. In order to determine the composition of the systemic agenda in education, a school leader might skim the tables of contents of several education journals, glance through some recent issues of *Education Week*, and add to them any education problems that the mass media are currently highlighting.

Within education's systemic agenda, three subagendas can be distinguished. The **professional agenda** consists of those issues under discussion within various interest groups, education policy networks, and education associations as well as among informed professional educators. School leaders frequently encounter these issues when they attend conferences or read current literature in their field. The **media agenda,** in contrast, consists of those education issues that editors and other decision makers in the communications industry have decided to emphasize (Mead, 1994). As most school leaders know, this agenda often bears little resemblance to the professional one. The mass media are businesses that must attract customers in order to survive; therefore, they focus on exciting issues, such as school violence and sex crimes among teachers. Finally, the third subagenda is the **public agenda,** which includes those education issues to which the general public are actually paying attention (Mead, 1994). This agenda is normally shorter than the other two, and may or may not overlap with them. Usually, although not always, the public agenda is greatly influenced by the media agenda. Together, the professional, media, and public agendas comprise the systemic agenda.

The Governmental Agenda. The **governmental agenda** consists of "the list of subjects or problems to which governmental officials . . . are paying some serious attention at any given time" (Kingdon, 1995, p. 3). An issue on this agenda is being seriously discussed by government officials or has been scheduled for official action. Obviously, many governmental policy agendas exist in education. The federal government has an agenda, as does each of the fifty states. Moreover, each of these agendas consists of several components, such as bills slated for introduction or legislative action; court cases on the docket or working their way through the system; and decisions pending in regulatory agencies.

How Agendas Relate to Each Other

The most important fact to understand about policy agendas is that access to them is highly competitive. As a result, most issues that have been defined never reach the governmental, public, or media agenda at all. The reason is simple: the "carrying capacity" of each agenda is severely limited (Hilgartner & Bosk, 1988). Members of the general public do not have enough time to inform themselves about every issue, much less discuss them all. Newspapers and Web sites have limited space for text; and television and radio have even more limited broadcasting time for education news. Above all, legislatures, courts, and administrative agencies have tightly limited resources and cannot introduce every conceivable bill, hear every conceivable case, or make a decision on every controversial point. Thus, the relationship among the items on the agenda is competitive; if a new item moves onto an agenda, an older one usually moves off. As items move from one agenda to another, a selection process occurs. Some issues remain on the systemic agenda for a long time and attract considerable attention, eventually winning this competition and reaching a governmental agenda. Most, however, are discussed for a short while and then vanish, losing the competition.

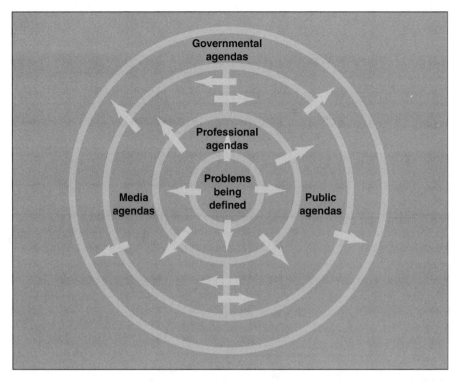

Figure 7.8 Policy agendas in relation to each other.

Figure 7.8 represents the policy agendas in schematic form and uses arrows to depict the most common patterns of movement.

Typically, far more education policy issues are on the professional agenda than the other agendas can accommodate. Some issues, however, do move from the professional agenda to the media agenda and spread from there to the general public. Policy makers—who are usually aware of all three systemic subagendas—select from them a few issues they wish to actively support. Other patterns of movement are possible, however. For example, in the late 1970s, the public in several states became incensed about escalating school taxes, and organized to put tax limitation initiatives on the ballot. This "tax revolt" is an excellent example of a situation in which an issue was both defined and placed on the policy agenda by the general public. In most cases, however, education policy issues follow the path of development suggested in Figure 7.2.

Getting on the Governmental Policy Agenda

The Story of School Choice.   Usually, a new idea languishes on the shelf for a long time before it reaches a governmental policy agenda, is acted upon, and becomes official policy. School choice is a good example. First seriously proposed in 1962 by Milton Friedman, a professor at the University of Chicago, it was considered an odd professorial type of idea throughout the 1960s. By the early 1970s, however, a few radicals and liberals had become interested in it, even though Friedman was a well-known conservative. Because it was an item on the professional agenda, people such as Christopher Jencks and James Coleman picked up the idea and advocated it as a way to empower poor parents and equalize educational opportunity for their children. In the early 1970s, school choice moved briefly onto a governmental agenda when the federal government funded a choice experiment in Alum Rock, California. This pilot program was generally considered a failure, and choice dropped off the governmental agenda, but remained on the professional agenda. In 1980, conservative Ronald Reagan was elected president. Propelled by the professional agendas of many of the conservative groups that had supported him, he moved choice onto the governmental agenda again by advocating tuition tax credits and vouchers in his speeches. Soon both forms of choice were introduced as bills in Congress . . . and introduced, and introduced, always going down to defeat. By the late 1980s, however, states such as Minnesota and Ohio had not only moved choice onto their governmental policy agendas, but had also adopted some forms of it as policy. Since then, three states have enacted public voucher programs and 37 have adopted charter school policies. Thus, after languishing on various agendas for 30 years, school choice rapidly moved onto governmental agendas and into official policy during the last decade of the twentieth century (Morken & Formicola, 1999; Viteritti, 1999).

Public Officials and Agendas.   The story of the movement of school choice from a newly defined policy issue to the professional agenda to various governmental agendas illustrates how many issues finally reach the governmental agenda. Major political leaders—especially the president and governors, but also prominent legislators—often play a central role in agenda setting (Anderson, 1984). Because they frequently give speeches and hold press conferences, they can call attention to an issue and keep attention focused on it. Moreover, because their public appearances are by definition media events, they can easily move an issue onto the media agenda. The school-choice issue stayed on the governmental agenda in part because in the spring of 1983, a presidential commission issued *A Nation at Risk*, an official report claiming that education was in a state of crisis. Although this report did not advocate school choice, it gave credibility to the claim that a crisis in education existed. One of the best ways to draw attention to an issue is to associate it with a real or perceived crisis (Hogwood & Gunn, 1984; Rochefort & Cobb, 1994). Therefore, school choice became a favorite item on all the policy agendas—because many people saw it as a cheap, but effective, way to deal with that crisis.

Other Paths to the Agenda.   Issues can reach the governmental policy agenda in other ways. Sometimes a "triggering event" occurs, clarifying or dramatizing an issue that has hitherto attracted little attention (Baumgartner & Jones, 1993). Triggering events are especially likely to propel issues related to health and safety onto center stage. In many states, for example, policy makers, school leaders, and education groups know that many school buildings are rundown and need repairs to bring them up to current health and safety codes. This issue has been on their systemic agenda for years. Yet, nothing happens. The reason is clear: Renovating buildings costs money and might necessitate a tax increase, so many politicians would rather think about something else. However, if the roof of a school building collapses and injures 50 children, this catastrophe may act as a "triggering event," attracting media attention, causing a public outcry, and almost forcing the state legislature to act. Or again, it may not; if the story about the collapsed roof has to compete with a major national news story for media attention, it may be buried in the back pages of the papers and in brief reports on the 11:00 p.m. news. Especially if education leaders are not ready to act swiftly as soon as a triggering event occurs, the issue may evaporate within a few days and things may continue as before.

Other forces can also put an issue on the systemic or governmental agenda. Interest groups often play a major role, providing information about their issues to key policy makers and mobilizing sustained pressure to draw attention to an issue through letter-writing and lobbying campaigns. Or they may use the same tactics to keep an issue off the agenda (Kingdon, 1984). Policy networks—such as the ECS, the Institute for Educational Leadership, and the Business Roundtable—also play a role. They usually focus on a few education policy issues of major importance to them; then, through their publications, programs, and conferences they repeatedly reinforce these key issues. This practice tends to narrow the systemic agenda, but it also increases the likelihood that their favorite issues will eventually reach the governmental agenda (Kaplan & Usdan, 1992). Issues sometimes reach the governmental agenda because bureaucrats in state agencies—who have good access to policy makers—point out problems to them (Elling, 1996). Finally, many policy actors stage events to attract media attention to an issue, hoping to move it onto the media agenda and from there to a governmental agenda. For example, in 2001 Jane Hirschman, founder of a New York state group called the Parents' Coalition To Stop High-Stakes Testing, brought 1,500 parents in 27 buses to the capital in Albany to demonstrate opposition to New York's increased emphasis on its venerable Regents examinations (Manzo, 2001, May 16).

The Problem of the Disempowered.   Up to this point, all the ways to get items on the agenda have involved exercising considerable power. Students of the agenda-setting process have long recognized that some people and groups have more influence on the agenda than others. In their seminal study of agenda setting, Cobb and Elder (1972) demonstrated that, where agenda setting is involved, all citizens are definitely not equal: the powerful have more influence on policy agendas than do the disempowered. They argued, however, that disempowered groups sometimes use violence or the threat of violence to draw attention to their issues. For example, students have been known to hold protest marches and sit-ins or even stage food riots to make their concerns known. African Americans used similar strategies in the 1960s to demonstrate their dissatisfaction with the pace of school desegregation. Even so, such demonstrations of power require a level of planning and support that makes them unrealistic tactics except in extreme situations. For the most part, powerless groups have little impact on agenda setting.

Staying on a Policy Agenda

Although gaining access to any of the policy agendas is difficult, dropping off them is extremely easy. Indeed, all policy agendas are marked by great instability; issues that were hot in January may be forgotten by June. Once an issue has faded, reviving interest in it is hard because it now seems out of date. Among political scientists this phenomenon is known as the *issue–attention cycle;* in every policy area issues suddenly become the center of enormous attention on several agendas . . . and then, as suddenly, "lurch" out of everyone's thoughts (Baumgartner & Jones, 1993). In part, this instability results from the tendency of the mass media to prefer new ideas to old. In part, too, it results from the tendency of the general public to prefer novelty. However, after several years off the agenda, old ideas may resurface in a slightly different form and with a new name and reach the agenda again. Anyone who has been in education for more than a decade is aware of how cyclical education policy is.

The vagaries of the issue–attention cycle mean that advocates of particular policy changes must work hard to keep their ideas on the agenda once they get there. Informal clusters of advocates develop around some issues, providing ongoing support for a new policy idea (Hilgartner & Bosk, 1988). The "policy entrepreneurs" associated with such communities churn out fresh material on the issue, develop new approaches to it, and may even develop new terminology in the attempt to keep the issue ever new and attractive. Communities of operatives have developed around education issues such as school choice, inclusion (which in a slightly different form used to be called mainstreaming) and national standards. Such ongoing support keeps an item on the agenda for long periods of time, enhancing the likelihood that it will eventually lead to official policy.

Nondecisions

As noted earlier in this book, the **failure to act** on certain problems is a dimension of policy just as surely as an official action is. The technical term for such failures is *nondecisions.* Most nondecisions occur, not in the legislatures, courts, or executive offices, but rather during the problem-definition and agenda-setting stages of the policy process. Often, being able to identify just exactly where nondecisions have occurred is important because they provide important clues to how official policies and official policy rhetoric should be interpreted.

In many states, school finance equalization is a nondecision that has occurred between the systemic and governmental policy agendas. In his yearlong study of state politics in Kansas, Loomis (1994) learned that the related issues of equalizing school funding and reforming the property tax were important items on the systemic agenda. In fact, for many years Kansas educators and various state interest groups had discussed these issues and pressured the governor and the legislature to change the taxation and school finance systems. Almost everyone in

Kansas politics considered them outdated and unjust. Yet, year after year nothing happened. Governmental policy actors simply refused to move property tax and school finance reform onto their agendas because they knew that dealing with these issues in a serious manner would be controversial. They also recognized that any meaningful solution would cost money. Kansas is not the only state in which school finance reform has been a nondecision. In fact, this is why in some states education leaders and parents finally formed organizations to challenge school funding systems in the courts. School finance reform is still a nondecision in many places, suggesting how unwilling contemporary lawmakers are to increase taxes or redistribute them.

SCHOOL LEADERS AND THE EARLY STAGES OF THE POLICY PROCESS

Following the Early Stages

By definition, the first stage of the policy process is never covered by the mass media. Also by definition, many aspects of agenda setting are not covered either, which makes following issue definition and agenda setting challenging for school leaders. It is not impossible, but it does require using specialized sources. Three of these are especially important.

Most accessible to education leaders are the journals of professional educational associations. Figure 7.9 lists several of the more important ones. Most of them carry regular reports on research as well as book reviews. Leaders interested in issue definition should scan these regularly, paying special attention to those publications produced by major foundations and think tanks. Articles that present new or unusual ideas are probably based on current issue definition discussions. Those that deal with the current crop of hot ideas are drawn from various agendas. A regular reader of these journal features therefore develops a good sense of what is going on at both stages.

A second valuable resource is *Education Week*, an education newspaper published throughout the year by Editorial Projects in Education in Washington, D.C.; its Web version is called *Education Week on the Web* and includes searchable archives. Although it covers all aspects of the education policy process, its coverage of the first two stages is particularly helpful. For example, *Education Week*

American School Administrator
American School Boards Journal
Educational Leadership
NASSP Bulletin
The Phi Delta Kappan
Principal

Figure 7.9 Some leading journals published by educational associations.

usually runs articles about major foundation grants and think-tank reports on education, permitting outsiders to follow the ongoing definition of issues within the EPPRC. These articles often provide information about related Web pages, making it easy to access details on the Internet. Just scanning the headlines of the articles each week suggests which issues are on the professional and governmental agendas. The ECS annual meeting is covered in detail, providing valuable information about which issues government officials are discussing. *Education Week* also publishes summaries of the sessions and workshops at the annual conferences of the major education associations. These summaries make identifying which issues are now on this portion of the professional agenda possible.

Finally, those with access to the Internet should find following both issue definition and agenda setting easy. The USDOE, several major think tanks, and all major education associations have Web sites that offer much information. The materials available include position papers, publication lists, reports on meetings and conferences, and speeches by organization leaders. As more Web sites are developed and as existing ones are refined, the EPPRC activities will become increasingly visible to those who wish to track them.

Influencing the Early Stages

Influencing National Issue Definition.   At the outset, school leaders should recognize that national issue definition is the least accessible stage of the policy process and therefore the most difficult to influence. Significantly, Burke (1990) calls the process and the institutions involved in it "para-private." This means that most of the discussions, debates, and meetings within the EPPRC are closed to the general public and thus to almost all education leaders. Even so, some ways exist to influence the process, even at the national level. One of the simplest is to respond to new issue definitions in writing. Publications put out by think tanks, foundations, and universities are easy to identify; and a reference librarian can quickly locate the addresses of these institutions. This means that education leaders who have concerns about a new policy idea and would like to react to it from a practitioner's perspective can do so by writing a letter to one or more of the people actively involved in defining that issue. Because the policy actors within the EPPRC, unlike elected politicians, are not accustomed to receiving letters from constituents, they would certainly notice one that critiqued their ideas. The Internet provides another channel for written responses. The USDOE, think tanks, foundations, and education associations do not usually provide elaborate feedback mechanisms such as chat rooms and bulletin boards with their Web sites. However, they often give e-mail addresses to use to convey questions and comments, so school leaders could use them to convey their opinion of an educational idea the organization advocates.

Challenging National Definitions Locally.   Although influencing issue definition at the national level is difficult for ordinary educators, they should find challenging a nationally defined issue locally easier. In the 1980s, Ray and Mickelson (1990) did a case study of a group of local business leaders who sought to reform a southern school district. Thoroughly imbued with the claims of the national business community about the failures of public education, these business people established a task force to study ways to make the district more "competitive." Their preferred solution to the school system's alleged failure was to establish a central vocational high school at which all students who did not plan to go to college could "be socialized as productive workers" (p. 127). However, as the task force continued to meet, school leaders presented more and more counterevidence to undermine the business community's claims. For example, they invited experts to address the group about successful local school programs and also about the social conditions that had caused many children to fail. At an important meeting, a high-ranking central office administrator presented evidence that many local business people were actually satisfied with the schools, and then shifted to the theme of "the widening gap between 'the haves and have-nots'" (p. 129). In short, school leaders repeatedly grabbed the issue away from the business leaders and redefined it. Ray and Mickelson summarize their behavior in this way:

> Throughout the final stages of the Task Force deliberations business leaders kept inserting remarks about the need for centralized vocational education. The ranking school district official, however, forcefully finessed each attempt by first reiterating the social and curricular drawbacks of centralized vocational education, and by consistently repeating the shortcomings of a particular population of students. The numbers of low income youngsters were expanding, he insisted, "it's going to get worse!" (p. 130)

Ultimately, the education leaders' redefinition of the issue prevailed. The final report of the task force said much about poverty and recommended more early childhood education programs rather than a centralized vocational high school. School leaders throughout the country should always remember that merely because an issue has been defined at the national level does not mean that it is final or beyond question. Those who understand issue definition and can use discourse skillfully can often reshape an issue when it surfaces locally.

Influencing Agenda Setting: Basic Prerequisites.   Because agenda setting occurs in more visible and more accessible arenas than issue definition does, it is easier to influence. Usually, affecting agenda setting involves either (1) getting an issue moved from the systemic agenda to the governmental one, or (2) keeping an issue on the systemic agenda off the governmental one. Effectiveness at this stage of the policy process requires developing one's power sufficiently to be able to exercise impact.

Three power resources are especially important. The first is knowledge. Education leaders who wish to affect agenda setting must systematically work to be well-informed about new trends in education policy at the state and national levels. This means keeping up with professional reading and attending professional conferences. Only by following the unfolding issues in these forums can one gather enough information to know which policy issues are most likely to reach a governmental agenda in the near future. The second essential power resource is allies. No principal, district office administrator, or superintendent should even consider working alone on such efforts. Effective action requires having allies in four arenas: in professional associations, at the state department of education (SDE), among government officials, and among colleagues in school leadership. Such networks do not just happen; they must be developed over time and in a systematic and reflective way. Part of Chapter 8 discusses how to develop relationships with various policy actors. Most of the recommendations made there are also relevant for influencing agenda setting. Finally, one must build enough organizational effectiveness to be able to respond quickly to events in agenda-setting arenas. Kingdon (1984) argues that windows of opportunity for moving an issue onto the governmental agenda open suddenly; they close quickly, too. This means that anyone who wants to influence this stage of the policy process must be prepared to act and to act fast.

Attracting Attention to an Issue.   Drawing the attention of the media, the general public, and policy makers to a policy issue is the most important method of influencing agenda setting (Hilgartner & Bosk, 1988; Kingdon, 1984). This method can be used at both the national and state levels. It can also work effectively at the district level when a superintendent wants to motivate a school board to take needed steps to solve a problem. Many techniques can be used to attract attention. Figure 7.10 lists several. Except for the most urgent situations, education leaders should avoid demonstrations and rallies and select one of the less dramatic techniques. An essential dimension of attracting attention today is obtaining media coverage; therefore, all special events designed to capture attention for an issue should be planned to include a public relations component from the start. Leaders should make sure the media receive notice of the event and accurate information about the issue. They should also plan ways to facilitate media attendance and provide opportunities for reporters to interview visiting experts, panelists, and guest speakers. A sequence of carefully planned activities may be needed to focus attention on an issue and persuade key players to give it serious consideration.

- Invite an expert to give a talk about it.
- Sponsor a workshop on it.
- Hold a mini-conference on it.
- Put out a press release explaining how the issue affects local schools.
- Ask the PTA or teachers' union to discuss it at a meeting.
- Present a multimedia program about it to civic organizations.
- Put it on the agenda for a faculty retreat.
- Send an article about it to legislators.

Figure 7.10 Ways to attract attention to a policy issue.

Reducing Attention to an Issue.   Sometimes leaders do not want to attract attention to an issue. Instead, they wish to reduce the amount of attention it is already receiving in order to keep it from reaching a governmental policy agenda. The most effective way to achieve this goal is to persuade policy makers that solving the policy issue or adopting the solutions advocated by proponents would be prohibitively expensive. The first step required in using this approach is a careful, realistic cost analysis. (Chapter 9 includes a method for determining the total cost of a policy.) Then, some of the methods listed in Figure 7.10 can be used to draw attention to the potential costs. Other, similar strategies should also be considered. A realistic estimate of the extent to which the policy would expand government bureaucracy might be carried out. Or a lawyer could be asked to specify those aspects of the policy idea that might open the door for litigation. Or key segments of the electorate most likely to oppose the policy idea (and vote against policy makers who support it) could be identified. These negative analyses must be *realistic;* unsubstantiated and exaggerated claims will look like scare tactics and may backfire. Of course, appropriate publicity for these analyses must be included as a key element of this strategy.

Exemplary Programs.   Edward St. John (1992) argues that one of the most effective things school leaders can do to influence agenda setting is to develop exemplary programs to address education problems at the local level. According to him, when high-level government officials want new ideas for education policy, they look for "examples of successful practice, then [develop] policy proposals that might encourage these new practices to develop elsewhere" (p. 97). For example, in the late 1970s Sequoia Union High School District in California developed a dropout prevention program funded by both the schools and private industry. This collaborative effort established Peninsula Academies, which provided computer and electronics instruction for students struggling in high school. The academies succeeded in graduating a high percentage of their students and in finding jobs for them. In the late 1980s this program attracted national attention and was widely cited as an example of a dropout intervention worthy of imitating across the country.

Although St. John (1992) does not provide a full analysis of the sequence of events, the leaders of Sequoia Union High School District were probably aware that dropping out of high school was being defined as a policy issue in the late 1970s (Martin, 1994). They probably also knew that it was beginning to be discussed on the systemic agenda. The fact that they received funding for the Peninsula Academies from "local foundations, corporations, and local, state, and federal programs" (St. John, 1992, p. 98) suggests that their idea was consistent with the emerging systemic agenda. However, by developing their own project at the local level and successfully operating it for a decade, they exercised considerable impact on the shape of the dropout programs the federal government eventually advocated. Their exemplary program also encouraged policy makers—never eager to risk highly visible failures—to place dropout prevention on the governmental agenda. They had demonstrated that a strong intervention

---

program can reduce the dropout rate, causing dropout prevention policies to seem feasible to those in government.

In a similar way, well-informed school leaders who are attuned to the emerging policy agenda can often advance the new issues they support. By keeping abreast of the professional literature and monitoring the projects that foundations are supporting, they may be able to establish a program truly on the cutting edge of the policy agenda. Eventually, their project may become exemplary, encouraging policy makers to place it on their agenda. It may even serve as a model for a whole state or for the nation. One should remember, however, that a decade passed before the California project attracted national attention. In agenda setting, as in other phases of the policy process, patience and persistence are the keys to ultimate success.

QUESTIONS AND ACTIVITIES FOR DISCUSSION

1. Select a current education problem definition. Identify the claims made about it and the evidence used to support those claims. Then suggest how this problem definition could be effectively challenged.

2. Select a current education problem definition. Identify the claims made about it and the evidence used to support them. Then suggest how the issue could be redefined.

3. Identify a nondecision in your district or state. In your opinion, why has it remained a nondecision? What does this nondecision reveal about the constraints on education policy making in your environment?

4. By skimming recent issues of publications put out by business and education groups, develop a list of the education issues on the professional policy agenda. Then, by skimming several recent local newspapers, develop a list of the education policy issues on the media agenda. Compare the two agendas. What differences do you notice? How do you explain them?

INTERNET ASSIGNMENT

Locate the Web sites of 10 of the organizations listed in Figures 7.5 and 7.6. Analyze them to determine the ideological orientation of each and be prepared to discuss them in class.

PRO-CON DEBATE: IS THERE REALLY AN EDUCATION CRISIS?

Yes: No one who is willing to look at the evidence can deny that there is an education crisis in the United States. Since standards were lowered in the Silly Sixties, student performance on tests such as the SAT and the ACT has plummeted. In almost every international comparison, U.S. students make a poor showing; it is a cause for rejoicing in the education establishment if they rank average rather than dead last. Our schools are not even safe anymore; both children and teachers fear for their lives as gang members roam the halls, looking for someone to bully or rob. Many schools even have metal detectors at the entrances these days to check students for weapons as they enter. Finally, school buildings are in a shocking state—they are filthy with graffiti scrawled everywhere and basic equipment in disrepair. How can children learn well in such settings? All these problems seriously hamper the ability of the United States to compete effectively in today's global economy.

No: There is a crisis in the United States today, but it's not an education crisis—it's an economic crisis. Real wages have stagnated for a quarter of a century now; middle-class families have a hard time buying a house and providing college educations for their children; the gap between the rich and the poor is constantly growing. The United States now has a higher rate of child poverty than any other developed country. Often these indicators are hard to see, but we can see more obvious ones. Decades of insufficient tax revenues have led to deferred maintenance, causing our inner cities to decline, becoming shabby crime centers in which few people would willingly live, work, or shop. And much of our once-prized interstate highway system is now pocked with potholes, again because of inadequate public funds for their repair. Of course, all these problems spill over into the schools, which simply reflect the larger society. Government and business leaders prattle about an education crisis, hoping we will not notice the real economic crisis . . . for which *they*, not educators, are responsible. Fix the economy and the schools will improve.

What do YOU think?

News Story for Analysis: **MAKING SCHOOLS MORE EFFICIENT**

Official government statistics make no attempt to measure productivity in public education. In particular, there's enormous dispute over how to measure the "output" of education.

But assuming that test scores are a reasonable measure of educational output, public schools are getting less productive by the year. In 1972–73, each $1,000 of spending per pupil "bought" 63 points on the National Assessment of Educational Progress math test for 17-year-olds, according to calculations by Harvard University economist Caroline M. Hoxby. By 1998–99, that same level of spending "bought" only 39 points. The trend is similar for other tests and ages. To correct for inflation, all spending is stated in 1999 dollars.

What's the solution? Hoxby argues that educational productivity rises if parents have more choice among schools. That forces schools to become more efficient to retain students. For example, in metro areas with many school districts, such as Boston and Pittsburgh, parents can easily switch school districts by moving to another town in the same area. In other areas, a large number of traditional private schools provides an effective alternative to the public school system.

By comparing test scores in areas with and without choice, Hoxby concludes that competition makes public schools more productive. She calculates that the productivity of American schools would rise 28% if all metro areas had ample inter-district competition and many private schools. She also finds good results from newer forms of choice, such as vouchers in Milwaukee and Arizona.

(Adapted by permission of the publisher from "Making Schools More Efficient," *BusinessWeek Online*, May 20, 2002. Paragraphs 1-4. Available: *http://www.businessweek.com/magazine*. Retrieved May 17, 2002.)

Questions

1. In one sentence, state the definition of the education policy issue presented in this article.

2. What claims does the author make? Identify the causal claim(s).

3. What evidence does the author provide to support the claims?

4. In your opinion, why did *BusinessWeek Online* think that its readers would find Hoxby's research interesting?

5. Challenge this issue definition and redefine the issue, using other evidence with which you are familiar and offering a different solution.

FOR FURTHER READING

Berliner, D. C., & Biddle, B. J. (1995). *The manufactured crisis.* **Reading, MA: Addison-Wesley.**

In a well-documented book the authors argue that the education crisis of the 1980s and 1990s was fabricated for political reasons. After challenging the evidence for the education crisis, they offer a redefinition of the education problems in the United States.

Dye, T. R. (1995). *Who's running America? The Clinton years.* **6th ed. Englewood Cliffs, NJ: Prentice Hall.**

Dye presents a detailed picture of the leading individuals and institutions in U.S. society in the mid-1990s. Although the entire book is relevant to issue definition and agenda setting, chapters 4 and 9 are especially pertinent.

Feulner, E. J. (2000). The Heritage Foundation. In J. G. McGann & R. K. Weaver (Eds.), *Think tanks & civil societies.* **New Brunswick, NJ: Transaction Publishers.**

In this book chapter, the president of the Heritage Foundation discusses the history, funding, and work of his conservative think tank. He also explains how his organization's marketing of its publications has influenced think tanks generally.

McGann, J. G. (1995). *The competition for dollars, scholars, and influence in the public policy research industry.* **Lanham, MD: University Press of America.**

McGann traces the history of think tanks and describes their current activity and the increasing competition among them, arguing that they are becoming increasingly ideological.

Weiss, C. (Ed.). (1992). *Organizations for policy analysis.* **Newbury Park, CA: Sage.**

This book opens with an overview of the history, functions, and influence of think tanks; a series of chapters on individual think tanks follows, each by a different author. It provides information about the program and ideological orientation of several major think tanks.

GETTING THE WORDS AND THE MONEY: POLICY FORMULATION AND POLICY ADOPTION

Focus Questions

In what government arenas are policies expressed in words and adopted?

Why are some policies mandated but not funded?

How can school leaders influence policy formulation and adoption?

THE HIGH VISIBILITY STAGES OF THE POLICY PROCESS

Although the first two stages of the policy process occur so quietly that they are almost invisible to the general public, the third and fourth stages—formulation and adoption—occur in more visible arenas. Indeed, when most people hear the word *politics*, this is one of the two political processes that they think of. The other, of course, is elections. Policy formulation and adoption constitute the heart of most government and political science courses and attract ongoing attention from the media. They are the parts of the policy process about which school leaders feel best informed and that they are most likely to seek to influence. Yet, even familiar territory can conceal unexpected surprises.

During policy formulation and adoption, three major processes occur. First, and in many ways most important, the policy is expressed in written language, taking the form of a statute, an administrative rule, or a court decision. This process is never easy because words have a range of meanings and can be interpreted in several ways. People who formulate policy language are acutely aware of the fact that such details as the choice of *may* rather than *must* or the definition of *day* will affect a law's range of possible interpretations. It will also affect the level of support available for the policy in the legislature and its chances of being adopted at all. During both policy formulation and policy adoption, mighty battles are often fought over word choice, the inclusion of a phrase, and punctuation marks. Although these battles may appear trivial to the uninitiated, they are not; major policy issues can hang on a preposition or a semicolon.

When a legislature formulates a policy, wording is not the only issue at stake; because legislatures control the government's purse strings, funding is equally important. Neither the U.S. Congress nor the 50 state legislatures are required to fund all the policies for which they adopt official wording. Alas, school leaders of today are all too familiar with the unfunded mandate. Legislators often have much to gain by voting for popular legislation—it gives them something to brag about when they make speeches back home. They have little to gain by generously funding such legislation; generous funding implies an eventual tax increase, which is always unpopular with voters. As a result, they tend to take the easy way out, adopting policy language but failing to adopt appropriate funding to support it. This means that in legislatures, policy formulation and adoption is always a battle fought on two fronts: words and money.

Finally, a policy as formulated in words must be adopted. In a legislature this means that a majority of both houses must vote for it and that the executive must sign it. Policy language is often adopted in two arenas other than legislatures: administrative agencies and courts. Administrative agencies write rules that guide the implementation of statutes; agencies write operating procedures indicating which panels, committees, or officials must approve their rules. In the courts, the majority of a group of judges sitting in a given court must approve a particular written decision. Sometimes a judicial decision must move through a series of courts, being scrutinized by several panels of judges in succession as an appeals process plays out before the final wording of the decision is determined.

In this chapter, the policy formulation and adoption processes in three arenas—legislatures, administrative agencies, and courts—are presented in detail. After the process in each arena is described, ways that school leaders can follow and influence the process are discussed.

POLICY FORMULATION AND ADOPTION IN LEGISLATURES

A Conservative Process

In a videotape developed to teach school leaders how to influence state legislatures, Ohio State Representative Mike Fox begins by emphasizing that the legislative process was designed to be conservative. By *conservative* he does not mean that it is ideologically conservative, but rather that it was deliberately constructed to make passing laws difficult. Because the Founding Fathers feared governments that could change policies speedily, they created a slow and cumbersome system (Ohio State University [OSU], 1991). Both the U.S. Congress and the 50 state legislatures still use the complex process developed in the eighteenth century; in all of them, a bill must cross numerous barriers to be enacted into law. Lorch (1987) counted 18 such barriers, or "battles" as he called them, in the Colorado legislature, observing: "It is jungle warfare" (p. 240). The Colorado legislature is typical, not unique. As a result of this complicated system, the large majority of bills introduced in legislatures in the United States never become laws at all. For example, in the 105th Congress (in session from 1997 to 1999) 7,732 bills were introduced, but only 1,296 (18%) were reported out of committee, and only 394 (5%) were eventually enacted into law (Oleszek, 2001).

In the following discussion, procedures common to most of the 50 U.S. legislatures are emphasized; the federal and state levels are combined to avoid repetitiveness. On occasion, however, distinctive features of one of the levels or of some state legislatures are pointed out.

Legislative Proposals and Where They Come From

The policy ideas developed and discussed in the first two stages of the policy process usually become **legislative proposals** before they become bills, then statutes, and finally official policy. A legislative proposal is a serious recommendation for a policy change in the current or next legislative session; it can be considered the first step in policy formulation. Usually in written form, it might appear in a governor's memo to her staff, in an interest group's current legislative program, or on a U.S. senator's list of new laws to sponsor in this session of Congress. Not yet a formal bill, it has nonetheless moved well beyond the systemic policy agenda and is on the verge of being drafted into legal language. Such proposals can come to a legislature from several sources. Obviously, legislators are frequently the originators of legislative proposals which may fulfill a campaign promise, meet constituents' needs, or further a cherished policy goal (Anderson, 1984; Lorch, 1987).

However, assuming that only legislators develop proposals is a mistake. One of the most common sources of proposals is the chief executive—the president at the federal level and the governor at the state level. Chief executives and their staffs usually develop several policy proposals for introduction in each session of the legislature. Naturally, legislators are acutely aware of the proposals originating in the White House or governor's mansion; because of their powerful backer, they are likely to give them careful consideration (Anderson, 1984). Administrative agencies are another common source of proposals. Most often, they propose new laws to plug loopholes in already existing laws; their role in policy implementation places them in an excellent position to know what "bugs" exist in the original law and how best to eliminate them. For example, after five years of working under a law establishing statewide proficiency testing, a state department of education (SDE) may realize that the testing dates need to be changed and that the third- and tenth-grade tests provide little new information and should be abolished. The SDE may therefore propose such legislation in order to improve the current law.

A third common source of legislative proposals is interest groups. Most interest groups have a long list of policy changes they would like to see; when they judge that the time is ripe, they develop them into legislative proposals. Most teachers' unions, for instance, have ideas about how their state's collective-bargaining law could be strengthened and how teacher compensation could be improved. Year after year they develop corresponding legislative proposals, hoping to advance their long-range goals (Anderson, 1984). Among the types of interest groups most likely to initiate education policy proposals are teacher organizations, administrator and school board organizations, and business groups. Increasingly, foundations and think tanks are also active at this stage of the policy process, often operating in national and state legislatures through "policy entrepreneurs" who usually advocate a specific policy change such as school choice, privatization, or higher standards (Mazzoni, 1993).

A major difference exists between legislators who develop proposals and everyone else, however. A legislator can develop a proposal, get it drafted as a bill, and introduce it directly into her house of the legislature. Chief executives, administrative agencies, and representatives of interest groups can develop a legislative proposal and get it drafted as a bill, but they cannot directly introduce it into the legislature. They must persuade two legislators—one in each house—to "sponsor" their bill by introducing it and shepherding it through the legislative process. Naturally, they usually have allies in the legislature who work closely with them and often "carry" their bills, as legislators would express it.

In a study of 20 Minnesota education issues that surfaced between 1971 and 1991 and eventually became state law, Mazzoni (1993) identified the originators of the initial policy proposals. Tables 8.1 and 8.2 summarize his findings. As Table 8.1 shows, although proposals were put forth by a single individual or by a single type of policy actor about one third of the time, usually proposals were developed by a coalition of actors. Given the legislative system's bias against change, this practice is strategically smart, guaranteeing that the proposal will enter the process with broad support. Table 8.2 summarizes the relative frequency of the involvement of each type of actor. In it, although the central importance of the legislature and its individual members emerges clearly, it is also clear that the governor and interest groups play major roles in initiating proposals. Education leaders may find it sobering that education interest groups were relatively unimportant; even more sobering is that both instances of education interest group influence involved teachers' groups. The noneducation groups were almost all either business groups or "policy entrepreneurs" representing members of the policy planning and research community; often they worked in alliance with each other. The SDE, although significantly less involved than the other actors, was more involved than many inexperienced people might expect. School leaders should never underestimate its potential importance in legislative policy making.

TABLE 8.1 Originators of 20 Minnesota Education Policy Proposals, 1971–1991

Originator	Percentage of the 20 Proposals
Legislator(s)	15%
Interest group(s)	15%
Governor + interest group(s)	15%
State department of education	10%
Legislator(s) + interest group(s)	10%
Governor + legislator(s)	10%
Governor	5%
Governor + state department of finance	5%
Interest group(s) + legislator(s)	5%
State department of education + legislator(s)	5%
Legislator(s) + state department of education + interest group(s)	5%

Note. Based on Mazzoni (1993).

TABLE 8.2 Cumulative Involvement of Various Policy Actors in Policy Proposals in Mazzoni Study

Actor	Percentage of Initiatives in 3Which Involved
Legislators	50%
Governor	35%
Interest groups	35%
Education	10%
Noneducation	45%*
State department of education	20%

*One noneducation group acted in alliance with an education group regarding one initiative.
Note. Based on Mazzoni (1993).

How Bills Are Drafted

The second stage in policy formulation is the transformation of a legislative proposal into a **bill**, or proposed law. Legislative proposals are expressed in the language of lay people, but bills introduced into a legislature must fit a specific format and be expressed in legal discourse. Writing a bill is a technical process, and few people—even among lawyers and legislators—know how to do it. Therefore, legislatures usually have a legislative drafting office staffed by lawyers who have the special technical skills required for drafting legislation. Legislators submit written versions of their proposals to this office, which edits them into correctly drafted bills. As part of this task, lawyers check the federal or state law code to determine how existing legislation would be affected if the new law were enacted. This used to be a time-consuming process; today, however, the entire law code for the federal government and each state is comput-

1. Title
2. Text that enacts the legislation
3. Definitions of key terms
4. Effective date
5. List of portions of existing legal code potentially affected

Figure 8.1 Major components of a correctly drafted bill.

erized. Lawyers can search their legal database rapidly, locating all related statutes and identifying the sections that might be affected (Anderson, 1984; Lorch, 1987).

People and organizations who frequently submit legislation usually have their own legislative drafting office or a specialized staff lawyer to transform proposals into bills. The president and most governors have drafting offices; administrative agencies and interest groups typically use the services of a lawyer they employ for this purpose. Groups who do not have a lawyer on staff often submit their proposal to the legislators who have agreed to sponsor it, and they in turn submit it to the legislature's own drafting office (Lorch, 1987).

Bills must conform to a specific format. Figure 8.1 summarizes the fundamental components of a bill. Although many bills are popularly referred to by their number (e.g., H.B. 70) or by a nickname (e.g., "the Grab 'Em by the Keys Bill") or by an acronym (e.g., KERA), they all have an official title. For example, the title assigned to a bill aimed at dropouts that Representative Charles Hays of Chicago introduced into the U.S. House of Representatives in 1985 was: "The Dropout Prevention and Reentry Act" (Martin, 1994). Although the text of the legislation is obviously crucial—and is the focus of the "jungle warfare" of the legislative process—definitions and the effective date are also important and may give rise to much debate before a bill is finally formulated and adopted (Rosenthal, 1981).

How Bills Move Through a Legislature

Most school leaders are familiar with the distinction between the formal and the informal organization. The formal organization consists of the official structure and power relationships including the communication system, rules, and procedures of the organization; the informal organization is the actual human culture that has grown up within that structure (OSU, 1991). As most people realize, actual power relationships are not necessarily identical to those depicted in a formal organizational chart; and actual practice does not necessarily conform to the official policy manual. In this respect, U.S. legislatures are no different from other organizations; they have both a formal and an informal face. In this section, the **formal procedures** that must be followed in order for a bill to become a law are described. In the next, the **informal political practices** that have arisen around the formal procedures are described. Understanding both is important. Figure 8.2 depicts the formal procedures

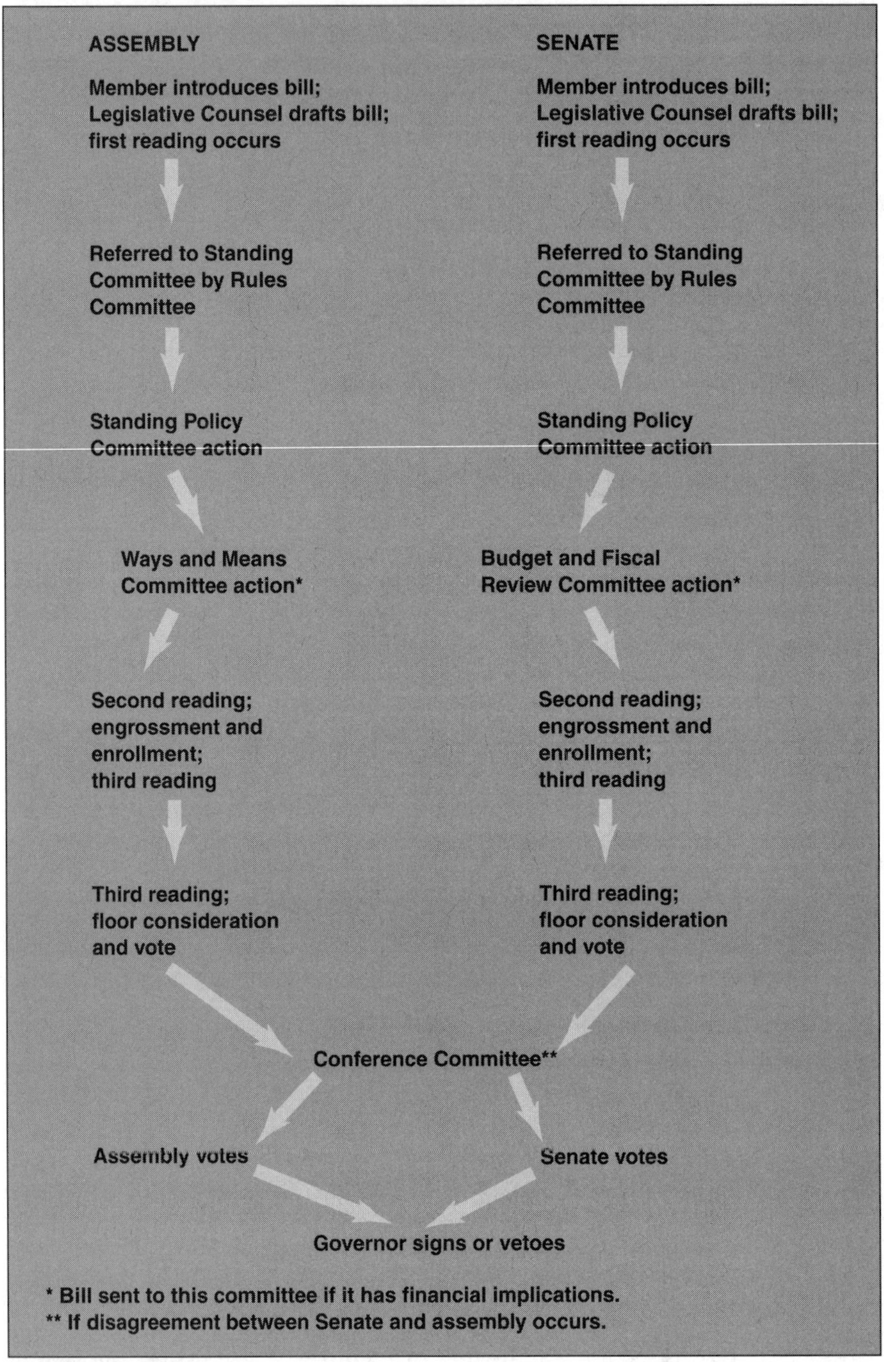

ASSEMBLY

Member introduces bill;
Legislative Counsel drafts bill;
first reading occurs

Referred to Standing
Committee by Rules
Committee

Standing Policy
Committee action

Ways and Means
Committee action*

Second reading;
engrossment and
enrollment;
third reading

Third reading;
floor consideration
and vote

SENATE

Member introduces bill;
Legislative Counsel drafts bill;
first reading occurs

Referred to Standing
Committee by Rules
Committee

Standing Policy
Committee action

Budget and Fiscal
Review Committee action*

Second reading;
engrossment and
enrollment;
third reading

Third reading;
floor consideration
and vote

Conference Committee**

Assembly votes

Senate votes

Governor signs or vetoes

* Bill sent to this committee if it has financial implications.
** If disagreement between Senate and assembly occurs.

Figure 8.2 The legislative process in the California state legislature.
Note. From *California Politics* by J. W. Lamare © 1994 by West Publishing Co., p. 120.
Reprinted by permission of Wadsworth Publishing Co., Belmont, CA.

followed in California's legislature; however, the procedures followed in Congress and in 48 of the other 49 state legislatures resemble it, differing only in minor ways. (The exception is the Nebraska legislature, which has only one house.) The procedure described below is a generic procedure; any specific legislature in the United States will conform to its overall outline but differ from it in unimportant ways.

Every bill must be sponsored by a member of the house of the legislature in which it is to be introduced. This **sponsor** introduces the bill by submitting it to an official—often called a "secretary" or "clerk"—who is responsible for handling new bills. This person assigns it an identifying number, which consists of two parts: (1) letters that indicate the house in which it was introduced, and (2) numerals that indicate its order among the bills introduced during this session. In the U.S. Congress, House bills receive the letters "H.R." and Senate bills, the letter "S." (*Congress A to Z*, 1999). Various lettering systems are used in the states. For example, in Ohio, House bills are labelled "H.B.," while Senate bills receive the prefix "S.B." The secretary or clerk also sees that the bill is printed and that copies are distributed to every member of the house.

Next, the bill moves to a committee—often called the Reference Committee—which assigns it to an appropriate standing committee for hearings, debate, possible revision, and a decision on whether it should proceed. If the standing committee votes favorably on it—or "reports it out," to use legislative jargon—the bill moves to yet another procedural committee, often called the Rules Committee. This committee schedules it for a debate on the floor of the house and a vote of the whole house. During this debate the bill may be amended.

If the whole house passes the bill, one of four things can happen. In the unlikely event that the **"companion bill"** (a similar bill that has been simultaneously progressing through the other house) has also passed in a form identical to the final form of the bill in this house, then it will pass directly to the chief executive—the president or governor. If no companion bill was introduced, then the bill will be sent to the other house to go through the same process there. If a companion bill produced in the other house differs from this bill—even by as little as one word or one punctuation mark—then those differences must be resolved. Most often, this is accomplished through informal negotiation. Increasingly, however, both bills go to a **Conference Committee,** which includes equal numbers of members from each house. This committee's task is to resolve the conflicts to produce a single, mutually agreeable version. If the Conference Committee succeeds, the revised bill returns to each house for a final vote.

Assuming that both houses have voted to accept an identical formulation of the bill, it is sent to the chief executive who can approve or disapprove—**veto**—it. If the bill is approved, it becomes law. If the bill is vetoed, it can be returned to both houses for an **override** vote—approval by a super-majority, usually of two thirds, in both houses. If the chief executive's decision is overridden, the bill becomes law. Overrides are rare.

In order to become law, a bill must successfully complete this process within a single session of a legislature—normally a two-year period. Bills that do not do so are said to have "died." However, the same bill or a similar one can be introduced during later sessions, including the next one. If so, then it must repeat the entire process from the beginning.

The Politics of Getting a Policy Adopted

The legislative process can best be understood as a series of hurdles over which every potential law must leap; therefore, legislative success demands political skill and a willingness to compromise. Anyone who introduces a bill with the idea that the current wording must not be altered is doomed to failure. The informal process of policy adoption involves negotiating with a succession of policy actors in order to get them to vote to adopt a bill, and those negotiations usually relate to the way the policy is formulated. As they move through the legislature, then, bills are repeatedly revised and amended. The final product usually differs considerably from both the original legislative proposal and the bill as first introduced. Although rewording can happen at numerous points, the following discussion focuses on a few particularly crucial hurdles.

Sponsorship. The person who has a legislative proposal must select sponsors with care. Although any legislator can introduce a bill into her own house, not every legislator makes a good sponsor. Obviously, the sponsor should be a person known to support policies similar to the one being proposed. A business group that wishes to have a bill introduced to increase the number of math courses required for high school graduation will probably look for sponsors among legislators who have supported higher academic standards in the past. Among this group, they will focus their attention on legislators who meet certain criteria. The ideal sponsor is a member of the majority party and of the standing committee to which the bill is most likely to be assigned. She has a good working relationship with the members of that committee and also with key officials in the house, such as the speaker or senate president, the majority leader, and the chair of the Appropriations Committee. Such a legislator is well suited to shepherd the bill through the legislative process, making the compromises necessary to obtain favorable votes. Of course, she may insist on changing the formulation of the proposal somewhat as a condition of sponsoring it; this may be the point at which the first reformulation occurs (Martin, 1994; OSU, 1991).

Reference Committee. After introduction, a bill is always sent to a committee or to a leader of the house who decides to which standing committee it will be assigned. This is an important decision because bills undergo their most important revisions in committee; in fact, most die there. This decision is so crucial that legislative policy actors do not leave it to chance; formally or informally, the leadership of the house always decides where a bill will be sent. If the leaders strongly oppose a bill, they will send it to one of those convenient committees known as "killer" or "death" committees, not to be heard of again. A lesser degree of opposition may be expressed by keeping a bill in Reference Committee for an unusually long time; after all, the later it is sent to a standing committee, the more likely it is to die at the end of a session. Or it may be sent to a standing committee whose composition is such that it will either be allowed to die there or be revised extensively before being reported out. Support by the leaders, on the other hand, is suggested when a bill emerges rapidly from the Reference Committee and is assigned to a committee whose majority is likely to look favorably upon it.

Standing Committee.   Many possible fates—mostly bad—await the flood of bills that surges onto the agenda of the typical standing committee of a U.S. legislature. An unlucky bill may be "laid on the table" (i.e., delayed), amended beyond recognition, indefinitely postponed, or sent to another committee. Bills that have a brighter future are scheduled for hearings. These are meetings—normally open to the public—at which experts on the substantive content of the bill testify before the members of the standing committee, providing them with information and answering their questions. Hearings may be held in or near the capitol building or out in the field, in which case they are called field hearings. For example, double hearings were held for the Dropout Prevention and Reentry Act with field hearings in Chicago supplementing those in Washington, D.C. After the hearings have ended, the committee usually revises and amends the bill extensively, using information obtained from the expert testimony. The thoroughgoing nature of this reformulation is suggested by the nickname given to it in Washington, D.C., *mark-up*, in reference to the extensive editing marks that now appear on the printed bill. If a majority of the committee votes to approve the marked-up bill, it is reported out, moving on to the next step (Martin, 1994).

Rules Committee.   A novice might imagine that the rest of the process will be smooth sailing for any bill that, triumphant over dozens of lesser bills, has finally managed to receive a majority vote from a standing committee. Not so. Although its prospects of becoming law are far brighter than when it entered the standing committee, it must now face another procedural hurdle, either the Rules Committee or an individual officer charged with the functions of a rules committee. The Rules Committee has been called the traffic cop of the legislature because it regulates the flow of legislation to the floor for debate and voting (Oleszek, 2001). In doing so, it decides on a "rule" for each bill, determining its priority among other bills scheduled to go to the floor of the full legislature, how long it can be debated, and the extent to which it can be amended. Supporters of the bill hope—and work—for a high priority ranking, a short debate, and limited possibilities for amendment, whereas opponents lobby for the reverse. Many bills meet their doom in the Rules Committee, either because they are scheduled late on the legislature's docket or because during a long floor debate they are amended beyond recognition. Nonetheless, most bills that the Rules Committee sends to the full legislature for a vote are passed. Passage should not be confused with enactment, however (Lowi & Ginsberg, 1994; Oleszek, 2001).

Conference Committee.   The last major hurdle many bills must cross is the Conference Committee. Obviously, even if identical bills were originally introduced in each house of the legislature, by the time they emerge from their respective houses months later, they are no longer the same. Yet, in order to

---

become a law, identical bills must be approved by both houses. Often this task can be accomplished informally, but controversial or major legislation frequently must go to a conference committee whose task is to work out disagreements. In the 103d Congress, 13% of the bills went to Conference Committee (Oleszek, 2001). State legislatures also use conference committees to resolve conflicts; in his analysis of Minnesota's legislative process, Mazzoni (1993) found that the importance of the Conference Committee had increased during the 20-year period he studied.

Composed of members from both houses, the Conference Committee tries to negotiate a version of the bill that will be acceptable to both houses. Although full meetings of the Conference Committee are open to the public at the federal level and in many states, in actual practice much of the hard bargaining is done in private. Unfortunately, both in Washington and in state capitals this bargaining process often degenerates into a power struggle between the two houses with conferees from both determined to make a point with members of the other house (Martin, 1994; Oleszek, 2001; OSU, 1991). Many bills die in Conference Committee not because of substantive differences between the two houses but because of power politics. Undoubtedly this is why one U.S. senator stated more than 35 years ago:

> I have been in this body long enough to beware of the chairman of a committee who says in an enticing voice, "Let me take the amendment to conference," because I think that is frequently the parliamentary equivalent of saying, "Let me take the child into the tower and I will strangle him to death." (R. F. Fenno, Jr., *The Power of the Purse* [Boston: Little, Brown, 1966], p. 610, as cited in Oleszek, 1996, p. 275)

The bill that does pass a conference committee has an excellent chance of becoming law. True, it must return to both houses for a majority vote and go on to the chief executive for approval, but those steps are rarely fatal. The bill that emerges from a conference committee belongs to that select group of bills that has jumped all the major hurdles; they are now in the home stretch of an arduous marathon. However, they may not be funded.

Obtaining Funding

Because the wording of a law and its funding are determined by separate legislation in U.S. lawmaking, the battle for any new policy must be fought on two fronts: words and money. For example, in her case study of the reauthorization of the Dropout Prevention and Reentry Act in 1989–1990, Martin (1994) recounts the complex legislative struggles required to obtain congressional approval of the extension of the wording of the law for two more years. Yet, even after the reauthorization bill had been signed into law on March 6, 1990, she frequently received frantic phone messages from a woman who directed a dropout program at a technical college in Milwaukee. The messages were always the same: "What about the funding?" (p. 78). This educator anxiously reminded

Martin—herself a political science professor—that although "it was fine that the program had been reauthorized . . . it meant nothing if appropriations were not forthcoming" (p. 78). The battle for dollars was still to be fought and, as usual, it was a tougher battle than the battle for words. Advocates of a new policy must simultaneously work for the wording they want and fight to see that money will be available for the project. The struggle for dollars occurs during the budget and appropriations process, which is described in the next sections.

The Budget Process. The government's budget for the next fiscal period is included in one of the most important laws passed during any legislative session. At the most superficial level, a budget is a detailed statement of how much revenue the government expects to receive and how it plans to spend that revenue. At a deeper level, it is a statement of the overall policy direction of the government, revealing the policy choices it has made and its true policy priorities. School leaders who want to know what their state's policy toward K–12 education really is should read its laws and its budgets simultaneously to determine if the government is "putting its money where its mouth is." Legislators frequently pass laws but fail to fund them, which is why the advocates of a policy must be vigilant during the budgeting and appropriations processes; if they are not, the law they fought to get adopted may be reduced to empty words. These processes cannot be brushed aside as boring procedures of interest primarily to accountants and tax lawyers; the financial decision making of a legislature "is a particularly important arena of politics because many policy decisions are meaningless unless they can be implemented through the budget process" (Rubin, 2000, p. 283).

The Federal Budget Process. The federal budget is adopted annually through a process that gives both the president and Congress important roles. Although developing a budget proposal for submission to the legislative branch is the chief executive's responsibility, most of the actual work is carried out by the Office of Management and Budget (OMB), one of the fourteen offices and permanent agencies comprising the Executive Office and to which the chief executive delegates management tasks. As the first step in the process, OMB economists estimate the probable economic climate and federal tax revenues for the next two years. Using these estimates as well as the current budget as their framework, they sketch out a preliminary budget. This tentative budget helps them develop guidelines for budget requests, which they send to all federal agencies and departments. After the departments and agencies send back their budget requests for the next fiscal year—using OMB guidelines to do so—the OMB bargains, negotiates, and argues with agency representatives until everyone agrees on a reasonable amount of money for each agency. Then the OMB, working closely with the president and his staff, develops the final budget proposal (Oleszek, 2001; Rubin, 2000).

Current federal law requires the president to send his budget proposal to Congress on the first Monday in February, known as Budget Day. The law also stipulates a series of deadlines for Congress, which Table 8.3 summarizes. The budget proposal goes to several specialized committees in Congress, which work on various portions of it. First, it goes to the budget committees of both houses,

TABLE 8.3 Important Deadlines in the Federal Budget Process

Date	Deadline to Meet
First Monday in February	President sends budget proposal to Congress
February 25	House and Senate committees send estimated costs of their bills to budget committees
April 1–15	Budget committees must submit budget resolution
June 10–15	Appropriations Committee must report out all appropriations bills and Congress must pass reconciliation bill
June 30	Appropriations bills must be adopted
October 1	Fiscal year is supposed to begin

Note. Based on T. J. Lowi and B. Ginsberg (1994), *American Government* (brief 3rd. ed.), p. 161. From *American Government: Freedom and Power,* Fifth Edition, by Theodore J. Lowi and Benjamin Ginsberg. Copyright © 1998, 1996, 1995, 1994, 1993, 1992, 1990 by W. W. Norton & Company, Inc. Reprinted by permission of W. W. Norton & Company, Inc.

which develop a concurrent budget resolution establishing the total amount of federal expenditures, the amount of revenue needed, and the projected amount of federal debt or surplus for the coming fiscal year. After this resolution has been adopted by both houses, the House Ways and Means Committee and the Senate Finance Committee begin to work on the revenue side of the budget, while the appropriations committees in both houses focus on the expenditure side. Ultimately, of course, everyone must agree and all the numbers must add up. The complex procedure used to reach these objectives in a cantankerous organization such as the U.S. Congress is called, appropriately enough, reconciliation. It involves much coalition building; many deals are made, and some of the fiercest battles fought in Congress are waged. Ultimately, however, a budget emerges, although in some years it is late. This budget will, of course, differ substantially from the proposal submitted by the president and the OMB, but usually its basic framework remains (Oleszek, 2001; Rubin, 2000; Wildavsky, 1988).

Education leaders must understand that this budget process is playing out simultaneously with the process of policy formulation and adoption described in the previous section. This means that people working for the adoption of a new policy through legislation must follow and try to influence both processes at the same time. Usually, they have carefully thought-out strategies for each. An attempt to obtain funding for a new education policy might start by seeking to persuade the U.S. Department of Education (USDOE) or an agency within it to include money for the new policy in its initial budget request in hopes that it will ultimately appear in the president's proposal. Even if it does not appear in his proposal, all is not lost; appropriations committees can be lobbied to allocate funds to it. Appropriations committees, however, are notoriously stingy, regarding themselves as stern "guardians of the Treasury" (Martin, 1994, p. 78). Usually composed of powerful legislators from safe districts, these committees have an adversarial relationship with the rest of Congress and cultivate a reputation for stinginess. This means that getting the funding one wants is usually harder than getting the words (Martin, 1994).

Even so, it can be done. Continuing funding for the Dropout Prevention and Reentry Act was not even included in the president's budget proposal for fiscal year 1991, and congressional novice Martin began working on funding for the policy late. Experts in Congress warned her that "nearly insurmountable odds [existed] against funding for [the] program" (p. 79). Nonetheless, she and other staff members built a broad-based, bipartisan coalition of support for funding both inside Congress and out, and (after a dramatic defeat in the Senate Appropriations Committee) managed to get funding through an amendment added on the Senate floor. Another well-orchestrated strategy helped the amendment survive the deliberations of a Conference Committee, and the program for dropout prevention was funded. In her final analysis, Martin suggests that their success was the fruit of a well-orchestrated grassroots effort to influence the appropriations process. Her case study illustrates not only the difficulty of the fight for funding but also the fact that the federal budget process can be influenced relatively easily.

Budgeting at the State Level. Like the federal government, each state government adopts a budget to guide its financial activities. Some differences exist, however, between the federal budget process and its counterparts in the 50 state capitals. Most important, state governments cannot engage in deficit spending; the revenue and expenditure sides of their budgets must balance. Another difference is that, although the federal government adopts its budget annually, not all states do—some adopt biennial budgets. Finally, unlike the president, most governors have the legal power to use a line-item veto to eliminate spending approved by the legislature (Gargan, 1994; Rosenthal, 1981; Rubin, 2000; Wildavsky, 1988).

The budget process also differs among states; the procedures used can be arranged on a continuum, ranging from a top-down, gubernatorially dominated process to a bottom-up, legislatively dominated one (Rubin, 2000). Ohio uses a top-down approach. Its biennial budget is developed by an OBM that works closely with the governor's office as it estimates future revenues and uses these estimates to develop guidelines for state agencies. The latter use the guidelines to formulate their funding requests for the next two years. Much of the negotiation surrounding the budget occurs during formal and informal meetings held by the OBM. Eventually, working with the governor, the OBM writes the budget proposal that will go to the General Assembly. Although members of the legislature can and do alter this proposal as they transform it into law, the top-down process severely circumscribes their margin of maneuver (Gargan, 1994). At the opposite end of the continuum is Texas, whose budget process centers in the legislature. Although the governor does have the power to set a ceiling on state expenditures, the legislature takes the lead in developing the budget. This decentralized process permits interest groups to play a large role and to exercise considerable influence on the outcome (Rubin, 2000). Because of the fiscal constraints of the last quarter of a century, the trend in state budgeting is toward a top-down process in which the governor plays a central role. Although this approach is less broadly participative than the bottom-up approach, controlling expenditures and keeping taxes down is easier (Rubin, 2000).

Obtaining funding for a state policy is more difficult than obtaining the enactment of the legislation that authorizes the policy. In the states, as in Washington, D.C., unfunded mandates have proliferated in recent decades. Part of the problem is the cost-conscious appropriations committees, which often look with jaundiced eyes at any program that is going to cost public money. Their attitude was beautifully captured by a politically experienced Midwesterner who, as early as 1981, claimed this about education politics in his state:

> They can have a nice time in house education and in senate education talking about textbook selection, competency-based education, and a lot of other things like that. Not much is going to happen on those things. It's the people who control the money who are calling the shots up and down the line. (Rosenthal, 1981, p. 291)

In the state capitals, then, obtaining money for new education ideas is difficult. This means that advocates for policy changes must always incorporate into their strategies not only plans for getting the wording that they want but also detailed plans for getting adequate funding approved.

POLICY FORMULATION AND ADOPTION IN ADMINISTRATIVE AGENCIES

Rule Making

Why Rules Are Needed.   Because U.S. legislatures write vague laws, administrative agencies must fill in the details by developing rules, regulations, and policy guidelines (Kerwin, 1994). Figure 8.3 contains most of the text of a 1994 Tennessee education law designed to establish coordinated children's services. Although the Tennessee General Assembly has clearly mandated cooperation between the SDE and the Department of Mental Health and Retardation (two administrative agencies), it has also granted them considerable authority to define and shape their efforts. In doing so, they will have to formulate numerous documents, identifying the responsibilities of several agencies, spelling out a funding process, defining their target population, and so on. If approved by the SBE, these texts will become rules and have the force of law (Kerwin, 1994).

Administrative rules can serve three different functions. First, and perhaps most important, they may fill in gaps in the law that lawmakers either did not recognize or left to the experts working in government agencies. A second possible function of rules is defining the key terms in a law or in the body of laws governing a specific domain. For example, SDEs often develop official definitions of such terms as *teacher, school,* and *secondary education.* Finally, administrative agencies also write the rules that define their own internal procedures, including procedures for writing rules (Anderson, 1984; Kerwin, 1994). Figure 8.4 contains

49-6-6101. **Improvement and coordination of services.**—The state departments of education and mental health and mental retardation shall take the following actions to improve and coordinate services for behavioral/emotionally disordered children. Any policy change required as a result of these actions will be presented to the state board of education for review and approval:

(1) Delineation of each state and local agency's responsibilities;

(2) Development of joint agency planning and training, especially between Tennessee's state and local agencies of mental health, mental retardation, and education;

(3) Development of a systematic process for securing funding for a continuum of related service options;

(4) Development of a definition of the target population;

(5) Development of ongoing needs-assessment process that addresses:

    (A) The complex and diverse needs of the children and their families; and

    (B) The resources of schools, mental health/mental retardation providers, and public/private agencies;

(6) Prepare an inventory of a continuum of existing services and options, known private or public agencies, and families;

(7) Development of an interagency agreement on the principles to be included in a plan of care as they relate to intervention and/or treatment goals. The plan of care shall have:

    (A) Child involvement if developmentally appropriate;

    (B) Measurable outcomes;

    (C) Identification of agency or agencies that shall monitor the plan of care;

    (D) Family involvement; and

    (E) Sensitivity to unique cultural needs; and

(8) Development of interagency training plan in the area of truancy prevention. [Acts 1994, ch. 985, § 4.]

Figure 8.3 A Tennessee education law.

Note. Copyright 1995. Michie. Reprinted with permission from *Tennessee Code Annotated, 1995 Supplement,* Vol. 9, page 164. LEXIS Law Publishing, Charlottesville, VA, (800) 446-3410. All Rights Reserved.

several rules from the section of the *Oregon Administrative Rules, 2002 Compilation* that covers district improvement plans. These rules spell out in detail how districts are to develop their plans and various procedures to follow in relationship to them, filling in gaps in the legislature's statute.

How Rules Are Written.   In formulating rules, agencies usually follow a three-step procedure: (1) gathering information, (2) providing for public participation, and (3) submitting their proposed rules to a designated individual or panel for approval. Agency workers consult several sources of information as they prepare to make rules. For example, they may study rules developed in other states with similar legislation, read research reports about the implementation of similar policies elsewhere, and informally discuss possible rules with people in the field (Hall, 1988; Kerwin, 1994). Public participation in rule making is a widely shared, but not always honored, ideal. At a minimum, most agencies publish some kind of notice to inform interested parties about when specific rules will be developed and to solicit some form of participation. This participation can take various forms: the agency may invite written comments on its proposed rules, hold public hearings during which interested parties can raise questions about

Assessment and Evaluation
581-022-0606
District Improvement Plan
Each district shall:
(1) Identify school and district needs for improvement of student achievement at the district and school levels by conducting self-evaluations that include a review of test results and other evaluative information (e.g., at a minimum demographics, other student performance data, student access to and utilization of educational opportunities and staff characteristics.)
(2) Based on the self-evaluation described in section (1) of this rule, develop and implement a written improvement plan for the district and each school to include, where appropriate, plans for:
  (a) Continuous short-term and long-term staff development;
  (b) Programs and policies to achieve a safe educational environment; and
  (c) Local efficiencies and efforts to make better use of resources.
(3) Revise and update the district improvement plan on a biennial basis.
(4) Annually review and report test results and progress on the district improvement plan to the community.
(5) Maintain copies of the school and district improvement plans as a public record.
(6) Submit the district improvement plan to the Department of Education when requested.
Stat Auth.: ORS 326.051
Stats. Implemented: ORS 326.051

Figure 8.4 Some administrative rules governing education in Oregon.
Note. From *Oregon Administration Rules 2002 Compilation.* Retrieved November 2002 from *http://arcweb.sos.state.htm* or *us/banners/rules.htm.* Used by permission of the State of Oregon.

them, establish an advisory committee to help with the initial formulation of the rules, or even negotiate the rules with the major interest groups concerned. Although private individuals may participate in these activities, the most frequent participants are interest groups, business representatives, and leaders of organizations affected by the rules. In education, teachers' unions, the major administrator and school board groups, business associations, and activist education administrators are often involved (Hall, 1988; Kerwin, 1994; Madsen, 1994).

Although administrative agencies often have considerable leeway in formulating rules, they must have them approved by someone external to the formulation process. Often, as in the example from Tennessee, education rules are adopted by a vote of the SBE; or a special committee of high-ranking officials who review new rules may have to approve them. Like all laws, administrative rules are subject to judicial review and so can be challenged in the courts; indeed, litigation over rules is common. Thus, although administrative agencies have broad discretion in formulating and adopting rules, important checks on their power exist (Hall, 1988; Kerwin, 1994).

Why Administrative Rule Making Is Helpful. Because administrative agencies (including SDEs) and their rule-making function evolved between 1887 and 1917 as part of the Progressive Era, they reflect progressive reformers' faith in expert "scientific" knowledge and in governmental bodies that are supposedly above politics and partisan conflict (Kagan, 1986; Sabatier, 1975). As the twentieth century unfolded, agencies became increasingly powerful and promulgated more and more rules, provoking attacks from both liberals and conservatives (Hall, 1988). Among the most common criticisms were complaints that the agencies and their rule making were undemocratic (e.g., Lowi, 1979) and accusations of inefficiency and rigidity (e.g., Wilson, 1989). Undoubtedly, many of these criticisms were valid; and most contemporary school leaders could cite numerous examples of "formalistic compliance, paperwork, and . . . meaningless legal procedures" (Kagan, 1986, p. 65). Even so, policy formulation and adoption by administrative agencies has a positive dimension as well as a negative one. Many agency employees formerly worked in the business or profession they now regulate; for example, both the USDOE and SDEs employ numerous former teachers, school administrators, and college professors. Because of their familiarity with education, these workers are better able to develop the details of education policy than are legislators, most of whom have never worked in a school. Thus, agency rule making provides an arena in which professional expertise can shape policy. When those who currently work in schools and school districts are permitted to participate in a meaningful way, the influence of professional expertise is amplified (Kerwin, 1994).

Administrative rule making serves two other important functions as well. First, it can facilitate a more responsive and flexible implementation of new policies. If legislatures wrote detailed laws, amending them in necessary ways might take years, and faulty programs could continue indefinitely even though everyone recognized their flaws. Because changing rules is easier than changing laws, an SDE that is establishing a new testing program or new teacher certification standards can revise its rules and clarify its policy guidelines as problems emerge during implementation. Finally, delegating some policy-making authority to agencies lightens legislatures' workload. Because all U.S. legislatures are overburdened with bills and other business, shifting detailed policy formulation to agencies such as the USDOE and the SDEs streamlines the legislative process, making it more efficient. In spite of widespread criticism of government bureaucracy, then, administrative agencies will probably continue to play a role in policy formulation and adoption for the foreseeable future. In fact, the importance of SDEs in policy development has increased since 1980 (Madsen, 1994).

Federal Rule Making. In 1946 Congress passed the Administrative Procedures Act, standardizing the rule-making procedures of federal agencies. This law requires agencies to base rules on information about a policy area and to give the public notice of their intention to write rules. It also requires them to permit public participation in rule making, although this participation can take several forms, ranging from submitting written comments to holding hearings (Kerwin, 1994).

Like other federal agencies, the USDOE publishes notices of its intention to write rules in the *Federal Register,* a volume of which is published in paperback form on most weekdays of the year. The *Federal Register*—also available on the Internet and on microfiche—publishes announcements of the USDOE's intention to develop rules, identifies the sections of the law for which rules will be made, and summarizes the general thrust of the proposed rules. Some form of public participation is always solicited; most commonly, interested parties are invited to submit letters

with their comments by a specific deadline. On occasion, however, broader participation is possible. For example, on January 18, 2002, the USDOE invited written
feedback in the form of "advice and recommendations" for rules to accompany the
No Child Left Behind Act of 2001, which reauthorized the Elementary and Secondary Education Act of 1965. It invited several specific categories of stakeholders,
including parents, teachers, and administrators to submit comments (*Federal Register*, January 14, 2002). Six weeks later the DOE announced it had received comments from 100 individuals and groups and published information about the time
and location of five public meetings of a group which would review the proposed
regulations. It also indicated that four regional meetings would be held throughout the country to give a broad audience a chance to offer feedback (*Federal Register*, February 28, 2002). Although the USDOE is not required to use the comments
which it solicits in writing new rules, it often does so. The final rules, as adopted
by the USDOE, are published in the *Federal Register* along with an analysis of the
comments received from the public and an explanation of how the comments were
used or why they were not. The final version of the rules is also available in the *Code
of Federal Regulations* (CFR), a multivolume collection that fills many shelves and is
also on the Internet; most education rules appear in the three volumes that cover
Title 34, although a few appear under other headings.

Rule Making in the States

As might be expected, the procedures used to develop rules and regulations vary
among states. However, the writing of rules for education policy is typically the
responsibility of the SDE; often the SBE formally adopts them. In her inside
story of three years as an employee in the SDE of an unidentified midwestern
state, Madsen (1994) devotes much of a chapter to the development of rules to
accompany the state's 1985 Excellence in Education Act. In her SDE she observed a variety of procedures for rule making. For example, the director of certification unilaterally developed the regulations for the Career Ladder Program
and prepared a handbook for school districts to use as they implemented the program. "He made most decisions regarding career ladder policies in isolation,"
Madsen later wrote, concluding: "This director greatly influenced how programs
were interpreted" (p. 50). The commissioner of education also unilaterally decided many rules.

Nonetheless, some rules were formulated with the participation of the education community. The law itself required advisory committees to participate in
formulating some rules, and the commissioner established several advisory committees not required by the law. The number of members of each committee
ranged from 15 to 30; the SDE selected them with care, seeking to balance them
by region and district size as well as by professional education position, including teachers, administrators, teacher educators, union representatives, legislators, and parents. Committees convened monthly, holding daylong meetings
with lunch provided by the SDE. The commissioner attended most of these sessions, and SDE officials were always present. The rules formulated by the committees were sent to the SBE for discussion and approval or rejection. Finally,

public hearings on the rules were held at several sites around the state so that people could comment on them. Those rules that provoked numerous complaints were then revised.

In Madsen's view, the SDE dominated the process of rule formulation; indeed, she describes the committees as "little more than rubber stamps" (p. 103). Nonetheless, at least some of the rules were developed in a way that potentially could lead to meaningful participation by educators and others.

POLICY FORMULATION AND ADOPTION IN THE COURTS

Judges as Policy Actors

A black-robed justice, seated at an elevated desk and routinely addressed as "Your Honor," provokes awed respect from most people. Indeed, the purpose of this traditional symbolism is to provoke awe and enhance the authority of judges, who must deal with many difficult, even dangerous people in the course of their work. Awe and respect should not obscure objective reality, however; judges are important policy actors in the U.S. political system (Baum & Kemper, 1994; Cronin & Loevy, 1993; Frohnmayer, 1986; Kirp, 1986; Lowi & Ginsberg, 1994). For those who did not already understand this, the presidential election of 2000 made it abundantly clear (Tapper, 2001).

Nor are they apolitical actors. Although insulated from the crassest aspects of the political hurly-burly by mechanisms such as appointment or low-visibility elections, long terms, and the secrecy of their deliberations in their chambers, judges are political figures just as much as members of Congress or governors are. Most have ties with one of the major political parties (otherwise they would never have become judges), and in most cases their ideological orientations are well-known in legal circles. Their appointment or election to office usually comes about because more visible policy actors hope that as judges they will make the right kind of decisions, however they may define "right" (Abraham, 1986). Of course, sometimes they surprise those who appoint them by developing an independent streak after they begin to hand down decisions on the bench. Nonetheless, the political stance of judges, regardless of whether they change their views, is important because a court "is more than a judicial agency—it is also a major lawmaking body" (Lowi & Ginsberg, 1994, p. 189).

When judges make decisions about the cases they hear, they are playing the crucial policy role of interpreting the laws passed by a legislature or the rules developed by an administrative agency. They write their interpretations in the form of **opinions,** the most important of which are collected and published in one type of law book, establishing **precedents** for future legal interpretations by other judges and lawyers. Judges' written opinions constitute **case law** and are part of the law just as legislation is. Additionally, judges can use their power of **judicial review** to invalidate the laws passed by a legislature or the rules written by an agency if they consider them unconstitutional (Abraham, 1986; Lowi & Ginsberg, 1994).

Although some courts behave in a restrained manner, showing great deference to precedent and the legislature, others are known for their activism and play a leading role in shaping the direction of policy (Hagan, 1988; Porter, 1982; Porter & Tarr, 1982). At the federal level, the Warren Court of the 1950s and 1960s was activist, outlawing school segregation in 1954 and blazing new trails in other civil rights areas (Hudgins, 1970; Kirp, 1986; Tyack, 1986). State court systems are often even more activist than federal courts, taking the lead in pressuring other branches of government to act. In New Jersey, for example, one Supreme Court justice publicly affirmed that he and his colleagues deliberately wrote decisions in such a way as to prod the legislature to move in specific policy directions—including reforming the school finance system (Porter, 1982). In fact, the New Jersey Supreme Court is well-known among school finance experts as the court that overturned its state's school finance system in *Robinson v. Cahill I* and then—in a series of cases numbered like horror films—rejected plan after plan developed by the state legislature in *Robinson v. Cahill II–VI* (Unfulfilled Promises, 1991). New Jersey is not alone; "many state courts are in the midst of political thickets in ways federal courts seldom are" (Porter, 1982, p. 18). For these reasons school leaders can never afford to overlook the importance of judges in formulating and adopting education policy. Ultimately, many education policy questions are decided by judges, not legislatures. And, sooner or later, most school administrators will find themselves dealing with a court.

Taking Cases to Court

Unlike the other two branches of government, the judiciary is reactive rather than proactive. Even if judges believe a piece of legislation is unconstitutional or that the legal rights of a segment of the population are being violated, they do not publicly announce this fact or search out aggrieved citizens to challenge the law in court. Instead, they must wait for someone to pursue a judicial remedy for unjust treatment (Beatty, 1990).

Legal principles govern who can bring suit in a court. A citizen who believes in the abstract that a law is being violated or that a statute or practice is unconstitutional is not enough; only those individuals or groups who have actually been injured in some way have what is called standing and can bring a court challenge. This injury may be physical, psychological, or economic, but plaintiffs must be able to demonstrate actual damage in order to successfully seek remedy through the justice system. In addition, a real **controversy** must exist and an **adversary** must be named as the defendant in the case (Alexander & Alexander, 1998; Lowi & Ginsberg, 1994). For example, parents who believe their child's school progress has been hampered by racial discrimination cannot simply file a general complaint. They must also identify individuals or groups they hold responsible—perhaps a superintendent and school board—and these individuals or groups must disagree with them. If the defendants agree with their charges and offer a settlement, no controversy exists and therefore no case exists, even though the plaintiffs might like to take it to court in order to publicize their point. This means that abstract, hypothetical, or theoretical cases are not tried in U.S. courts;

if such cases are filed, they are dismissed at an early stage of the process (Abraham, 1986; Lowi & Ginsberg, 1994).

Organizations can, however, advance specific causes by bringing **test cases** to court as part of a broader strategy for causing policy change. Usually such groups have concluded—often with good reason—that they have little chance of obtaining the policy changes they seek from the legislative branch. Therefore, they turn to the courts and, over a period of years, bring many cases into the court system in an attempt to change policy gradually. One decision that such groups (and all litigants) must make is in which court system—federal or state—they will seek redress. Because the two systems have different jurisdictions, this decision is often clear-cut; some suits, however, fall under both jurisdictions and a choice must be made. Although state court decisions are binding only within a single state, decisions in state court systems are widely read and often have a broad impact. Decisions handed down in other states may, for example, encourage a legislature to take action because it fears a lawsuit (Porter, 1982). Of course, each of these cases must satisfy the legal criteria of standing, adversary, and controversy, and the attorneys who work with such groups make sure they do (Abraham, 1986).

How Judges Formulate and Adopt Policy

In the **trial courts** at the lowest level of both the state and federal court systems, a single judge hears the evidence in a case. In the kinds of cases that most often change education policy, usually no jury is present. Nonetheless, as trial court judges weigh evidence and seek to apply the law to an individual case, they do not act in total isolation. They are supposed to follow the precedents laid down by other judges in similar cases, and they realize that their decisions may be appealed to higher courts where other justices will evaluate the accuracy of their findings. Thus, their concern for their professional reputation, if nothing else, encourages trial court judges to avoid eccentric and implausible rulings (Abraham, 1986; Lowi & Ginsberg, 1994).

Above the trial court level, a panel of judges hears each case. In the **U.S. Supreme Court** this panel has nine members; in many **state supreme courts,** seven; and in most **appellate courts,** three. This makes procedures for reaching consensus necessary. Although the secrecy of judges' deliberations means that few citizens ever observe this policy formulation and adoption process, the general practices followed are well-known.

Courts with several members have a **chief justice** who chairs their closed meetings and facilitates decision making. After hearing several cases, the justices hold a **conference** in which they discuss these cases and argue about them. Such meetings are often tumultuous; a California Supreme Court justice once commented: "[Conference] is . . . like a battleground where opposing philosophies meet in hand-to-hand combat" (Abraham, 1986, p. 204). Periodically, tentative votes are taken on the decisions. When a clear majority position seems to have emerged on a particular case, a final vote is taken and the outcome is recorded. Then the chief justice assigns a member of the majority to write an **opinion,** stating the decision and the court's reasons for it. The first draft of the opinion is circulated among the other justices for comments and suggestions. The members of the court may negotiate with each other over the inclusion or exclusion of specific points, phrases, and reasoning. Judges who disagree with the majority can write a **dissenting opinion.** This procedure can take a long time. The Warren Court took more than one year to decide and draft an opinion in the *Brown v. Board of Education* (1954) school segregation case because the chief justice wanted a unanimous decision and a single opinion for this controversial issue. After having reached a number of decisions, a higher court announces them to the public on a designated date often called **Opinion Day.** At that time, the authors of the opinions read them—or summaries of them—aloud to the audience assembled in the court room. Later, these opinions are published in law books called **reporters** and become part of the case law that attorneys and judges consult (Abraham, 1986).

Examples of Education Policy Making by Judges

In State Courts.   State court judges have played an important role in education policy making since the earliest days of the nineteenth-century Common School Movement. In a study of the history of judicial lawmaking in education, Tyack (1986) found that 90% of nineteenth-century state courts' decisions about education dealt with school finance and governance. For example, in 1882 an Illinois court found the state compulsory attendance law constitutional; and in 1886 an Indiana court upheld school boards' power to require the teaching of a specific curriculum. In other important cases, courts upheld the authority of states to use tax money to support public education and the power of school boards to go into debt to fund building construction (Alexander, 1998). Of course, court decisions handed down in one state are not binding in other states; even so, Tyack (1986) concluded that legal precedents set in states that established school systems early strongly influenced what other states did.

As the twenty-first century begins, state courts are still making important decisions on school finance policy. Table 8.4 summarizes the state court cases challenging the constitutionality of school finance systems litigated between 1971 and 1997. It vividly illustrates how a judicial decision in one state can encourage people in other states to file similar suits; in fact, challenges have been brought in almost every state—44, to be exact. What the table does not show is that the overturning of finance systems in a few states has encouraged state legislatures across the country to adjust their own school finance formulas either to head off litigation or to place themselves in a stronger position if they are taken to court.

In Federal Courts.   Only seven education cases reached the U.S. Supreme Court during the entire nineteenth century (Tyack, 1986), but after World War I federal judges began to play an important role in education policy. For example, in 1923 the high court struck down a Nebraska law prohibiting the use of any language other than English for instruction in grades K–8; two years later it declared unconstitutional an Oregon statute that required all children to attend public

TABLE 8.4 Summary of School Finance Litigation by State, 1971–1997

Successful Litigation	Unsuccessful Litigation	Continuing Litigation	No or Dormant Litigation
Arizona	Colorado	Alabama	Delaware
Arkansas	Georgia	Alaska	Hawaii
California	Idaho	Florida	Indiana
Connecticut	Maine	Illinois	Iowa
Kentucky	Michigan	Louisiana	Kansas
Massachusetts	Minnesota	Maryland	Mississippi
Montana	Nebraska	Missouri	Nevada
New Hampshire	North Dakota	New Mexico	Oklahoma
New Jersey	Oregon	New York	Utah
Ohio	Rhode Island	North Carolina	
Tennessee	Virginia	Rhode Island	
Texas		South Carolina	
Washington		South Dakota	
West Virginia		Vermont	
Wyoming		Wisconsin	

Note. Based on College of Education, Illinois State University Web page, "Status of School Finance Constitutional Litigation." Retreived June 19, 1997 from *http://www.coe.ilstu.edu/boxscore.htm*.

schools. These two decisions foreshadowed the education policy role the federal courts would play throughout much of the twentieth century: protector of the rights of teachers, students, and various minorities (Hudgins, 1970). This role was greatly enhanced by the 1954 *Brown v. Board of Education* decision, which "sparked a revolution in the role of American courts" (Jensen, 1985, p. 18). Over the next two decades, the federal courts shaped education policy actively, championing civil rights and equality under the law but creating considerable controversy as well (Kalodner, 1990; Kirp, 1986).

As with the state court systems, the federal courts often make decisions that have a ripple effect, influencing the behavior of the legislative branch (Frohnmayer, 1986). A good example is provided by the 1971 case, *Pennsylvania Association for Retarded Children v. Commonwealth*, in which a coalition of parents brought suit against Pennsylvania in federal district court, alleging that it had failed to fulfill its legal obligation to provide public education for handicapped children. After a single day of testimony in court, the state conceded and signed a consent agreement in which it affirmed that in Pennsylvania mentally handicapped children between ages six and 21 had a legal right to "a free and appropriate public education" (Jensen, 1985, p. 29). During the next three years, 899 bills related to the rights of handicapped children were introduced in state legislatures and more than 200 passed. Moreover, the U.S. Congress also reacted, passing relevant legislation in 1973 and 1974 and P.L. 94-142, the Education for All Handicapped Children Act of 1976 (Alexander, 1998; Jensen, 1985). Thus, judges shape education policy not only directly by their decisions but also indirectly by stimulating legislative action.

INFLUENCING POLICY FORMULATION AND ADOPTION

General Principles

Know the Process. Any school leader who wishes to influence education policy must understand the policy process; otherwise, she will make foolish mistakes and waste valuable resources. For example, those who are ignorant of the legislative process often contact their congressional representative just as the bill is going to the floor for a final debate and vote. Although some bills are stopped or altered at that time, it is not the best point of intervention. Rather, the earlier one can intervene, the more likely one is to be effective. Likewise, the legal codes are full of laws whose advocates worked earnestly to obtain the passage of the language they wanted, but did not realize that fighting for funding was also necessary. The first part of this chapter provides a thorough overview of the process and contains enough information to permit intelligent thinking about it. School leaders should not expect to fully grasp the process from reading this book, however. They should anticipate a period of learning, and this book and others will provide useful resources for them to return to when they are unsure of what is going to happen next.

Follow Government Activity. As the earlier parts of this chapter have made clear, the policy formulation and adoption processes operate within a time frame that includes numerous official deadlines. This means that often those who wish to influence these processes not only must be aware of what is happening but must also respond in a timely manner. Of course, all government bodies publish official records of their schedules and actions; these are available in large libraries and, increasingly, on the Internet. However, most school leaders will find using the resources of their professional organizations to monitor policy formulation and adoption easier than using either.

Organizations such as the American Association of School Administrators (AASA), National Association of Secondary School Principals (NASSP), and National Association of Elementary School Principals (NAESP) as well as their state affiliates provide three important resources to facilitate keeping informed about policy events. First, they publish information about government activities, especially in the legislative branch. Often, in addition to a monthly magazine they put out a weekly legislative update while Congress or the state legislature is in session. Although they may not send the update to all members, they will usually add any member to their mailing list upon request. An advantage of these updates is that they include only legislation relevant to education and highlight especially key issues, often explaining them in some depth. If a major case is moving through the courts, such updates often include information about that as well. A second service associations usually offer is a Web site, part of which is devoted to the organization's legislative agenda, to major bills introduced into the legislature, and to other policy events. Finally, professional associations usually have a government relations office with one or more staff members. These experts are usually more than willing to provide additional information to members who have been unable to obtain enough detail from the organization's publications and Web site.

Work With Others.   No reader of this book needs to be told that school administrators are busy people with little time to spare. Influencing policy formulation and adoption is an essential part of education leadership, but it does not have to be done alone, and indeed should not be, because "lone rangers" are rarely effective in politics. In large school districts a district office administrator often has the responsibility for developing and maintaining liaisons with government officials at the local, state, and federal levels. Such a government relations officer plans and coordinates the policy activities of the whole district. Naturally, administrators employed in such districts should establish a good working relationship with this individual, communicating their major policy concerns to him and using this district resource as much as possible.

Smaller districts usually cannot afford to employ a government relations specialist; nonetheless, working together to influence policy is important in these districts, too. Superintendents, central office supervisors, and principals should strive to create a professional climate in which everyone is aware of major trends in state and national education policy and understands that on occasion, becoming active will be necessary. Much of the day-to-day monitoring of policy developments can be delegated to those who are most directly concerned. For example, in many districts the federal Title I program is an important source of district funding and of remedial curriculum initiatives. As with all federal programs, Title I must be reauthorized and re-funded periodically; in addition, the regulations governing it frequently change. These are important policy issues for such districts, and should be followed closely. However, superintendents and principals need not assume the major responsibility for doing so; rather, the person who supervises Title I and the teachers who work in the program could do the daily tracking and contact federal officials as necessary, working within general guidelines determined by the district. In this and other ways, school leaders should try to build a broad base of policy awareness and involvement among their colleagues.

Set Priorities.   In any given year, dozens of bills related to education are introduced in Congress and in one's state legislature; many regulations are written or revised; and several relevant court decisions are handed down. No single education leader, school, or district can have an impact on all of them. Setting clear priorities for one's activity and learning to ignore issues of lesser importance is therefore essential. Priority setting can take many forms. For example, in a large metropolitan district, the government relations office may have a written list of priorities developed with the central office staff and divided into three categories labeled: First Tier Policy Priorities, Second Tier Policy Priorities, and Third Tier Policy Priorities. At the other extreme, in a small rural district the superintendent may carry her list in her head: "First, protect district funding. Second, expand the vocational agriculture program. Third, obtain more realistic school lunch regulations." The form of the list and the process of developing it may vary, but priorities should be developed and respected. Otherwise, attempts to influence policy will be scattered, diffuse, and ineffective.

Influencing Legislatures and Agencies

Three Approaches. Three general approaches to influencing policy formulation and adoption exist: government relations, working through professional organizations, and "lobbying." These approaches are complementary rather than mutually exclusive. Skillful education leaders use all three, building a strong foundation of solid relationships with other public officials, participating in and networking through professional organizations, and "lobbying" by contacting officials about specific bills or rules as necessary. Many school leaders make the mistake of neglecting the first two components; and then, whenever they become good and angry about a proposed policy change, they aggressively "lobby" legislators or agency administrators who are strangers to them, hoping somehow to influence them. This approach is worse than ineffective; it antagonizes those it is intended to sway (OSU, 1991; Turner, 1995). This is why "most legislators view educators as whiners who show up only when they want something—usually more money" (Turner, 1995, p. 1). Educators must, then, learn a better way to relate to public officials. In this section the three approaches that together constitute a better way are detailed. Before beginning a discussion of each, a concrete illustration or vignette of how this approach might be used in real life is presented.

Government Relations. This is the indispensable foundation on which the other two approaches are built, which will become clear in the following sections.

Vignette I: Making the Case for Technology. Elementary school principal Jennifer O'Malley strongly believed in the importance of building positive relationships with the community, and she interpreted the community as including local and state government officials as well as the congressman who represented the district. She sent all of them copies of the school newsletter and invitations to special school events such as graduation and the December holiday pageant.

Over the years, Jennifer had come to know most of these people by sight and they knew her. However, a somewhat closer relationship had developed between her and Cynthia Hernandez, the woman who represented the area in the lower house of the state legislature. Jennifer and Cynthia belonged to the same chapter of the Soroptimist Club, and sometimes they sat together at a club dinner. Jennifer had once arranged for Cynthia to participate in a panel discussion about the new state graduation requirements that her school board had sponsored. She also occasionally sent her representative an article from a professional journal about inclusion, one of her special concerns.

One evening at Soroptimist Club everyone at the table where Jennifer and Cynthia were sitting began to talk about the sad state of education in the United States today. Jennifer tried hard to be unbiased but also to defend schools against some of the more unreasonable criticisms. At one point in the conversation, Cynthia exclaimed, "I don't know why I'm talking so much! You know, I don't have kids of my own, and I haven't been in an elementary school since the day I finished sixth grade!" The words popped out of Jennifer's mouth before she could stop them: "Why don't you come visit my school, then?"

Two weeks later, she was surprised when Cynthia called to schedule an appointment to visit her school. On the morning of the visit, Jennifer took her on a tour of the building and grounds, introduced her to teachers and staff, and presented her with a giant greeting card one of the first-grade classes had made for her. Over coffee in Jennifer's office, Cynthia asked, "Jennifer, do elementary kids need computer education?" "Oh, yes!" the principal replied. She went on to explain why young children need to learn about computers, how computers can support classroom instruction in basic subjects, and the importance of thorough professional development for elementary teachers. Cynthia asked a few questions and accepted a copy of a special issue of *Principal* devoted entirely to computer education.

Several months later Jennifer noticed in a legislative update from the state affiliate of the NAESP that Cynthia was cosponsoring a bill to fund more computers for grades K–12; it included a strong professional development component. Jennifer quickly wrote a short note thanking her for sponsoring such important legislation. Two years later, after the bill had finally become law, Cynthia laughingly told her at Soroptimist: "That bill should be named the Foxx, Hernandez, and O'Malley Bill because of the way I picked your brain about computers that day!"

Influence Through Building Relationships. President Lyndon Johnson, one of the most skillful politicians of the twentieth century, was fond of saying, "The time to make friends is before you need them" (Turner, 1995, p. 1). Yet, far too many school leaders neglect this fundamental principle of politics, contacting government officials only when they have a complaint or want money. Above all, legislators, officials in administrative agencies, and judges are human beings. Like all human beings they feel suspicious of people who approach them only when they need something. Like all people, they trust those who show an ongoing interest in them. Thus, the indispensable foundation of all policy influence is building relationships. Education leaders need to broaden their understanding of the school community beyond students, teachers, parents, the school board, and district taxpayers to include those government officials who potentially have direct influence on education in their school or district (Turner, 1995; Wiget, 1995). Figure 8.5 lists the major officials to include in this expanded concept of the school community.

- Mayor*
- City council member*
- County executive*
- County commissioner*
- Representative and senator in state legislature
- Congressional representative
- Selected officials in state department of education
- Selected officials in federal agencies
- Local judges
- Appellate and Supreme Court justices who live in the area

Figure 8.5 Officials to consider including in a government relations program.
* Especially in fiscally dependent districts.

> **Provide information to them:**
>
> - The district or school directory
> - The district or school newsletter
> - The district's legislative agenda
> - Newspaper clippings about special school or district programs and events
>
> **Receive communication from them:**
>
> - At town hall meetings
> - At legislative hearings
> - At political receptions and dinners
> - At their speaking engagements in the area
>
> **Involve them in schools:**
>
> - Arrange a school visit
> - Invite them to attend a special school or district function
> - Invite them to a school open house
> - Invite them to speak to faculty, the district leadership team, the school board retreat, a class, and so forth
> - Ask them to present awards to students at graduation or an awards ceremony

Figure 8.6 Ways to communicate with public officials and involve them in schools.
Note. Based on Turner (1995); Wiget (1995).

Relationships are built through regular, two-way communication. The easiest, least time-consuming way to open communication channels with government officials is to send them the district or school directory and to place them on the mailing list to receive the newsletter and other communications designed for a general audience. In the first mailing sent to an official, the school leader should include a short letter of introduction. Other ways to build these relationships include extending appropriate invitations. Figure 8.6 summarizes ways to communicate with public officials and to involve them in school activities. Readers should note that good communication includes a willingness to receive messages as well as to send them; therefore, Figure 8.6 also includes suggestions for making oneself available to listen to government officials. School leaders should either attend these meetings or send an appropriate representative to report back on what was said and how the audience responded. Approaching the official before or after the affair to introduce oneself and one's professional affiliation is appropriate. A school leader might also express appreciation for the official's presence and willingness to receive feedback (if such willingness has been apparent) at such events.

School leaders usually have numerous opportunities to listen to SDE officials and other administrative agency workers at the meetings and workshops they sponsor. Educators should perceive these occasions not just as times to learn about how the rules have changed and all the new paperwork, but also as opportunities to build positive relationships with agency administrators and to gain a better understanding of their perspective.

Over time, relationship building can bear much fruit. A chance to influence policy directly may result as it did for Jennifer O'Malley. Obviously, too, legislators with questions about education issues or practices are likely to contact school leaders who are known to them rather than strangers. Similarly, when SDE department heads or federal agency administrators are establishing a task force to study a problem or an advisory committee to work on new rules, they usually invite school leaders with whom they are already acquainted to participate. Even judges, deliberating over a tricky decision in an education case, will recall communication from and contacts with those education leaders who have included them in their government relations programs; they will have no reason to think of the many schools and districts that have not.

Another, more subtle result often becomes apparent over time. School leaders will gradually find themselves dealing with government officials who understand schools better than before, express more sympathy for the work of educators, and recognize that both schools and children have changed since their own days in the classroom. A good government relations program educates those politicians involved. As Turner (1995) says: "Legislators will make laws with you or without you. They will make better ones with you. If they don't get information about education from you, they'll get it from someone else" (p. 2).

The politicians are not the only ones who will be educated, however. An even more subtle result—but possibly the most important one—is that school leaders who implement a government relations program learn a great deal about the policy process and those involved in it. They will shed naive and uninformed popular attitudes such as, "All politicians are crooks" and "You can't fight City Hall." They will gain an increased appreciation of (and skill at) the policy-making game. Their respect for the political process will grow, and they will begin to model informed, active, and responsible citizenship for the entire school community. For all these reasons, a good government relations program represents a sound investment of money and time.

Working Through Professional Organizations

Vignette II: Working for Higher Mathematics Standards. After nine years as a high school mathematics teacher, Bruce Jensen was selected to serve as the mathematics supervisor for his large suburban district. Bruce was delighted with this opportunity to make a broader impact on mathematics education because he had identified several serious problems during his years in the classroom. His concerns included the small number of mathematics courses required for elementary certification, the high percentage of people without certification teaching high school math classes, and the emphasis on rote learning in his state's mathematics curriculum. He recognized that these problems could not be addressed at the school or district level. In fact, he had reached the conclusion that the best way to solve them would be for his state to officially adopt the mathematics standards developed by the National Council of Teachers of Mathematics (NCTM).

Bruce believed that as a professional mathematics educator he had an obligation to work for this policy change, but he hesitated to do so through his school district. Although the NCTM standards were not inconsistent with his district's legislative agenda, they were not mentioned in it either. Moreover, some school board members had recently expressed opposition to national standards. Deciding that pursuing his commitment through district channels would be ineffective and possibly unethical, Bruce turned to one of his professional organizations, the state Council of Teachers of Mathematics (CTM). He volunteered to serve on the CTM's Government Relations Committee. Because Bruce's district was known for its effective government relations program and especially because he had gained a certain amount of experience in it, the state CTM leaders gladly appointed him to the committee.

During the next three years, Bruce became a leader in this group. He arranged training workshops for the committee and helped draft its first legislative proposal. He spearheaded a letter-writing campaign and visited numerous members of the state legislature and SDE officials. In the third year, he was invited to testify before the House Education Committee. Bruce did not hide the fact that he was a mathematics supervisor in his district, but in all his activities he clearly stated that he was working with the state CTM and representing its positions.

Bruce is still fighting for curriculum policy changes in his state, but he does not feel that he has wasted his time. He now realizes that a broad effort to educate policy makers must precede a change of such magnitude. He also understands that policy victories usually go to the persistent. Right now, Bruce believes that the education of his state's policy makers is almost complete, and he looks forward to the day when they will adopt the NCTM standards.

Professional Organizations—A Powerful Resource. Many reasons exist for joining one or more professional organizations. For school leaders who wish to influence the policy process, such memberships are essential. Selecting the best organizations with which to affiliate is an important decision that requires careful analysis and reflection. Table 8.5 presents some of the major education organizations active in the United States; it is a representative, rather than all-inclusive, list. It divides education organizations into three broad categories: (1) specialized administrator groups, (2) subject-matter groups, and (3) general associations. All school leaders should affiliate with the specialized administrator group most appropriate for their school role. In addition, they should consider joining one or two other groups. For instance, as with Bruce Jensen in *Vignette II*, they may continue to have a strong interest in the subject they taught and wish to remain involved in shaping its development. Joining a subject-matter group is one way to do this. Belonging to one of the general associations also has advantages because they accept a variety of professional educators as members and concern themselves with a wide spectrum of policy issues. For example, the Association for Supervision and Curriculum Development (ASCD) welcomes all types of educators as members, including administrators, teachers, and professors in colleges of education. Similarly, the Greek letter societies—which are education honoraries—accept a wider segment of the education community than do the specialized administrator and subject-matter organizations. Such groups provide a venue for meeting and working with a variety of education professionals. Although in some states the National Education Association (NEA) refuses membership to administrators, in others (especially in the South) it does not. In

TABLE 8.5 Representative Professional Education Organizations

Administrator and Related Organizations	Subject-Matter Organizations	General Organizations
American Association of School Administrators (AASA)	American Vocational Association (AVA)	Association for Supervision and Curriculum Development (ASCD)
National Association of Elementary School Principals (NAESP)	Council for Exceptional Children (CEC)	Delta Kappa Gamma
National Association of School Business Officials (NASBO)	International Reading Association (IRA)	Kappa Delta Pi
National Association of Secondary School Principals (NASSP)	National Association for the Education of Young Children (NAEYC)	National Education Association (NEA)*
National School Boards Association (NSBA)	National Association of School Counselors	Phi Delta Kappa
National School Public Relations Association (NSPRA)	National Council for the Social Studies (NCSS)	Pi Lambda Theta
	National Council of Teachers of English (NCTE)	
	National Council of Teachers of Mathematics (NCTM)	
	National Science Teachers Association (NSTA)	

*In some states.

these inclusive states, the NEA may be the most effective general education group at work, especially because it also accepts college professors. Thus, in deciding which groups to join, school leaders must weigh numerous factors, including their professional responsibilities, interests, and the nature of each group's recruitment and activity in their own state. There is no single best choice.

The benefits professional organizations provide school leaders who wish to influence policy making are numerous. First, they offer a rich source of information and expertise. As discussed in Chapter 7, most organizations publish journals, and in many of them policy developments are regularly featured. Many of these organizations also retain lobbyists who work in Washington, D.C., and in the state capitals; some even have full-fledged government relations offices. The most active groups put out a steady stream of useful policy updates—in printed newsletters, on the Internet, on telephone hot lines, and in special mailings. They usually sponsor informative policy sessions at their state and national conferences. As noted in Chapter 6, the regular print and broadcast media cover education news intermittently, especially at the state level; therefore, school leaders will find these information sources indispensable if they go far in trying to influence education policy.

Moreover, professional organizations provide a valuable forum in which administrators can meet other people who share their policy interests and discuss them. Such interactions clarify and solidify policy positions. They also break down feelings of isolation, sometimes leading to joint action either within the organization or outside it. Many professional organizations have official legislative agendas that they try to advance in each session of Congress or the state legislature. Like Bruce Jensen, some school leaders will find—or help develop—an agenda compatible with their own views. Others may discover that they need to work outside the organization, perhaps because working within it would split the group. Even so, they may locate allies within the organization and use them to build a new network. In several states, for example, challenges to school finance systems have been brought by coalitions of school superintendents who originally met through the state AASA affiliate. Learning that many other school leaders shared their frustrations about the ongoing financial crisis, they worked together to try to bring about a solution through the courts. Although they considered working outside the official group wise, that group provided the original basis for their organizing efforts.

"Lobbying"

Vignette III: Avoiding a Financial Loss. Superintendent Harry Levinson was answering e-mail when Business Manager Suzanne Matsuo rushed in.

"Have you seen this, Harry?" she demanded, shoving a "legislative alert" published by the state affiliate of the National Association of School Business Officials (NASBO) into his hands.

Harry looked at it. She had circled one item in bright red; it concerned companion bills that had been introduced into both houses of the state legislature last week. One of its provisions would reduce the state subsidy for students transported by bus by increasing the minimum distance for which the state would reimburse districts from 1.5 to 2 miles.

"How much will we lose?" Harry asked.

"We figure about $63,000," Suzanne replied. "But the real problem is that almost all the kids affected live in San Pedro. We'll have to transport them no matter what."

San Pedro was a mining town, located halfway up a mountain, and only accessible by a steep and narrow road with many sharp curves. San Pedro had operated its own school system for decades; but after several mine closures had brought the district to the brink of financial disaster, the state had consolidated it with Harry's district.

"How far is it to San Pedro?" he asked Suzanne.

"I had Ted check the bus routes—he says 1.7 miles for the elementary kids and 1.9 miles for the high schoolers."

Harry groaned. "Well, the good news is that this bill has just been introduced. We have plenty of time to get it amended."

That afternoon Harry developed a lobbying plan. He would write a letter to the representative from his district, asking him to urge an amendment to the bill. Because his state senator served on the Senate Education Committee, Harry decided to pay a personal visit to her local office. During the twenty minutes he spent with Senator Blackstone, he described the San Pedro situation to her and presented a one-page financial fact sheet that Suzanne had put together the day before. Senator Blackstone said she would do what she could. Harry also telephoned two SDE people with whom he had an especially good working relationship and several area superintendents, asking for their support.

In May, when the heavily amended bill narrowly squeaked through the legislature, it contained the provision that districts with hardship cases could apply for a waiver of the two-mile requirement. While this was not exactly what Harry had hoped for, he was glad that the new law recognized exceptional cases. The next year, his district applied for a waiver for San Pedro and received it.

When to "Lobby." Most readers have probably noticed that the word *lobby* has been enclosed in quotation marks up to this point. That is because under federal law and many state laws, public officials who contact legislators or agency workers in an official capacity about issues that directly affect their work are not lobbying, technically speaking. They are performing a fundamental part of their job responsibility. For most other people, however, *lobbying* means contacting an executive or legislative branch official, orally or in writing, about the formulation, adoption, or modification of a statute or rule (deKieffer, 1997). School leaders must be prepared to contact officials as their job requires. In *Vignette III*, for example, Harry Levinson was either going to lose part of the district's state funding or he was going to have to endanger children's lives by requiring them to walk on a treacherous road. This issue clearly related to the best interests of the district and his students; he was right to contact legislators and agency officials as part of his responsibility as superintendent.

Issues are not always so clear-cut, however. The line between a personal conviction and the best interests of children is sometimes blurred. "Lobbying" can easily shade over into real lobbying, which is covered by detailed laws. Before contacting political figures about a specific bill or rule, therefore, school leaders should ask themselves a series of questions and answer them with brutal frankness. Figure 8.7 summarizes some questions that might be asked. If a leader has any doubts about the answers, she should move with caution and consider working through a professional organization with registered lobbyists. Another possibility, of course, is for the district to retain its own lobbyist. Regardless of the course of action chosen, school leaders must understand that lobbying is a

- Does this issue clearly relate to my job responsibilities or is my interest in this issue really a matter of personal taste or commitment?
- Would the school board see contacting this official about this issue as clearly a part of my job? would parents? would area newspaper editors? would the teachers' union?
- How long would explaining to someone how this action relates to my job take me?

Figure 8.7 Questions for reflection before "lobbying" government officials.

heavily regulated political activity, requiring registration and the filing of much paperwork. School leaders who become active in contacting officials about specific rules and laws should therefore be absolutely sure that they understand the most current federal and state regulations governing lobbying. As Wiget (1995) warns: "No matter how honest we are, no matter how pure our motives or how solid our principles, there are rules to be followed—particularly regarding lobbying" (p. 37).

Written Communication. Three of the most effective ways to "lobby" public officials are written communication, telephone calls, and personal visits. Written communication is discussed in this section and telephone calls and personal visits in the next two.

Although writing a letter is the most traditional method of contacting a government official, it is still one of the most effective, especially as made easier by faxes and e-mail. The most effective letter is a unique, handwritten one—that is, the only one exactly like it that the official receives. Unique, word-processed communication is also effective (deKieffer, 1997). Letters that meet these descriptions are likely to be read, although not by the official. The staffs of government officials usually read them before entering them in a log, noting the issues they addressed and the positions of their authors. A summary of correspondence is eventually given to the official. Such letters are often answered, too, although the answer will almost certainly be a computer-generated letter.

Members of the U.S. Congress and state legislatures have long had e-mail addresses that are readily available to the public, usually on a Web site maintained by the legislative body of which they are part. Not surprisingly, then, e-mail has supplanted much of the "snail mail" which legislators used to receive. E-mail can be an effective way to communicate with policy actors if certain considerations are kept in mind. An e-mail message should be brief—even briefer than a letter—and the message should not include an attachment; many legislative staff members routinely delete any e-mail correspondence which includes an attachment. Even though the message is an electronic one, the sender's address should be included; legislators always want to be able to distinguish constituents from non-constituents. Finally, the e-mail should be sent to only *one* address; a message addressed to a long list of recipients is ineffective (Casey, 1996).

Mass-produced correspondence—such as when 50 people all send the same letter to an official—is less effective. Usually it is not read; it is weighed (deKieffer, 1997). This means that producing 50 or 60 such letters and getting different people to sign them is a waste of time and money. Generating several hundred or several thousand, however, might have an impact—at least that many letters would weigh a significant amount.

Figures 8.8 and 8.9 detail the norms that govern letters, including e-mail, to legislators. Professional educators should keep in mind one additional rule: only send letters whose spelling and grammar are flawless; the reasons are obvious. Special norms also cover written communication to agencies in response to their calls for comments on proposed rules. Usually, these are provided in the

U.S. Senators

Address: The Honorable Jack R. Clemmons
         U.S. Senate
         [Office number and building]
         Washington, D.C. 20510
Salutation: Dear Senator Clemmons:

U.S. Representatives

Address: The Honorable Bernice Cohn
         United States House of Representatives
         [Office number and building]
         Washington, D.C. 20515
Salutation: Dear Representative Cohn:

State Senators

Address: The Honorable Stanley Cernak
         State Senator
         State Capitol
         City, State, ZIP
Salutation: Dear Senator Cernak:

State Representatives

Address: The Honorable Iris Wong
         State Representative
         State Capitol
         City, State, ZIP
Salutation: Dear Representative Wong:

Figure 8.8 How to address legislators.
Note. Based on Bootel (1995); deKieffer (1997); Wiget (1995).

- Include your name and address on the envelope and in the letter.
- Deal with one issue or bill.
- Keep letters short; one page is ideal.
- Identify the legislation by number in the first paragraph.
- Clearly state your position and give your reasons for it, drawing on your expertise and experience.
- Ask the legislator to support your position.
- Be pleasant, polite, and constructive.
- Sign your name by hand.
- Write a letter of appreciation if the legislator does support your position.

Figure 8.9 Tips for effective letters to legislators.
Note. Based on Bootel (1995); deKieffer (1997); Wiget (1995).

- Before calling, prepare a short written outline of the points you want to make.
- Identify yourself and where you live at the beginning of the call.
- State what issue concerns you; identify the issue by bill number as well as a brief description.
- Tell your own position and explain your reasons for holding it.
- Ask for the legislator's support.
- Be pleasant, polite, and constructive.
- Follow up with a letter if time permits.

Figure 8.10 Tips for telephoning legislators.
Note. Based on Bootel (1995); deKieffer (1997); Wiget (1995).

official notice of the proposed rule making. They should be followed to the letter; otherwise, agency officials will probably disqualify them.

Telephone Calls. Especially when time is short, the most effective way to contact a legislator is by telephone. Calls can be directed either to the legislator's office in the capital or to her district office. Needless to say, busy legislators rarely answer their office telephones; a secretary or receptionist handles that task. Because members of legislative staffs often specialize in specific policy areas, callers should indicate why they are calling so that they can be referred to the right person. The tips in Figure 8.10 are helpful in preparing for and structuring a telephone call. As with letters, calls should be brief—no more than five to ten minutes (Bootel, 1995; deKieffer, 1997; Wiget, 1995).

The telephone is often the best way for a school leader to contact an agency administrator. Although agency administrators do not answer their own telephones either, they are usually willing to return a call. As with legislators, callers should be prepared either to give the number of the rule they wish to discuss or to identify the area where they are having problems. Contacting agency workers with questions, requests for clarification, and complaints about new policies or rules is appropriate. Offering to help develop new rules in your area of expertise is also appropriate. Often they value honest input that can help them plan the implementation of a new policy (Bootel, 1995).

Personal Visits. Sometimes talking with a legislator face to face is advisable; such a personal visit can be extremely effective. An appointment must always be arranged well in advance, and planning to visit early in a session of the legislature rather than later when calendars are packed and days are full is wise. Appointments can be arranged with the legislator's secretary. Staff members may ask about the purpose of the visit; their questions should be answered fully and accurately.

A typical appointment with a legislator lasts only about 15 minutes; therefore, to get the most value from a visit, it should be carefully planned, which means knowing exactly what needs to be said and being ready to say it. Educators should prepare a brief outline of major points to make. Many people also put together information to leave with the lawmaker. Frequently, these include a fact sheet that summarizes their position and the reasons for it.

Educators must arrive punctually for an appointment with a legislator. Sometimes, however, the legislator is not able to keep the appointment personally and has arranged for a staff member to handle it. Naturally this is disappointing, but school leaders should not interpret it as either an insult or an indication of a lack of interest. Rather, this is one of the ways in which legislators manage the heavy demands on their time and the unpredictability of legislative work. A visitor should talk to the legislative staff member sitting in for the legislator just as he would speak with the legislator—after all, the staff member will be the one to report on this conversation to the legislator. Whether meeting with the legislator or a staff member, taking notes is always appropriate. As in letters and telephone calls, the tone of the visit should be polite and constructive.

After a visit, education leaders should write letters thanking the legislator and any staff members involved in scheduling the appointment and holding the meeting. The letter should also briefly recall pertinent facts from the conversation. This is often a suitable time to send information items, especially if the legislator or a staff member expressed an interest in having them (Bootel, 1995; deKieffer, 1997; Wiget, 1995).

Special Comments on Influencing the Judiciary. Attempting to influence the policy formulation and adoption process of the court systems raises some delicate issues that do not arise in relation to the other two branches of government. Although school leaders should include judges in their government relations programs, they must also understand that they should never "lobby" a judge. The professional norms of those who sit on the bench dictate that they should reach decisions through the impartial application of the law, precedent, and legal reasoning (Abraham, 1986). Therefore, they will regard any attempts by laymen to sway them in one direction or the other as an insulting violation of their judicial prerogatives. Although school leaders may frequently encounter judges at civic and political functions, they should carefully avoid bringing up any education cases pending in their courts. Should a judge raise the issue, school leaders should speak carefully, letting the judge set the parameters of the conversation.

This does not mean, however, that one cannot express views about an important case. The formal, institutionalized method for expressing an opinion to a panel of judges is the **brief amicus curiae,** or friend of the court brief. This is "a partisan brief filed by an outside individual or group . . . who is not a litigant . . . but is vitally interested in a decision favorable to the side it espouses" (Abraham, 1986, p. 248). Such a document typically presents an argument couched in legal terms in support of its position. Important limits exist on the use of the brief amicus curiae. Individuals and groups who wish to submit one must file applications with the relevant court, and permission to file a brief amicus curiae is not always granted. Education leaders who are considering taking this route should seek legal counsel and also advice from one or more professional organizations.

Danger—Beware! Influencing the policy process is not an activity for the naive or the uninformed. People who become involved in political activity of any sort need to be aware of several possible legal pitfalls. The major ones are discussed in this section.

Partisan Activity. Many school leaders belong to a political party or at least feel strong sympathy for one. They should understand, however, that in their capacity as professional education leaders, their behavior must be carefully nonpartisan. Relationships must be built with all relevant policy players, regardless of their party affiliation or ideological orientation. Invitations must be extended to officials representing a variety of views, not just the ones with whom school officials agree. Education leaders must avoid favoring one party or party faction over another or even appearing to do so. Many states have laws governing partisan activity by public officials (Wiget, 1995). This is an area where knowing the rules and playing by them is important.

Campaign Contributions. Sooner or later, most school leaders will be approached for a campaign contribution. Needless to say, school funds must never be donated for political purposes, which means that all contributions will have to come from the individual's own resources, and professional educators rarely have excess funds. Also, contributing to one campaign often means feeling obligated to contribute to others. Unfortunately, no single, universal, hard-and-fast rule exists; politics is rarely that simple. Nonetheless, the following advice should be helpful.

All aspiring and new education leaders should try to decide how they will respond to requests for contributions before they are asked. Their two major considerations should be the law and local professional norms. Their professional organization will be able to provide information about federal and state laws; it may even publish a brochure summarizing legal guidelines. Aspiring and new leaders should also ask practicing administrators in their district what the local norms are. These may be even more restrictive than the law. For example, although in one state contributing up to $100 to each campaign may be legal, in one school district everyone may have quietly decided not to make any contributions at all. In an adjacent district the practice may be to give a token sum—$5, perhaps—to everyone who asks. A special situation arises when a new or aspiring leader learns that local professional norms violate the law. In such a case, she should first make sure, by consulting outside sources, that the practice in question is actually illegal. If outside sources confirm that it is, hard choices must be made.

Gifts. Gifts to politicians, like campaign contributions, are heavily regulated. Under 1995 federal laws, the following guidelines seem appropriate for federal officials. Normally, paying for lunch, giving a book that relates to your issue, offering an award that includes a plaque, or giving a small item costing less than $5, such as a pennant or paperweight, is acceptable. Larger or more expensive gifts will probably be refused. Federal law in this area is rapidly evolving and should be frequently checked. States also have legislation regulating gifts; school leaders should know it and follow it, updating the information annually. In most states, for example, taking a state representative or SDE official out for lunch is acceptable. Small gifts clearly related to your school or district—such as a cap, bumper sticker, poster, or decorated mug—will probably fall within the acceptable range. However, leaders should check carefully before offering gifts such as an expensive warm-up jacket, season tickets to the high school's football games, or a district-funded weekend at a state conference.

FINAL POINTS

Hopefully, the last few paragraphs were not so disconcerting that some education leaders are now inclined to avoid interacting with government officials. School leaders cannot stay away from the policy formulation and adoption processes. As public officials, part of their responsibility is to work to obtain the best possible policies for schools. As education leaders, part of their responsibility is to model effective citizenship in a democracy. One reason that education policies are often unrealistic or even harmful is that too many school leaders have decided to avoid politics. But to eschew politics is to become the victim of politics and to see ineffective policy after ineffective policy visited on the schools by people who know little about them or the children they serve. Influencing policy formulation is hard and often risky work. But it is part of the work of anyone who wants to be an education leader.

QUESTIONS AND ACTIVITIES FOR DISCUSSION

1. Identify three sources in your state that provide information about the activities of the state legislature. Contact them and discuss your findings with your class.
2. Contact the SDE in your state and ask what provisions, if any, it makes for the participation of educators in rule making. Discuss your findings with your class.
3. Visit a public or university library and list the most useful government documents related to policy formulation and adoption in your state that you can find in the collection.
4. Develop a plan for building better relations between your school district or building and area government officials involved in policy formulation and adoption.

INTERNET ASSIGNMENT

Search the Internet for Web sites maintained by the legislative, executive, and judicial branches of your state's government. Then, evaluate them by assessing them in terms of these criteria: (1) user-friendly design; (2) up-to-date information; (3) accurate and complete information; (4) provision of information about how to contact government officials.

CASE STUDY

THE GADFLY

As he moved into the last decade of his professional career in a midwestern state, Superintendent Jack Donato became increasingly disgruntled about education policy trends. Although he was comfortably ensconced in a district with several booming shopping malls and no financial woes, all around him he saw school systems on the verge of bankruptcy and increasing poverty among schoolchildren. Yet, at both the national and state levels, politicians were blaming educators and developing policies to reward high test scores and punish low ones.

Jack launched his first attack about seven years before his retirement, when the state legislature passed an education reform act establishing an interdistrict open enrollment program to improve schools through competition. He worked with the regional section of the state superintendents' association to create workshops on the new law, inviting legislators, SDE representatives, and out-of-state critics of open enrollment to speak to school administrators about it. Next, he persuaded another superintendent to file suit against the state with him; they challenged the portion of the law that required every district to send demographic data about students and their test scores to the SDE, alleging a violation of privacy rights. In the state capital, these activities earned Jack the nickname, "the Gadfly," but Jack didn't care.

Although he lost his court case, Jack continued his crusade. In order to raise questions about the way political and business leaders had defined education problems, he and his district sponsored a lecture series, inviting national figures such as Gerald Bracey, David Berliner, and Bruce Biddle to speak about alternative perspectives on public education and its problems.

During the year he retired, Jack was distributing information about the legislature's proposed voucher plan to his teachers and urging them to let legislators know their opinion of it. Of course, the teachers were well aware of Jack's strong opposition. When the Gadfly retired, the legislature was still considering vouchers, but Jack felt that he had fought the good fight.

QUESTIONS

1. What aspects of Jack's personal and professional situation permitted him to take strong stands? Describe a more subtle campaign that a differently situated leader might have waged.
2. Describe Jack's use of coalitions and allies as well as his attempts to influence all three policy formulation and adoption arenas.
3. To what extent did Jack choose the best stage of the policy process for his interventions? How might he have sought to influence the policy process at an earlier stage?
4. What legal and ethical questions might be raised about Jack's activities?

[*Note.* Jack Donato is based on a superintendent with whom the author is personally acquainted.]

PRO–CON DEBATE   SHOULD SCHOOL SERVICES BE PRIVATIZED?

YES: Public schools perform many services that have little to do with educating children—food service, janitorial work, transportation, management, and so forth. Everyone knows that the private sector is more efficient than the rigid and bureaucratic public one, so why not just privatize all the noneducational aspects of education? Let the market work its magic, motivating school service providers and administrators to provide good service at the lowest possible cost. Soon we would see a more businesslike atmosphere and a keener concern for customers and their needs. They would have to be responsive to the market, or they would not survive. Privatization would therefore improve our children's education and save taxpayers money at the same time.

NO: Most arguments for the privatization of school services and management are based on ideology rather than on evidence. The growing body of research on privatization—especially the privatization of school management—suggests that it neither improves education services nor saves money. The fact is that the private sector is not well suited to carry out some activities, and the provision of universal education is one of them. The reason is clear: Children are not packages to be transported from place to place or cows waiting to be fed. Every aspect of their schooling is potentially educational. Therefore, these services should not be under the control of private corporations whose overriding concern is making a profit.

What do YOU think?

FOR FURTHER READING

Martin, Janet M. (1994). *Lessons from the hill.* **New York: St. Martin's Press.**
    A political science professor, Martin won a fellowship that permitted her to spend a year working in a congressional staff position. Her book explains the inner workings of Congress, focusing on her experiences as she moved a piece of federal education legislation through the legislative process, managing to get it both funded and adopted.

Oleszek, W. J. (2001). *Congressional procedures and the policy process.* **5th ed. Washington, D.C.: CQ Press.**
    Oleszek provides an inside picture of how the U.S. Congress does its work, from the budget process to how conflicts are resolved. Although he describes the functioning of the Congress, much of his information can also be applied to state legislatures.

Rosenthal, Alan. (1981). *Legislative life.* **New York: Harper & Row.**
    This classic, widely cited study of the culture and behavior of state legislatures is rich with insights into how legislators think and feel, as well as the mechanics of passing laws in legislatures.

Turner, D. W. (1995). Building legislative relationships: A guide for principals. *Here's How, 13* **(5), 1–4.**
    Turner, a principal for 20 years before becoming the executive director of the Illinois Principals Association, explains how to build positive relationships with legislators and makes concrete suggestions about writing letters, telephoning, and making personal visits.

Wiget, L. A. (1995). *Effective government relations for public education.* Bloomington, IN: Phi Delta Kappa Educational Foundation.
This PDK "Fastback" provides detailed advice in booklet form for establishing a government relations program. Up-to-date and well written, it would be a valuable resource for school leaders who are just beginning to recognize the importance of government relations.

9

LOOKING AT POLICIES: POLICY INSTRUMENTS AND COST EFFECTIVENESS

Focus Questions

How can leaders anticipate what kind of politics will develop around a new policy?

How can they select the best instrument for achieving a policy goal?

How can they determine the true costs of a policy?

LEARNING TO ANALYZE PUBLIC POLICIES

Just knowing about policy development, formulation, and adoption or about the roles of various policy actors is not enough for school leaders. They should also know how to take policies apart and scrutinize them closely. This analytical process can yield clues about how well a policy will work and predict with some accuracy who will support and oppose it. School leaders need this skill for two reasons. First, as administrators they must develop policies themselves. Principals are responsible for adopting policies that will permit their schools to operate as positive learning environments for children. Superintendents must draft policy proposals on many subjects and recommend them to the school board. Dress codes, tardiness, strategies for raising test scores, unruly behavior in the cafeteria—in these areas and more, administrators often find themselves formulating policies. Yet, unless they are familiar with the forms that policies can take, they will probably address all problems with the same type of policy—usually a rule with a penalty attached. Sometimes a rule with a penalty attached is the best policy. But not always. When leaders understand several policy options, they can choose among them, matching the policy to the problem and its context. Second, education leaders today often find themselves implementing policies developed by others. Chapter 10 discusses implementation in depth, but the first step toward skillful implementation is understanding the structure of the policy. How likely to work is this policy? How will various stakeholders react? What problems are most likely to arise? What will it really cost? These are questions that policy analysis can help answer.

This chapter, then, presents three lenses through which school leaders can critically examine policies, both their own and others'. Although these analytical approaches are different, they are complementary. Each brings a slightly different aspect of policy structure into focus. Together they constitute a powerful instrument for closely examining education policies. Unlike the other chapters, the exercises in this one are provided after each major section to permit readers to apply each framework to concrete examples immediately.

LOWI'S TECHNIQUES OF CONTROL

In a 1964 article, Theodore Lowi advanced the thesis that three basic types of policies exist—**distributive, regulatory,** and **redistributive**—and that each generates a distinctive political arena. Thirty years later, he and Benjamin Ginsberg (1994) slightly refined the original thesis, calling the policy types *techniques of control* and renaming *distributive policy, promotional policy.* This discussion draws ideas from both the 1964 and 1994 writings but retains the 1964 terminology because it is widely used.

Distributive Policies

Distributive Defined.   Distributive policies bestow gifts on citizens; these gifts may be goods, services, or special privileges. Although the idea of a government giving gifts may seem strange to some, this practice is actually an old one. In ancient times kings used gifts to consolidate the loyalty of their followers and build their power. In the Anglo-Saxon epic *Beowulf,* synonyms for *king* include *ring-giver* and *dispenser of treasure* (Abrams et al., 1962). Although contemporary governments do not bestow jewelry on their citizens, they have other ways to distribute wealth and privileges. Lowi and Ginsberg distinguish three: (1) subsidies, (2) contracts, and (3) nonregulatory licenses.

Subsidies.   A **subsidy** may consist of "cash, goods, services, or land" (Lowi & Ginsberg, 1994, p. 389). For example, both the federal and state governments subsidize the building and repair of roads. A county government that needs to fill the potholes in some of its roads usually applies to a higher level of government for a subsidy. If the application succeeds, county officials are overjoyed. They brag to county residents about this proof of their effectiveness and even erect signs at construction sites, proclaiming how much money they received for the project.

Contracts. **Contracts** are another form of distributive policy. Under a contract, a private firm agrees to provide a product or service to the government in exchange for a specific amount of money. Lowi and Ginsberg (1994) argue that many policies commonly called *privatization* are actually forms of government contracting. Current proposals to privatize education functions such as transportation, custodial services, and even management fall into this category. Although the businesses that enter into contracts with school districts must perform work in exchange for their gift, nonetheless the school district is bestowing upon them a privilege with a substantial cash value attached.

Nonregulatory Licensing. "A license is a privilege granted by government to do something that it otherwise considers to be illegal" (Lowi & Ginsberg, 1994, p. 391). **Licenses** can be obtained by paying a fee without having to meet many requirements. For example, in most states people who have reached a certain age can obtain a hunting license with little difficulty. All licenses allow license holders to perform activities for which they could otherwise be charged with a legal violation. Through them the government distributes privileges that those who do not hold licenses lack. Currently, nonregulatory licenses are rarely used in education.

Distribution as Control. In ancient times chieftains bestowed jewelry and land upon their followers to keep them loyal, but they usually did not seek to control their behavior in other ways. Today, of course, governments have broad public purposes in mind when they use distributive policies. They use them to influence behavior. For example, the federal school lunch and milk program, first established in 1946, is distributive. Although some children qualify for "free" or "reduced" food based on family need, all students (and school staff as well) receive subsidized meals from the government. For the last 50 years, this program has served to improve child nutrition, especially among the poor, but probably among the middle class as well. At the state level, governments often provide flat grants based on enrollment to subsidize school services such as transportation and testing. Their distributions encourage districts to provide these services to children; otherwise, they might not. Figure 9.1 lists some typical distributive policies used in education; this list suggests the many ways that distributive policies can shape behavior.

Distributive Politics. A return to the metaphor of the ancient king will clarify the nature of the political arena generated by distributive politics. Rulers of long ago needed the support of their vassals in battle; they also wished to discourage them from revolting. Distributing gifts was an excellent way to achieve these goals. As long as a ruler was both generous and fair, his followers were likely to remain uninterested in challenging his power. Wise distribution practices encouraged followers to focus on nurturing their relationship with the king, not on

Subsidies

- Many professional development programs
- State subsidies for school transportation
- State programs for upgrading computer technology in schools
- State programs supporting capital outlay
- School lunch and milk program
- State or federal block grants
- Flat grants as part of school funding
- Some foundation formulas used to allocate state funds to districts

Contracts

- State or district contracts with textbook companies
- State or district contracts with testing companies
- Contracting out transportation, custodial, or cafeteria services
- Contracts for designing and constructing school facilities

Nonregulatory licenses

- Parking permits issued to students
- Parking permits issued to staff
- Library cards issued to community users of a school library

Figure 9.1 Examples of distributive policies in education.

paying attention to the other followers. Among themselves, followers tended to practice mutual noninterference. The wise distribution of gifts also made inciting a rebellion difficult for the occasional malcontent because contented followers usually calculated their probable gain from joining a rebellion and decided the costs would outweigh the benefits. Of course, rulers did not always distribute gifts wisely. In that case, their gift-giving policy became redistributive rather than distributive. As we shall see, redistributive politics generates a different political game.

In contemporary U.S. politics, distributive policies create a political arena similar to that of the wise king. When the government is distributing "gifts"—such as grants for remedial education or school transportation money—potential recipients focus their attention on the relevant government agency, largely ignoring each other. If the agency is skillful in its distribution, the political arena is stable and conflicts are rare. Of course, skillful distribution requires constant concern for "equality, consistency, impartiality, uniformity, precedent, and moderation" (Schattschneider, 1935, p. 88). Politicians like pork barrel policies precisely because they are distributive, providing them with an opportunity to reduce conflict among their constituents . . . and discourage potential challengers in the next election.

Regulatory Policies

Regulatory Defined. **Regulatory policies** are formalized rules expressed in general terms and applied to large groups of people. They either reduce or expand the alternatives available to those regulated. Rules imply enforcement by the government and penalties for those who break them. Although regulatory policies appeared early in history, Lowi and Ginsberg (1994) argue that not until the nineteenth century did governments rely heavily upon them. The reason is clear: Until recently, government's ability to enforce rules was limited. The communication and information revolutions have changed this, however.

Types of Regulatory Policies. Most regulatory policies take the form of laws or administrative rules that explicitly require or prohibit certain behaviors. A special type of regulatory policy is **regulatory licensing.** A regulatory license makes practicing a profession illegal until people have met specific requirements set by the government. Teachers' and administrators' licenses are regulatory licenses.

Educators often feel that they are swimming through a sea of regulations. As Figure 9.2 suggests, they have good reason to feel that way. From the day that they enter a teacher education program that leads to a regulatory license, professional educators deal with government regulations. Many federal grant programs involve such heavy regulation of recipients that Lowi and Ginsberg (1994) categorize them as regulatory rather than distributive. State governments seem to have a strong preference for regulatory policies. They use rules and laws to prescribe how many days a year schools must be in session, what subjects they must teach, how school buildings must be constructed, under what conditions a teacher can be dismissed, and so on. At the local level, school boards and educators follow in the footsteps of higher levels of government. No smoking policies, dress codes, disciplinary handbooks, and teachers' classroom rules are all regulatory policies.

Regulatory licenses

- Teacher certification
- Administrator certification

Laws, rules, regulations, and guidelines

- Graduation requirements
- State or district curriculum frameworks
- State or district textbook adoptions
- State or district rules regarding school day, week, and year
- Dress codes
- Fire and safety codes
- Compulsory attendance requirements
- School discipline codes
- Federal or state grants with detailed guidelines
- Required criminal record checks
- Prescribed teacher evaluation procedures
- Some foundation formulas used to allocate state funds to districts

---

Figure 9.2 Examples of regulatory policies in education.

Regulatory Politics. Regulatory policies create a political arena different from that generated by distributive ones. Several social groups with conflicting interests are usually concerned about regulatory policies. For example, if a state legislature is proposing to increase the length of the school year, several groups will be interested in this legislation. Teacher and administrator groups will be concerned about the possibility that their members will be expected to work more days without a commensurate pay increase. School board groups will fear that the longer school year will generate additional expenses, which will fall on them rather than on the state. Some business groups will favor the legislation as a way to raise standards and possibly reduce their on-the-job training requirements. The tourist industry, however, will oppose the bill because it depends upon the cheap summer labor of young people. Parent groups will probably be split with some favoring more schooling (and supervised care) for their children and others concerned about lost opportunities for family trips and camping experiences. No single regulatory policy will please all these groups. In such an arena the political actors pay a great deal of attention to each other, both competing and seeking to find allies. This arena is unstable and filled with conflict. Coalitions form quickly and fall apart quickly; participants bargain and negotiate. These conflicts, however, are largely nonideological with most participants willing to concede points in order to make a deal.

Redistributive Policies

Redistributive Defined. A **redistributive policy** is one that shifts resources or power from one social group to another. By doing so, the government "seek[s] to control conduct . . . indirectly by altering the conditions of conduct or manipulating the environment" (Lowi & Ginsberg, 1994, p. 397). The policy goal may be economic, such as shifting income to the middle class in order to stimulate consumer buying. It may also be social or political, such as providing a modest income to the unemployed in order to keep social unrest from becoming a problem.

Types of Redistributive Policies. Redistributive policies fall into two broad categories: those that shift economic resources and those that shift power. The government usually shifts material resources by manipulating taxation or the monetary system. A good example of such a policy is Social Security, which is not a form of insurance or old-age annuity but rather a redistribution of income through taxation. The federal government deducts a special tax from the paychecks of most U.S. workers and channels this money to Social Security to pay benefits to the elderly, the disabled, and some children. Thus, Social Security taxes "redistribute wealth from higher to lower income people and from . . . workers to . . . retirees" (Lowi & Ginsberg, 1994, p. 401). Redistributive policies may also shift power, usually by granting new rights to a large social group.

Redistributive policies are often used in education. Figure 9.3 lists major redistributive policies of the past and present.

Obviously, these are the hot topics of education policy. Redistributive policies of the 1960s and 1970s shifted resources and power from dominant so-

---

- Affirmative action programs
- Desegregation
- Education for All Handicapped Children Act
- Privatization of school management
- Privatization of teaching special subjects
- School finance systems based on power equalizing
- School finance systems based on full state funding
- Site-based management
- Title I (remedial programs for the poor)
- Title IX (gender equity)
- Vouchers

Figure 9.3 Examples of redistributive policies in education.

cial groups to groups that had been, or felt they had been, oppressed. Among the major beneficiaries were African Americans, residents of the South and inner cities, the poor, women, and those with handicaps. As one would expect, these redistributive policies sparked much controversy and were subjected to much criticism. Today, most redistributive education policies shift power within the education establishment. Vouchers reallocate the power to assign pupils (and state funds) to schools, removing it from school administrators and giving it to parents. Site-based management moves power from the school board and district office to the school site. Reagan's New Federalism shifted much authority over education from the federal to the state level. Like the redistributive policies of the past, these have generated conflict and intense ideological debates.

Redistributive Politics. Redistributive policies are usually controversial and "cut closer than any others along class lines" (Lowi, 1964, p. 707); therefore, they generate a political arena marked by conflict. Precisely because of this conflict, the groups involved—usually large associations—form two stable coalitions and face off against each other. They are unlikely to negotiate or "cut deals" because each is convinced that it alone is right. The attitudes and discourse of the participants in this arena are deeply ideological. In a redistributive political arena, the government often plays the role of mediator and umpire. In the 1960s, for instance, the civil rights movement and the laws that it pressured Congress to pass created a redistributive political arena. The National Association for the Advancement of Colored People and its allies stood on one side, calling for equal rights and dignity for African Americans. On the other side white southerners and many northerners as well spoke with equal passion for preserving states' rights and their traditions. This conflict frequently erupted into violence. Meanwhile, behind the scenes, government officials tried to find ways to convince both groups to accept legalistic approaches to resolving the conflict. Although most redistributive policies do not spark violence, all redistributive political arenas are marked by sharp divisions and ideological intensity.

Do Lowi's Categories Overlap?

When one tries to apply Lowi's categories to specific policies, one often feels that they overlap. For example, what seems at first to be a purely distributive policy, such as the school lunch and milk program, reveals aspects of regulation and redistribution when thoughtfully analyzed. The rules controlling lunch content have the effect of regulating the cafeteria staff's behavior. Also, providing subsidized lunches to schoolchildren redistributes public money to farmers; indeed, this was one of the original purposes of the policy. Lowi (1964; Lowi & Ginsberg, 1994) anticipates this criticism, arguing that these categories should be understood as describing the short term, rather than the long. Because most citizens and politicians think and act in the short term, the categories describe short-term perceptions of policies. In the long term, all policies are both regulatory and redistributive.

Using Lowi's Categories in School Leadership

Anticipating Political Situations. Lowi's basic policy types provide a way to anticipate the political environment that will develop around a policy both when it is under consideration and after its adoption. Moreover, the relationship between the techniques of control and their political arenas suggests ways to manage policy change at the local level. Lowi's framework can also make developing strategies for influencing the policy process easier. In this section, each of these uses of Lowi's categories is considered in turn.

Managing Policy Change. Analyzing policy ideas using Lowi's techniques of control can help leaders at the district level plan several policy changes over a period of years. Generally, one should not introduce too many policies of the same type simultaneously, especially if the changes are redistributive. The following example clarifies this principle.

Imagine a school board, superintendent, and central office team who, after much discussion and argument, have agreed that numerous policy changes need to be made over the next few years, including:

1. Requiring teachers to submit lesson plans to their principal;

2. Using a large reserve fund to repair buildings;

3. Adopting a uniform dress code for students;

4. Reducing class size to 15 in grades K–3;

5. Implementing a pay-to-play policy for the athletic programs;

6. Applying for a grant to support a dropout prevention program;

7. Applying for federal funding for a preschool program;

8. Providing a day of release time for teachers to attend a computer workshop;

9. Moving to an intradistrict open enrollment plan; and

10. Requiring more frequent evaluations of teachers whose students have low scores on the state proficiency test.

Using Lowi's categories to analyze these policies makes it clear that numbers 2, 6, 7, and 8 are distributive; numbers 1, 3, and 10 are regulatory; and numbers 4, 5, and 9 are redistributive. In planning how to introduce these changes over a period of a few years, district leaders should reflect about the political arenas they will generate and especially about which people and groups they will activate. For instance, implementing changes 4 and 5 simultaneously would probably arouse middle school and secondary teachers, coaches, and the parents of secondary students. They might well form an alliance, making common cause around the issue of unfair treatment of secondary schools. Such a coalition, fired by redistributive politics, could create a volatile situation that leaders could not handle. Less dramatically, but with equal potential for political harm, trying to put regulatory policies numbers 1 and 10 in place at once could so activate the teachers' union that it might be able to build unprecedented power among angry teachers. At first, no political risks might seem to be attached to putting several distributive policies in place at once. This perception is mistaken, however. The fact that distributive policies are often referred to as *pork* and *patronage* suggests why. Excessive use of such policies appears weak at best and corrupt at worst. This situation, too, is one to avoid.

In general, then, wise education leaders should plan a gradual introduction of several changes, taking care to use a judicious mix of policy types. Above all, they should avoid: (1) making too many policy changes of the same type close together; (2) making too many policy changes that will activate the same individuals and groups at about the same time; and (3) making a combination of changes that will activate too many people and groups in the policy arena at the same time.

Planning Influence Strategies.   As suggested in Chapter 8, education leaders should play an active role in policy adoption and formulation, contributing their professional knowledge and bringing their influence to bear on those issues that concern them. But because different policies establish different political configurations, leaders need to select appropriate strategies. Lowi's categories suggest ways to do this.

As an illustration, let us imagine a superintendent who feels strongly about three bills the state legislature is considering and wishes to support them. The bills are the following:

1. *Computers for Our Schools Bill.*   This bill proposes that $250 million in unexpected tax revenues be used to upgrade computer systems in schools across the state. Funds will be allocated proportionally on the basis of enrollment. Districts will be able to use them to rewire old buildings and to purchase approved hardware and software.

2. *H.B. 203.*   This bill would modify teacher certification requirements, mandating more field experience and exposure to diverse educational contexts. It would also require a stronger academic background in the content areas to be assessed by a nationally standardized test.

3. *A Bill to Expand Education Choices for Families.* This proposal would establish a statewide open enrollment program. Parents would be able to apply to enroll their children in any public school in the state; each child's share of state foundation moneys would be sent to the receiving district. Schools could not discriminate on the basis of race, gender, handicap, or native language.

As a first step in planning to influence politicians, the superintendent should analyze these bills by applying Lowi's categories to them. Such an analysis would suggest that the *Computers for Our Schools Bill* is basically a distributive policy, H.B. 203 is regulatory, and *A Bill to Expand Education Choices for Families* is redistributive. Unless complicating factors exist in state politics, each will generate a different sort of political arena; the superintendent should strategize accordingly.

Strategies for Distributive Arenas. Distributive policies generate stable arenas in which little conflict exists; the recipients of "gifts" focus most of their attention on the distributor rather than on each other. During the policy formulation phase, therefore, the superintendent should focus on communicating to lawmakers information about how the bill as introduced would shortchange her district. If necessary she should suggest ways to amend the bill to help her district more. No conflict within the K–12 education community should arise over this bill. Any opposition will come from other state-level players, such as the board of regents or the prison system, who may perceive the bill as redistributive. The superintendent might therefore indicate to the bill's sponsors her willingness to help obtain passage by contacting those legislators most likely to be influenced by the other groups. After passage, the superintendent should focus on seeing that the rules written by the state department of education (SDE) are fair to her district. She should also work to develop and maintain a good relationship with those in the state agency who will administer the program.

Strategies for Regulatory Arenas. H.B. 203, however, is a regulatory policy. It will probably generate a competitive but pragmatic political arena in which most major players are connected with K–12 education. Therefore, the superintendent should first tentatively identify these competitors and their probable positions. Hypothetically, one would expect the teachers' unions, subject-matter associations, administrators' groups, and teachers' colleges to be most interested in this policy. Each will have a different agenda but be willing to enter coalitions and negotiate. A good second step would be for the superintendent to contact her professional association to gather information about its position and discuss her views with the lobbyists who will work on this bill. She might offer to help the association in its efforts to see that the final law reflects administrators' concerns. She should expect that as the bill is being formulated and adopted as official policy, deals will be cut and alliances will form and fall apart. She should not waste her or anyone else's time by castigating people for selling out. She should understand that this is a pragmatic arena, not an ideological one; in it, unyielding positions are out of place. Nor should she lose interest after the bill is passed. The groups that worked to influence the law will compete to influence its accompanying rules. Only after rules have been formally adopted should she and her association relax their vigilance.

Strategies for Redistributive Arenas. A *Bill to Expand Education Choices for Families* is a redistributive policy, which would reallocate the power to decide which districts and schools children attend from public officials to parents. It would also reallocate some state foundation funds to those districts that, for whatever reason, can attract students from outside their boundaries. This proposal will probably generate an intensely ideological arena in which two opposing sides will emerge. As a first step toward participating in this arena, the superintendent should identify who is most likely to join each side. The supportive side will probably include districts that expect to gain students, parents who are interested in transferring their children, businesses, and conservative groups. On the opposing side, one would expect to see those districts that fear they would lose students, associations that represent cities' interests in the state capital, and liberal groups. The African American community may be split, with those who live in inner cities supporting the bill and others opposing it. Districts that anticipate no major impact from the policy—large rural districts, for instance—will probably remain uninvolved.

Such an analysis would suggest to the superintendent where she is most likely to find individuals and groups who share her position. They might consider forming an ad hoc umbrella organization, combining all supporters of the bill. Such an organization would magnify the power of supporters and provide a vehicle within which people from diverse backgrounds could work together. She should realize that building a strong coalition will require much ideological work such as developing appropriate slogans, flyers, news releases, and speeches. She should understand, too, that ideological battles are often won by the side whose discourse most resonates with the public. Finally, she should recognize that getting this policy adopted may require a campaign of several years during which supporters will have to educate legislators and the public, build an effective organization, and raise funds to support their efforts. Long-term persistence is often the key to passing redistributive policies.

EXERCISES ON THE TECHNIQUES OF CONTROL

1. Identify each of the following policies as distributive, regulatory, or redistributive.
   a. A federal preschool program for poor children.
   b. A school board policy detailing the procedure for expelling students.
   c. A legal requirement that minority teachers be hired to staff an inner-city dropout prevention program.
   d. A bill to require all children in grades K–6 to study the dangers of drugs.
   e. A law requiring the development of state content standards in all major subjects, grades K–12.
   f. A bill to require a certification procedure for teachers' aides.

g. A state program that gives high schools $100 for each student enrolled in driver's education.

h. A state law that grants school districts funds to provide a mentoring program for first-year teachers.

i. A federal court decision requiring girls' athletic programs to be funded equally with boys' athletic programs.

j. A school board's plan to contract with an educational management company to operate five schools in the district.

2. For policies a, d, f, and h, describe the political arena that each policy will probably generate. Identify probable supporters and opponents as well as the nature of the conflicts that will ensue.

3. For policies c, e, g, and j, decide whether you support or oppose each policy. Then outline a strategy for influencing the policy process in the direction you prefer.

4. Do any of the policies in Question 1 have the characteristics of more than one technique of control? If so, which? How would these mixed characteristics affect the politics surrounding the policy?

MCDONNELL AND ELMORE'S POLICY INSTRUMENTS

McDonnell and Elmore (1987) argued that four "alternative policy instruments, or . . . mechanisms [exist] that translate substantive policy goals . . . into concrete actions" (p. 134). Those four instruments are **mandates, inducements, capacity building,** and **system changing.** Seven years later, McDonnell (1994) added a fifth instrument to the framework: **hortatory policy,** or **persuasion.** Although Lowi's three techniques of control are based on the impact of policies on society, McDonnell and Elmore developed their framework of policy instruments by considering "the conditions under which these instruments are most likely to produce their intended effects" (McDonnell & Elmore, 1987, p. 133). Lowi's categories can be understood as a wide-angle lens for looking at policies, bringing the whole society into view. McDonnell and Elmore's resembles a close-up lens, permitting a detailed view of how a particular policy type functions. This section first discusses each policy instrument. Table 9.1 summarizes the highlights of this discussion. Next, the use of multiple policy instruments is illustrated by a discussion of education reform in California between 1983 and 1994. Finally, this section explores ways that school leaders can use McDonnell and Elmore's ideas.

Mandates

A **mandate** is a "rule governing the actions of individuals and agencies" (McDonnell & Elmore, 1987, p. 138). It usually consists of two components: (1) language that spells out required behavior for all people in a specified social group, and (2) a prescribed penalty for those who fail to comply. These components may take the form of a statute, an administrative rule, a court decision, a school board

TABLE 9.1 McDonnell and Elmore's Policy Instruments

Policy Instrument	Components	Best Context	Costs	Major Drawback
Mandates	1. Language requiring behavior 2. Penalty	1. Uniform behavior desirable 2. Strong support	1. Enforcement 2. Compliance 3. Avoidance	Adversarial relationships
Inducements	1. Short-term transfer of resources 2. Guidelines	Diverse behavior desirable	Oversight	Excessive diversity
Capacity Building	1. Long-term investment 2. Guidelines	Existing institutions unable to respond	1. Investment 2. Administration	Intangibility of short-term results
System-Change	Shift of authority	Existing institutions unwilling to respond	Countering resistance	Unpredictable results
Hortatory Policy	1. Information 2. Symbols, images 3. Appeal to values	Target population most likely to act on information	Disseminating information	Danger of manipulation

Note. Based on L. M. McDonnell and R. F. Elmore (1987), "Getting the Job Done: Alternative Policy Instruments," *Educational Evaluation and Policy Analysis,* 9, pp. 137 & 141; McDonnell (1994).

policy, or a school or classroom rule. A good example of a mandate is a compulsory school attendance law. Such a statute requires the parents of children between certain ages to send their children to school or arrange for their home schooling. Most school districts have district-level administrators—who used to be called *truant officers* but now have more pleasant titles—who monitor attendance figures and check up on children who are not attending school. They usually start by issuing a warning to the parents, but if necessary can take them to court where a judge may impose a fine.

Mandates are appropriate policy instruments only in certain situations. A mandate functions best when one wants to encourage all members of a group to behave in the same way and when the mandate can be enforced. Mandates also require strong political support. Compulsory attendance laws meet both criteria; almost all people, both average citizens and political leaders, believe that children should be educated, and school attendance can easily be enforced. However, like all policy instruments, mandates imply costs. These include the cost of enforcing a mandate, the cost of complying with it, and the cost of avoiding compliance. School districts must pay the administrators who enforce attendance and provide them with offices, clerical help, and automobiles. The families incur costs, too. School attendance entails expenditures for items such as suitable clothing, required fees, and necessary materials. The family also loses the domestic labor or supplementary income that older children could provide. Noncompliance involves costs as well. Tactics to elude the truant officer—such as frequent moving and time spent persuading friends and relatives to cover for the family—impose a toll.

The ideal result of a mandate is widespread, uniform behavior of a socially desirable sort. Compulsory attendance laws have led to a society in which almost everyone has received some education. Less desirable results may also occur. Mandates may encourage uniform behavior in a situation where diversity would be preferable. Finally, mandates usually create an adversarial relationship between the enforcing agency and those who do not wish to comply. The comic antics of children playing hooky as they try to avoid a pursuing truant officer are a frequent theme in popular culture; they illustrate in amusing fashion the hostile relationships that can develop around a mandate.

Inducements

An **inducement** is a "transfer of money [or in-kind grants] to individuals or agencies in return for the production of goods or services" (McDonnell & Elmore, 1987, pp. 137–138). Inducements consist of two components: (1) the money, services, or in-kind materials to be transferred, and (2) guidelines that spell out how they are to be used. These guidelines may be broad, as with block grants, or detailed, as with categorical grants. Most often, the language in which an inducement is formulated appears in a statute or administrative rule. Theoretically, however, it could also be included in a school board policy or in school or classroom rules. A good example of the use of inducements in education is Title I of the Elementary and Secondary Education Act of 1965. Passed as part of President Johnson's War on Poverty, Title I has evolved through numerous mutations, changing its name from Title I to Chapter I and back again. For more than three decades, it has offered federal grant moneys to public and private schools in exchange for their provision of remedial education services. The guidelines have changed over the years, but they have always required schools or districts or both to serve a certain percentage of poor children in order to qualify for grants (Spring, 1986).

Inducements are appropriate only in certain situations, however. First, because accepting inducements is voluntary, leaders should not use them to encourage a behavior so desirable that everyone should display it. For example, inducements would be a poor policy instrument to use in implementing compulsory school attendance. The most appropriate contexts in which to use inducements are those in which diverse behavior is desirable or at least acceptable. Second, inducements work best when large numbers of potential implementers are willing to implement the policy but currently lack the resources to do so. Finally, since adopting inducements does not require strong political support, they are the ideal policy instrument for situations in which it may be difficult to pass a mandate, a system change, or a capacity building program. Title I represents an appropriate use of inducements. Its main purpose was to provide educational support for poor children; however, since many schools and districts have few poor children, diverse behavior in the area of remedial education for the underprivileged was acceptable. Moreover, public school professionals were generally willing to provide such remedial services but could not afford to hire additional teachers without financial assistance. Finally, because the passage of Title I in 1965 was hotly contested, those who formulated the bill believed that Congress was more likely to approve inducements than mandates.

Naturally, inducements entail costs. Money must be provided to fund grants or provide in-kind contributions such as teaching materials and testing services. Oversight is required to make sure that guidelines are followed, and this cannot be provided free of charge. Moreover, grant recipients are usually expected to contribute some of their own resources to a project—at a minimum, space, utilities, and administrative overhead. Sometimes they must provide matching funds. Title I has been a costly program with the federal government providing grant money and local districts contributing classroom space, furnishings, materials, supervision, and other tangible and intangible goods.

The ideal result of inducements is diverse behavior in policy domains where diversity is acceptable. Because school districts and schools serve different populations and must therefore meet different needs, inducements offer an opportunity to develop flexible, responsive programs tailored to local situations. Excessive diversity can pose problems, however. Inducements should be used to advance broad, coherent policy goals; otherwise, a patchwork quilt of unrelated and contradictory programs may evolve.

Capacity Building

Capacity building can be defined as "the transfer of money for the purpose of investment in material, intellectual, or human resources" (McDonnell & Elmore,

1987, p. 134). The word *investment* indicates the major difference between inducements and capacity building. The latter policy instrument is designed to bring about a major, permanent change in the functional ability of an individual or an organization. Therefore, it represents a long-term investment, whose full impact will not be apparent for years. A major component of capacity building is a large sum of money that is transferred to the implementing agency as a grant or as an appropriation of earmarked funds. The other major component is investment guidelines. A good example of capacity building is the Venture Capital program in Ohio. Under it, schools can apply to the state for a grant of $25,000 a year for up to five years. The narrow purpose of these grants is to support "long-term, evolving efforts focused on a particular dimension of school improvement" (Ohio Department of Education [ODE], 1995, p. 1). The broader purpose is "to build organizational capacity" (p. 6) through professional development. The guidelines encourage schools to build organizational capacity by adopting one of eleven well-established school improvement programs or by inventing a school improvement program of their own (subject to state approval).

Capacity building is well suited to situations in which the currently employed staff and existing institutions cannot carry out desired policies because they are incapable of doing so. This incapacity may result from insufficient training, a lack of appropriate experience, inadequate equipment, or some combination of these. The Venture Capital program in Ohio is an appropriate use of capacity building. The Ohio State Board of Education has a vision of schools in which "conditions for learning are right" (ODE, 1995, p. 1), but it recognized several years ago that teachers are unaccustomed to working together and lack training in school improvement models. Therefore, through the grants it hopes to build "a professional development infrastructure" (p. 6) across the state to make achieving this long-term goal possible. Capacity building is extremely expensive, however. Figures given in *Venture Capital in Ohio Schools: Building Commitment and Capacity for School Renewal* (ODE, 1995) suggest that in 1994–1995 the grants alone cost $8,675,000. Operating and publicizing the program also require expenditures.

The ideal result of capacity building is people and institutions capable of implementing desirable new programs and policies. However, capacity building has a major drawback. Precisely because it is expensive and yields results only in the long term, its political support may evaporate before sufficient capacity has been built. As the booklet by the ODE warns: "The state's commitment . . . is to fund schools for $25,000 a year for as many as five years. This commitment is contingent upon funding from the legislature beyond 1995" (ODE, 1995, p. 54).

System Change

System change is a policy instrument that "transfer[s] . . . official authority among individuals and agencies" (McDonnell & Elmore, 1987, p. 139). Its central component is a statute, administrative rule, or board policy that weakens or eliminates the authority of an official or agency over a specific decision-making area while simultaneously shifting that authority to different individuals or agencies. As a secondary effect, a system change may reallocate resources; however, in a true system change the shift of resources follows the shift of authority. Voucher plans offer a good example of system change. In their much discussed book, *Politics, Markets, and America's Schools*, Chubb and Moe (1990) recommended vouchers, which they called *scholarships*. Under their plan, state governments would shift the authority to decide which schools children attend from state and local officials to parents. After parents have chosen schools, the state government would allocate funds, in the form of scholarships, to schools on the basis of enrollment. Thus, parents would individually select their own child's school; collectively, acting through market mechanisms, they would also determine how much state funding each school would receive.

System change is an appropriate policy instrument when new behavior is needed but the currently employed staff and existing institutions are unresponsive to demands for change. In their book, Chubb and Moe (1990) explained at length why public schools, as institutions, cannot provide high-quality education to children in the United States. Therefore, they argued, an institutional change is needed. They considered vouchers the best way to improve education because they believed vouchers would stimulate competition among schools. Advocates of system changes often believe their policy reform will save money, leading to greater efficiency in the use of resources. However, a high, although intangible, cost is associated with system change. People who stand to lose power and resources (and perhaps their jobs) through a system change will not stand idly by while it occurs. They will probably mount resistance to the proposed change, and if change comes anyway they may work to sabotage it. Such resistance can entail costs in both morale and lowered productivity. In 1990 Chubb and Moe anticipated strong opposition to their plan from professional educators. Since then, reactions in states where voucher legislation has been proposed have confirmed their expectations.

The ideal result of a system change is a revolutionized institution able and willing to meet the new demands placed upon it. The major drawback is its unpredictability. The individuals or agencies to whom authority has been shifted may be as unable to meet new demands as the previous ones were. Unforeseen consequences may also arise, causing problems equal to or worse than those that existed under the older system. Voucher opponents base their central arguments on this unpredictability. They claim that parents will not be able to choose schools well and that competition will lead to educational winners and losers by causing resegregation and the development of "dumping-ground schools."

Hortatory Policy, or Persuasion

Hortatory, or **persuasive, policies** "send a signal that particular goals and actions are considered a high priority by government" (McDonnell, 1994, p. 398). Because they are intended to persuade, hortatory policies are primarily discursive, using symbolism and imagery to appeal to values in order to encourage citizens to act on their values. The major components of hortatory policies are written, spoken, or graphic texts that communicate information and suggest that people should behave in a certain way. Common examples in schools include campaigns to encourage children to recycle trash and "Just say no" drug education programs. Simply providing information to the public may play a hortatory role. Many states release district-by-district or school-by-school test results to the media as a way of persuading educators to take the tests seriously and, if necessary, change their curriculum. The Clinton Administration's proposed voluntary national tests to assess fourth-grade reading and eighth-grade mathematics provide another example of a hortatory policy. Because the tests were to be completely voluntary, some questioned their usefulness. These objections overlooked their potentially persuasive nature, however. The test scores would have permitted comparisons of states, districts, and schools, making it possible for some parents to compare their own child's results to average results in other places (Lawton, 1997). Such information, if widely disseminated, would have persuaded some educators to alter their teaching to make a better showing. As Lyle Jones, a North Carolina psychology professor, observed, "The pressures to teach what is being tested are bound to be very large . . . particularly . . . where teachers and principals know the results will be published . . . " (Hoff, 1997, p. 34).

Hortatory policies are appropriate when the desired change can be readily linked with symbols and information and when people are likely to act on new information. They are especially suitable as the first step in a long sequence of policies designed to change behavior gradually. Often, when political support is weak, a hortatory policy is the only one with a chance of being adopted. President Clinton's voluntary national tests meet these three criteria. Linking the rhetoric of education excellence to test scores is easy, and educators do tend to modify their practice in response to tests. Finally, considerable opposition to national tests exists. Among the groups attacking them were the Eagle Forum and the Christian Coalition, which feared the tests might be part of an agenda leading to centralized control over education (Lawton, 1997). In this context, a hortatory policy was the only politically feasible one.

The major cost of a hortatory policy is the dissemination of information. Hortatory policies usually involve public relations techniques such as posters, radio and television commercials, and printed flyers—all expensive. Moreover, distributing such materials is costly, too. The ideal result of a hortatory policy is successfully persuading the targeted population to act differently. The major drawback of hortatory policies is the ease with which persuasion can slip into propaganda and other forms of manipulation. Those who adopt hortatory policies should bear in mind the principles for the ethical use of discourse discussed in Chapter 2.

Combining Policy Instruments

Although for analytical purposes McDonnell and Elmore distinguish five policy instruments, education leaders must understand that in practice, policy instruments are often combined. Indeed, combining several instruments within a single policy can work quite effectively to bring about change. Using McDonnell and Elmore's instruments as a framework for analyzing California's curriculum policy between 1983 and 1994, Chrispeels (1997) discovered a consistent pattern of combining policy instruments. In her study, she identified twelve state initiatives designed to change classroom instruction to make it more "meaning-centered" (p. 466) and interdisciplinary. She found that although California employed all the policy instruments over the course of the decade and almost always used two or three together, it preferred mandates. In fact, it began its curriculum reform by enacting S.B. 813, which mandated several new standards for the entire state. These included increased requirements for high school graduation, a longer school year, and new criteria for textbook selection. Yet mandates did not stand alone, even in this initial legislation. In S.B. 813, the state employed three other policy instruments: inducements, hortatory policy, and capacity building. For example, it required the SDE to develop model curricula for different subjects. School districts did not have to adopt these; rather, the models played a persuasive role. The law also provided for capacity building, primarily in the form of professional development.

This pattern of combining policy instruments continued throughout the period under study. Over and over, California passed laws that included more than one policy instrument. Chrispeels concluded that this approach was successful because it "created multiple leverage points and a common language used by teacher leaders" (p. 471). Moreover, because the different instruments were used *coherently*—that is, they all aimed at the same broad policy goal—their use in combination facilitated the implementation of curriculum reform by the state's teachers and principals. Another of Chrispeels's major conclusions was that capacity building was a critical component of the reform effort. Without capacity building policies, many educators would not have understood how best to put the mandated policy changes into effect. Nor would they have made the best use of inducements.

As is often the case in education, the 10-year period of curriculum reform that Chrispeels documented came to an abrupt halt in 1994. In that year, the governor vetoed a funding bill that would have continued to implement the California Learning Assessment System (CLAS), a key component of the reform. Even so, three years later many of the state's educators were still using significant portions of CLAS, explaining to Chrispeels in focus groups that it made sense to them. She decided that this continued adherence to the policy in spite of its lack of official sanction demonstrated the power of a coherent set of diverse policy instruments to change both beliefs and practice.

Using McDonnell and Elmore's Ideas in School Leadership

Diversifying Policy Instruments. Benveniste (1986) argues that for many reasons policy formulators overuse mandates with negative penalties. They often regard such policies as foolproof, are ignorant of the contexts in which their policies will be implemented, and find devising punitive mandates easy. Benveniste blames overuse of these policy instruments for "the general malaise and ineffectiveness" (p. 151) prevalent among teachers, as well as for much teacher burnout. Federal and state officials are not the only ones who overuse mandates. Superintendents, school boards, and principals usually consider mandates first when faced with a problem.

McDonnell and Elmore's theories about policy instruments provide a way to conceptualize policy alternatives and also suggest criteria for assessing their probable effectiveness. For illustrative purposes, let us imagine a superintendent who discovers the reading levels in several primary classes are much too low. In reflecting on this problem, he will immediately think of several possible mandates. He could require all primary teachers to submit detailed reading lesson plans to their principals, increase the hours of required reading instruction, or mandate a new phonics program. McDonnell and Elmore's framework suggests, however, that such an approach would be inappropriate. In the first place, he does not need to change the behavior of all the primary teachers, but only some. Moreover, the costs of requiring principals, who usually have little free time, to check more lesson plans may be high, including both neglect of other important duties and lowered morale. Finally, this approach may not even achieve the desired policy goal. After all, if some teachers simply do not know how to teach reading well, requiring all teachers to submit lesson plans, teach more reading, and use phonics workbooks will not address the root problem.

Deeper reflection on this problem, using McDonnell and Elmore's framework, suggests that capacity building would be a more appropriate instrument. The superintendent could identify individual teachers with problems and require them to spend several in-service days at special workshops on reading pedagogy. He could ask the language arts supervisor to locate several recent articles on effective reading instruction and use them in discussion groups with weak reading teachers. He could purchase a set of videotapes on reading and urge these teachers to look at them several times and use them to change their instruction. This approach should build capacity in the teachers. As a side effect, it would probably also exercise a hortatory impact on other primary teachers. Noting their colleagues' supplementary activities, many would undoubtedly decide to devote a little extra attention to reading instruction if only to avoid extra activities next year.

Combining Policy Instruments in School Leadership. McDonnell and Elmore's framework, especially as illuminated by Chrispeels (1997), suggests ways that education leaders can combine policy instruments for maximum impact. The effective combination of several instruments depends upon **coherence:** all instruments must be used to achieve the same broad policy goal. Failure to keep this principle in mind leads to a confusing set of policies that undercut each other.

As an illustration, let us imagine a middle school principal who wishes that her building looked cleaner and more attractive. At the moment, the school's halls are littered, the floors near eating areas are stained, and graffiti cover desk tops as well as the booths in student restrooms. Her first reaction to this mess might be to crack down by announcing several new, punitive mandates. Any child caught littering, spilling food, or defacing school property might automatically be given a detention. Deeper reflection should suggest problems with this approach. It would have to be enforced by faculty and staff, so it would probably increase hostility between teachers and students—always undesirable. Moreover, it would pose enforcement problems. Although youngsters often commit the relatively minor offenses of littering and spilling food in the presence of adults, the more serious offense of damaging school property is usually committed privately. Therefore, vigorous enforcement could lead to a blatantly unfair situation in which minor infractions are punished and major ones are not. Of course, middle school students would be quick to perceive this injustice and point it out.

A more effective approach would be to combine policy instruments in a long-term strategy. This strategy might begin with several hortatory policies. For example, the first day of school, the principal might declare this year Make Our School Beautiful Year. A special assembly program and posters and banners in the halls could be used to reinforce this message. Littering, careless spills, and petty vandalism could be identified as some of the barriers to a beautiful school while focusing on the positive theme. Next, the principal might utilize inducements. Middle school youngsters are unlikely to relish writing grant proposals, but they do enjoy contests. Each month classes could submit a plan for beautifying some part of the building. The winning class could be given free time to carry out its proposal, a pizza party upon its completion, and publicity to celebrate its achievement. The principal should not overlook capacity building, either. She should seriously consider the possibility that the custodial staff or its equipment are inadequate. Are enough trash cans placed in the halls? Are they located in the most crucial places? Do the custodians need training on how to organize their work or remove spills and graffiti? All these possibilities should be explored.

After two or three months, the principal might issue some mandates; by this time support for them should be stronger than it would have been with a sudden crackdown. Of course, ideally, the penalties for violation should advance the broader policy goal. Instead of sitting in a detention hall for thirty minutes, children caught littering might pick up trash in the restrooms. Those caught writing on walls might be given a bottle of household cleaner and told to remove their own graffiti and others'. Most children would perceive a certain fairness in such penalties, reducing resentment and adversarial attitudes.

With a carefully planned combination of several policy instruments all aimed at improving her school's appearance, the principal will probably have a more attractive building at the end of the year than she had at the beginning. Possibly even more important, she will have sensitized her pupils to an important environmental issue and improved school climate. In schools, as in California, the simultaneous use of several instruments can "create multiple leverage points and a common language" (Chrispeels, 1997, p. 471).

EXERCISES ON THE POLICY INSTRUMENTS

1. Write three brief policies designed to reach each of the following goals. Each policy should use a different instrument.
   a. Improve district test scores on the state proficiency examination.
   b. Expand the use of computers in schools across the state.
   c. Increase the number of young women enrolled in engineering programs.
   d. Reduce student tardiness in a high school.

e. Encourage students in the district to become more interested in mathematics.
2. For two of the policy goals in Question 1, develop a long-term set of coherent policies designed to reach the central objective over five years.
3. Analyze part of a school handbook or a board policy manual. Describe its use in the five policy instruments.
4. Analyze education legislation introduced in the last session of your state legislature to determine which policy instruments the legislature uses most often and least often.

COST ANALYSIS AND COST-EFFECTIVENESS ANALYSIS

Thinking About Costs

School leaders feel daily pressure to use school funds wisely. Yet, the best way to utilize resources is not always clear. In *Cost-Effectiveness Analysis* Levin and McEwan (2001) describe a 1987 study of four approaches to raising students' scores on mathematics achievement tests: (1) adding an hour to the school day, (2) computer-assisted instruction, (3) cross-age and adult tutoring, and (4) reducing class size. Although the tutoring program was more expensive than the other alternatives, it was also far more effective. In fact, when costs were divided by effects to obtain a cost-effectiveness ratio, researchers found that the tutoring programs were almost ten times more effective than adding an hour to the school day. This illustration points to a serious issue. Many school leaders adopt new policies without realistically analyzing either their cost or their cost-effectiveness. This can lead to wasted time and money as well as poor educational results. Therefore, leaders need ways to analyze costs in order to choose wisely among educational alternatives.

In this section both **cost analysis** and **cost-effectiveness** analysis are presented as tools for educators to use. In thinking about both types of analysis, one must understand the terms *cost* and *benefit*. Many people think *cost* is synonymous with *expenditure*, but this is untrue. **Costs** are closely related to **benefits**. A **benefit** is "anything you gain by undertaking a particular course of action" (Coplin & O'Leary, 1981, p. 129). A **cost** is "anything you must give up in order to obtain those benefits" (Coplin & O'Leary, 1981, p. 129). Costs therefore include both expenditures and those potential benefits lost by following a course of action. For example, if a room in a school is transformed into a student lounge, the costs include not only expenditures for fresh paint and new furniture, but also the lost opportunity to use the room for something else, or an **opportunity cost.** Both costs and benefits may be either **tangible** or **intangible.** A **tangible** cost or benefit can be quantified. Higher test scores and lower dropout rates are examples of tangible benefits; stronger community support is an intangible one. Examples of tangible costs include the number of dollars spent or hours worked on a project. **Intangible** costs include teacher burnout and lower student morale. In thinking through the potential costs and benefits of a policy, considering both the tangible and the intangible ones is essential (Coplin & O'Leary, 1981).

Cost Analysis

Levin and McEwan's Ingredients Method.   Levin and McEwan (2001) recommend a system for estimating the tangible costs of a policy or program. It requires calculating the expenditures and opportunity costs involved in providing five ingredients: personnel, facilities, equipment and materials, client inputs, and miscellaneous inputs. Each of these ingredients is explained below.

Personnel includes all people who will work on the program, full time and part time, paid employees and volunteers. The cost of the services of each should be expressed in dollars. For paid employees, this figure should be based on their salary plus fringe benefits. For part-time workers, a percentage of this is calculated. Volunteer work should be assigned a price comparable to what the work would cost in the marketplace.

Facilities include all space used to house the program, such as offices and classrooms. The price assigned could be the cost of an actual lease or mortgage or what it would cost to lease a similar facility. Facilities are normally stocked with **equipment and materials,** which include necessary office machinery, audiovisual equipment, and furniture. To calculate annual costs, actual prices should be divided by the number of years of anticipated use. Thus, the annual cost of a $500 microscope that should last five years is $100.

Required client inputs should never be forgotten. This ingredient reflects costs imposed on the participants or their parents. If additional transportation is required, its cost should be estimated; driving time for parents should not be overlooked. Other required client costs include books, materials, or clothing that must be purchased and food that will be donated for special events. **Miscellaneous inputs** do not easily fall into the other four categories. They include utilities, maintenance, administrative overhead, and added insurance costs.

The Ingredients Method Applied.   Tables 9.2 and 9.3 analyze the costs and expenditures involved in setting up a new computer laboratory in a middle school. In this hypothetical case, the school serves grades five through eight and enrolls 700 children. The staff includes a principal, assistant principal, 28 teachers, two secretaries, five cafeteria workers, and three custodians. The school already has one computer lab, and seventh and eighth graders are required to take two hours of computer science in the lab each week. The district leadership wishes to take advantage of a state technology grant to create a second laboratory, permitting the 350 fifth and sixth graders to take two hours of computer science each week also. An empty classroom currently storing district audiovisual equipment would be used for space. A new media specialist would be hired to operate the laboratory and teach the classes.

TABLE 9.2 Cost Analysis of a Computer Laboratory

Ingredients	Total Annualized Costs	Total Costs, First Year	Costs to School District	Costs to Other Government Agencies	Private Contributions	Required Client Costs
Personnel						
Media specialist	$47,350.00	$47,350.00	$47,350.00			
District technical support (5%)	1,906.50	1,906.50	1,906.50			
2 parent volunteers (5 hrs./week)	3,751.20	3,751.20			$3,751.20	
5 student assistants (5 hrs./week)	4,635.00	4,635.00			4,635.00	
Facilities						
800 sq. ft. classroom	3,600.00	3,600.00	3,600.00			
Materials and Equipment						
30 PCs	7,200.00	36,000.00	10,000.00	$20,000.00 (state grant)	6,000.00 (Local business)	
5 printers	299.95	1,499.75	1,499.75			
20 inkjet cartridges	280.00	280.00	280.00			
10 tables	200.00	2,000.00	2,000.00			
30 student chairs	225.00	2,250.00	2,250.00			
1 teacher desk	12.50	250.00	250.00			
1 teacher chair	5.00	100.00	100.00			
1 metal file cabinet	6.25	125.00	125.00			
252 reams paper	998.00	998.00	998.00			

TABLE 9.2 Cost Analysis of a Computer Laboratory (*Continued*)

Ingredients	Total Annualized Costs	Total Costs, First Year	Costs to School District	Costs to Other Government Agencies	Private Contributions	Required Client Costs
Client Inputs						
350 workbooks	3,500.00	3,500.00				$3,500.00
3500 diskettes	900.00	900.00				900.00
Miscellaneous						
Administrative overhead	3,665.40	3,665.40	3,665.40			
Maintenance	2,000.00	2,000.00	2,000.00			
Utilities	500.00	500.00	500.00			
Added insurance	250.00	250.00	250.00			
Total	$81,284.80	$115,560.85	$76,774.65	$20,000.00	$14,386.20	$4,400.00

TABLE 9.3 Analysis of District Expenditures

Ingredients	Totai First Year Expenditures	Total Annual Expenditures After First Year
Personnel		
Media Specialist	$47,350.00	$47,350.00
Materials and Equipment		
PCs	10,000.00	
Printers	1,499.75	
Inkjet refills	280.00	280.00
Tables	2,000.00	
Student chairs	2,250.00	
Teacher desk	250.00	
Teacher chair	100.00	
File cabinet	125.00	
Paper	998.00	998.00
Miscellaneous		
Utilities	500.00	500.00
Added insurance	250.00	250.00
Total	$65,602.75	$49,378.00

In making calculations, the following procedures were used. Most personnel costs are based on the annual salary plus 23% in fringe benefits. The cost of parent volunteers is based on the salary of teachers' aides; the cost of student assistants is calculated at minimum wage with no fringe benefits. The PCs and printers were annualized over five years; student furniture, over 10; and teacher furniture, over 20. Administrative overhead, maintenance, and utilities were calculated on the assumption that the lab would absorb 2% of the overall costs of the school.

The usefulness of such a cost analysis is apparent. First, and perhaps most important for the pressured administrator, it reduces the chance of unanticipated expenditures. Such a procedure makes conceptualizing exactly what the financial impact of a new project is likely to be easy and permits decision makers to plan accordingly. A second advantage is that it makes seeing ways to save money easy. For example, perhaps appropriate furniture is available elsewhere in the district or could be purchased at a lower cost from a business that is closing. Finally, cost analysis can also alert leaders to potential problems. This computer lab will add to the workload of the district's technical support staff as well as to that of the building's administrators, secretaries, and custodians. If they have some spare time during the day, this should not matter. However, if their workloads have been increased at other times, reevaluating them may be necessary. If additional responsibilities are repeatedly added to certain positions, eventually more employees will be needed. Failure to recognize this situation and intervene early can lead to morale problems. Another potential problem is the imposed student costs. Under this plan, each fifth and sixth grader would have to pay an additional $15 in fees. In some districts, this would be an unrealistic burden for families. School and district leaders should reflect carefully on the wisdom of imposing such a requirement.

Analyzing Tangible and Intangible Costs and Benefits. As a supplement to Levin and McEwan's (2001) ingredients method, leaders should also carry out the analysis of both tangible and intangible costs and benefits recommended by Coplin and O'Leary (1981). Table 9.4 presents such a cost-benefit analysis of the computer lab. The meaning of this type of analysis must be interpreted within its context. In many districts these intangible costs would have to be taken seriously. If rapid staff turnover is a problem and a parent group has recently complained about high fees, these costs should weigh heavily in leaders' thinking. On the other hand, if school leaders see no indicators of staff dissatisfaction and fees are low, leaders would not need to feel particularly concerned about these intangible costs. Benefits must also be understood in context. Improving public image and raising scores on accreditation reviews are not important issues everywhere. Such an analysis should be related to a specific context in order to answer this key question: Do the potential benefits of adopting this policy outweigh the potential costs? Only if the answer is in the affirmative should the policy be adopted. As Coplin and O'Leary (1981) warn: "A project should be undertaken only if its benefits are at least equal to its costs" (p. 130).

Cost-Effectiveness Analysis

Thinking About Effectiveness. No policy, even a low-cost one, should be adopted if it is unlikely to be **effective.** And an existing policy should be changed or dropped if it is proven **ineffective.** An **effective policy** is one that leads to the intended outcomes, such as higher reading achievement scores, better attendance, or increased parent involvement. **Cost-effectiveness analysis** is a systematic way to compare alternative methods for reaching the same goal in terms of cost and effectiveness. The most desirable alternative is the one that costs the least while also reaching the policy goal. In the absence of a cost-effectiveness analysis, leaders often make the mistake of selecting the least expensive policy or program. If a policy is ineffective, it is too costly, even if its cost is low.

Steps in Cost-Effectiveness Analysis. Levin and McEwan (2001) outline several steps for a good cost-effectiveness analysis. The first, and most important, step is to accurately identify one's **true policy objective.** This is often harder than one might think. For example, consider a school board and superintendent who face a common problem: they need to cut the budget. Too often, they hastily identify their policy objective as cutting the budget, whereas their real objective should be cutting the budget in the way that will least reduce the effectiveness of the educational program. Starting with the wrong objective, they limit their ability to see all the alternatives and their true costs. The result is typically the selection of an ineffective policy—such as closing small schools.

TABLE 9.4 Potential Costs and Benefits of the Computer Lab

	Tangible	Intangible
Costs		
	$76,774.65	1. Excessive workloads for some staff 2. Burnout among some staff 3. Parent resentment of fees
Benefits		
	1. Higher level of student computer literacy 2. Improved scores on accreditation reviews 3. More team planning time for fifth- and sixth-grade teachers	1. Improved public image 2. Higher morale among fifth- and sixth-grade teachers

The next step is to select an appropriate measure of the effectiveness of the available alternatives. This might be the number of dollars saved, results of a school climate assessment, or a dropout rate. After that, all alternatives should be identified, ideally in a group brainstorming session in which no ideas are rejected as outlandish. Such a session may yield creative alternatives with much potential for enhancing the quality of education. For example, at least three cost-saving alternatives to closing a small school may exist: (1) sharing teachers and administrators among small schools; (2) sharing resources with a nearby community college; and (3) leasing empty space in the school building to groups such as senior citizens' organizations.

After all the viable alternatives have been specified, a thorough cost analysis of each should be carried out. This analysis should consider both tangible and intangible costs. When small schools are closed, the savings are not always as great as anticipated. Savings will be partially offset by increased transportation costs. Moreover, consolidating schools often discourages parent involvement, reducing the number of volunteer hours available and the number of in-kind contributions. Over the long term, a district that has closed several small schools may lose financially as bond issues fail, opposed by resentful citizens in the areas that lost schools.

Next, the effectiveness of each alternative should be carefully considered. A staff member should locate research on each, taking care that the research selected relates to the effectiveness measures chosen earlier. The research on many widely adopted policies contains surprises. For example, the research literature raises serious doubts about the educational effectiveness of closing small schools. School consolidation seems to jeopardize student learning, faculty morale, school climate, and participation in extracurricular activities (Levin & McEwan, 2001). In considering closing a school, these intangible costs should be carefully weighed. Finally, after carefully comparing the costs and effectiveness of each alternative, one should make a choice. The best choice is not necessarily either the cheapest alternative or the most effective one. Rather, cost must be balanced against effectiveness, keeping in mind the context in which the policy must be implemented.

FINAL POINTS

In recent years, many have stressed that school leaders must reflect before acting. Reflection and thoughtful analysis are especially important when one is developing policies or implementing policies adopted by others. Making policy mistakes is easy. As demonstrated in Chapter 10, most policy implementations fail primarily because those in charge of developing the policy or planning the implementation did not think enough about their decisions. The three types of analysis presented in this chapter—Lowi's techniques of control, McDonnell and Elmore's policy instruments, and the analysis of costs and effectiveness—are useful tools for guiding reflection. Education leaders who use them intelligently will find that they can smooth both policy change and policy implementation.

EXERCISES ON COST ANALYSIS AND COST-EFFECTIVENESS ANALYSIS

1. A midwestern state legislature passed a law requiring all school districts to gather data on 78 demographic, financial, and educational variables, enter them in a special computer program, and send them via modem to the SDE each spring. Legislators bragged to the newspapers that this bill had a $0 "fiscal note." However, local school leaders did not believe this plan would cost *them* nothing. Using Levin's ingredients method, calculate a reasonable cost for district compliance.

2. A southern school board is considering a policy which would require every third grader who fails the state reading test to repeat the third grade. Children who fail the test during their second year in third grade would be promoted to fourth grade, however. Assume that the district has 2,000 third graders each year, that 10% fail the test each year, and that every student who fails third grade eventually completes the twelfth grade in this district. Assume also that the district spends an average of $3,000 of local money on each student annually. Do a cost analysis of the cost to the district during the first 20 years of implementing such a policy.

3. A large East Coast district with an enrollment of 25,000 has the lowest scores on the state's twelfth-grade proficiency test. The school board wants to raise the scores over the next two years. Using cost analysis and cost-effectiveness analysis, develop and evaluate three possible plans for reaching this goal and make a recommendation to the board.

4. A large suburban district in the Southwest is receiving $1 million in new revenues each year because of taxes generated by a new power plant. The school board is considering the following ways of using the money to improve student

learning: (1) raising teachers' salaries, (2) reducing average class size K–12 from 25 to 21, (3) adding a half-day kindergarten program for four year olds to the existing full-day program for five year olds, and (4) establishing a merit pay plan for teachers, awarding significant pay raises to those whose classes score in the top 25% on a standardized achievement test. Using the research literature, which alternative would you recommend as the most cost-effective plan for improving student learning?

FOR FURTHER READING

Chrispeels, J. H. (1997). **Educational policy implementation in a shifting political climate: The California experience.** *American Educational Research Journal, 34,* 453–481.

Chrispeels analyzes 10 years of curriculum reform legislation in California to determine which policy instruments were used. Her findings suggest that using multiple instruments to achieve the same goal improves the quality of policy implementation.

King, J. A. (1994). **Meeting the educational needs of at-risk students: A cost analysis of three models.** *Educational Evaluation and Policy Analysis, 16,* 1–19.

King uses cost analysis to determine the true costs of three intervention programs for at-risk children and makes recommendations based on her findings. Her study illustrates the usefulness of cost analysis.

Massell, D. (2000, September). **The district role in building capacity: Four strategies.** *CPRE Policy Briefs,* RB32.

Massell describes the four capacity building strategies most often used by school districts: (1) using data; (2) teacher in-service; (3) curriculum alignment; and (4) targeted interventions for underachievers. She also discusses the pros and cons of each.

Newmann, F. M., King, M. B., & Youngs, P. (2000). **Professional development that addresses school capacity: Lessons from urban elementary schools.** *American Journal of Education, 108,* 259–299.

Based on a study of nine urban elementary schools, the authors identify five ways to build school capacity through teacher in-service. They argue that the effectiveness of specific approaches is mediated by school context and that school leaders should be careful to choose appropriate programs for their setting.

Pruslow, J. T. (2001, November). **What do we spend to educate a child? The student resource allocation model.** *School Business Affairs,* 33–36.

Pruslow, an educational cost analysis specialist, describes a method for determining educational costs for individual students based on Levin's ingredients approach. He suggests that this method can be used for analyzing the costs of proposed instructional changes.

10

POLICY IMPLEMENTATION: GETTING PEOPLE TO CARRY OUT A POLICY

Focus Questions

Why is implementing new policies difficult?

What does research tell us about successful and unsuccessful implementation?

How can a school leader plan a policy implementation that increases the likelihood of success?

What courses of action are open to school leaders who are expected to implement a policy that they or important stakeholders oppose?

THE SURPRISING DIFFICULTY OF IMPLEMENTATION

In *Presidential Power*, Richard Neustadt (1960) tells how President Truman chortled about the transition from military to government leadership that General Eisenhower would have to make when he took office. " 'He'll sit here,' Truman would remark (tapping his desk . . .), 'and he'll say, "Do this! Do that!" *And nothing will happen.* Poor Ike—it won't be a bit like the army' " (p. 9). As an experienced political leader, Truman knew that the mere fact that a president, legislature, or court has promulgated a policy does not mean that people will immediately execute their orders; in fact, many official policies are never implemented at all, and many others are implemented only partially or incorrectly. Implementation can never be taken for granted. As with the other stages of the policy process, school leaders in charge of implementing a policy must think about what they are doing and plan carefully.

Of all the stages of the policy process, implementation is the one with which education leaders can least avoid involvement. Conceivably, they could work for years without contacting a member of the state legislature or paying attention to issue definition or agenda setting. But they cannot work for even one year in a leadership position without being required to implement a policy. Indeed, to a great extent their jobs can be summarized in two words: *policy implementation*. Whether a new attendance policy adopted by the school board, an interdistrict open enrollment law passed by the legislature, or federal grant money for vocational education—all are policies that others have chosen but education leaders must implement. Today, especially, with policy changes emanating from most state legislatures onto local school districts with amazing speed, education leaders must be prepared to guide districts, schools, and teachers through the often difficult task of changing to meet new expectations.

This chapter, then, explores policy implementation. Many policies are easy to implement. New regulations that involve only minor changes and can be easily enforced pose few problems (Murphy, 1990). Therefore, this chapter concentrates on more difficult implementation situations in which redistributive, capacity building, or system changing policies are involved. The first part of the chapter presents the research on implementation from the early 1970s until today and discusses the implications of this body of research for school leaders. The next section provides practical guidelines for implementing a policy. The final section addresses a dilemma that school leaders face more and more often: having to implement an unpopular policy or one that they find objectionable.

THE RESEARCH ON IMPLEMENTATION

Defining *Implementation*

Implementation is the stage of the policy process in which a policy formally adopted by a governmental body is put into practice. It is "the process of carrying out authoritative public policy directives" (Nakamura & Smallwood, 1980, p. 1). The major actors in the implementation arena are the **implementers. Formal implementers** are government officials who have the legal authority to see that a new policy is put into effect. In education, the formal implementers are often administrators who work in the U.S. Department of Education (USDOE) or in a state department of education (SDE). However, if a local school board has adopted a new policy, the formal implementers are the superintendent and possibly other central office administrators. **Intermediaries** are implementers to whom the formal implementers delegate the responsibility to help with implementation. They are all the people and groups who operate between the formal implementers and the point at which the policy impacts the target population, usually students. When the USDOE is implementing a policy, the intermediaries include SDEs, school boards, district administrators, and—most preeminently— classroom teachers. During the implementation of a policy that originated at the state level, the professional employees of local districts (both administrators and teachers) are the intermediaries. Locally developed policies are implemented by intermediaries such as building principals and teachers.

Successful implementation depends upon developing and maintaining both the **will** and the **capacity** of the intermediaries. The individuals and agencies who must cooperate in order to implement a policy must have reasons for doing so— in other words, they must be willing. Motivation can be encouraged in many ways, but formal implementers should never take it for granted. Moreover, motivation, although necessary for good implementation, is not sufficient. All the will in the world cannot overcome lack of capacity, or inability to do what the policy requires. As with will, formal implementers must constantly keep in mind the capacity of the intermediaries (McLaughlin, 1987).

A Rapidly Growing Field

In the preface to their 1971 case study, *Implementing Organizational Innovations*, authors Gross, Giacquinta, and Bernstein observed that "the implementation phase of the process of planned organizational change . . . has received little attention in the social science and educational literature" (p. v). However, 30 years later, in the preface to the third edition of *The New Meaning of Educational Change*, Fullan (2001) could assert: "the 'knowledge base' is becoming more profound and . . . is absolutely indispensable to dealing with the relentless ubiquity of innovation and reform . . . . Individuals [must] arm themselves with knowledge of the change process . . . . " (p. xii). In the intervening three decades, then, researchers have produced much new knowledge about how to implement policies in education settings. Today we can say, without exaggeration, that of all the stages of the policy process, implementation is the second best understood, after policy evaluation.

This implementation research grew out of practical concerns. In the 1950s and 1960s, the federal government provided new funding for numerous education reforms, such as revised science curricula and compensatory education for disadvantaged children. Naturally, federal officials wanted to know if these millions of dollars were achieving the intended results. Therefore, they commissioned quantitative evaluations of the programs. The results were surprising. Many of the statistical findings were so puzzling that researchers decided to observe what was actually going on at the program sites—in other words, they wanted to study them using qualitative research methods. They found that their statistical results were peculiar because many federal programs were nonevents. Nothing had changed because nothing was happening. This discovery stimulated research on implementation itself (Firestone & Corbett, 1988).

The implementation research can be divided into two generations. The first generation began to appear in print in the early 1970s; the second, in the late 1970s. Like the generations of a family, who are born at different times but continue to live side by side for decades, both generations of implementation research are very much alive today.

First Generation Research—The Difficulty of Implementation

Overview. First-generation implementation research focuses on the difficulty—in some cases the impossibility—of policy implementation. Researchers attribute the extreme difficulty of implementation to various causes. For example, after synthesizing several studies of Title I of the Elementary and Secondary Education Act of 1965 (ESEA), Jerome Murphy (1971) concluded that politics and federal bureaucracy had hindered the implementation of compensatory education programs. He found that the USDOE was woefully understaffed and, even if it had employed enough personnel to oversee implementation, agency workers probably would not have supported the goals of compensatory education for ideological reasons. His major conclusion was pessimistic: "The federal system . . . not only permits but encourages the evasion and dilution of federal reform, making it nearly impossible for the federal administrator to impose program priorities" (p. 35).

Other first-generation studies focused on cultural barriers rather than political ones. In his influential book *The Culture of the School and the Problem of Change*, first published in 1971 and reissued in 1996, Seymour Sarason argued that most education reforms fail because reformers do not take school culture into account. They devise new policies as if they will be implemented in a vacuum rather than in an institutional setting with more than a century of cultural traditions. One of Sarason's examples of misguided reform was the New Math of the 1950s and 1960s. Developed in universities (whose institutional culture differs markedly from that of schools), the New Math curricula were inconsistent with many of the most fundamental features of school life. The failure of this reform was predictable. Sarason's thesis inspired many later researchers to study how culture interacts with implementation efforts, posing difficulties.

In-Depth Look at a Typical Study. In the late 1960s, Gross et al. (1971) conducted a yearlong case study of an attempt to introduce a policy change in an elementary school located in the slums of a New England city. The reform required teachers to modify their pedagogy and classroom role. They were supposed to stop running teacher-centered classrooms and become "catalytic role models." "Catalytic" teachers "assisted children to learn according to *their* interests throughout the day in self-contained classrooms" (Gross et al., 1971, p. 12). Children's activities were supposed to include lots of "fun" learning kits and games.

Before they began their fieldwork, the researchers expected that the major barrier to implementation would be teacher opposition. On the contrary, however, all the teachers at Cambire School (a pseudonym) supported the innovation because it was consistent with the open education movement, whose ideals they espoused. Nonetheless, by the end of the year the teachers had lost their enthusiasm for the change. Almost all reverted to their former teaching methods. One commented in a May interview:

> I have to admit . . . I am failing to make as much effort as I was
> in the past because of my doubts about the assumptions and val-
> ues . . . and also the effect of this thing on the kids when you let
> them go. (Gross et al., 1971, p. 120)

In their analysis of the situation, the researchers identified five barriers to effective implementation. The first four caused the last one to develop. They were:

1. The teachers never really understood the change.

2. The teachers did not know how to use the new pedagogy.

3. The materials needed to establish open classrooms were not available.

4. The culture and institutional organization of the school were not consistent with the requirements of the new policy.

5. The teachers became discouraged and lost their motivation to implement.

Gross et al. (1971) concluded their book with a call for more research; over the next decades, hundreds of researchers responded.

Lessons From the First Generation.   The major lesson that first-generation research teaches is that implementation is difficult. Before the early studies of implementation appeared, many people assumed—like Truman's caricature of Ike—that when people receive authoritative policy directives, they naturally follow them. Nothing could be further from the truth. The fact that a government body has come up with a new policy does not mean that it will be followed. The implementers may not want to follow it, or they may not be able to. Moreover, change is hard and the status quo comfortable. Policies are implemented only if the formal implementers and the intermediaries are willing and able to work hard to put them in place.

First-generation research also suggests why policy implementations often fail. Indeed, the 1971 account of Cambire School contains in embryonic form all the major reasons that later studies confirmed. First, implementers frequently do not understand what they are supposed to do. Too often education policy changes are introduced at a short in-service session at the beginning of the school year. A pep talk by a consultant precedes the distribution of glossy materials to a room full of apprehensive teachers and principals. This approach leaves the intermediary implementers confused. At Cambire School, teachers had no idea what a "catalytic" teacher was supposed to do because they had never observed one teach. Not surprisingly, then, they were unable to behave "catalytically."

A second problem revealed by the first generation of implementation research is that intermediary implementers often lack the knowledge and skills necessary to implement a policy. The effective operation of an open classroom does not happen by chance. It requires a high level of planning and organizational ability. Yet, no one thought to teach these skills to the Cambire teachers.

Finally, first-generation implementation research underscores the critical importance of resources in implementation. The two key resources are materials and time. At Cambire, teachers lacked the abundant materials essential for running an open classroom. The problem was twofold: they did not have enough materials, and the materials they did have were of poor quality. Although the formal implementer had explicitly recognized the key role of materials during the planning process, he never made them available. Gross et al. (1971) do not explain why, but the most likely reason is that teaching materials—especially games and kits—are expensive. Probably the true cost of the program had not been calculated before implementation began.

Time is as important as are materials, and it, too, is a cost factor, as pointed out in Chapter 9. At Cambire, teachers were asked to take on many new tasks simultaneously. They were also required to do a great deal of additional paperwork. The effect was to increase greatly the length of their workday without increasing their salaries. Not surprisingly, then, by the third month of implementation, many of them were visibly "exhausted and short tempered" (Gross et al., 1971, p. 180). Fatigue and overwork undercut their motivation—the intangible cost of basing an implementation on the assumption that teachers will work extra hours to compensate for insufficient personnel.

The lessons from the first generation of implementation research have been available for more than 30 years. Researchers would like to be able to report that policy makers and implementers have learned them so well that they no longer repeat the errors of the past. Sad to say, this is not the case. In education, many contemporary policy implementations—perhaps most—continue to make the same mistakes that were made at Cambire School in the late 1960s, which is why the first generation of research is relevant today.

Second Generation Research—Analyses of Failure and Success

Overview. Second-generation research studies both successful and unsuccessful implementations, attempting to determine why some policies are fully implemented and others are not. The best known early research of this type was the Rand Change Agent Study, whose principal investigators were Paul Berman and Milbrey McLaughlin. In 1973, under contract with the U.S. Office of Education (USOE), Rand researchers began a multiyear investigation of the implementation of 293 federal projects in 18 states. Like first-generation researchers, the Rand team drew a largely negative conclusion: "In most cases, the innovations funded by federal seed money had not taken root" (Berman & McLaughlin, 1978, p. 12). Even so, they did find some success stories among the 293 projects. In the official report to the USOE, Berman and McLaughlin sought to explain these differences among the projects. They decided that successful implementation was not a mechanical process of following recipes from a policy "cookbook." Rather, a process of "mutual adaptation" had occurred in the successful projects. Mutual adaptation involved changes in both the implementers' behavior and in the details of the policy design, which was modified to fit local circumstances (McLaughlin, 1976). The Rand Change Agent Study clearly found that implementation, though difficult, was possible. Soon other implementation researchers began to report similar findings.

First-generation studies had suggested that the education policies put in place during the War on Poverty were failures that had made little impact on schools. However, in 1980, Kirst and Jung challenged this view. Thirteen years after the passage of the ESEA, they conducted research on the implementation of Title I compensatory education programs. They discovered that by the late 1970s substantial implementation had, in fact, occurred. They concluded that short-term implementation studies magnify the proportion of failures and argued that researchers should study a policy implementation over the course of a decade. Several years later Peterson, Rabe, and Wong (1986) further refined Kirst and Jung's thesis. They suggested that implementing Title I had taken a long time because it was a redistributive policy. Although its early implementation had been tumultuous, the quality of Title I implementation had improved significantly as the policy matured. They argued that because redistributive policies are complex, they are eventually implemented only if those who direct the programs are highly skilled (Peterson et al., 1986).

In 1990, Joseph Murphy reported on the implementation of a different set of education policies: the reforms of the 1980s, such as increased graduation requirements. Many policy scholars—drawing largely on first-generation implementation research—had predicted the failure of these reforms. Yet, after analyzing a large body of research on them, Murphy (1990) concluded that they had been implemented quickly and were already influencing schools in the United States. He understood this success as the result of the design of the policies. Most important, the policies of the 1980s were regulatory; therefore, they were easier to implement than the policies of the 1960s and 1970s had been. Moreover, they built on existing school structures and "emphasized quantitative increases" (Murphy, 1990, p. 35). These landmark studies and many others conducted during the 1980s and 1990s laid a solid foundation for understanding policy implementation.

In-Depth Look at a Typical Study.   In the late 1970s and early 1980s, Huberman and Miles (1984) conducted a USDOE-funded, three-year study of the implementation of various "school improvements." Although their study looked at 146 schools, they selected 12 schools for in-depth, comparative case studies. Their book, *Innovation Up Close: How School Improvement Works* (1984), reports their findings from these twelve sites. The schools were located "in rural, urban, and suburban settings in 10 states from Maine to California" (p. 1), and they achieved a range of results. Huberman and Miles concluded that two of the implementations were extremely successful, two were miserable failures, and the rest fell somewhere in between. They were not content, however, with merely chronicling success rates. Rather, they described their purpose in writing the book as "to show just *what happened* in the course of these school improvement efforts, to explain *why* it happened, and to suggest the *implications* for changes . . . elsewhere" (p. vi).

Consistent with the findings of the first-generation research, Huberman and Miles discovered that implementation—especially early implementation—was difficult. Common problems reported by teachers were similar to those observed 15 years earlier at Cambire School. At the sites where implementation succeeded, however, this painful early period eventually ended. After teachers had mastered the components of the change, they felt proud and self-confident. At the unsuccessful sites, feelings were quite different; discouragement and burnout were often reported. At the conclusion of the implementation period, the policy change had been institutionalized at the five most successful sites. It was there to stay. At the other schools, various scenarios were played out. Turnover in the project's leadership, the loss of administrative support, and budget crises were among the factors contributing to the demise or declining importance of the failed policies.

In their book, Huberman and Miles (1984) divided the 12 schools they studied in-depth into four "families": (1) highly successful implementations, (2) relatively successful implementations, (3) relatively unsuccessful implementations, and (4) unsuccessful implementations. The story of what happened in each family is illuminating.

Both **highly successful** implementations had been initiated by central office administrators who were deeply committed to the new program. Both projects were ambitious ones requiring substantial change in teachers' classroom practice. However, although much change was demanded, the new policy fit well into the district and was consistent with its philosophy. Although the central office administrators who advocated the innovation pressured principals and teachers to implement it, they offered strong assistance in the form of materials, training, and consultants throughout implementation. The researchers commented about these two schools: "Local administrators used muscle along with tutoring and tenderness" (Huberman & Miles, 1984, p. 277).

The four **relatively successful** schools followed a different path. Because the new policies addressed well-recognized problems in these districts, a crusading atmosphere developed among the teachers. They were strongly committed to making the programs work in order to solve the problems. Both central office support and leaders' preparation for implementation were adequate, but the real key to the success of these projects was the willingness of many teachers to work long hours to master new skills. Although district administrators exerted little pressure and also provided little assistance, the teachers in the schools helped each other a great deal. As time passed, however, many teachers experienced burnout and opted to weaken the innovations.

The four **relatively unsuccessful** schools had adopted modest policy changes that demanded little of them. Their district leaders, who had been supportive at first, quickly lost interest after implementation began. They offered little assistance, and when principals and teachers approached them with requests for permission to downsize their projects even further, they readily agreed. "The administrators 'helped' most by granting latitude to make changes," Huberman and Miles (1984) observed (p. 265). The result, however, was that the policy changes were never truly implemented.

The researchers considered two projects pitiful **failures.** In both instances, district-level administrators had launched policy changes as part of broader strategies for personal career development. Their programs were poorly designed, and these leaders were never really interested in implementation. They neither prepared carefully for implementation nor offered assistance to principals and teachers. Considerable resistance to both policies developed; the building principals spearheaded it. Before long, implementation ground to a halt. Huberman and Miles (1984) did not criticize the uncooperative principals, however. They concluded: "In a sense, these two 'failures' can be seen as a successful effort by users to protect their schools against poorly conceived ideas" (p. 269).

Lessons From the Second Generation. Like first-generation implementation research, the research of the second generation suggests that implementation is difficult. Many policies—perhaps most—are never really implemented. Among those policies that are not implemented, a watered down version is often put in place. Sometimes nothing changes at all. This means that the people responsible for an implementation can never take it for granted that those under them will put a policy into effect simply because they are supposed to.

Unlike first-generation research, however, the research of the second generation suggests that implementation is possible. Although in successful implementations a process of "mutual adaptation" occurs, which changes both the design of the policy and the behavior of the implementers, the core and the spirit of the new policy do take effect (McLaughlin, 1976). Success requires hard work and pressure. It may cause some implementers to burn out. But success can and does happen.

Most important, second-generation research suggests why some implementations succeed whereas others fail. Using carefully constructed quantitative and qualitative research designs, second-generation researchers have teased out many of the common characteristics of strong and weak implementation. As a result, making concrete recommendations to school leaders about how to plan and carry out a policy implementation is now possible. The rest of this chapter draws on both first- and second-generation research to suggest how to implement a new education policy and what to avoid.

HOW TO IMPLEMENT A NEW POLICY

Implementing policies is one of school leaders' most important tasks. Moreover, as the last section made clear, central office staff and principals play a crucial role in the implementation process; without their support implementations are likely to fail. This section, then, presents some general guidelines for implementing new policies. It describes the process chronologically, starting with mobilization for implementation, moving on to implementation proper, and concluding with the institutionalization of the new policy. A fundamental assumption is that the school leaders and other major implementers either support or accept the policy. The last section of this chapter addresses a more challenging situation: dealing with a policy that the leaders or other major implementers oppose.

Mobilizing for Implementation

Mobilization is probably the most crucial step in policy implementation; serious errors here almost always doom a project to failure. This section is therefore unusually long in relation to the other two sections, reflecting the author's conviction that investing time and energy in mobilization is important. Therefore, leaders who hope to bring about a lasting change should pay careful attention to each step of mobilization: policy adoption, planning, and the gathering of resources. They should also understand that mobilization is not a short phase; Huberman and Miles (1984) found that mobilization typically lasted 14 to 17 months.

Adopting a New Policy. Many readers are undoubtedly surprised by this heading. After all, much of Chapter 8 dealt with policy adoption. Although many new policies are adopted outside school districts and then passed down to them for implementation, new policies are often adopted at the district or even building level. For example, a central office staff may decide to recommend to the school board that the district's junior high schools be transformed into middle schools. Or a principal and her faculty may decide to establish a peer tutoring program. Other policies are initiated at the state or federal level, but are voluntary for schools and districts. Most policies based on inducements fall into this category. For example, a school or district might apply to its SDE for a grant to change from traditional to authentic assessment. In all such cases a local adoption process must occur, and it should be more than a decision by a small group of people who have the authority to impose their ideas on others. A misguided or faulty adoption process will undermine the entire implementation. In fact, poor approaches to policy adoption are a common cause of implementation failure. Therefore, school leaders who are considering adopting a policy should be sure that they can answer three key questions in the affirmative. If they cannot, they should alter or abandon their plans for policy change. The remainder of this discussion is organized around these key questions.

Motives for Adopting a New Policy. The first, and most important, question is, **Do we have good reasons for adopting a new policy?** The research on implementation suggests that both good and bad reasons for adopting policies exist. The worst reason for adopting a policy is that a few leaders want to build their reputations as innovators in order to advance their careers. Typically, when a policy is adopted as part of a career building scheme, the key leaders receive job offers in the middle of implementation and leave. When that happens, the implementation falls apart, leaving disillusionment in its wake. Even when the hoped-for jobs never materialize, such implementations are usually poorly planned and consist of more image than substance (Berman & McLaughlin, 1978; Fullan, 2001). Another poor reason to adopt a new policy is the belief that it will enhance the district's reputation as a progressive, cutting edge system. Innovation for the sake of innovation frequently fails because the implementers sense (accurately) that the new policy is just this year's fad. As a result, they never take it seriously. Innovation for the sake of innovation also creates an atmosphere of skepticism about all change (Fullan, 2001). Experts find that not attempting any policy change is better than adopting a new policy for either of these poor reasons.

Only two good reasons exist for adopting a new policy (Berman & McLaughlin, 1978). The first is that it will help solve a bona fide, well-recognized problem. For example, district leaders might choose to change from junior highs to middle schools in order to address the growing alienation of preadolescents. If they are able to articulate this genuine problem clearly and explain how the proposed policy change will address it, they should find that building support for adopting the new policy is relatively easy. Such support will improve the likelihood of a successful implementation. The second strong reason for adopting a new policy is to build the capacity of the implementers so they can eventually introduce other changes. For instance, a superintendent may decide that, in order to encourage the development of stronger leadership skills among teachers, the district should introduce site-based decision making. After some experience with decision making, the faculty will have, one hopes, developed the capacity for handling other changes, such as working in teams and mentoring beginning teachers.

Appropriateness of the New Policy. The second question leaders should consider before adopting a new policy is, **Is this policy appropriate for our school or district?** Finding new ideas about how to do things in schools is not hard. Every education journal, every education conference, and many politicians' speeches abound with suggestions. What is hard is determining which of these many possible policy changes are suitable for the specific context within which one works (Fullan, 2001).

Figure 10.1 lists the major issues that should be considered. Although all are important, two merit special emphasis. Some education leaders develop plans for policy changes as if they worked in a social vacuum. Learning about an exciting program that has achieved dramatic success in New York or San Francisco, they rush to put it into place in another setting—perhaps in a rural southwestern community or a small New England town. Of course, sometimes such transplanted policies work well. But often they do not, attracting the anger of the community, whose values have been ignored. Mirel (1994) recounts the story of such an attempted implementation in Illinois. The Bensenville school district was awarded a $1.5 million grant to develop and implement a "break-the-mold" New American School. However, the controversy that erupted from the teachers' union and the community revealed, a little tardily, that Bensenville was not interested in breaking any molds, which ultimately led to the withdrawal of funding.

Another common mistake is adopting a policy that does not match the resource level of a school or district. Analyzing the resources needed both to implement a new policy and to continue it over the long term is essential. As pointed

---

- Is the proposed policy consistent with the school's or district's vision statement or philosophy?
- Is it consistent with the school's or district's assessed needs?
- Is it consistent with the school's or district's priorities?
- Is it consistent with the level of available and potentially available resources?
- Is it consistent with the values of the community?
- Does evidence exist that it has been effective with student populations such as the school's or district's in terms of:
    —age?
    —racial or ethnic background?
    —gender composition?
    —socioeconomic class?
    —English language proficiency?
    —life experience?

Figure 10.1 Determining whether a policy is appropriate for a specific context.

---

out in Chapter 9, the resources needed are not just monetary. Issues such as the availability of extra time, volunteer workers, and space must also be thought through. When policies that do not match the resource level of the organization are adopted, one of two things usually happens. If the mismatch is very large, the implementation fails from the outset. Prestine and McGreal (1997) describe a case of this sort. Teachers in four schools were told to implement authentic assessment. However, this new policy was not appropriate to their situation. Although numerous problems existed, a major one was that the teachers' classes were already overloaded; they averaged 130 students each. They did not have enough time in the day to prepare for classes, teach all day, and implement authentic assessment for 130 students. As a result, the large majority of them never put it into effect.

Alternatively in such implementations, all goes well as long as the extra resources provided by a grant are available. As soon as the extra funding ends, however, so does the new policy. The implementers are left with a sense of futility and are likely to develop a reluctance to invest time and energy in future changes.

In trying to determine whether a policy is appropriate for their own setting, school leaders should consult several sources. An Educational Resources Information Center (ERIC) search may uncover articles and other reports on what has happened in places where the new policy has been tried. The SDE and professional associations may have useful information. Visiting schools and districts similar to one's own where the policy is already in place is especially helpful. By exploring these avenues, leaders should be able to gather enough information to determine whether a new policy is appropriate for their own setting.

Adequate Support. The third question leaders should ask themselves is, **Does the policy we are considering have sufficient support among key stakeholders?** Policy implementations are as political as policy formulation and adoption in a legislative arena; this means that a policy can be derailed by unwilling stakeholders as quickly as it can be killed in a hostile committee. Therefore, assessing the level of support the proposed policy enjoys is important (Berman & McLaughlin, 1978; Fullan, 2001). Above all, considering the level of support among the major implementers is essential. If members of a central office staff advocate adopting a new policy, they need to make sure that the principals and teachers who will have to implement it accept it. Principals play an unusually important role in implementation; ideally, they should strongly support any new policy they must implement. The support of teachers is not quite as crucial because they will often fall in line behind a principal who is convinced of the value of change. Even so, they are likely to resist any new policy to which they strongly object even if their principal supports it. Therefore, ensuring that the new policy is at least acceptable to most of them is important. Berman and McLaughlin (1978) found that top-down implementations "generally met with indifference or resistance at the school level" (p. 15).

On the other hand, if educators at the building level are the primary advocates of a change, assessing support is even more important for them than it is for central office staff. They must be especially certain that the central office and school board solidly backs their plans. Research suggests that implementing a policy change in the face of opposition from high-level management is almost impossible. Such policy adoptions usually remain "isolated . . . within the district," (Berman & McLaughlin, 1978, p. 15) receiving little assistance from central office staff. They are also likely to be among the first victims in a round of budget cuts. Depending on the details of the proposed policy, obtaining the support of other stakeholders, such as parents, social service agencies, unions, and students may also be necessary.

In determining the level of support, leaders should not merely guess. The adoption process should include an ongoing dialogue with all the groups and individuals who will be asked to play a role in implementation or who could derail it. Some of them may have to be persuaded. Many will not be willing to accept the exact change proposed but will suggest modifications of it; such negotiations are an important component of the adoption process. Leaders should put aside any notions that they know best and listen carefully to what other stakeholders say. As Fullan (2001) observes:

> Do not assume that your version of what the change should be is the one that should or could be implemented. On the contrary, assume that one of the main purposes of the process of implementation is to *exchange your reality* of what should be through interaction with implementers. . . . (p. 108)

Not until the proposed policy change has gone through this transformative process should leaders move to adopt it officially.

Planning for Implementation.   After making the decision to implement a new policy, leaders must plan the implementation. Although **planning** is essential, the research somewhat paradoxically suggests that leaders can also overplan (Fullan, 2001; Louis & Miles, 1990). Because detailed, long-range plans almost always represent the ideas of one person or a small group, such rigid plans are not likely to succeed. This does not imply, however, that leaders should embark upon a policy implementation with a casual "let's just see what happens" attitude. Rather, they should engage in what Louis and Miles (1990) call *evolutionary planning*. By all means they should have a plan, especially for the crucial first weeks of implementation, but they should be prepared to revise it as experience suggests needed changes. As the project evolves, they should modify their plan, adapting it in response not only to experience but also to changes in the environment such as altered levels of resources or shifting political configurations.

Who Should Participate in Planning? Two schools of thought exist about who should take part in planning a policy implementation. One approach is to form a large steering committee that represents all the stakeholders interested in the project. Such a committee would include administrators, teachers, parents, support staff, community representatives, officials from local government, and possibly students and social service workers. The other approach is to form a smaller steering committee, comprising a few people who have volunteered to work on the project and who are strongly committed to it. Both types of planning groups can succeed. However, the large, broad-based steering committee is most effective in settings where the stakeholders share a general consensus about education policy and work harmoniously together. In contexts with a history of conflict, the smaller committee will probably work best.

Regardless of which form is chosen, eventually it *must* include representatives of two key stakeholder groups: building principals and teachers. Because they will be the grassroots implementers, their input is essential. If they are unrepresented in the initial planning group, they should be added later as plans become more concrete. More than any other participants, they will understand both the opportunities and potential difficulties the policy change brings with it. If representatives of the school board and community are not included in the initial planning group, then systematic channels of communication between the planners and those two groups must be established at the start and maintained throughout. Otherwise, the steering committee will appear to be acting secretively (Louis & Miles, 1990).

Planning by Forward Mapping. The group in charge of planning should try to anticipate all the major prerequisites for beginning the implementation. This is not easy to do. Putting most new policies into practice requires first mustering a broad range of resources—such as materials, equipment, trainers, consultants, and suitable spaces. The exact nature of what is essential to the project is not always obvious during planning. Yet the absence of some resources in the early weeks of implementation can prove fatal. Therefore, school leaders are wise to anticipate as much as possible.

One technique for identifying implementation needs ahead of time is forward mapping (Weimer & Vining, 1992). The first step in forward mapping is developing a written scenario that describes what the new policy will look like when fully implemented. A scenario could be produced by the planning group as a whole, or one member could write it and then present it to the larger group for critique. Once the participants have reached agreement on the scenario, they use it as the basis for developing practical questions about it. Table 10.1 presents a short scenario that describes a fully implemented site-based decision-making policy and lists some of the questions it might generate.

These questions are then used by the group to develop a plan, which should be a general outline rather than a detailed blueprint. A sample, based on the scenario and questions in Table 10.1, appears in Figure 10.2. A tentative draft of the plan should be presented to all building principals and a representative sample of the teachers who will be involved in implementation. Because they will be the grassroots implementers, they know the real context for implementation better than anyone else and will be able to offer realistic advice. After their suggestions have been used to revise the plan, it should provide a useful guide for the next (and final) stage of mobilization. It may also provide some clues for things that will need to be done during implementation itself.

Gathering Resources for Implementation. The third aspect of mobilizing for policy implementation is **gathering resources.** As Table 10.2 indicates, many of the problems in implementation are caused by insufficient resources. In fact, of

TABLE 10.1 A Scenario With Practical Questions

Scenario	Practical Questions
*Principal** (1) Smith *checks her watch* (2) and then calls the *regular* (3) meeting of her school council to order. Almost all the *representatives* (4) are present, seated around a large *conference table* (5). "The meeting of the Maple Grove Elementary School Council is *called to order,*" (6) she announces. "The first *agenda* (7) item is the minutes of the last meeting. They were distributed to you last week. Do I hear a motion to approve them?" "*So move,*" (8) responds a teacher. This motion is seconded promptly and passed unanimously, but the meeting bogs down on the next agenda item, a change in planning periods. The upper- and lower-grade teachers *disagree on this issue and spend the better part of an hour discussing it, sometimes heatedly* (9). At length, however, *they reach a compromise* (10) that all can accept. At this point they decide to hold another meeting to discuss the rest of the agenda and vote to adjourn.	1. Should principals chair the councils? 2. When will these meetings be held? Will representatives need release time for them? 3. How often should meetings be held? Does a potential conflict exist with the master contract? 4. What groups should be represented and how should representatives be selected? 5. Do all schools have a room of the right size for council meetings and furniture appropriate for participative decision making? 6. How has the principal learned to use parliamentary procedure? 7. How much extra clerical time and materials will be required to prepare for meetings? 8. How have the teachers learned parliamentary procedure? 9. How have the teachers learned to be assertive and to manage conflict? 10. How have the teachers learned to negotiate their differences?

*Portions that have triggered questions are italicized.

all the major problems that principals in Louis and Miles's (1990) study mentioned, fully two-thirds of the major problems (lack of time, lack of money, inadequate staff development, and poor facilities) and one minor problem (lack of skills) related to resources. Moreover, several of the other problems were probably caused or made worse by resource shortages. A frequent cause of implementation failure is the lack of or unwise allocation of resources (Fullan, 2001; Louis & Miles, 1990; Miles & Huberman, 1984). This means that leaders who wish to bring about genuine policy changes must carefully analyze what resources will be necessary and obtain them both before and during implementation.

Money. This resource is important because it can be used to obtain other resources. Many policy implementations are supported by grants obtained from a government or a private foundation. Needless to say, grant opportunities should be fully explored. However, other sources of money may also be available. For

```
Planning for Governance Issues

1. Discuss parameters with superintendent.
2. Discuss parameters with school board president.
3. Based on (1) and (2), convene a governance committee.
4. Governance committee develops recommended governance document
   detailing: council composition, meeting frequency, chairmanship,
   (s)election processes, and so forth.

Planning for Staff Development Issues

1. Identify possible trainers in parliamentary procedure, assertiveness,
   conflict resolution, negotiating, and so forth.
2. Schedule preimplementation training sessions.
3. Discuss times for later training sessions.

Planning for Improving the Setting

1. Check available rooms and furniture in each building.
2. Discuss meeting times with superintendent and both contract
   managers.
3. Are release time or common planning periods or both possible?
4. Discuss clerical implications with clerical supervisors and selected
   secretaries.
5. Increase budget for clerical supplies as needed.
```

Figure 10.2 Plans for implementing site-based decision making.

example, by reallocating portions of the school or district budget, implementers may be able to free up funds. Area businesses should not be overlooked, either; some of them, especially those that have a partner relationship with the school or district, may be willing to contribute funds.

Although a certain amount of money is essential, many education leaders overestimate the importance of abundant fiscal resources (Berman & McLaughlin, 1978). Even more crucial than the total budget available is how money is spent. The research suggests that the best use of one's money is to pay for ongoing assistance for the implementers and to hire someone to direct the project. Providing modest salary supplements or stipends for a lot of people involved is wasteful (Louis & Miles, 1990).

Time. Time is another crucial resource (Fullan, 2001; Louis & Miles, 1990; Prestine & McGreal, 1997). Inevitably, all policy changes make great demands on the time of everyone involved. In part, this is because performing new behaviors is more time-consuming than acting in routine ways. Therefore, expecting that the implementers will spend additional hours each week working on the change project is reasonable. What is not reasonable, however, is expecting that they will work 12- to 15-hour days or devote weekends and vacation periods to it. Excessive demands of this sort are a sure recipe for failure. Therefore, when leaders muster resources, they must take steps to ensure more hours of work for the project than they can expect teachers and principals to add to their already full workdays.

TABLE 10.2 Implementation Problems Identified by Principals

Major Problems*	Other Problems*
Teacher time and energy	Lack of skills among staff
Money	Slow progress
Arranging staff development	Disagreement over goals
Ongoing communication	Maintaining interest
Limitations of facilities	Overambitious project
Teacher morale/resistance	Unexpected crises
	Competition with other new projects

*Problems are arranged in order of importance with the most important first.
Note. Based on Louis and Miles (1990).

This can be done in several ways. One is to provide some release time for key implementers. Employing part-time or substitute teachers is one approach. Another is to explore some of the innovative forms of scheduling that can be used to free teachers for team meetings or planning sessions. School leaders should try to avoid wasting the precious time of highly skilled employees on tasks that minimum-wage workers could easily perform. Teachers and principals should not be asked to set up meeting rooms, make coffee, stuff envelopes, meet consultants at the airport, or perform similar routine chores. Ideally, some funds are used to hire less-skilled people to perform such tasks. Alternatively, volunteer workers (if available) can be used. Solving the time problem is always a challenge, but a combination of realism and creativity will enable leaders to do so.

Personnel. Although few policy implementations can afford to hire large staffs, certain personnel are necessary in order to achieve even a modest change. One important personnel decision is the selection of a project director or coordinator. In their study of policy change in large urban high schools, Louis and Miles (1990) found that a major predictor of success was the presence of someone who had assumed major responsibility for the project. This person performed such essential tasks as monitoring progress, handling communication, and taking the initiative to solve problems. Louis and Miles recommended that the project director work at least half time on coordinating the implementation. Even where a half-time position is not feasible, specifically designating a director and providing at least some release time for him is advisable. Other necessary personnel are people to provide training and other forms of assistance to the implementers. The SDE, professional organizations, and universities are useful sources of people who can lead workshops or act as consultants. Because such people often have full calendars, contacting them early about a date for them to work with the implementers is wise. Training will be necessary just before implementation begins and also throughout the process, so more than one date will have to be scheduled.

Space. In Louis and Miles's 1990 study, two thirds of the principals who responded to their survey identified "constraints of the school's physical plant" (p. 146) as either a major or a minor problem during implementation. Such constraints can

```
_____  1. Classrooms are large enough for new teaching methods.
_____  2. Classrooms/offices have sufficient storage space for new
          equipment or materials.
_____  3. Classrooms/offices are wired for modern technology.
_____  4. Adequate office space can be provided.
_____  5. Secure storage areas for new equipment can be provided.
_____  6. Facilities are adequately maintained.
```

Figure 10.3 Checklist for assessing space needs.

take many forms: not enough classrooms; too small classrooms; substandard maintenance practices; and, in some cases, no space at all. At one high school, for example, the policy change involved hiring nine new counselors . . . but not enough space was available for them to have offices! These findings suggest that education leaders in charge of overseeing a policy implementation should not deem space issues too trivial to talk about. Inadequate or inappropriate space can seriously undermine the quality of an implementation. In assessing space needs, school leaders should have someone—preferably someone who will be a grassroots implementer of the project—visit each building that will be involved to assess space needs. If possible, visiting a site in which a similar policy has been successfully implemented and noting how space is used would also be helpful. The checklist in Figure 10.3 can be used to assess how appropriate the existing space is for the project and to determine how it needs to be altered.

Equipment and Materials. At Cambire School, the implementation of a new teaching methodology failed in part because of the lack of materials (Gross et al., 1971). Policy changes often depend heavily on the availability of specific machines and materials. For example, a policy that includes a computer-assisted instruction component will require the use of computers. In fact, it will probably require a large number of computers, and some of these will probably have to be rented, purchased, or borrowed from other programs. Sometimes the materials required by a new program are less apparent. A hands-on science curriculum may obviously require the gathering of wire, batteries, test tubes, and chemicals for experiments. However, the fact that each week students will have to use two or three photocopies of the lab sheets may escape some leaders. This program feature means that, in addition to the materials for experiments and projects, extra paper and copier toner will have to be ordered. Nor should extra wear and tear on copying machines be overlooked. Skillful implementers will make sure they order additional cases of paper and toner cartridges and provide funds for extra copier maintenance. Otherwise, the project could come to a halt in midyear when teachers can no longer reproduce the lab sheets.

Implementation Proper

Implementation itself should begin only after a solid foundation has been laid during the mobilization period. Implementing a new policy at a logical point in time, usually at the beginning of the school year or a semester, is best. This section considers implementation from two perspectives. The first is chronological. Implementation researchers usually identify two stages in the process, early and late, and each of these is described. Then several crosscutting themes relevant to both the early and late stages are discussed.

Stages of Implementation.

Early Implementation. In their comparative study of twelve implementations in education, Huberman and Miles (1984) found that the early months of implementation are invariably rough. Although solid preparation during mobilization does permit things to run somewhat more smoothly than they would otherwise, even well-prepared projects encounter serious problems. The reason for this difficulty is that the grassroots implementers must learn how to act in new ways. Even if they have been well trained, they have not yet had to actually perform the new behaviors day in and day out. Because they are learning, the implementers—usually classroom teachers—will most likely feel overloaded, tired, anxious, and confused. They will make many mistakes and wonder if they are failing. They may feel demoralized and depressed. Said one teacher in Huberman and Miles's (1984) study: "I got into it. I fell down and I had to pick myself up. That happened a lot of times. I'm just beginning to walk" (p. 73). Huberman and Miles found, however, that several factors helped teachers surmount their earliest difficulties and begin to experience some success. Not surprisingly, two of these were rooted in the mobilization stage: "the general degree of preparedness . . . [and] the provision of resources and materials" (p. 88). Also helpful was making ongoing in-service training available throughout early implementation and offering other assistance.

Unfortunately, some negative ways to help teachers survive this trying period exist too. In some of the districts, school leaders responded to complaints by agreeing to downsize the magnitude of the required policy change. These modifications in the adopted policy were not true mutual adaptations, but rather what Huberman and Miles dubbed *midgetizing.* By making the policy change smaller, leaders also made it less meaningful and worthwhile. Huberman and Miles comment: "Such 'midgetizing' eliminated most of the potential headaches but also threw out most of the potential rewards" (p. 88). They conclude that a smooth early implementation is actually "a bad sign" (p. 273). Although a rough start does not necessarily predict ultimate success, a smooth one does predict one type of failure—the failure that comes when a genuine change is transformed "into a modest, sometimes trivial, enterprise" (p. 273). Three factors stand out as predictors of ultimate success: (1) a rough start, (2) pressure by leaders to continue trying the new approach, and (3) ongoing assistance of various kinds. In short, the key to surviving early implementation with both the policy change and the implementers intact is a judicious combination of pressure and support.

Late Implementation. Not surprisingly, the nature of **late implementation** depends on the extent to which early implementation has been successful. In this case, *success* means making a genuine change in an education policy. As noted earlier, many implementations fail. Therefore, two scenarios are sketched here: (1) late implementation in failed projects, and (2) late implementation in "midgetized" and successful projects.

When a policy implementation fails, negative feelings are left in its wake; the onset of these feelings and the behavior that usually accompanies them signal the beginning of late implementation. Typically, failed implementations are characterized by much disappointment and discouragement. Burnout is often apparent. The implementers scale back their personal investments of time and energy at this point. Many revert to their earlier practices . . . if indeed they ever abandoned them. One common cause of negativism is the withdrawal of funding for the policy change. Other causes include resentment of a poorly designed project and anger at leaders. In many ways, things gradually return to the status quo, but in one important respect they do not. The next time the leaders suggest implementing a new policy, they will probably be met with cynicism, the usual legacy of a failed implementation (Gross et al., 1971; Huberman & Miles, 1984; Louis & Miles, 1990; Prestine & McGreal, 1997).

Midgetized implementations often enter the late implementation stage after five or six months; truly successful ones usually do not mature to this stage until about 18 months have elapsed. But in both, similar phenomena are apparent. The implementers now feel comfortable with the new policy and confident in their ability to use the new behaviors it requires. They also feel in control and proud of their accomplishments. During this stage they usually begin to refine the project and debug it. Some ineffective components may be eliminated and more effective ones substituted in their place. Implementers may write a manual describing some of the routines they have developed. They may adapt the policy for a different student population or they may begin to use some of its features in other parts of the curriculum (Huberman & Miles, 1984). One should not think, however, that by this point all problems should have been solved. Problems are less frequent and less severe than during early implementation, but they still exist. Nor should one expect otherwise. As Louis and Miles (1990) caution their readers, "Implementing serious change . . . is a problem-rich enterprise. . . . Problems of the program itself are easiest to solve; 'people' problems come next; and 'setting' problems of structures and procedures are most difficult to solve" (p. 272).

Thus, late implementation is not a time for school leaders to relax and congratulate themselves, even if their project has been successful. Problems still exist that they must face. Most of all, as we shall see, they must resolve some critical issues if their policy is to endure or be institutionalized.

Cross-Cutting Themes. Most studies identify three components that run through successful implementations from beginning to end: (1) monitoring and feedback, (2) ongoing assistance, and (3) coping with problems. Each of these is discussed below.

Monitoring and Feedback. In education, the sink-or-swim approach is an old tradition. Far too often, new teachers are shown the way to their classrooms and then left on their own to struggle to survive. Similarly, new principals are sometimes handed the keys to a building and told, "It's all yours now." Not surprisingly, then, many school leaders adopt this method when they find themselves in charge of an implementation (Louis & Miles, 1990). Although probably not an effective way to induct new educators, it is definitely not an effective way to manage a policy implementation.

Successful implementations depend on continuous **monitoring and feedback.** Someone—ideally a project director—should be responsible for keeping a close watch on the implementation process. This leader's monitoring task should include frequent visits to the site(s) involved and frequent conversations with implementing teachers. He should also regularly communicate what he learns to the central office and building administrators. In addition, a good project director coordinates actions to resolve problems. For example, the director might invite a consultant in to work with several teachers who are experiencing the same difficulty (Fullan, 2001; Louis & Miles, 1990).

Although the project director should manage the daily details of monitoring the project, school administrators should not remain detached from the implementation. The research indicates the importance of pressure from above in successful policy changes. This means that principals and central office leaders should not only stay well informed about the course of the project, but should also be visible at the sites where implementation is occurring. Their presence, questions about progress, and encouraging words will communicate an important message to the implementers about the seriousness of their efforts (McLaughlin, 1987).

A final reason exists for involving administrators. Principals and central office leaders should be actively engaged in the evolutionary planning process that characterizes good implementations (Fullan, 2001; Louis & Miles, 1990). Evolutionary planning requires flexibility and an experimental attitude, but it also depends on accurate knowledge about what is going on. Such knowledge cannot be gained by sitting at a desk; it can only be obtained by listening closely to the implementers and visiting them in the field. Only leaders who are in touch with the implementation will be able to revise old methods and develop new ones, making needed changes as the process unfolds. Their ability to respond to the dilemmas that emerge as the abstract policy confronts the concrete setting of the implementation will help guarantee that mutual adaptation occurs, rather than either midgetization or failure.

Ongoing Assistance. Although pressure is essential in successful implementation, so is support. Probably the most important form of support is **assistance** (Berman & McLaughlin, 1978; Fullan, 2001; Louis & Miles, 1990). "One of the clearest findings in recent research on educational improvement . . . is that it benefits sharply from assistance," write Louis and Miles (1990). An in-service program the week before the project begins is definitely not sufficient. People who are struggling to learn new ways of working need help, and that help should be "intense, relevant to local needs, varied, and sustained" (Louis & Miles, 1990). It should also continue throughout implementation—during the mobilization period; through the entire implementation, early and late; and until the completion of institutionalization. The only way leaders can know when help is needed and what kind it should be is by monitoring the project and gathering regular feedback as described earlier. As soon as the grassroots implementers begin to flounder or get confused,

```
Pre-start-up training
Follow-up sessions
External consultants
Internal consultants
External trainers
Internal trainers
Visits to other sites
Off-site conferences
Regular meetings with other implementers
Printed materials
Easing of schedules
Teaching aides
Demonstrations
Chances to exchange materials and tips
Workshops
Formative evaluations
A sympathetic ear
```

Figure 10.4 Seventeen types of assistance for implementers.

TABLE 10.3 Most Common Implementation Problems by Category

Program Related	People Related	Setting Related
Weak coordination	Unresponsive target population	Competition from other organizations
Delays	Lack of skills	Outside pressures
Conflicts	Negative attitudes	Unexpected emergencies
Lack of planning	Resistance	Powerlessness regarding key decisions
Contradictory goals	Skepticism	Physical environment Insufficient resources

Note. Based on Louis and Miles (1990).

school leaders at either the building or district level should make sure that they receive assistance. This help can take many forms; Figure 10.4 lists some of the most widely used. No single best type of help exists. What is essential, however, is that the assistance be relevant to the problems the implementers are experiencing.

Problem Coping. Multiple problems are inherent in every policy implementation. According to Louis and Miles (1990), they can be divided into three categories: (1) program related, (2) people related, and (3) setting related. Table 10.3 summarizes the most common problems of each type. Research suggests that program-related problems are the easiest to solve, whereas those that are setting related are the most difficult. However, the ultimate success of every implementation depends on how well its leaders can identify and cope with problems of each type.

Two general approaches exist to implementation problems. One is to consider them unwelcome intruders in an otherwise idyllic world and to refuse to see them (much less deal with them) until they have mushroomed into crisis proportions. The other is to recognize that problems are not unexpected intruders, but as a normal part of the process. This realization encourages skillful leaders to scan the implementation environment actively in order to detect problems in their earliest stages. They do this by speaking with the key implementers every day and welcoming open, honest discussion in meetings. As soon as they detect new problems, they begin to work to resolve them. They do not procrastinate or waste time looking for someone to blame. Nor do they eliminate problems by midgetizing their project (Fullan, 2001; Louis & Miles, 1990).

Leaders can find many ways to cope well with implementation problems. Louis and Miles (1990) found that in the most successful change, project leaders used a wide range of coping strategies and chose actions based on a deep, rather than a shallow, analysis of the problem. They also selected approaches that were appropriate to the specific problem with which they were dealing. Table 10.4 lists several ways to cope; they have been divided into three broad categories. **Technical** strategies involve carefully analyzing the problem area and targeting the necessary resources to it. **Political** strategies involve mobilizing power to encourage people to act in desired ways. **Cultural** strategies "focus on the shared beliefs, values, and symbols that are the key to the problem" (Louis & Miles, 1990, p. 272). Of the three, technical approaches are usually the most effective; political and cultural methods typically achieve moderate success. Good education leaders thoughtfully employ a mixture of all three.

TABLE 10.4 Methods for Coping With Implementation Problems

Technical	Political	Cultural
Break the project up into smaller parts	Create a representative task force to deal with problems	Have frequent discussions of project at meetings
Create task forces to work on problem areas	Mandate staff participation	Have frequent informal discussions with implementers
Phase in implementation gradually	Use incentives to encourage participation	Work to increase consensus on goals
Train staff to train other staff	Transfer unsupportive staff	Publicize the project
Tailor training to staff needs	Insulate implementation from community pressures	Work to improve organizational climate
		Use motivational techniques (e.g., slogans, t-shirts, etc.)

Note. Based on Louis and Miles (1990).

Institutionalization

The final stage of implementation is **institutionalization,** "the period during which an innovation is incorporated into the organization" (Gross et al., 1971, p. 17). A policy has been fully institutionalized when it has been seamlessly integrated into the routine practices of the school or district. No longer perceived as new or special, it has become "the way we do things around here." Institutionalization does not occur because it is the natural end product of implementation. It occurs because advocates of the new policy—most commonly district and building administrators—work deliberately to modify the formal rules and procedures of the organization in order to accommodate the policy change permanently. As with the other stages of implementation, it requires both thought and planning. Figure 10.5 provides a checklist about institutionalization. It can be used to assess the extent to which a policy has already been institutionalized, and it can serve as a planning guide, suggesting the next steps in the institutionalization process.

Although institutionalization is usually described as the third phase of implementation and is discussed last in this section, in practice it often overlaps with late implementation. Skillful leaders of a project should be alert throughout late implementation for opportunities to accomplish any aspect of institutionalization. For example, if the district's procedures for evaluating teachers come up for routine review, they should try to get them modified to make them more consistent with the new policy. Institutionalization is rarely accomplished all at once; it is usually a piecemeal process. If advocates of the policy are alert, early in the implementation they identify all areas of the organization's routine procedures that do not support their project. Therefore, as late implementation begins, they are ready to watch for opportunities to institutionalize their new policy a little at a time. They know when any of the inconsistent routine procedures are scheduled for review and read meeting agendas carefully to find other openings for needed changes.

Although all the issues in Figure 10.5 are important, the last one is especially crucial. Many policy innovations are made with temporary funding, often re-

---

_____	1. The policy is included in appropriate portions of the school board's policy manual.
_____	2. Necessary changes have been negotiated in the master contract.
_____	3. Teacher and administrator evaluation procedures are consistent with the policy.
_____	4. Student evaluation procedures are consistent with the policy.
_____	5. Necessary training in practices associated with the policy is included in the orientation and induction programs for new teachers and administrators.
_____	6. All cost items associated with the policy are included in line items of the district's/school's regular operating budget.

Figure 10.5 Checklist for assessing degree of policy institutionalization.

---

ferred to as *soft money*. As long as major components of the new policy are supported by such funds, it is vulnerable. Extra money may be available for special materials, supplementary staff, and release time during periods of financial prosperity. But few things are more certain than this: as soon as the business cycle turns downward, those special funds will be cut. This means that policy advocates must work conscientiously to move every essential component of their innovation from soft money to a line item in the regular budget of the organization. This will not be easy because as a policy change moves through late implementation, competitors from within the organization will probably surface, hoping to capture some extra dollars as the project comes to an end. The struggle to move the policy into the regular budget will probably be as difficult as any other part of implementation. Even so, only when it has been incorporated into the regular budget does the new policy have a chance to be fully institutionalized and, therefore, fully implemented (Firestone & Corbett, 1988; Huberman & Miles, 1984).

IMPLEMENTING UNPOPULAR POLICIES

Throughout the last section we assumed that no major groups of implementers, including the school leaders themselves, opposed the policy being implemented. Of course, this assumption is not always valid. Often policy changes are imposed by high-level administrators or those outside the school organization. In these cases large numbers of implementers—sometimes most or virtually all of them—may oppose the new policy. Dealing with opposition and resistance is one of the greatest challenges school leaders face. The challenge is compounded when the leaders themselves have serious reservations about the required change. Although no easy answers are ever found in these situations, this section explores the problem, explaining why opposition occurs and suggesting some ways to deal with it as well as with open and covert resistance. It also discusses occasions when school leaders feel that they too must take the path of resistance.

Why Some Policies Are Unpopular

Self-interest. Implementers are unlikely to support policies that they perceive as contrary to their own self-interest (McDonnell, 1991). In particular, they will almost certainly oppose changes that appear to threaten their job security, chances for promotion, or status in the workplace. For example, if a state legislature mandates site-based management throughout the state, central office administrators will probably not feel enthusiastic about it (Malen & Ogawa, 1988). They will suspect that as decision-making authority is devolved to school sites, their jobs will become unnecessary. No one should be surprised, then, if they resist implementing the policy even though their resistance may not be open. Another aspect of self-interest that often becomes important is the desire to maintain current compensation and working conditions. Readers may recall that in Prestine and McGreal's (1997) study, an outside organization insisted that teachers implement authentic assessment. Although authentic assessment requires considerably more time than traditional assessment, no one proposed raising the teachers' salaries or reducing class size. In effect, the teachers were asked to accept a longer workday without a commensurate salary increase. Not surprisingly, Prestine and McGreal found that teachers were skeptical of the value of the new policy and that "both across and within these schools, authentic assessment never achieved anything close to systemic implementation" (p. 390).

Professional Values. Educators are also likely to oppose implementing policies that conflict with their basic professional values (McDonnell, 1991). Grace (1995), an English researcher, describes such a situation in the United Kingdom. During the 1980s a number of government reforms changed the roles of both head-teachers (principals) and teachers. Previously, head-teachers had been expected to exercise pedagogical and moral leadership in their schools; however, government policy reforms dramatically altered their mission. By the end of the 1980s they were expected to work as managers in a competitive market environment, publicizing their schools' scores on examinations. Although some head-teachers made this transition easily, and even welcomed it, others experienced considerable difficulty because they disagreed in fundamental ways with the reform. Many of them dealt with the contradiction between their own understanding of their profession and the demands of new policies by downplaying those aspects of the reforms with which they disagreed. A few resisted openly, however, primarily by voicing their disapproval and completely ignoring some aspects of the reforms. For example, a primary school head-teacher stated, "One has to fight harder and harder to maintain one's professionalism as more and more is imposed from above. As a staff we resist 'jumping through hoops' and fix our own priorities within the parameters of the national curriculum" (Grace, 1995, pp. 104–105). Although the resistance of school leaders was usually relatively discreet, teachers in Great Britain sometimes acted more forcefully. For instance, in 1983 primary teachers boycotted a new government test. The British experience demonstrates that many educators are deeply attached to professional values and are unwilling to surrender them lightly. McDonnell (1991) argues that in the United States such value conflicts, whether recognized or not, are at the root of many incomplete or failed policy implementations.

Issues Surrounding Resistance

Exit, Voice, and Disloyalty. Weimer and Vining (1992), drawing on Albert Hirschman's classic *Exit, Voice, and Loyalty* (1970), argue that three responses are possible when asked to implement a policy with which one disagrees: (1) exit (leaving the organization), (2) voice (speaking up about problems), and (3) disloyalty (quietly or openly failing to conform to the policy). Of course, a single individual may combine these approaches. For example, a middle school principal who disagrees with a new district policy that creates excessive paperwork for teachers may first use voice. He may speak out at the superintendent's regular meetings with principals and schedule an appointment to discuss the issue with his immediate superior, the middle school supervisor. If these approaches fail, three courses of action are open to him.

The first is simply **compliance.** He may decide that the issue is not important enough to try exit or disloyalty and implement the new policy to the best of his ability, perhaps sympathizing openly with his teachers, but explaining to them that this is just the way things are. However, if his value conflict is very intense, he will have to consider the other two options. Various forms of **exit** are also possible. The principal may decide that this is a good time to retire or to initiate a search for a job in another district. Less satisfactory types of exit would include returning to classroom teaching or moving into a central office job that did not require implementing the new policy. If exit is not a feasible or desirable option, the principal may choose among various forms of **disloyalty.** While Weimer and Vining's (1992) term *sabotage* conjures up images of spies and terrorists, many less dramatic ways exist to sabotage a policy. The principal may prioritize the new paperwork and indicate to the teachers that he will require them to fill out only some of the forms. He may simplify or streamline the forms without obtaining district approval. He may close his eyes to various shortcuts devised by the teachers. All of these approaches constitute **token compliance** (Bardach, 1977). Or he may have the teachers do all the paperwork, but give them extra time to complete it, perhaps letting them use vacation periods to work on their already late reports. This approach is **delayed compliance** (Bardach, 1977). Outright sabotage includes fabricating the required reports or "losing" all of the necessary forms and directions. Obviously, all types of disloyalty are risky and some are unethical. Nonetheless, some people choose these courses of action when faced with implementing a policy they strongly oppose.

Coping With Resistance. Although the strategies of opposition described above were attributed to a principal, during an implementation any or all of the implementers in a school district or SDE may use them, from the chief state school officer on down. In fact, because much resistance is covert, school leaders should suspect its presence any time that one thing after another just "happens" to go wrong with an implementation. School leaders, then, must be prepared for resistance and should have devised some ways to head it off or to minimize its impact. One reason that it is essential to involve representatives of all the major implementers in the adoption process is that this approach reduces the likelihood of widespread resistance. However, even if a policy has been adopted through a participative process, some resistance may occur.

The first strategy to use with strong opponents of the policy is **persuasion.** Attempts at persuasion should be preceded by some nonjudgmental listening to opponents as they voice their objections. Next, school leaders should analyze these objections to determine the root of the problem. More often than not, opponents will feel either that their self-interest is threatened or that the policy change is inconsistent with their values. They may have objections on both counts. Possibly they do not fully understand the policy change, so their objections are partially or totally unfounded. In this case, the leaders of the implementation should provide them with more information, helping them to see that they really have no legitimate grounds for opposition. If attempts at persuasion are successful, then leaders should be sure to maintain good channels of communication with these people throughout implementation to detect other misunderstandings early.

Another possible approach is to modify the policy to meet some objections. Although leaders must be careful not to midgetize the policy change (Huberman & Miles, 1984), all policy implementations involve some mutual adaptation between the policy and the setting (McLaughlin, 1976). Modifications to meet the legitimate objections of some implementers may be part of the necessary mutual adaptation. Leaders should certainly be ready to consider this possibility, especially if it will considerably reduce resistance.

Finally, moving strong opponents out of the implementation or excluding them from the outset is often possible. This can be accomplished in several ways. Unhappy teachers and principals can be transferred to schools or grade levels not included in the policy change. Administrators who object can be moved into positions that are not crucial to the implementation, perhaps being promoted or assigned to another administrative position. If a group or office that is important to the implementation is a problem, supervision of the process often can be assigned to another, more supportive group. Sometimes creating a special steering committee to assume an oversight role may be necessary. When these methods are used, however, they must be used in a limited fashion and with respect for the law, the master contract, and the right of all individuals to hold dissenting views. Overuse of these approaches or a heavy-handed application of them can cause the people who are moved to appear as martyrs, thereby actually increasing opposition to the policy change.

Choosing to Resist. A school leader's decision to resist implementing a policy with which she disagrees is not one that she should take lightly. After all, resistance can lead to the loss of her job and professional reputation. It may irreparably damage her organization. It may take a heavy toll on family, friendships, and health. Nonetheless, sometimes it is necessary. Any notion that administrators are always obligated to obey orders from their superiors is contrary to most ethical systems and was declared invalid by the Nuremberg Tribunal after World War II. School administrators are not ethically obligated to obey every order; they are, however, obligated to carefully think through their situation, their motives, and the possible effects of their resistance before deciding to take such a strong stand.

Probably the first question that a school leader contemplating resistance should ask is this: "Is this objectionable policy just a symbolic one?" Symbolic policies are adopted for purely political, rather than substantive, reasons (Fullan, 2001). Legislatures sometimes adopt them in order to please a noisy constituency and encourage it to stop pressuring them. Presidents, governors, and other prominent leaders may push for a policy that they think will be popular and sound good in the publicity for their next campaign. The fact that the policy has been formally adopted does not necessarily mean that anyone cares much about its implementation. The implementation of symbolic policies is often pro forma—poorly planned, underfunded, and understaffed. This means that implementation almost always fails anyway. Thus, wise leaders should consider this possibility when faced with an objectionable policy. If it is symbolic, resistance will probably be widespread and individual acts of opposition will go unnoticed. Risks will be low, and leaders may find the best course of action is a quiet failure to comply. Symbolic policies are usually quickly forgotten, and within two or three years no one will even notice that noncompliance occurred.

If, however, the evidence suggests that the new policy was motivated by substantive reasons, resistance becomes more serious, especially if the degree of compliance will be aggressively monitored. In this case, leaders contemplating resistance must think through their own motives. The best motive for resistance is commitment to a professional, philosophical, or religious principle, especially one that directly relates to the best interests of students. Issues of self-interest must be carefully analyzed to determine if a bona fide conflict of interest exists and if perhaps the best interests of students do not outweigh one's personal self-interest. The worst reasons for resistance are dislike for the proponents of the policy, the desire to settle an old score, or a scheme to damage the career of one of the implementation leaders. Resistance arising from such questionable motives will probably backfire, damaging both the resister and the organization.

Finally, anyone considering resistance should think through the probable outcome. The basic question is, "Will resistance force the abandonment or major amendment of the policy?" Sometimes it will. Huberman and Miles (1984) write of a principal who blocked the implementation of a poorly conceived and pedagogically unsound curriculum change in his school. Far from considering the principal's actions wrong, they observe that although the implementation failed, the principal was successful in protecting his school from a potential policy disaster. However, many times, as in the schools in Great Britain that Grace (1995) studied, opposition changes nothing; the power balance is such that the implementation rolls right over all resistance. In such cases, resisting to make a point and defend an important principle may still be right. Or engaging in quiet token compliance while conserving one's strength for even more important battles may be wiser. Principled resistance to implementation should always be the fruit of much reflection and soul-searching. Leaders should be prepared to lose their jobs because of it.

FINAL POINTS

Implementation is an important part of the work of all school leaders and one that they often dread. They have good reason to dread it—the implementation of any new policy is hard work at best and an embarrassing failure at worst. However, today no good reason exists for failure in policy implementation. This is one of the best researched stages of the policy process; the standard errors are well-known; workable approaches have been identified and field tested. This means that as leaders begin to plan for the implementation of any new policy, they can and should have the confidence that comes from knowing they are entering a well-mapped territory. Today no excuse exists for failure; a good knowledge base, combined with thought and planning, will lead to success in this difficult endeavor.

QUESTIONS AND ACTIVITIES FOR DISCUSSION

1. Reflect on the implementations in which you have been involved. Which ones went smoothly? Why? What errors were apparent in those that encountered serious difficulty?

2. Assume that you work in an SDE and that next year you will be involved in implementing a statewide voucher plan. Using a scenario and forward mapping, develop a tentative plan for this implementation.

3. Assume that you are going to lead the implementation of portfolio assessment in your district. Identify the resources that will be needed and develop a plan for gathering them.

4. Select one of these policies: site-based management, vouchers, inclusion, or detracking. Be prepared to discuss the value conflicts that some educators might feel when implementing this policy and the types of resistance they might try.

INTERNET ASSIGNMENT

Using a search engine such as AltaVista, Google, or HotBot, search the Internet for implementation *and* No Child Left Behind Act, *or another recent federal education law. Explore several of the sites you located and be prepared to report to your class on what you found.*

CASE STUDY

THE REFORM THAT WENT AWRY

In the mid-1980s, the state of Tennessee set out to change its curriculum policy for elementary schools. Committees dominated by college professors, SDE officials, and representatives of wealthy city districts developed the new policy, which was called the Basic Skills First Program (BSF).

These committees devised a comprehensive system for monitoring student progress in the basic skills. The mathematics and reading components alone included seven manuals, 112 tests, 180 individual student charts, and 15 pages of class record sheets for each grade. Teachers' record-keeping work was supposed to be facilitated by computers. However, the state provided only one computer per school, and it arrived five months after implementation had begun. The SDE did offer computer training, however: a two-hour session for one representative from each school. This person was supposed to go back and teach the others how to enter the data in the special software developed for BSF.

The state's teachers, who enjoyed making jokes about the program's acronym, did not enjoy the prospect of doing the many extra hours of paperwork that full compliance would require. In fact, because many of them had neither planning periods nor duty-free lunch periods, they deeply resented the state's new demands on their time. Eventually, most decided not even to do the BSF record keeping. They had divided the number of teachers in the state by the number of monitors for the program and figured out that at most they would be monitored once every three years. Moreover, they had detected a distinctly cool attitude toward BSF among their principals and superintendents, too.

In Nashville, SDE officials and politicians knew that the BSF implementation was not going as it should but blamed the traditionalism of Tennessee teachers. They did not think to blame themselves.

Note. Based on Fowler (1985).

QUESTIONS

1. Identify the errors that the Tennessee SDE made during the adoption stage of this policy.
2. How could the SDE have modified its approach to increase the chances of a successful implementation of BSF?
3. Using the premise that successful implementation requires creating and sustaining the will and the capacity of the implementers, analyze the weaknesses of this implementation effort.
4. Describe the forms of resistance Tennessee educators used and explain the role school administrators played in this resistance.

NEWS STORY FOR ANALYSIS: **PASCO PONDERS TEACHING ISSUE: PARAPROFESSIONALS FACE NEW FEDERAL STANDARDS**

Land o'Lakes, FL—A federal mandate to improve the qualifications of teacher assistants who work with low-income children concerns Pasco County School officials. They say the intent is good, but the implementation could prove difficult and costly.

Under the No Child Left Behind Act of 2001, new paraprofessionals hired at Title I schools must hold at least an associate degree, or take a test to demonstrate they meet a "rigorous standard of quality" for assisting in teaching reading, writing, and mathematics. Paraprofessionals already employed in Title I schools must meet the new standards within four years. Paraprofessionals assist teachers by tutoring students or by helping with other classroom duties.

Seventeen of Pasco's 56 schools are Title I schools. Just 44 of the paraprofessionals they employ meet the new requirements, while about 220 don't, said Kathleen Vito, the district's Title I supervisor. Schools are given the Title I designation, which qualifies them for extra money from the federal government, when they have a high number of students from low-income families. The federal government mandated the new paraprofessional requirements to make sure the nation's poorest children aren't receiving much of their instruction from unqualified adults, school officials told Pasco County School Board members during a workshop last week. "I don't think there's anything wrong with that intent," said Susan Rine, the district's administrative assistant for elementary schools. "If you're going to teach someone to read, you need to know how to read." But officials say the district may need to revisit the $6.50-an-hour starting salary for paraprofessionals if it wants to attract people with the education level now required. School districts are also waiting to get clarification on what kind of test would qualify as rigorous enough to allow paraprofessionals to bypass the two-year requirement, Assistant Superintendent Sandy Ramos said.

The act didn't change the qualifications for paraprofessionals at schools that don't receive Title I money. But Assistant Superintendent Sandy Ramos and the Title I supervisor said they would recommend that the school board implement the more stringent qualifications at all schools so that requirements are uniform throughout the county. Ramos said the district could grandfather in paraprofessionals already working at non-Title I schools, but make the higher qualifications a requirement for any new people hired. But board member Marge Whaley expressed skepticism about whether the district could find enough job candidates who meet those qualifications.

(Used by permission of the publisher. From R. Blair, "Pasco Ponders Teaching Issue: Paraprofessionals Face New Federal Standards," *Tampa Tribune*, April 21, 2002, Pasco Section, pp. 1, 5. Copyright 2002 by the *Tampa Tribune*.)

Questions

1. What policy values are implicit in the portion of the No Child Left Behind Act discussed here?
2. To what extent does the Pasco County School District have the will and the capacity to implement this new policy?
3. Discuss resource differences among districts and how these might affect implementation.
4. What do you think will happen if the school district is unable to find enough qualified job candidates for positions as teachers' assistants?

FOR FURTHER READING

Berman, P., & McLaughlin, M. W. (1976). **Implementation of educational innovation.** *Educational Forum, 40,* 345–370.

> This article is a shortened version of the major findings of the Rand Change Agent Study and provides a good introduction to this influential early investigation of policy implementation in education.

Jacob, B. (2001). **Implementing standards: The California mathematics textbook debacle.** *Phi Delta Kappan 83,* 264–272.

> Jacob describes in fascinating detail the heavy-handed, top-down manner in which California implemented a part of its new "standards-aligned" mathematics curriculum. His story reveals the impact of politics and ideology on a statewide policy implementation.

Pankake, A. M. (1998). *Implementation: Making Things Happen.* **Larchmont, NY: Eye on Education.**

Part of the publisher's School Leadership Library, this short volume is a practical guide to implementation for building administrators. It covers such topics as routine and nonroutine implementation, coordinating implementations, and monitoring an implementation.

Prestine, N., & McGreal, T. L. (1997). Fragile changes, sturdy lives: Implementing authentic assessment in schools. *Educational Administration Quarterly, 33,* **371–400.**

The authors recount an attempt to implement authentic assessment in the Essential Schools of a midwestern state. Failure to provide adequate resources and assistance contributed to poor implementation.

Tyack, D., & Tobin, W. (1994). The grammar of schooling: Why has it been so hard to change? *American Educational Research Journal, 31,* **453–479.**

In this article the authors analyze five school reform policies from U.S. history including two that succeeded and two that failed. They conclude that those who would implement new policies in schools must take their underlying organizational patterns into account.

POLICY EVALUATION: DETERMINING IF THE POLICY WORKS

Focus Questions

Why should education leaders be knowledgeable about policy evaluation?

How can one tell if a proposed or completed evaluation is of high quality?

Why are evaluations always political?

How can a leader facilitate the evaluation process?

A NERVOUS-MAKING TOPIC

Evaluation is an integral part of the professional lives of all educators. Teachers regularly evaluate students; principals regularly evaluate teachers; and, increasingly, administrators themselves are subjected to regular evaluation. Broader forms of institutional evaluation are also common. Accrediting teams visit schools and districts, observing, interviewing, and collecting data. Many states have established **indicator systems** in order to gather information from school districts in dozens of performance areas, analyzing and comparing these figures, and then issuing official reports on their findings. In some cases state departments of education (SDEs) even use evaluation results to categorize districts, perhaps labeling them *excellent, effective,* or *deficient* and attaching rewards and sanctions to those labels. An age of accountability such as our own is inevitably an age of evaluation.

Not surprisingly, then, policies are often evaluated, too. In an ideal world, not only would all policies be thoroughly and fairly evaluated; but policy makers would also act on evaluation findings, modifying or terminating policies on that basis. Of course, our world is far from ideal. As a result, many policies are never evaluated at all; some are evaluated poorly; and, although some others are evaluated carefully, no one ever acts on the findings. But sometimes, of course, the final stage of the policy process unfolds as it should: after an appropriate length of time, the new policy is carefully evaluated and then either maintained as it is, changed, or terminated.

Like every other stage of the policy process, evaluation is difficult, in large part because it is political; the major reason is that it threatens people. Stufflebeam (1983), a leader in education evaluation in the 1960s, 1970s, and 1980s, observed that Michael Scriven, another leader in education evaluation, "once said that 'evaluation is nervous making,' and it is. I have often been reminded of the biblical warning to 'Judge not, lest ye be judged' " (p. 140). This means that school leaders cannot take a smooth, problem-free policy evaluation for granted any more than they can take a smooth, problem-free implementation for granted. But neither can effective leaders avoid or ignore policy evaluation. Stufflebeam continues:

> We cannot make our programs better unless we know where they are weak and strong. . . . We cannot plan effectively if we are unaware of options and their relative merits; and we cannot convince our constituents that we have done good work and deserve continued support unless we can show them evidence that we have done what we promised and produced beneficial results. For these and other reasons, public servants must subject their work to competent evaluation . . . . (p. 140)

As public servants, then, education leaders must expect to be active participants in policy evaluation. Sometimes they will have to provide leadership while a school or district policy is undergoing evaluation. On other occasions they may have to plan and implement an evaluation themselves. In either case, they need to know how and why policies are evaluated.

Chapter 11 provides a knowledge base about some of the fundamental issues in policy evaluation and offers recommendations about making key decisions regarding it. Chapter 11 will not, however, provide detailed directions for designing and executing an evaluation. Many books are available on this subject, some of which are suggested at the end of this chapter. Instead, this chapter offers background for understanding the general principles of evaluation and the choices that must be made as evaluations are implemented. In order to accomplish these goals, some definitions and a brief history of education policy evaluation are provided first, followed by discussions of the general characteristics of policy evaluations, the politics of evaluation, and ways to facilitate a meaningful evaluation. The last section discusses acting on the findings of an evaluation.

DEFINITIONS ASSOCIATED WITH POLICY EVALUATION

As with any specialized field, policy evaluation has developed its own language, and its practitioners use professional terminology that may not be familiar to outsiders. This section defines four key terms: (1) *evaluation,* (2) *project,* (3) *program,* and (4) *stakeholder.*

Evaluation is "the systematic investigation of the worth or merit of an object" (Joint Committee on Standards for Educational Evaluation [Joint Committee], 1994, p. 3). A policy evaluation is a type of applied research in which the practices and rigorous standards of all research are used in a specific setting for a practical purpose: determining to what extent a policy is reaching its goals.

Policies are often first put into effect through **projects,** which are "educational activities that are provided for a defined period of time" (Joint Committee, 1994, p. 3). For example, when the federal government adopted compensatory education as a national policy, it funded short-term Head Start and Title I projects in many school districts. When projects are institutionalized, they become **programs:** "educational activities that are provided on a continuing basis" (Joint Committee, 1994, p. 3). Thus, most districts have an ongoing reading program or professional development program that reflects their basic policies in these areas. These programs are often based on earlier projects.

In any evaluation, a number of **stakeholders** exist: "individuals or groups that may be involved in or affected by a program evaluation" (Joint Committee, 1994, p. 3). In a school system, major stakeholders generally include teachers, administrators, support staff, students, parents, the teachers' union and other unions, school board members, and any important interest groups.

A BRIEF HISTORY OF EDUCATIONAL POLICY EVALUATION

Early Evaluation

Evaluation has been defined as "the systematic assessment of the worth or merit of some object" (Stufflebeam, 1988, p. 571). Because the phrase *systematic assessment* has a contemporary ring to it, assuming that educational evaluation is a recent phenomenon would be natural. This is not true, however. In the United States, educational evaluation can be traced to pre–Civil-War Boston where Horace Mann and the board of education gathered examination data in order to compare schools. In the late 1880s, the first large-scale educational evaluation was conducted by Joseph Rice, who used test scores from many districts to evaluate spelling instruction. Because Rice found that children who spent 200 minutes a week on spelling drills scored no better than those who spent only ten minutes, the teaching of spelling changed across the country. The development of standardized testing during the first quarter of the twentieth century made evaluating schools and districts by comparing test scores even easier. In the 1930s, educational evaluation as we know it began to come into its own when

Ralph Tyler, then a professor at Ohio State, directed the Eight-Year Study, a comparative evaluation of the college performance of graduates of progressive and traditional high schools. Tyler's idea that educational programs should be evaluated in terms of their objectives was widely influential, encouraging most of the evaluators who followed him to adopt the same perspective (Madaus, Stufflebeam, & Scriven, 1983; Popham, 1988).

The War on Poverty

The passage of the Elementary and Secondary Education Act of 1965 (ESEA) was a watershed event in educational evaluation. Because this law represented an unprecedented outlay of federal funds for education, some lawmakers, including Senator Robert Kennedy, insisted that it contain language mandating evaluation. As a result, Titles I and III of the ESEA required that every program funded under their provisions be evaluated; reports of the findings were to be sent to the federal government. Because of the ESEA, educational evaluation became a growth industry. Several people who eventually made major reputations in policy evaluation, such as Michael Scriven and Robert Stake, actually switched from other fields into this one in order to participate in this unusual opportunity to develop and refine the evaluation of education policies.

Over the next decade thousands of evaluations were conducted by enthusiastic recruits to the field. Soon their enthusiasm waned, however, for their results were disappointing. When their findings were not contradictory, they were negative. As indicated in Chapter 10, one result was that education researchers began to look more closely at implementation. Another was that people began to take a closer look at evaluation. Early Title I evaluations had used standardized test scores as indicators of program success; experience quickly revealed that these tests inadequately measured the progress of disadvantaged children. The situation became so serious that in 1971 the education honorary, Phi Delta Kappa (PDK), established a national committee to study educational evaluation. Concluding that the field was in crisis, the committee recommended that new evaluation methods be developed (Madaus et al., 1983; Popham, 1988).

The Professionalization of Evaluation

About 1973, evaluation began to mature as a field and to emerge as a distinctive profession within education. One sign that the discipline was coming of age was the establishment of several professional journals, including *Educational Evaluation and Policy Analysis* and *Evaluation Review*. Another was the publication of numerous books, including textbooks, on evaluation. Many universities began to offer courses in evaluation, and a few even established graduate concentrations in it. Moreover, the federal government and several major universities established centers to conduct research and development in policy evaluation. The existence of these forums for discussion facilitated the exchange of research findings and the development of new approaches to evaluation, as recommended by PDK. During the next fifteen years, numerous evaluation "models" were developed and tested in the field. By 1983, Madaus et al. were able to include chapters on ten different "models," including Stufflebeam's CIPP Model, Provus's Discrepancy Evaluation Model, and Eisner's Connoisseurship Model in their book, *Evaluation Models*. At the end of the decade, Popham (1988) observed:

> Although devout kitten-lovers may be offended by the notion, there is substantial truth embodied in the adage that "there is more than one way to skin a cat." Similarly, there is more than one way to conduct a defensible educational evaluation. (p. 21)

Today, education leaders who want to know how well a policy works are in a very different situation from that of their predecessors in the 1960s and early 1970s. Policy evaluation is a well-established field with numerous professional practitioners and a wealth of experience. Whether the policy in question is a national one or confined to a single school building, it is possible to determine with a fair degree of accuracy how well it is accomplishing its objectives. Increasingly, SDEs routinely collect data for use in assessing the performance of the state as a whole, of districts, and even of individual schools. Increasingly, too, education administrators are expected to have some practical knowledge of evaluation and to be able to use it. Evidence for this trend is the fact that in the mid-1990s, both the Association of Supervision and Curriculum Development (ASCD) and PDK published handbooks for district and building leaders who need to conduct an evaluation (Beyer, 1995; Brainard, 1996). Educational policy evaluation has clearly moved out of universities and policy centers and into the daily lives of practicing educators.

CHARACTERISTICS OF POLICY EVALUATIONS

The Evaluation Process

Whether a large national organization evaluates a policy in fifty states or a building principal evaluates a program in a single school does not matter: All policy evaluations follow the same general procedures. These are briefly summarized in this section and in Figure 11.1. The first step is to determine as precisely as possible the **goals** or **objectives** of the policy. After all, as Ralph Tyler pointed out more than sixty years ago, it is legitimate to evaluate a policy only in relationship

```
1. Determine the goals of the policy
2. Select indicators
3. Select or develop data-collection instruments
4. Collect data
5. Analyze and summarize data
6. Write evaluation report
7. Respond to evaluators' recommendations
```

Figure 11.1 Basic steps in the policy evaluation process.

to the goals that it is supposed to achieve (Madaus et al., 1983). As an example, if the objectives of a district's new award system are to improve student attendance and morale, then evaluators should assess only the extent to which those two goals have been attained. The impact of the policy on other aspects of school activity—such as test scores—is irrelevant. Because whether objectives have been reached is usually not readily apparent, evaluators must next select **indicators,** which are measurements or signs that a goal has been reached. In evaluating the award system, for example, comparative attendance figures for five years and scores on a school climate survey administered at the beginning of each year of implementation might be selected as indicators.

The third step in conducting an evaluation is to select or develop **data collection instruments.** In assessing the award system, evaluators might develop a form to use for recording data from district attendance records for the last five years. They might also select a commercially available survey of school climate to administer to all students. Next, the evaluators **gather data.** In studying the award system, someone would have to locate attendance records and transfer relevant information from them to the form prepared for that purpose. Someone would also have to administer the school climate survey each time it was given. After the data have been collected, they must be analyzed. Numerical data (such as test scores) are usually analyzed statistically; means, ranges, and frequencies are calculated and used to determine if any differences are statistically significant. Such findings are often summarized in the form of graphs, trend lines, and tables. Verbal data (such as interview transcripts) are usually analyzed by identifying recurrent themes in the entire set of transcripts and coding them so that all the occurrences of each theme can be located. Computer programs are available for analyzing both numerical and verbal data.

After the data have been carefully analyzed, the evaluators **write a report,** presenting their findings and making recommendations based upon them. For instance, an evaluation of the awards system discussed throughout this section might reveal that attendance has improved since the awards policy was implemented but that student morale has not. The evaluators might, then, recommend that the awards be continued but that another approach be tried for raising morale. After district leaders receive the report, they should use it to either modify the policy or terminate it (Brainard, 1996; Nakamura & Smallwood, 1980).

Criteria for Judging Evaluations

Although evaluations are designed to judge the effectiveness of policies, they can be evaluated themselves. In fact, education leaders need to know how to assess the quality of a proposed or completed evaluation. If they have contracted for an evaluation to be implemented, they need to know if the recommended research design is sound. If they are using a completed evaluation, they need to be able to determine how seriously to take it. In 1975, to meet the need for recognized criteria for evaluation, 12 research associations established a joint committee, assigning it the task of developing standards for assessing educational evaluations; the result of its work was published in 1981. Revised during the early 1990s to reflect new trends in evaluation, the most recent version appeared as *Program Evaluation Standards* in 1994. The 30 standards were grouped under four broad categories, which serve as general criteria: (1) **usefulness,** (2) **feasibility,** (3) **propriety,** and (4) **accuracy.** This section, drawing heavily on *Program Evaluation Standards*, discusses each of these four criteria (Joint Committee, 1994).

Usefulness. In order to be useful, an evaluation must be conducted by an individual or team well qualified to do evaluations. Qualified people include consultants who work for evaluation firms, college professors, and workers in district or SDE research offices; however, regardless of where an evaluator works, her individual credentials should be carefully scrutinized.

The usefulness of an evaluation also depends to a great extent on stakeholder identification and the collection of meaningful data. Early in the study, a good evaluator identifies all the stakeholders, the people and groups involved in the program under study or those that might be affected by the outcome of the evaluation. Representative stakeholders should be interviewed so that their needs can be identified at the outset and addressed throughout the evaluation process. Moreover, data sources that are relevant to their needs should be selected. All data gathered should relate to the major purposes of the evaluation; information sources should not be used just because they are convenient or inexpensive, but because they help answer questions important to the stakeholders.

Interim and final evaluation reports should also be useful. They should be written in clear language that the stakeholders can understand and should avoid overly technical words and incomprehensible statistics. If necessary, different versions should be prepared, expressed in the various languages of the stakeholders. For example, a version designed for central office administrators might include more technical words and graphs than a version aimed at a parent group. All reports for all audiences should include adequate information about the policy under study and the general design of the evaluation. The major findings should be clearly related to practical situations, and all recommendations should be specific rather than general. Finally, reports should not be excessively long and should include an executive summary at the beginning.

Feasibility. The second criterion is feasibility; the evaluation must be doable without imposing unreasonable strains on the school or school district. An important aspect of feasibility is practicality. The evaluation should be designed so that it can be completed within the required time frame and implemented without unduly disturbing the professional responsibilities of the educators who are involved. An evaluation that requires that learning come to a halt for a week or two so that interviews can be conducted or tests administered is not practical. Another dimension of feasibility is political. As suggested at the beginning of this chapter, evaluations are "nervous making"; nervous people are more likely to try to block portions of the study in order to protect themselves or their jobs. This means that evaluations are always political. A good evaluation does not ignore this fact, but rather plans the evaluation with this in mind. One way to minimize the political controversy that often erupts around an evaluation is for the evaluators to meet with all the interest groups and stakeholders during the planning process to discuss their concerns and hear their suggestions. During the evaluation, leaders must also avoid favoring, or appearing to favor, one group over another in interviewing, observing, collecting data, and so on. Moreover, evaluators with good political skills are careful to maintain communication with all stakeholders throughout the process so that no one has any unpleasant surprises when the final report is issued. Finally, a feasible evaluation is financially responsible. It has a definite budget, which is sufficient to carry out the study but not exorbitant in relation to the environment.

Propriety.   Issues of propriety are legal and ethical; a good evaluation must conform to accepted norms for research. First, evaluators selected should not be in a conflict of interest situation regarding the study. They should not have a personal, professional, or financial interest in the outcome of the evaluation, nor should they be close friends of any of the people who wish to commission the evaluation. Next, a written contract should be signed between the evaluator(s) and the organization commissioning the study, spelling out the purposes of the research, what it is to entail, and when it is to be completed. Evaluators should respect the rights of human subjects as they conduct their work, maintain appropriate confidentiality, and inform each participant of the purposes of the research. Moreover, they should be careful to treat everyone courteously and to solicit a range of opinions, not allowing themselves to be blinded by individuals' status in the organization, race, gender, or age. The final report should fully disclose the findings of the evaluation, even if evaluators include the discovery of financial fraud or other questionable behavior.

Accuracy.   Finally, an evaluation should be accurate. In order to produce an accurate report, evaluators must first study the context in which the policy has been implemented, familiarizing themselves with its cultural and socioeconomic characteristics. In their report, they should provide enough detail about their sources of information that readers can determine the value of their information and thus of the conclusions based upon it. Data collection should be systematic rather than haphazard, drawing on a range of sources. In the report, evaluators should explain exactly how they reached their conclusions and specify the data upon which each conclusion is based.

Purposes of Evaluations

Summative Evaluation.   Policy evaluations can serve at least four purposes. Many are **summative;** they assess the quality of a policy that has been in force for some time, especially when it has reached a critical juncture in its history. For example, many federal policies are evaluated just before they are due to be reauthorized. A negative evaluation could mean the end of the policy because Congress might vote not to reauthorize funding for it. Or, alternatively, negative findings might mean that the policy would be re-funded, but only with the condition that major changes be made in it. The primary purpose of summative evaluation, then, is to hold the implementers of a policy accountable, which is why the stakes are high when summative evaluations are conducted and why external evaluators are normally used. However, although summative evaluation was popular in the 1960s and 1970s, more recently, formative evaluation has been preferred (Popham, 1988).

Formative Evaluation.   The purpose of a formative policy evaluation is to enable the implementers of a policy to make necessary changes throughout the life of a policy in order to improve it. As a result, formative evaluation is an ongoing, recurrent process. Although the evaluators write formal reports only at predetermined intervals, data are usually collected regularly. Because a formative evaluation is designed to help implementers make good decisions about what they are doing, it is not as threatening as a summative evaluation. And, because the stakes are not as high, sometimes internal evaluators are used (Popham, 1988).

Pseudo-evaluations.   Unfortunately, policy evaluations are not always conducted in good faith. Often, what appears on the surface to be a bona fide evaluation is actually what has been called a pseudo-evaluation (Stufflebeam & Webster, 1983). Pseudo-evaluations are of two types. The first is *"the politically controlled study"* (p. 25, emphasis added). Such an evaluation is politically motivated; its purpose is usually communicated, directly or indirectly, to the evaluators, who must then decide if their ethical standards permit them to continue with the project. In such a pseudo-evaluation, the data collection and dissemination of the final report are carefully controlled to create the desired impression of the policy. The desired conclusions about the policy may be either negative or positive, but they reflect not the truth about the policy's success, but the outcome that those who commissioned the evaluation sought for political reasons.

The second type of pseudo-evaluation is *the public relations evaluation*. Its purpose is to "create a positive public image for a school district, program, or process" (Stufflebeam & Webster, 1983, p. 26). As with politically inspired pseudo-evaluations, those who commission a public relations study usually clearly indicate what the findings must be. In this case, the conclusions in the final report not only must be positive, but also must add luster to the public image that has already been created. In order to bring about this result, the commissioners of the evaluation carefully shape and select the data that they make available to the researchers, limiting where they can go, to whom they may talk, and what questions they may ask. Needless to say, either commissioning or participating in a pseudo-evaluation is unethical.

Methodologies Used in Policy Evaluation

Quantitative Methodologies.   **Quantitative research designs** involve the collection and statistical analysis of numerical data. Many types of numerical data are available in schools and school districts. Figure 11.2 lists some of the most common. Quantitative policy evaluations are sometimes based on experimental or quasi-experimental designs that investigate the statistical differences between a group that participated in a program and a group that did not. For example,

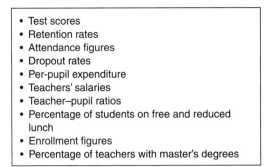

- Test scores
- Retention rates
- Attendance figures
- Dropout rates
- Per-pupil expenditure
- Teachers' salaries
- Teacher–pupil ratios
- Percentage of students on free and reduced lunch
- Enrollment figures
- Percentage of teachers with master's degrees

Figure 11.2 Examples of quantitative educational data.

evaluations of Head Start have compared children who participated in the preschool program to those who did not, seeking to determine if Head Start graduates score higher on achievement tests and are less likely to repeat grades. However, many quantitative evaluation designs are not experimental. Some use quantitative data to determine if specific objectives have been achieved and others use surveys to assess attitudes or opinions. Quantitative evaluations have several advantages. Perhaps the most important is the high level of credibility of a well-constructed quantitative study. Most Americans respect findings that are presented in statistical terms or depicted in graphs. A second major advantage is that quantitative evaluations can often be carried out relatively quickly and at a relatively low cost. The major disadvantage of a quantitative evaluation is that because of its tight structure and precise research questions, it is not well suited for discovering unexpected facts about the policy under study (Brainard, 1996; Stufflebeam & Webster, 1983).

Qualitative Methodologies.   Although almost all early policy evaluations were quantitative, in recent decades **qualitative approaches** have become popular (Guba & Lincoln, 1989). Qualitative research designs involve the collection of verbal or pictorial data. Many types of such data are available in schools and school districts or can easily be generated by a researcher. Figure 11.3 lists some

- Transcripts of interviews
- Transcripts of focus group discussions
- Notes on observations
- Open-ended surveys
- Personal statements
- Diaries
- Minutes from meetings
- Official reports
- Legal documents
- Books and materials
- Photographs

Figure 11.3 Types of qualitative data.

of the most commonly used. Qualitative research designs often involve collecting several types of data and comparing them, a process called *triangulation*. For example, a qualitative evaluation team assessing a dropout prevention project might interview students and teachers, observe in classes, and analyze books and other materials associated with the program. Like quantitative evaluations, qualitative ones have certain advantages. When the policy under consideration is very new or is a pilot program, a qualitative study can yield valuable insights into a problem. Moreover, qualitative evaluations sometimes make unexpected findings that quantitative ones miss; for example, in the late 1960s qualitative evaluations determined that some federal education policies were not being implemented. The major disadvantage of qualitative evaluations is that they are more time-consuming than quantitative ones and therefore more costly. Additionally, because most people trust numbers more than apparently subjective findings based on interviews and observations, qualitative evaluations are less credible than quantitative ones (Brainard, 1996; Guba & Lincoln, 1989; Stufflebeam & Webster, 1983).

Holistic Evaluations.   The choice between quantitative and qualitative evaluation is not an either—or one, however. Designing evaluations that include elements of both is possible; these are sometimes called holistic **evaluations.** For example, many case studies draw on both numerical and verbal data. An evaluation of the implementation of middle schools across a state might include in-depth case studies of several schools and analyze numerical data such as test scores, attitude assessments, and attendance rates as well as verbal data such as interviews, observations in classrooms, and open-ended surveys. Such an evaluation would permit the use of multiple indicators of several types and could provide a rich understanding of the challenges involved in making the transition from junior highs to middle schools as well as its relative success. The major advantage of the holistic evaluation is implied by its name; it provides a holistic view of what is happening. This means that the findings are often more valid than the findings of a study that uses only qualitative or only quantitative data. The major drawback is the time and cost required for the collection and analysis of qualitative data. No one best type of evaluation exists; the choice of methodology depends on the purpose of the study and the nature of the questions asked (Brainard, 1996; Joint Committee, 1994; Wolf, 1990).

Indicators

As an essential step in any evaluation process, the evaluators must define the **indicators** they will use to determine to what extent the policy is achieving its objectives. The exact definition of *indicator* is disputed by practitioners within the field. This one is typical: "An indicator is an individual or a composite statistic that relates to a basic construct in education and is useful in a policy context" (Shavelson et al., 1987, cited in Nuttall, 1994, p. 18.) This definition, of course, excludes qualitative evaluations. Nuttall suggests that indicators can be qualitative, but that even so they must be quantified to a certain degree in order to be meaningful. For example, in a qualitative evaluation of a school-to-work program, one indicator of success might be that the majority of participants interviewed stated that because of the program they had obtained a job. The purpose of all indicators, quantitative and qualitative, is to provide reliable information about the quality of a policy so that well-informed decisions can be made about it.

In designing an evaluation, selecting indicators for each policy objective and, if possible, using more than one indicator in relation to each is important. For example, in determining if a new mathematics program has increased students' competence in mathematics, evaluators might use three indicators: (1) student scores on a multiple-choice test; (2) student scores on an open-ended problem-solving test; and (3) interviews with selected students in which their mathematical thought processes are discussed (Joint Committee, 1994). By using these three indicators, evaluators could obtain a detailed, in-depth picture of the impact of the program. Using just one of them—the multiple-choice test, for example— would not provide complete information and would, therefore, be less valuable.

Careful thought must be given to the selection of indicators because of the potentially pathological effects of inappropriate ones. Continuing with the previous example, the use of multiple-choice test scores in isolation would probably have a detrimental effect on teachers' pedagogy as they implemented the mathematics curriculum. Multiple-choice examinations encourage a broad but superficial coverage of content as well as an emphasis on facts. Teachers teach differently when they know that measures of problem-solving and thinking ability will also be examined. Sometimes the indicators selected actually encourage educators to stop serving the population for which a policy was designed. For instance, one danger of simple reward systems that give schools or individuals extra money if their test scores are high is that they motivate principals and teachers to find ways to remove those students whose scores are most likely to be low. They may find ways to refer large numbers of youngsters to special education or vocational schools so that they will not reduce their chances of receiving funds. The way to avoid setting up an unintended pathological dynamic in which misguided indicators drive a program is to use several types of indicators and to discuss them and their probable effects with important stakeholders (Joint Committee, 1994).

FACILITATING MEANINGFUL POLICY EVALUATIONS

No educator can exercise a leadership role for long without having to deal with an evaluation. It may be an evaluation that the state, federal government, or a private foundation requires as one of the conditions for accepting their money. It may be an evaluation of a locally initiated policy, requested by the school board or central office staff. Or it may be a more limited study that addresses questions of interest only within a single building or a high school department. Regardless of how broad or limited its scope is, it will pose characteristic challenges to those who must play leadership roles during its course. The leader's responsibility is simultaneously to facilitate a useful evaluation and to provide ongoing guidance for the overall educational program—no easy task. Moreover, the leader's environment will probably be more turbulent than usual because evaluations threaten the status quo and thus almost always "occur in a hostile setting" (Brewer & de Leon, 1983, p. 361). This section, then, offers practical guidance for making this challenging job easier. After a discussion of the politics of evaluation, it suggests ways to reduce the conflicts that often surround the evaluation process and provides a setting in which a useful evaluation can be implemented.

The Politics of Evaluation

Why Evaluation Is Political.   The inherently political nature of policy evaluation has long been recognized. As Weiss, nationally known for her evaluation work, observed in 1973: "The politics of program survival is an ancient and important art" (Weiss, 1988, p. 49). Fifteen years later she affirmed that statement, saying: "I find that I still agree with almost everything I wrote then" (p. 66). Nor is the political nature of evaluation likely to evaporate with the beginning of a new century. In a 1997 volume entitled *Evaluation for the 21st Century* (Chelimsky & Shadish, 1997) the editors devoted their third chapter to a discussion of the politics of evaluation. Evaluations are political for three reasons. First, the programs and projects that they assess are the products of the political process. Second, evaluation reports influence what happens in the political arena, often affecting whether a policy is continued and how much funding it receives. Finally, the careers, professional reputations, and educational benefits of many individuals depend on the outcome of any evaluation (Weiss, 1988). This means that politics—often politics of the crassest sort—surrounds every evaluation. Wise education leaders do not deny the political aspects of the process, hoping they will not emerge in their setting. Instead, they anticipate and plan for them (Joint Committee, 1994).

The Players in the Evaluation Arena.   Planning for the politics of evaluation requires understanding who the players in this arena are and what motivates them. Each of the following short sections discusses the interests of a major group of stakeholders: the **policy makers,** the **policy implementers,** the **clients,** and the **evaluators** (Nakamura & Smallwood, 1980).

The Policy Makers.   Usually the policy makers are the people who have requested the evaluation and will use it to make important decisions about the future of the policy. Although they are most likely to be members of a school board, state legislature, or Congress, they may also include bureaucrats in an SDE. At one level, policy makers want good information that they can use to improve the policy in question or terminate it. However, being motivated by a mixture of values, they are also driven by self-interest: They want to keep their current positions. This means that they must win their next election or, in the case of bureaucrats, help their bosses win their next election. Therefore, policy makers are not necessarily interested in seeing that a technically excellent evaluation is carried out, but rather in guaranteeing that the program is maintained if it is popular with their constituents or cut if it is not (Nakamura & Smallwood, 1980).

The Policy Implementers. The policy implementers are all those within the school district who are involved in putting the policy into practice. They are likely to include administrators in central office, one or more principals, and numerous teachers. Although the implementers usually want to run a good program that benefits children, they also have personal interests at stake. Their professional reputations, chances of career advancement, and (in some instances) jobs may depend on the results of the evaluation. Therefore, they want it to be favorable (Nakamura & Smallwood, 1980).

The Clients. Although students are the direct clients of most policies in education and of the programs or projects that embody them, their parents are the indirect, behind-the-scenes clients. The parents become players in the evaluation arena much more frequently than their children do and those parents who are relatively well educated and affluent are most likely to be active. If the policy confers special benefits or status on their offspring, they will probably want a favorable evaluation just as the implementers do. Even if the program is failing to achieve its official objectives, they will be reluctant to see it changed in significant ways or discontinued because even if ineffective, it does provide some special services for their children and may save them a certain amount of money (Nakamura & Smallwood, 1980).

The Evaluators. Finally, the evaluators themselves have an interest in the outcome of the evaluation. One of their motives is to produce a thorough and accurate evaluation that will permit good policy decisions to be made. However, their self-interest also demands that they produce an evaluation that will enhance, rather than undercut, their careers as evaluators. In many instances this means that they seek to produce a sophisticated, technically correct evaluation report that will impress their colleagues and future clients rather than the type of evaluation that is really needed in a specific context. In others it may mean that they hesitate to report extremely negative findings for fear that they will gain a reputation as hostile evaluators and find their job opportunities dwindling (Nakamura & Smallwood, 1980).

Maneuvers to Prevent a Good Evaluation. Because all the players may use maneuvers to reduce the chances of a good evaluation, education leaders need to be aware of the standard approaches to derailing a successful study. School leaders involved in an evaluation should expect to see one or more of these deployed; well in advance they should develop tentative plans for how they will respond to them. The first broad tactic is simply to block the evaluation and prevent it from occurring at all. Policy makers, acting independently or responding to pressure from the implementers or clients (or both), may vote to cancel an evaluation or reduce funding for it. Those school leaders who do want a fair evaluation of a program should therefore be on the lookout for evidence that lobbying against the evaluation is occurring and move quickly to present the case for a serious study to policy makers.

A second tactic is to so shape the criteria that are to be used for the evaluation that the desired outcome is virtually guaranteed. For example, a group of parents who want a program for gifted students continued might pressure a school board to identify parental satisfaction as a major standard for judging the effectiveness of the program.

Once an evaluation is underway, a third favorite approach will probably surface: mobilizing the clients against the evaluators. The implementers are most likely to use this trick because they have ready access to parents and can fill their ears with frightening tales of the unsympathetic evaluation team that is gathering data on the program. Their objective is to incite conflict between the clients and the evaluators and also to persuade the clients to contact the policy makers to voice their complaints.

The fourth scheme is also usually put into action by the implementers. They may make data gathering impossible or difficult for the evaluators. Statistical records may mysteriously disappear; scheduled interviews may be abruptly cancelled; the return rate on surveys may be pitifully low. Because the implementers control most of the information about the program, they are in a good position to exercise their power in this fashion. Finally, after the evaluation has ended and the report has been issued, any of the stakeholder groups (except the evaluators) may choose the last approach: attacking the quality of the evaluation. The charges made can vary, but the most frequently heard are that the evaluators were biased or unqualified and they chose inappropriate indicators. By discrediting the evaluation, critics hope to discourage policy makers and implementers in leadership roles from using its findings to make any changes in the policy.

Clearly, the evaluation arena can be accurately described as a political minefield where many buried bombs wait to explode at the approach of unwary school leaders. Reducing (although not eliminating) the danger of this arena is possible, however, by taking some common-sense steps that can increase the likelihood of a sound evaluation. These are described next.

Suggestions for Achieving a Sound Evaluation

School leaders can do several things to increase the likelihood of a sound evaluation that is neither overwhelmed by politics nor undercut by insufficient data. In this section, five key steps to a good evaluation are discussed.

Building Evaluation in Early.   No good teacher would surprise unwary students with the evaluation plan that will be used to determine grades at the end of the course. Good teachers explain the evaluation plan at the beginning of the course, provide a rationale for it, and help students meet its objectives. Similarly, school leaders should not use an evaluation as an unexpected punishment that catches the implementers off guard. Such unpleasant surprises create an adversarial climate and encourage political game playing of the worst sort. Instead of using evaluation as a surprise strategy, leaders should build it in at the start. Often, a new policy, project, or program comes with a built-in evaluation system; this is frequently the case with government and foundation grants. In such instances, school leaders should not keep this information a secret. Rather, it should be shared and discussed with all the stakeholders from the beginning. On other occasions, the evaluation is not built in. This does not mean that it should be dispensed with—far from it. Instead, school leaders themselves should develop a general plan for evaluation, both formative and summative, and communicate it to stakeholders. Failure to do so may set the stage for a "surprise evaluation" several years later, creating a tense and unpleasant situation.

Communicating With Stakeholders.   Establishing open lines of communication with stakeholders at the beginning of the implementation of a new policy and maintaining them throughout is essential. A major subject of this communication should be the evaluation of the policy. Two important reasons exist for communicating freely with stakeholders.

First, good communication helps head off major political problems. Where communication is lacking, stakeholders consider the evaluation plans secretive and cherish multiple suspicions about leaders' true intentions. In such a mistrustful atmosphere, they will react defensively, seeking to derail the evaluation if possible. However, if leaders involve them in planning the evaluation, they are less likely to try such tactics. This means that, at the outset, leaders should hold meetings with the major stakeholders or their representatives. If representatives are used, they should be selected by their own groups rather than handpicked by the leaders. In meetings with them, the objectives of the new policy should be discussed and the stakeholders should be given a chance to ask questions and raise concerns. Leaders should also ask them what information they would like to obtain from the evaluation and incorporate their ideas into the evaluation. Throughout the evaluation process, leaders should regularly inform the stakeholders of what is going on; any preliminary findings should be communicated to them. Leaders should also make sure that the final evaluation report is understandable to stakeholders and should hold one or more meetings with them to discuss its implications for them (Joint Committee, 1994).

A second reason for strong communication with stakeholders is that it improves the validity and worth of the final evaluation. After all, the stakeholders are often closer to the grassroots implementation than are the leaders and know more about it than they do. But they will provide thorough information only in a climate of trust. Moreover, as suggested earlier about implementation, multiple perspectives surround all policies and knowing what those perspectives are is helpful. Leaders can discover them only through an interactive evaluation that involves much communication. As Guba and Lincoln (1989) state:

> The findings [of an evaluation] are not "facts" in some ultimate sense but are, instead, literally created through an interactive process that includes the evaluator . . . as well as the many stakeholders that are put at some risk by the evaluation. What emerges from this process is one or more constructions that are the realities of the case. (p. 8, emphasis in the original)

Selecting Indicators.   Even if outside evaluators will be used, school leaders should select indicators to monitor at the beginning of an implementation, fully realizing that the evaluators will probably add others. Selecting indicators early will reassure the implementers and also make determining what data to collect easier. As suggested earlier, choosing indicators that will not distort the implementers' behavior is important. Open discussions with all stakeholder groups will help leaders avoid serious errors in determining the best indicators (Hogwood & Gunn, 1984).

Building in Data Collection.   School leaders should not defer data collection until the summative evaluation is due. Just as indicators should be selected early, data collection should be ongoing because it can be used as part of formative evaluation throughout implementation. The results of frequent monitoring can provide leaders with ideas for improving the policy and also give them an important accountability tool. Later, when a formal, summative evaluation is conducted, the evaluators will have a rich existing information base to use in conjunction with the data that they generate themselves (Hogwood & Gunn, 1984).

Choosing Evaluators.   The choice of the individuals who will conduct a policy evaluation is an important one. Any school leader who is responsible for this decision should think it through carefully because it will seriously affect the quality and credibility of the final evaluation report. Basically, four alternatives exist, each with its own advantages and disadvantages.

The first possibility is an **internal evaluation conducted by the implementers.** The great advantage of this approach is that insiders have access to a great deal of information about the policy. Moreover, if they conduct the evaluation themselves, they will be more willing to act on negative findings than they will be if someone else has been in charge. However, this choice has serious disadvantages, too. First, the implementers may lack the research skills needed to carry out a high-quality evaluation. In addition, most outsiders will feel skeptical about their evaluation findings because of the strong probability that they are biased in favor of the policy.

A second alternative, then, is to use **internal evaluators from a specialized evaluation staff.** Many large districts, and some medium-sized ones, have a research office with personnel trained in evaluation. Such evaluators are well qualified in research methodologies and will also be more impartial than the implementers. However, some credibility problems may surface with such an evaluation; after all, the evaluators and the implementers work for the same employer and may even know each other personally. In addition, a negative evaluation could possibly incite conflict within the district.

Using external evaluators is also possible. The school or district can contract an **outside agency or consultant.** Universities and specialized evaluation firms are the most usual sources of researchers to conduct such evaluations. The advantages of using an external service are that the researchers are qualified and, as outsiders, will have considerably more credibility than any insiders. However, certain drawbacks exist. First, outside evaluators will not know the sociopolitical environment in which the policy has been implemented. This deficiency can be partially remedied by the research methods chosen, but not all professional evaluators are sensitive to this problem. Second, they may design an evaluation oriented toward making themselves look like experts in the eyes of their colleagues rather than toward providing truly useful information to their clients. Sometimes, too, their desire for future contracts with this or other districts leads them to gloss over problems rather than address them frankly. Finally, their services are usually costly.

The fourth alternative is to let the **organization that has funded the new policy** evaluate it. This organization might be a state legislature or a foundation; in fact, sometimes school leaders have no choice—under the terms of a grant they must permit the funding organization to conduct the evaluation. The major advantage of this option is that such organizations usually employ skilled, professional evaluators who are capable of doing a good study. Also, of course, their evaluation is likely to be more credible than any internal one. However, the major drawback is that the funding body may have its own evaluation agenda. The result may be an evaluation that is not useful to educators or one that is patently unfair to the policy and its implementers.

Education leaders must understand that no perfect choice exists, nor does a single choice that is always the best one exist. In making this decision, school leaders must weigh many factors—including the political situation, the nature of the information that they want about the policy, and the amount of money available for evaluation. Taking into account the needs of their particular program and the overall context in which it operates is especially important. Often the best solution is to choose not one but two evaluators: an internal one to conduct formative evaluations throughout implementation and an external one to do all summative evaluations. This approach balances the advantages and disadvantages of internal and external evaluation while also providing two relatively independent opinions of how well the policy has worked. As a result, when the time comes to make major modifications in the policy or even to terminate it, school leaders will have a broad range of data available to them that comes from different sources, thereby increasing their ability to make informed decisions (Hogwood & Gunn, 1984).

ACTING ON AN EVALUATION REPORT

After school leaders have received and studied an evaluation report, they must decide what to do about it. The first step in this process should be carefully assessing the quality of the report, using the criteria presented earlier in this chapter. Because evaluations vary greatly in quality, leaders should never uncritically accept them but should instead attempt to determine how good the study was. Only then can they know how seriously they should take its findings and recommendations. The second step should be convening the major stakeholders to discuss with them their perceptions of the report's quality. Trying to reach consensus on the general value of the evaluation before progressing further is wise. Only after some level of agreement has been achieved should leaders decide what to do with the report. Basically, four courses of action are open to them: (1) do nothing, (2) make minor modifications, (3) make major modifications, or (4) terminate the policy (Brewer & de Leon, 1983; Hogwood & Gunn, 1984). Each possibility is discussed in turn.

Inaction

Often, the wisest course of action is to do nothing, thus maintaining the current policy in place. Two especially valid reasons exist for choosing this course of action. The first is that, in the judgment of the leaders and other stakeholders, the evaluation was questionable and they therefore do not wish to accept its recommendations. Unless obligated by a funding agency to act on a questionable evaluation, no good reason to do so exists. The second solid justification for inaction on an evaluation is that it is not politically feasible. Sometimes waiting for a propitious moment to act on the recommendations of an evaluation is necessary (Hogwood & Gunn, 1984).

Minor Modifications

Deciding to make only minor modifications in a policy, either because only a bit of fine-tuning was recommended in an evaluation report or because more sweeping changes are impossible for political reasons, is also possible. Minor modifications do not affect the spending or staffing levels of the program, nor do they alter the objectives of the policy. Examples include changing the tests used to monitor student progress, modifying schedules, or providing additional materials similar to those already in use. Because minor modifications do not alter the substance of the policy or threaten the jobs of stakeholders, they are relatively easy to make (Brewer & de Leon, 1983).

Major Modifications

Table 11.1 summarizes the four broad types of major policy or program changes. They have been arranged so that the first one is the least thoroughgoing and each

TABLE 11.1 Major Methods for Modifying Policies

Method	Explanation
Replacement	A new program that has the same objectives is put in place of the old program.
Consolidation	Two or more entire programs or parts of programs are put together.
Splitting	One aspect of the program is removed and developed into a separate program or project.
Decrementing	A substantial cut in funding is imposed on the program by reducing the amount of money available to most components of the old program.

Note. Based on Brewer and de Leon (1983).

successive change is increasingly serious. Clearly, all of these are threatening because they could eliminate some stakeholders' jobs while reducing services to others. This means that in order to make them, leaders must be in a strong position: They should have both a well-conducted evaluation by expert researchers to legitimate their recommendations for change and the support of some of the stakeholders, particularly the policy makers. When trying to bring about major changes after an evaluation, leaders should anticipate political turbulence and plan for dealing with it (Brewer & de Leon, 1983).

Termination

When a policy or program is terminated, it is discontinued and nothing is put in its place—usually because the government's objectives have shifted. Obviously, terminating policies is extremely difficult because most of the stakeholders will fiercely resist discontinuation and fight hard to protect the policy. Often, therefore, an ineffective policy must be continued until an opportune moment presents itself; then leaders can move swiftly, discontinuing policies whose demise is long overdue. Figure 11.4 lists several situations favorable to terminating policies (Brewer & de Leon, 1983; Hogwood & Gunn, 1984).

FINAL POINTS

We live in an age of accountability. Policy makers are not generous with tax dollars; before spending public money on education policies, they want to know how well they work and what can be done to make them more effective. They expect education leaders to act prudently, allocating funds where they will make the most difference and eliminating worthless programs. This expectation is not an unreasonable one. To meet the demands of an age of accountability, however, school leaders must be literate about evaluation. They should take the lead in applying modern evaluation techniques to their own work and in acting upon the findings of sound evaluations. The children in our schools, as well as the general public, deserve no less.

- When the administration changes
- When the economy turns down
- When budget difficulties happen
- When other jobs are available within the organization
- When the old program can easily be replaced by a new one

Figure 11.4 Situations conducive to policy termination.
Note. Based on Brewer and de Leon (1983); Hogwood and Gunn (1984).

QUESTIONS AND ACTIVITIES FOR DISCUSSION

1. Discuss why people feel nervous about evaluations.
2. Find an evaluation that used quantitative methods and one that used qualitative ones. What methods of each type were used? Contrast the kinds of information yielded by each approach.
3. Find an evaluation report and evaluate it, using the criteria discussed in this chapter.
4. List the evaluation and monitoring techniques used by your SDE and identify the major indicators. Do they distort the behavior of your state's educators in any way? How would you improve them?

INTERNET ASSIGNMENT

Locate the Web sites of your state government and those of two neighboring states. Search for evaluations of education policies and be prepared to discuss your findings in class. (If you are not sure of how to locate the Web sites of state governments, refer to Appendix B.)

CASE STUDY

THE MIDDLE SCHOOL PROPOSAL GOES DOWN IN FLAMES

A school superintendent decided to evaluate the curriculum and organization of the district's junior high schools (grades 7–9) and formed a panel of evaluators consisting of the elementary, junior high, and senior high school principals and a teacher at each level. They were requested to complete a written report for the superintendent within five weeks of commencing the evaluation.

The panel prepared the report for the superintendent based on their own knowledge and beliefs about the school system and its needs, supplemented by limited staff and student perceptions collected with a survey instrument. Included in the report were sections on academic achievement of local junior high school pupils, national trends in junior high school organization (stressing the advantages of the middle school concept), present and projected enrollments, gaps in the junior high school curriculum, and the physiological and social development of students in the junior high age group. The report recommended that the school system shift to a middle school organization, with grades 6, 7, and 8 in the middle schools, and grade 9 going to the senior high schools.

When the report was published, elementary and senior high parents were disturbed that specific concerns of theirs had not been addressed in the report. Elementary parents, especially, were upset about the prospect of the loss of the school leadership provided by sixth-grade students. They suggested, among other things, that many parents looked to sixth graders to escort their younger children safely to and from school. Senior high parents were alarmed at the potential overcrowding that would be brought about by the addition of grade-9 students.

Representatives of both parent groups complained to the school board. The board itself was irritated because the report did not assess the disadvantages and cost implications of the suggested reorganization and the advantages and disadvantages of other possible organizational changes. The board supported the parent groups and rejected the middle school concept.

Note. From *The Program Evaluation Standards, 2nd ed.*, (pp. 38–39), Joint Committee on Standards for Educational Evaluation, 1994. Copyright 1994 by Sage Publications, Inc. Reprinted by permission of Sage Publications, Inc.

QUESTIONS

1. Using the criteria provided in this chapter, what were the weaknesses of this evaluation?
2. If you had been a member of the school board, how would you have voted on the panel's recommendation? Why?
3. What could the superintendent have done to encourage a more credible evaluation? What could the panel of evaluators have done?
4. Reading between the lines, how do you think that the politics of evaluation affected this situation?

NEWS STORY FOR ANALYSIS: DISTRICT BELIEVES IN BILINGUAL EDUCATION

Austin, TX—Any time a school administration undertakes significant change, rumors and half-truths inevitably circulate. As expected, this has occurred with the launching of the Austin Independent School District's blueprint to address the needs of chronically under-performing schools. Among the current rumors and half-truths, the notion has surfaced that this administration does not support bilingual education. As the district administrators responsible for bilingual education, we want to lay that idea to rest right now. Make no mistake—AISD unequivocally supports effective bilingual education as the best means to successfully educate students who speak little or no English.

Our philosophy is based on several important tenets:

- The primary language is the most powerful tool a student has to attain full intellectual and social development.
- The patterns of the language learned at home are the foundation for academic achievement in all-English classrooms.
- The use of the primary language to develop vocabulary, comprehension and the mechanics of language in bilingual education and in English as a second language programs are powerful in raising academic achievement.

Fluency and literacy in the native language commensurate with a child's age is vital for academic success in the second language. We can't be any more straightforward than that. That's what we believe, and that's what we practice every day in our 575 bilingual classrooms.

Undoubtedly, the cause of the recent confusion has been a misunderstanding by some members of the Harris Elementary community. A number of teachers at Harris practiced a dual-language bilingual education program, this year, funded by an outside grant. We aren't opposed to a dual-language approach in which Spanish speakers learn English and English speakers learn Spanish—if it is done well. Success requires every child to have both a command of their home language and to be on grade level in literacy skills in the native language if they are to fully benefit from the second language.

We've engaged national experts in bilingual education and literacy, Dr. Alba Ortiz of the University of Texas and Dr. Diane August of the Center for Applied Linguistics, to work with our staff in analyzing the dual-language program at Harris, and to suggest ways to make it more effective for the 2002–2003 school year, the last year of the grant. Review of the 2000–01 dual-language program evaluation revealed no single, comprehensive, cohesive approach to implementation being used at Harris. A number of dual-language approaches were being used with varying degrees of effectiveness. There was also no continuity from grade to grade. A significant number of students were performing below grade level in their native language because they weren't given the opportunity to have a good, solid basis for literacy before going to a second language. They, therefore, weren't developing their literacy in either language.

We believe a dual-language approach can be effective if properly applied. We want to establish the efficacy of dual-language programs. We certainly don't want them to fail. There are several sound approaches to bilingual education, but they must be properly implemented. That's our bottom line. We believe in bilingual education. But we believe in doing it well, so that all our students attain great academic success, opening up worlds of opportunity for them in their adult lives.

(Adapted by permission of the authors from E. Fuentes and D. M. Moore, "District Believes in Bilingual Education," *The Austin American Statesman*, May 24, 2002, p. A23. Copyright 2002 by E. Fuentes and D. M. Moore.)

Questions

1. What problems did the evaluation of the dual-language bilingual program at Harris reveal?
2. Was the evaluation summative or formative?
3. What players in this evaluation arena can you identify? What other players may be involved?
4. What tactics have the implementers used to discredit the evaluation?

FOR FURTHER READING

Beyer, B. K. (1995). *How to conduct a formative evaluation*. Alexandria, VA: Association for Supervision and Curriculum Development.
   In this slender volume, the author (an experienced educator and evaluator) offers practical guidelines for educators who want to conduct a formative evaluation.

Brainard, E. A. (1996). *A hands-on guide to school program evaluation.* Bloomington, IN: Phi Delta Kappa Educational Foundation.

Brainard outlines the process of conducting a program evaluation in a school or district from beginning to end. His chapter on methods of data collection is especially useful.

Chelimsky, E., & Shadish, W. R. (1997). *Evaluation for the 21st century: A handbook.* Thousand Oaks, CA: Sage.

This book provides an overview of current trends in policy evaluation. School leaders should find the chapters on the new methods of evaluation and monitoring used by governments especially valuable.

Guba, E. G., & Lincoln, Y. S. (1989). *Fourth generation evaluation.* Newbury Park, CA: Sage.

Guba and Lincoln give the reader a good overview of qualitative evaluation and also of the importance of involving stakeholders throughout the process.

Joint Committee on Standards for Educational Evaluation. (1994). *The program evaluation standards: How to assess evaluations of educational programs* (2nd edition). Thousand Oaks, CA: Sage.

This handbook contains a detailed discussion of each of the thirty standards for evaluation, including convenient summaries entitled "Guidelines" and "Common Errors" for each of them. Each standard is further clarified with one or two illustrative cases drawn from real life.

EDUCATION POLICY IN THE UNITED STATES: RETROSPECTIVE AND PROSPECTIVE

Focus Questions

How has education in the United States changed through history?

How do the policy proposals of today relate to those of the past?

Why is the policy environment today so turbulent?

What will education policy probably be like in the future?

IF WE AREN'T IN KANSAS, WHERE ARE WE?

This book opened with a quotation from *The Wizard of Oz*. "Toto, I don't think we're in Kansas anymore," the puzzled Dorothy commented to her little dog. The first chapter suggested that public education in the United States and those who lead it are no longer in quiet, stable Kansas, but in an unpredictable policy landscape that is hard to understand. Indeed, education leaders may often feel that their situation is worse than Dorothy's: Although the young heroine confronted witches and talking animals, at least she knew that the Emerald City was her destination and had magic shoes and a Yellow Brick Road to help her reach it. But at the beginning of the twenty-first century, school administrators often feel perplexed by the seemingly endless streams of proposals for education reforms from politicians, business people, think tanks, and universities. They ask themselves questions such as: What is happening? Why is everyone so dissatisfied with our schools? Where is it all leading?

This chapter, then, sets today's policy environment in its historical context, using four theoretical frameworks to illuminate the past and present and also to suggest what the future may hold. Two of these analytical frameworks—competing values and Lowi's policy types—have been presented earlier. The third and fourth—institutional choice and international convergence—have often been implicit in previous discussions. Together these four theoretical concepts can provide important clues to what is happening in education policy today and why. Although trying to predict the future is always risky, they can also suggest the most likely scenarios for the first decades of the new century. This chapter provides a general map of Oz so that, although it will never feel as comfortable as Kansas did to those who knew Kansas well, education leaders will at least have an understanding of the terrain through which they are traveling.

The first section, then, briefly presents each of the theoretical frameworks. Next, each framework is used to analyze education policy during three historical periods: the Young Republic, the Common School movement, and the "Scientific" Sorting Machine. Then, the same frameworks are applied to our own era, from 1983 to the present. Finally, the most likely scenario for the future is discussed. Because of the special nature of this chapter, only two sets of activities appear at the end.

FOUR THEORETICAL FRAMEWORKS

Competing Values

"Policy . . . [rests] . . . upon value-laden public beliefs—interpretations of the American creed or dream," insists Iannaccone (1988, p. 49). Chapter 5 of this book discussed these public values, grouping them in three categories: general social values (order and individualism), democratic values (liberty, equality, and fraternity), and economic values (efficiency, economic growth, and quality). As explained there, although all these values are always factors in education policy in the United States, their relative importance changes over time. People who analyze policy using the competing values framework argue that because only two or three values can be dominant at any given time, proponents of particular values compete with each other to move their preferred values into the top positions (Boyd, 1984). Once a value becomes the highest priority in education policy, it tends to hold that position for a long time, causing a cyclical alternation among the public values in U.S. history. Because the policies driven by each value differ considerably from each other, this means that periodically a rather dramatic shift occurs, sometimes called a *realignment*. This happens about every 40 years (Iannaccone, 1988).

Lowi's Policy Types

As discussed in Chapter 9, political scientist Lowi (Lowi, 1964; Lowi & Ginsberg, 1994) has developed a typology of policies (distributive, regulatory, and redistributive), arguing that each generates a distinctive political arena around itself. Although Lowi does not claim that preferred policy types move in cycles, he does assert that in different historical periods, different policy types have been favored. For example, up until the nineteenth century, governments mostly used distributive policies; but in the nineteenth century, regulations became common. In the twentieth century, on the other hand, many governments around the world pursued social goals by putting redistributive policies, such as welfare and Social Security, in place. This means that one way to understand policy shifts over time is to analyze them in terms of which policy types have been preferred in different historical periods.

Institutional Choice

Kirp (1982) argues that one way to compare and contrast the school systems of different nations is to examine the extent to which their organization reflects five types of institutions: (1) bureaucracy, (2) legalization, (3) professionalization, (4) politics, and (5) the market. He suggests that few systems are purely of one form, but that most incorporate elements of all five. However, one or two will be dominant, setting the tone of the overall organization and shaping its policy direction. Although he uses this framework to compare the school systems of different countries, it can also be used to compare the same system to itself across historical periods.

The first of the institutional forms that a school system can take is that of **bureaucracy.** A bureaucracy is a hierarchical organization in which everyone has a clearly defined role and directives flow from the top down. Rules and standard operating procedures are important in a bureaucracy, as are written documents such as policy manuals and minutes from meetings. Advancement within the organization is supposed to be determined by merit, as measured by a supposedly objective instrument such as a test or standard evaluation form.

A highly **legalized** institution is one in which laws are the ultimate instruments of control. Disputes are settled by taking complaints to court and letting judges make the final decision. Legalized institutions have an adversarial flavor, and all participants are concerned about protecting their rights. Probably no organization exists that is predominantly legalized in structure. Nonetheless, many exist that are so torn with conflict that recourse to the judicial system is common within them.

The organizational structure encompassing the members of some occupations is that of the profession, achieved through **professionalization** at some point in the past. Members of a profession are controlled internally by norms to which they were socialized by older people working in their field. Typically, entry into a profession is competitive and highly selective; the training is long and arduous; and learners must go through various rites of passage such as difficult examinations or exhausting field experiences. Upon graduation from the training program, professionals have a period of supervised practice during which they are further socialized. In a profession, the members decide who gains admission to it and who must leave because of incompetency. Professionals work autonomously, without direct supervision; medicine is a good example of a profession (Lortie, 1975).

Politics can also be the fundamental structural principle of an education system. In political situations, people build power in order to advance their own interests or values. Political game playing usually requires negotiating to reach compromises and is frequently based on exchanging favors. Clearly, all organizations without exception include some political elements, but politics is more pronounced in some than in others. The legislative branch of democratic governments is one of the most political of institutions, and in many countries legislatures make a high percentage of the education policy decisions. School systems vary in the extent to which policy making is politicized.

Finally, institutions can be organized as **markets.** In a market, goods and services are produced by competing providers, who try to attract customers by offering attractive prices or distinctive product features. In a market that functions well, the presence of competing providers leads to efficient operations and high quality products because businesses that cannot please customers lose them. While the economic system is heavily based on market principles, many other organizations in modern societies, including school systems, use some elements of the market.

International Convergence

Comparative education specialists theorize that the school systems of the nations around the world are "converging"—becoming more like each other in structure, curriculum, and goals. The process is not new. As early as the eighteenth century, Thomas Jefferson and the Marquis de Condorcet, a French leader, corresponded about the type of schools necessary to promote democratic government; the ideas of both men were later reflected in the public schools of each nation. Cross-national influence continued in the nineteenth century. To mention just one example, under the Meiji Restoration, Japanese leaders visited schools in Europe and North America, gathering information to use in establishing their own school system as part of a broader modernization effort. Today, as the world's economies globalize, no nation can escape the impact of international forces that affect many aspects of national life, including education. The result is that, around the world, school systems are becoming increasingly similar (Coombs, 1984; Wirt & Harman, 1986). Two Canadian scholars, Davies and Guppy (1997), describe the process:

> Nation-states must increasingly react to [economic] pressures and battle constantly to improve their comparative advantage, which leads to a key proposition: the ever expanding web of market relations fosters a standardization of knowledge systems in all core industrialized nation-states. Since nation-states organize and distribute knowledge through formal education, this logic implies a tendency for school systems to converge across these developed nations. (p. 436)

RETROSPECTIVE ON U.S. EDUCATION POLICY

The Young Republic, 1783–1830

Overview. The first decades of the U.S. republic were shaped by the struggle to establish a viable nation—to develop political institutions, to lay the foundation for a strong economy, and to resolve the inevitable conflicts that arose among a conglomeration of former colonies with different cultures and traditions. One important cultural difference lay in their attitudes toward education; this was the major reason for omitting all mention of education from the U.S. Constitution. Thus, each state was free to follow its preferred course with regard to education, and even within states much diversity existed. Although compulsory attendance laws had not yet been passed, literacy was growing and most citizens wanted to obtain at least a rudimentary education for themselves and to provide one for their children. Parents who sought a school for their offspring could choose among a rich variety of options. Youngsters often mastered the alphabet and early elements of reading in dame schools, informal "home" schools where a neighbor woman taught a few children in her own residence, often in her kitchen. Special "private venture" schools offered somewhat more advanced instruction in single subjects, such as handwriting and English. Most denominations also operated elementary schools for the children of their adherents. In rural areas, semipublic "district schools" operated for two or three months annually, teaching farm children some simple notions of reading and writing. For the small number of children who pursued academic learning beyond the basic level, private academies and boarding schools provided both classical and practical curricula. Although public subsidies were available in some areas, children's parents had to bear most of the costs of these schools: paying tuition, purchasing books and materials, feeding the schoolmaster, and contributing fuel for winter heating.

Toward the end of the period, cities began to sponsor public schools for poor children. Often called *charity schools*, they had high pupil–teacher ratios and, although they taught the rudiments of reading and arithmetic, they emphasized hard work and obedience, the character traits needed in the new factories that were springing up. Because public schools were considered inferior, middle- and upper-class parents rarely chose them for their children. For example, Edward Everett Hale, son of a middle-class Boston family, attended private schools until age 9, when his parents enrolled him in the Boston Latin School that, although operated by the city, was very prestigious. Hale later wrote about his educational path: "There was no public school of any lower grade to which my father would have sent me, any more than he would have sent me to jail" (Perkinson, 1991, p. 14). His comment reveals the attitudes of this period.

The Competing Values Perspective. Viewed from the perspective of the competing values framework, the values that drove education policy in the Young Republic were individualism and freedom. Memories of the Revolutionary War were fresh in people's memories, and the distrust of government that had developed during the late colonial period still flourished. As a result, most citizens were skeptical of proposals that the government operate schools, such as those that Thomas Jefferson was advocating in Virginia. Rather, they prized local—and parental—control of education and enjoyed being able to choose among many types of schools. Some parents also wanted to maintain the option of not sending children to school at all; their labor was essential on the family farms of the period. The idea that the government should establish a public school system that all or most children would attend was therefore unappealing during this period. It reminded people too much of the high-handed ways of the British king against whom they had so recently rebelled.

The Policy Types Perspective. The overall education policy orientation between 1783 and 1830 can best be described as inaction. For the most part, the local, state, and federal governments did little to either promote or discourage education. Nonetheless, some policies did exist, particularly at the local level and particularly in New England. Cities, towns, and townships did provide some resources for education; and, toward the end of the period, they were beginning to operate schools for poor children. These policies were distributive with no regulatory strings attached other than that the funds be used for education. Similarly, the *Northwest Ordinance*, passed by Congress in 1787, was distributive, stipulating that one of the 36 plots in every township in the newly opened territory be rented out and the proceeds used for schools. No regulations were included in the law, and no federal monitors were provided to exercise oversight. Although these plots were often used for education as Congress had intended, misuse and fraudulent diversion of the funds were not uncommon (Kaestle, 1983).

The Institutional Choice Perspective. One historian of this period observes that "schooling remained a local, voluntary, and largely entrepreneurial undertaking" (Kaestle, 1983, p. 184). The market was far and away the most dominant institutional form. Under this system, the other institutional forms were relatively insignificant. To be sure, some degree of bureaucracy had to exist within the larger schools, and parochial schools had a church hierarchy with which to contend. But no central offices, no superintendents, no state departments of education, and certainly no education agencies at the federal level existed. Because few laws existed relative to education, little possibility existed for legalization either. Nor were teaching or school administration at all professionalized; anyone who could attract students could establish a school. Teaching was regarded as a good temporary pursuit—ideal for women who wanted to earn a few dollars, for literate farmers who needed something to do in the winter months, and for young men not quite ready to enter business or read law. Finally, education policy was not particularly politicized yet. Occasionally debated in legislatures or Congress, it was not an ongoing concern. The market was clearly dominant, leading to a rich

TABLE 12.1 Institutional Choices in Education Policy in Four Historical Periods

	Historical Periods			
Institutions	Young Republic	Common School	Scientific Sorting Machine	New Paradigm
Bureaucracy	Weak	Strong	Strong	Unsettled
Legalization	Weak	Weak	Strong	Unsettled
Professionalization	Weak	Moderate	Moderate	Unsettled
Politics	Weak	Moderate	Weak	Unsettled
Market	Strong	Weak	Weak	Unsettled

variety of choices for parents and many entrepreneurial opportunities for would-be teachers and principals. Table 12.1 summarizes the relative importance of the five institutions during this period (and the others).

The International Convergence Perspective. Because education in the United States was diverse and uncentralized, no formal exchanges could take place between U.S. educators and those from other parts of the world. Furthermore, international communication was so poor that little opportunity arose for sharing ideas through print. Nonetheless, even at this early date, the influence of other countries on U.S. education was considerable. After all, the European settlers in the New World were immigrants who had come from older, more established societies. One of the things they had brought with them was the conception of schooling that they had known in the Old World. For the most part, this influence was British; however, immigrants from Germany, France, and other countries had also come with ideas about what constituted proper schools. Naturally, when they established schools for their children in North America, they followed these old patterns. Thus, from the start, education in the United States reflected a strong, and mixed, international influence.

Concluding Reflections. Political scientist Seymour Lipset (1996) observes that "the American Creed can be described in five terms: liberty, egalitarianism, individualism, populism, and laissez-faire" (p. 19). Measured against those criteria, the education policy orientation of the Young Republic can be described as quintessentially American. The high value it placed on liberty and individualism was discussed earlier. Its populism, or distrust of experts, was apparent in its relaxed attitude toward who was capable of teaching. The government definitely took a laissez-faire, "let citizens do whatever they want to," approach to education. In a strange sense it was even egalitarian, for all types of schools and teachers were considered good enough to participate in the education market although they might not survive for long. But ultimately it was not egalitarian enough because the education services it provided were quite uneven, which is one reason why it came under severe attack in the 1830s.

The Rise of the Common School, 1831–1900

Overview.   By the early 1830s, the Young Republic was no longer young, and the United States was changing rapidly. The major cause of the widespread transformations of this period was industrialization. Factories sprang up throughout the Northeast, and young men and women who had grown up on farms flocked to cities to work in them. They were not the only ones who came; immigrants from Europe, primarily Ireland and Germany, joined them. Many of these were Roman Catholic, much to the dismay of the overwhelmingly Protestant population. As a result of this population growth, cities burgeoned, spreading out across the former farmland, bringing with them increased crime rates and poverty. These rapid changes deeply disturbed many Americans, particularly in New England, and they responded in typically American fashion—by launching a variety of reform movements, each conceived as a way to save the country from the perils that threatened it. Prohibition, women's suffrage, abolition, prison reform—all these movements blossomed during the 1830s. Among them was the Common School movement, whose goal was to reform education in the United States.

The central leader of the movement was the New Englander Horace Mann, a tireless lecturer and prolific writer. He was also an educator with a reform agenda. Deeply distressed by the increasing social diversity and crime rate in the United States, Mann conceived of the Common School as a way to unify the heterogeneous population, thereby reducing the crime rate. In his view, the current school system was pitifully inadequate, "each [school] being governed by its own habits, traditions, and local customs" (cited in Perkinson, 1991, p. 22). The result was an uncoordinated educational hodgepodge, destined to remain ignorant and backward unless transformed. Mann's solution was the Common School, which would provide an elementary education for all white children of both sexes and of every ethnic, religious, and socioeconomic group. He and his fellow reformers developed a detailed agenda for transforming education in the United States into a highly coordinated system; Figure 12.1 lists the individual planks of that platform.

The battle for the Common School was a long one because the advocates of the old system did not surrender without a struggle. Nor did all citizens enthusiastically welcome paying taxes to support common schools. Nevertheless, by

---

- More regular school attendance
- A longer school year
- Graded schools
- The weakening of the district system
- Creation of state education agencies
- Creation of county superintendencies
- Improved occupational status for teachers
- Teacher training in normal schools

Figure 12.1 The platform of the Common School movement.
Note. Based on Kaestle (1983).

1860 the Common School was virtually universal in the North; in the South it took considerably longer to establish, but a racially segregated version of common schooling prevailed by the end of the nineteenth century (Kaestle, 1983; Perkinson, 1991; Spring, 1994). A very large part of the "Kansas" that many of today's educators take for granted was in place.

The Competing Values Perspective. Between the Young Republic period and the Common School era, the values that drove education policy in the United States shifted dramatically: from liberty and individualism to fraternity, order, and economic growth. Fraternity, defined as a sense of national unity, was the foremost value for Horace Mann and many of his fellow reformers. They feared the fragmentation of U.S. society along the lines of cleavage that had become apparent by 1830—ethnic background, religion, and, above all, social class. Their fears were dramatically reinforced by the Boston riots of 1837, during which Catholics and Protestants fought each other in the streets. In their opinion, the Common School would help prevent such conflicts by giving children from different backgrounds the opportunity to become acquainted with each other in school. All would develop a common sense of identity as Americans, forgetting the barriers that divided them. Clearly, order was also an important value for the leaders of the Common School movement. One historian even refers to "Mann's morbid fear of social unrest and instability" (Perkinson, 1991, p. 23). Although this severe judgment may reveal more about the author's inexperience with social disorder than it does about the legitimacy of Mann's fears, it does suggest the extent to which the desire for social order permeates his writings.

Somewhat less important to Mann, but a central concern for many of his supporters, was economic growth. Workers were needed for the new factories; employers wanted them to possess the rudiments of reading and arithmetic and insisted that they be hardworking, self-restrained, and obedient. Thus, the Common School emphasized the development of a particular kind of character. Its textbooks were studded with inspirational slogans such as, "The idle boy is almost invariably poor and miserable," and "Idleness is the nest in which mischief lays its eggs" (cited in Kaestle, 1983, p. 82).

The Policy Types Perspective. Distributive education policy had been dominant prior to the 1830s, but the Common School reformers advocated the enactment of many regulatory policies, as indicated in Figure 12.1. Compulsory attendance laws were passed, the school year was lengthened, and a standard school organization was mandated. Moreover, a governance apparatus was instituted at both the state and county levels to enforce the new requirements and to gather statistics on school performance. Schools lost their previous freedom to do whatever they wanted; now they were carefully controlled by government officials in agencies above them. The broad policy goal of the Common School movement was "systematic uniformity—uniform textbooks, a uniform curriculum, uniform teaching methods, uniform management, uniform discipline, and uniformly trained teachers" (Kaestle, 1995, p. 19). This uniformity was achieved through regulation.

The Institutional Choice Perspective.   The market was the dominant institution under the Young Republic, but its importance in the institutional mix dropped dramatically during the Common School era. Bureaucracy was the reformers' preferred institution; they established it at both the local and state levels. Under their guidance, state departments of education were established, directed by superintendents of public instruction. At the local level, superintendents and other supervisors made sure that state mandates were implemented. By the end of the period, bureaucracy was even beginning to appear in schools, where the roles of principals and teachers were gradually differentiated. Thus, a hierarchical, bureaucratic organizational structure was in place in U.S. education by 1900.

Although bureaucracy was the reformers' preferred institutional choice, politics and professionalism were also important to them. The education system was much more embroiled in politics during this period than it had been earlier. The fight to establish common schools was a political struggle of the first magnitude, requiring that legislatures enact statutes establishing agencies, creating the superintendency, and—above all—taxing the citizenry to support schools. All these issues were controversial. Moreover, because public education was now conceptualized "as an instrument of public policy" (Spring, 1994, p. 19), politicians were more interested in it than they had been previously. They saw it as a tool that could be used to shape docile workers, build patriotism, and solve a variety of youth problems. This meant that education policy issues and policy issues of other types often became intertwined. Professionalism also increased under the Common School. Although teaching was not fully professionalized, some professional elements were introduced into it. These included training in normal schools for teachers; better salaries; and journals, associations, and conferences designed especially for them. However, because teaching in common schools was feminized during this period, it remained an occupation that was relatively easy to enter. Teacher turnover was also high because many young women "kept school" only until they married (Lortie, 1975).

Although legalization and the market were the least important institutions, they were not completely missing. Numerous school laws were passed during this period, and some were challenged in the courts. Taxation to support common schools was frequently litigated; the courts almost always upheld it. As for the market, the Common School reformers had just weakened the old district system, not eliminated it. This meant that parents, especially in urban areas, could still choose schools for their children by choosing in which district they would live. Table 12.1 summarizes the relative importance of the five institutions during the Common School era.

The International Convergence Perspective.   The government and business leaders of the Common School era worried about international economic competition, just as they do today. Great Britain was the dominant world power, and Americans did not idealize the mother country as they sometimes do now; their memories of the Revolutionary War and the War of 1812 were too vivid. They perceived Great Britain, with her navy and global ambitions, as a persistent threat. A newer concern was Prussia (the northern region of modern Germany), which was building both economic and military might. Of less concern but also worrisome were France,

Japan, and Russia. The leaders of the period were convinced that education was a major weapon for winning the international competition that was developing. Therefore, Mann and other Common School reformers made a point of visiting European schools, especially those in Prussia and France, to obtain ideas. The European influence is apparent in many elements of the common schools and of the early normal schools, which trained teachers. Indeed, the very term *normal school* is a literal translation of the French term, *école normale* (Kaestle, 1983). Thus, the Common School reforms can be understood as a movement away from a distinctively American educational institution and toward emerging international norms for school systems.

Concluding Reflections. In many respects the Common School was a typical nineteenth-century institution. As with many other organizations developed during the period, including the business firm and the government agency, its structure was bureaucratic and hierarchical. In its reliance on regulations as its preferred policy type, it was also typical; in general, the nineteenth century saw a geometric increase in the number of government regulations in effect and also in governmental ability to enforce them (Lowi, 1964). Finally, its nationalistic goals were characteristic of an age during which nation-states grew in power, self-consciousness, and influence on the world stage. But the twentieth century presented challenges that the Common School could not fully meet. Therefore, the early 1900s, like the 1830s, would be a period of school reform.

The "Scientific" Sorting Machine, 1900–1982

Overview. Like the 1830s, the early twentieth century was a period of change; indeed, many of these changes paralleled those of the earlier era. For example, immigration reached high levels with 8.5 million immigrants entering the United States between 1900 and 1910, and another four million between 1910 and 1920 (Perkinson, 1991). The now highly industrialized economy was booming, conferring upon business a high degree of credibility with the public and great influence upon civic affairs. Numerous scientific inventions and advances had made daily life more comfortable and dramatically improved health and life expectancy. However, storm clouds were gathering over Europe as the new century began. International tensions were mounting since the competition among the European powers had intensified during the late nineteenth century. This period was marked by major international conflict, with World War I breaking out in 1914, World War II raging between 1939 and 1945, and the Cold War driving policy after that. The major result for Americans was the changed international status of the United States. It emerged from World War I as a major world power and from World War II as one of two superpowers dominating the world stage. Inevitably, all these changes made an impact on education policy (Perkinson, 1991; Ravitch, 1983; Spring, 1994).

At the beginning of the century, the two central education policy issues were modifying the governance structures of public education and deciding how to deal with growing enrollments in secondary schools. The Progressive reformers of the turn of the century sought local government reforms, including reforms of school governance, because they believed that in recent decades city governments had become thoroughly corrupt. Therefore, they advocated a number of legal changes, all designed to reduce partisanship, nepotism, and graft. Unfortunately, they also had the effect of reducing public participation in local politics. In education, the Progressive reforms involved reducing the size of school boards, making school board elections nonpartisan, and expanding central office staffs by adding to them various experts trained in the scientific management approach then popular in business circles. Confidence in experts—especially if they claimed to be "scientific"—was high, and many decisions that elected officials, teachers, and principals had previously made were shifted to central office (Callahan, 1962; Tyack, 1974).

Burgeoning enrollments in secondary schools also posed a major policy problem. Two distinctly different proposals for dealing with it were offered. The first was best represented by the recommendations of the Committee of Ten on Secondary School Studies that—significantly—issued its report in 1892, late in the Common School era. The Committee of Ten proposed a high school in which all children would pursue the same curriculum, which would be academically oriented. In short, it proposed the extension of the Common School concept into secondary education. The alternative proposal was for a differentiated secondary curriculum, all of whose components (or "tracks") would be offered in the same building. A concrete example of this policy proposal was the *Cardinal Principles of Secondary Education*, a report published by the National Education Association (NEA) in 1918. It called for a differentiated secondary curriculum that would be driven "by the needs of the society to be served, the character of the individuals to be educated, and the knowledge of educational theory and practice available" (cited in Ravitch, 1983, p. 48). This was the position that won out because the federal government, which was becoming increasingly active in education policy, supported it with both rhetoric and money. In 1917, for example, it had passed the Smith–Hughes Act, providing federal resources for vocational education. During the first quarter of the twentieth century a number of other policy mechanisms developed to facilitate and support the differentiation of the secondary curriculum into tracks; Figure 12.2 lists some of the major ones.

Throughout the rest of this period, leaders considered the public schools a major instrument of public policy, which the government could (and did) use to meet a broad range of social and economic needs: training future workers, identifying

---

- Ability grouping
- Extracurricular activities
- Guidance counseling
- I.Q. testing
- Junior high schools
- School psychology
- Standardized achievement tests
- Vocational guidance

Figure 12.2 Policy mechanisms in support of the differentiated curriculum.

young people's ability levels and channeling them into the "right" career directions, helping the United States maintain its economic and military supremacy, and encouraging most youngsters to "adjust" rather than to develop high-level cognitive skills that would not be needed in their workplace (Perkinson, 1991; Ravitch, 1983; Spring, 1989). Historian Spring (1989) has aptly dubbed this version of the American school "the great sorting machine." This was the other half of the school system that many educators consider their "familiar Kansas." It was largely in place by 1930.

A major contradiction lay at the heart of the Scientific Sorting Machine, however. Although it was surrounded by the rhetoric of equal educational opportunity for all children, people did not have to score at the genius level on one of the new intelligence tests to be able to figure out that a considerable gap separated rhetoric from reality. In both the North and South, African Americans attended racially segregated schools that were almost always inferior to those that white children attended. Moreover, in some parts of the country, Hispanic, Native American, and Asian American children were required to go to separate, unequal schools. The Scientific Sorting Machine also discriminated against girls, who, in the eyes of the writers of the *Cardinal Principles*, did not need to prepare for college but rather for lives as homemakers. This gender discrimination was expressed both in the courses that guidance counselors urged young women to take and in the fact that they had unequal access to some aspects of the extracurricular program, especially athletics. As for children with handicaps, they were originally excluded, shunted off into special schools or deprived of education altogether. After World War II, these incongruities were experienced as increasingly unacceptable and, one by one, they were either reduced or abolished. Such changes did not occur without a struggle, however, and the federal government had to play an increasingly important role in enforcing the new policies designed to enhance equal educational opportunity. Unfortunately, the continued existence of multiple school districts, especially in metropolitan areas, allowed families to "vote with their feet" by moving to the suburbs, where school populations were more homogeneous. The result was school systems that were increasingly segregated by class and in which a new form of racial segregation continued (Perkinson, 1991; Ravitch, 1983; Spring, 1994). By the end of the period, dissatisfaction with public education was mounting, suggesting that another period of reform might be on the horizon.

The Competing Values Perspective. During the era of the Scientific Sorting Machine, efficiency was the dominant value, with equality second most important. Efficiency was so paramount in the thinking of this period, that Callahan (1962) entitled his classic study of the transformation of school administration in the early twentieth century, *Education and the Cult of Efficiency*. This preoccupation with efficiency was manifested in many ways. The superintendency evolved into a job having more to do with school finance than with education leadership. Decisions about children's learning were increasingly based on test scores rather than on teachers' professional judgment. Testing itself changed; as time passed, essay examinations (which were time-consuming to evaluate and therefore costly) were progressively replaced by multiple choice tests (which could be quickly and cheaply scored by machines). In fact, the whole purpose of the sorting machine was to improve social efficiency by expeditiously channeling young people into tracks that would lead them into the occupations that U.S. society most needed (Perkinson, 1991; Ravitch, 1983). As the period moved toward its end, however, equality assumed ever greater importance. Understood as equal opportunity to succeed in the Scientific Sorting Machine, it became the driving value behind the various rights movements of the 1960s and 1970s. However, none of these movements seriously challenged the basic assumptions of the sorting machine or argued that other types of equality should be pursued by U.S. schools.

The Policy Types Perspective. During the Scientific Sorting Machine period, the preferred policy types were regulation and the redistribution of resources. Early in the period, regulations were emphasized; and many new ones were put on the books. For example, in line with the era's confidence in expertise, the requirements for teacher certification were substantially increased and administrative certification was introduced. As time passed and redistributive policies became increasingly popular, detailed regulations were usually attached to them. Title I, one of the compensatory education sections of the Elementary and Secondary Education Act of 1965, was accompanied by complex guidelines that changed frequently. Legislation governing children with handicaps, passed in the 1970s, also came with numerous guidelines. As regulations accumulated, the redistributive policies of the 1960s and 1970s also began to shift many educational resources away from the "regular" classroom and toward poor children, children with handicaps, non–English-speaking children, and others. As was to be expected, the political arena became increasingly turbulent as the dynamics of regulatory and redistributive policies were simultaneously set in motion. Ravitch (1983) describes the politics of the last decade of the period this way:

> Whoever the claimant, whether representing blacks, women, the handicapped, or non–English-speaking minority groups, the avenue of political remedy was the same: to bypass educational authorities by working directly with sympathetic congressional committees and by gaining judicial supervision. Each victory led to the imposition of mandates on school . . . officials, requiring them to do promptly what they otherwise would have done slowly, reluctantly, or not at all. By their very nature, these outside interventions diminished the authority of educational administrators. . . . (p. 311)

The Institutional Choice Perspective. Even more than the leaders of the Common School movement, the key figures during the Scientific Sorting Machine era preferred bureaucracy, for it was consistent with their great faith in expertise. Therefore, they not only maintained the bureaucracy that had been put in place during the nineteenth century but also extended and strengthened it. Their additions increased the specialization and division of labor that already existed. By the 1960s, a host of experts of various kinds worked in school systems—guidance counselors, school psychologists, reading teachers, special education teachers, curriculum specialists, vocational placement officers, and so forth. Increasingly, educational roles and authority were moved out of the classrooms and principals' offices and into the domains of these specialists.

Professionalization was also used, but within clear limits. As people who admired knowledge and those who possessed it, the leaders of the period had great confidence in credentials. Not surprisingly, therefore, they raised education requirements for teachers, developed administrator preparation programs, and emphasized inservice education. At the same time, however, their tendency to increase specialization and reinforce the existing division of labor undermined the professional autonomy of principals and teachers. Increasingly, the former were managers rather than education leaders, while the latter found themselves carrying out the directives of others and basing their instruction on supposedly "teacher-proof" curricula devised by experts (Ravitch, 1983; Spring, 1994).

The leaders of this period distrusted politics; but, ironically, this distrust led to the legalization of education in the United States, which in turn sparked fierce political controversy. The Progressive reforms of the early twentieth century had sought to "get the politics out of education," and to a great extent they had succeeded. The nonpartisan school boards established at that time were so removed both from ordinary citizens and from the mainstream of state and federal politics that exercising much political influence on them was difficult. As a result, citizens bypassed them, taking their grievances into the state and federal court systems. The degree of the legalization of education is suggested by the fact that, although federal courts decided only 112 education cases in the decade between 1946 and 1956, they decided 729 between 1956 and 1966, and 1,200 in the four years from 1966 to 1970 (Ravitch, 1983). Not surprisingly, this judicial activism was deeply resented in many quarters, setting the stage for political revolt on the part of both legislators and citizens' groups (Perkinson, 1991; Ravitch, 1983).

Although education leaders of the Scientific Sorting Machine period also distrusted the market, they unwittingly reinforced it. Urban parents who were disgruntled with court-ordered desegregation and busing policies fled to the suburbs where many small, competing school districts sought to lure them with shiny new facilities and low tax rates. The result was the development of an education market around most large cities in which suburbs competed for residents, drawing most middle-class children out of the city school districts (Weeres, 1988).

The International Convergence Perspective.   As with the education system of the Common School era, that of the Scientific Sorting Machine period reflected international influence. The major developed nations of Europe as well as Japan had established highly differentiated school systems during the nineteenth century. Although both bipartite and tripartite systems existed, the same basic concept prevailed in all of them: children whose probable career paths differed should pursue different education programs, and these should be offered in different, separate schools. Typically, youngsters who would ultimately seek professional positions studied in prestigious schools that prepared them for university admission. The others pursued less academically oriented curricula in vocational and technical schools. Although all these schools were funded by the government and were therefore public, they did not have equal status. Not coincidentally, pupils' social class background was a major determinant of the type of school they attended (Fowler, 1995a). Thus, the adoption of "tracks" in U.S. schools represented a movement toward the dominant international education model of the time. In fact, those who established vocational programs in the United States were especially influenced by the tripartite German school system.

International convergence was not a one-way street, however. As time passed and the United States became increasingly powerful in world affairs, other countries became familiar with the comprehensive high school found in the United States and adopted their own versions of it. In the 1950s, 1960s, and 1970s, many of them reformed their systems, bringing them closer to the U.S. Common School model. Indeed, by the end of this period, Japan and several nations of Western Europe, including France, Italy, and the Scandinavian countries, were actually closer to having common schools than was the United States (Fowler, 1995a).

Concluding Reflections. In many ways, the Scientific Sorting Machine was the ideal school system for most of the twentieth century. Organizationally modeled on the factories of the time, it produced the sort of workers that both business and the military wanted. It offered an intellectually challenging curriculum to the top 20% of youngsters while providing the rest with a basic education that emphasized rote memory, "adjusting" to society, and practical skills (Reich, 1991). Considering the great economic and military success of the United States during the period, this education system cannot be regarded as a complete failure. Nonetheless, times change, and by the 1980s the Scientific Sorting Machine was under sustained attack.

In Search of a New Paradigm, 1983–Present

Overview. By the 1980s, dissatisfaction with public education was growing again; much of it crystallized around a federal commission report, *A Nation at Risk*, which appeared in 1983. Blaming most of the problems in the United States on the failure of schools to prepare their graduates adequately for the competitive global economy, the writers of the report sketched a broad outline of the reforms that they thought necessary to save the endangered nation. Many leaders of education reform movements rallied to its call, even though they did not always agree with the report on the exact nature of the required changes (Lugg, 1996). The result was a vigorous education reform movement (or, rather, several overlapping and contradictory reform movements) that flourish to this day.

The movements of the 1980s and 1990s have to be understood against the backdrop of the 1970s. During that decade the economic boom launched by the end of World War II ended. This event—which was not immediately recognized—brought with it disquieting economic symptoms: double-digit inflation, unexpectedly high unemployment, and a slowing of economic growth. At the same time, Americans began to realize that the economic gap between them and other developed countries was narrowing. Although they still had the highest standard of living in the world, the Japanese and the Western Europeans were catching up, and in a few areas they were moving ahead. The success of the

Japanese in selling automobiles in the United States and the growing presence of European products in U.S. stores jolted many out of their previous complacency. The world was shrinking; our long-time allies were emerging as competitors for global markets; obviously something had to be done to solve the problem (Reich, 1991; Thurow, 1992). One solution was school reform.

Several observers have argued that the school reform movement was a red herring, designed to divert public attention away from the errors of business and political leaders (see, e.g., Berliner & Biddle, 1995). Some truth is probably inherent in this position; Americans have long regarded education as a cure-all for whatever ails the nation (Perkinson, 1991; Tyack & Cuban, 1995) and would therefore be particularly receptive to the notion that economic problems can be solved by tinkering with the school system. Nonetheless, dismissing the school reform movement as merely a "manufactured" crisis, to use Berliner and Biddle's (1995) term, would be simplistic. For one thing, education reform is not a purely U.S. phenomenon; it has international dimensions, and virtually all developed countries have implemented major changes in their school systems since 1980 (Fowler, 1995a). This suggests that deeper reasons exist for the movement in the United States than purely political ones. Undoubtedly, one of these is simply that because most of the school systems in the developed world were established in the nineteenth century, as institutions they were beginning to show their age by the 1980s.

In the United States several proposals for updating the school system currently coexist in the policy arena. Joseph Murphy (1990) groups them in three broad categories: (1) intensifying the old bureaucracy, (2) restructuring, and (3) redesigning. His basic concept has been adapted with some alterations for the following discussion. The first set of reforms, summarized in Figure 12.3, was proposed earliest and advocates the least thoroughgoing changes. Basically, the proponents of these reforms, although sometimes dubious about certain aspects of the Scientific Sorting Machine, accept the basic structure of the U.S. school system, especially its Common School components. Implicitly, however, they believe that the Common School model has never been fully achieved and advocate its completion. Thus, some of them push for reforms such as national standards and

---

• Curriculum alignment
• Detracking
• Inclusion
• Increased graduation requirements
• Longer school day/year
• New technology
• Paideia Proposal
• School finance reform
• State/national standards
• State/national subject matter tests
• State proficiency tests
• Subject-matter standards
• Systemic reform

Figure 12.3 Reforms to complete, restore, or update the Common School.

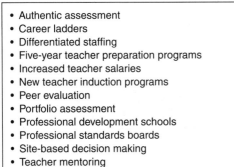

- Authentic assessment
- Career ladders
- Differentiated staffing
- Five-year teacher preparation programs
- Increased teacher salaries
- New teacher induction programs
- Peer evaluation
- Portfolio assessment
- Professional development schools
- Professional standards boards
- Site-based decision making
- Teacher mentoring
- Teacher teams

Figure 12.4 Reforms to professionalize teaching.

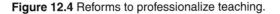

curriculum reform, which would further systematize education. Some are more interested in reforms such as school finance equalization, detracking, and inclusion, which would bring the school system closer to the old Common School ideal.

The second set of reforms, summarized in Figure 12.4, calls for the restructuring of the school system in the direction of greater professionalization. Those who advocate these reforms argue that children cannot be taught to be critical, creative thinkers by teachers who are required to conform to the old factory model of teaching. They believe that if teachers are given more autonomy within the classroom and more power to make decisions inside their school and to govern their profession outside it, they will be better able to educate the type of workers that the United States will need in the twenty-first century.

Finally, proposed reforms of the third type, summarized in Figure 12.5, advocate restructuring education to make it more like a market. According to advocates of these changes, the main cause of the problems of public education is that it is a government monopoly and therefore unresponsive to consumer demands. They suggest making it into a market or at least introducing market elements into it, so that the resulting competition can increase its responsiveness and efficiency.

Different policy networks and coalitions advocate these reforms, competing in Congress and in state legislatures to gain official acceptance for their ideas. Lawmakers freely borrow from all three groups of reforms, unaware that in practice they are not always compatible. So far, no single one of the three types has won out over the others; apparently, Americans are still in search of a new education paradigm. But for those who lead schools and school systems, the constant flood of new policies and policy proposals has created an education landscape that is sometimes very Oz-like indeed.

The Competing Values Perspective.   Some observers identify freedom and excellence as the two core values of the education reform movement of the late twentieth century (Boyd & Kerchner, 1988; Iannaccone, 1988). Certainly, freedom—understood primarily as freedom of choice—is central to the movement. Not only is freedom the value that drives every aspect of most school choice

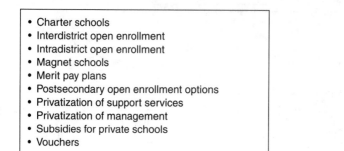

- Charter schools
- Interdistrict open enrollment
- Intradistrict open enrollment
- Magnet schools
- Merit pay plans
- Postsecondary open enrollment options
- Privatization of support services
- Privatization of management
- Subsidies for private schools
- Vouchers

Figure 12.5 Reforms to marketize education.

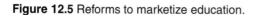

proposals, but it is also implicit in many policies that would increase teacher professionalism, understood as professional autonomy. Certainly, too, the rhetoric that surrounds the movement resonates with the discourse of excellence—whether it is conceived as higher standards, greater emphasis on critical thinking, or more challenging forms of assessment. Nonetheless, few advocate excellence for the sake of excellence; rather, what they really seek is economic growth, and higher standards of excellence are seen as a way to produce a workforce better able to compete in the global economy. Thus, the dominant core values seem to be freedom and economic growth with excellence seen as the best way to achieve the latter.

The Policy Types Perspective. Different branches of the reform movement prefer different policy types. Consistent with their fundamental loyalty to the old Common School, those who advocate completing it often express their policy choices through regulatory mechanisms. During the 1980s, for example, many legislatures increased graduation requirements and lengthened the school day or year by voting in laws that imposed new mandates on schools (Murphy, 1990). However, those who advocate either form of restructuring back redistributive policies. Unlike their predecessors in the 1960s and 1970s, they wish to reallocate power rather than money. Advocates of greater professionalism wish to shift power from central offices to school buildings and from principals to teachers. School choice proponents, on the other hand, seek to shift power away from educators of all types toward parents.

The Institutional Choice Perspective. Each of the three branches of the school choice movement favors a different institutional choice for the new education paradigm. Those who advocate the completion of the old Common School model wish to perfect several aspects of its bureaucracy, clarifying its rules, requirements, and organizational hierarchy. Proponents of increased professionalism argue for the greater professionalization of the teaching occupation, making it more like law and medicine. Choice supporters favor the market with its diversity of producers and products as well as its competition. Although all three movements are currently politically active, only the first implies the ongoing use of politics as an institution; the perfected bureaucracy would continue to be part of the government, and its basic mandates would have to be voted by legislatures. However, although some proponents of the old Common School model rely heavily on the courts today—especially advocates of school finance equalization and inclusion—no proposals imply the ongoing use of legalization as an ideal.

The International Convergence Perspective.   From an international perspective, all three branches of the current reform movement can be interpreted as movements toward greater conformity with international education norms. As those who push for the completion of the Common School model like to point out, most other developed countries and many developing ones have national or state standards, a national or state curriculum, and national or state tests. Moreover, most other school systems in the world are more "coherent," "systemic," or "aligned" (that is, more fully bureaucratic) than ours (Fuhrman, 1993). Similarly, teaching is more fully professionalized in most other developed countries than it is in the United States, a point that the American Federation of Teachers (AFT) has demonstrated through its research and publicity (AFT, 1995). Finally, although the education market is not particularly favored on the European continent or in Japan, the "marketization" of education has been popular throughout the English-speaking world since the early 1980s (Cooper, 1988). Each group, then, draws on international models for ideas.

Concluding Reflections.   The current education reform movement can be seen as a revolt against the aging school organization inherited from the nineteenth and early twentieth centuries and as a search for a new paradigm. The revolt against the Scientific Sorting Machine elements of the old system has been particularly strong with all three movements rejecting many of its components. Both the people who advocate the completion of the Common School and those who favor "marketization" somewhat idealize a past phase of the United States school system, with the former preferring the Common School era and the latter, the approach of the Young Republic. Proponents of increased professionalization cannot readily refer to an earlier period because teaching in the United States has never been fully professionalized (Lortie, 1975). They must look abroad for models, but both other groups have international connections as well. This is not surprising because school reform is an international movement, not peculiar to the United States. The final education paradigm that emerges from the ferment of today will almost certainly reflect not just American elements but also the results of education experimentation elsewhere.

WHITHER EDUCATION POLICY?

Although the contemporary education policy arena is filled with diverse and contradictory policy proposals, eventually it will settle down, leaving a reformed education system behind it. Of course, trying to predict the future is always dangerous. Nonetheless, history, theory, and the current balance of power do suggest the most likely outcomes. This chapter—and this book—will close, then, with five cautious predictions and some suggestions for school leaders.

Prediction 1: The new education paradigm will not be widely accepted for many years.

Structural change takes a long time primarily because it is redistributive and therefore encounters strong resistance. After all, putting in place the Common School model, which also involved substantial restructuring of the previous system, took approximately 70 years. Therefore, anticipating that the new education paradigm will also take a long time to emerge clearly and be widely implemented seems reasonable. The change probably will not require seven decades, however; modern communication and transportation have made disseminating ideas easier than it was 150 years ago. Nonetheless, the transition period will probably be longer than the average career of an education leader, and many educators will spend their professional lives grappling with change.

Prediction 2: Although teaching may become somewhat more professionalized, professionalization will not dominate under the new paradigm.

Appealing as the full professionalization of teaching may be to many educators, it would be inconsistent with core American values. As indicated in Chapter 5, freedom and individualism are deeply cherished in the United States. One expression of individualistic freedom is populism, the belief that common people know as much as supposed experts, and possibly more (Lipset, 1996). Populism is the major reason that Americans like to elect a wide array of local officials, including some whose posts require specialized knowledge, such as sheriffs and judges. Most U.S. citizens are therefore unlikely to support the full professionalization of teaching because it would reduce the scope of public control over education. Certainly teaching is much more professionalized in countries such as Germany, France, and Japan than in the United States, but citizens in those countries respect expert authority more than do Americans (Lipset, 1996). Thus, in this area, the degree of international convergence will be constrained by core national values.

Prediction 3: Numerous elements of the updated and completed Common School will be widely accepted, but this paradigm will not ultimately dominate.

The Common School ideal is more consistent with core American values than is professionalization. Its appeal to the ideals of fraternity and equality is broadly attractive as is its emphasis on order. Moreover, its call for a systematic approach to curriculum and testing provides a plausible method for achieving excellence, which many political leaders feel is the prerequisite for economic growth. And the updated Common School ideal strongly resembles the current school systems of France, Germany, and Japan, whose high performance in international education comparisons intrigues U.S. politicians. This model also has had support in high places, including both Bush Administrations and the Clinton Administration and several prominent think tanks. Even so, it has one glaring weakness. Freedom is the dominant policy value of our time, yet the updated Common School model would do little or nothing to advance it. This shortcoming will probably be sufficient to prevent it from dominating and becoming the new paradigm.

Prediction 4: Numerous elements of marketization will be widely accepted, but this paradigm will not ultimately dominate.

The introduction of market elements into the school system is also more consistent with core American values than is professionalization. Unlike the updated Common School ideal, the market paradigm does advance freedom; and because of the free-wheeling, competitive atmosphere of the market, it provides an ideal arena for expressing individualism as well. Moreover, marketization has powerful proponents in today's political arena; various forms of school choice and privatization have been introduced in most state legislatures and passed by many. And in 2002, the U.S. Supreme Court upheld a public voucher plan in *Zelman v. Simmons-Harris*. However, marketization has some problems that reduce the likelihood that it will be the unchallenged paradigm of the future. First, its ability to advance the goals of excellence and economic growth is uncertain. Although choice advocates insist that parents know how to choose good schools for their children, skeptics insist with equal fervor that considerable distance exists between most parents' conception of a good school and the type of education needed in the twenty-first century. Their skepticism has been supported by research that reveals that academic quality, although important to most parents, is not their central consideration when they choose schools (Cookson, 1994). Second, if the United States adopted a completely marketized system, as envisioned by some (Perkinson, 1991), it would stand alone in the developed world. No developed country uses such an approach to education; on the contrary, loosely organized market-oriented approaches to schooling are more characteristic of developing countries. Therefore, given the U.S. history of paying close attention to international education models because of concerns about economic competition, the adoption of a completely marketized system seems unlikely.

What, then, is left? All three proposed paradigms have been excluded. However, a combination of two or more of them has not been. So we move on to the fifth prediction.

Prediction 5: The emergent paradigm will incorporate elements from both the updated Common School and the marketization models.

Together, these two models fulfill all the requirements for the new paradigm: they express the dominant values of freedom and economic growth based on excellence, they have broad political support from a range of constituencies, and they are consistent with the theory of international convergence. Nor are the updated Common School model and marketization necessarily incompatible. Many school choice proposals include provisions to give detailed information about schools to parents; the implementation of state or national standards, curriculum, and tests would make accomplishing this goal easier. Moreover, the existence of national or state expectations that all schools would have to meet would make the public feel more comfortable about policy proposals such as vouchers and charter schools because guaranteeing that schools offer a worthwhile academic program to all students would be possible. Thus, several elements of the updated Common School could easily be combined with diverse forms of school choice, creating a new paradigm that would simultaneously advance the policy values of freedom, excellence, and economic growth. The possibility of fusing the two in this way is by no means mere theoretical speculation. Under the Thatcher government, the United Kingdom adopted precisely such a paradigm in the 1980s (Cooper, 1988). Of course, the fact that it exists as an international example in an English-speaking country increases the likelihood that it will eventually be adopted in the United States. In the author's view, this is the most likely outcome of the current school reform movement.

The prediction in the previous paragraph was originally written in late 1997; by late 2001 it was apparent that federal education policy was moving in precisely this direction. The 2001 reauthorization of the ESEA—the No Child Left Behind Act—included *both* mandatory statewide tests in mathematics *and* reading for grades 3–8 *and* the requirement that the parents of children attending poorly performing schools be provided with public school choice options (Robelen, 2002). This combination of an element of the updated Common School model with a market-based reform probably foreshadows what is to come.

Meanwhile, what are school leaders to do? A popular way to break a mixed message is to announce, "I have good news and bad news." This book will close with just such a mixed message. The bad news for school leaders is that they cannot reasonably expect a return to Kansas. Unlike Dorothy, they are not going to meet a wizard or find magic shoes that will carry them back to the world they once knew. For the foreseeable future, the education policy scene will be turbulent with many new policy proposals, many changes, and many failed experiments. Leading in such a stormy environment will be difficult and stressful. But there is also good news. When systems are in flux, individuals have a chance to exercise influence that they do not have when systems are stable. Thus, those school leaders who want to will be able to identify those trends in their state or district that they support and work to advance them. Over the span of a career they will be able to bring about some of the education changes that they consider most needed. Looking back over a lifetime of work, they should be able to feel a genuine sense of accomplishment as they think about how they helped construct the new Kansas. Whether school leaders choose to steer their institutions through the stormy waves of change, or to exercise influence over the storm, or some combination of both, this book should be a useful guide. Although no Yellow Brick Road, it does provide some useful ways to think about the Oz-like policy landscape of today and to act reflectively within it.

QUESTIONS AND ACTIVITIES FOR DISCUSSION

1. What elements of the education policy of the Young Republic, the Common School movement, and the Scientific Sorting Machine are evident in your school district?

2. What elements of the education policy of the Young Republic, the Common School movement, and the Scientific Sorting Machine are evident in your state?

3. List the major education reforms and reform proposals that have emerged in your school district in the last decade. Group them into the three categories discussed in this chapter. What tendencies do you notice?

4. List the major education reforms and reform proposals that have emerged in your state in the last decade. Group them into the three categories discussed in this chapter. What tendencies do you notice?

5. Identify the individuals and groups that have advocated reform in your district during the last decade. For which type of reforms has political support been strongest?

6. Identify the individuals and groups that have advocated reform in your state during the last decade. For which type of reforms has political support been strongest?

7. Using Figures 12.3, 12.4, and 12.5, make a list of the reforms you like best. How could you work to get these adopted in your district or state?

FOR FURTHER READING

Callahan, R. E. (1962). *Education and the cult of efficiency.* **Chicago: University of Chicago Press.**
This book is the classic study of the efficiency revolution of the early twentieth century, which transformed schools and education administration.

Chubb, J., & Moe, T. (1990). *Politics, markets, and America's schools.* **Washington, D.C.: Brookings Institution.**
This very readable book critiques the current institutional structure of schools and argues that school choice (in the form of vouchers) would solve many of the current ills of public education in the United States.

Fuhrman, S. H. (1993). The politics of coherence. In S. H. Fuhrman (Ed.), *Designing coherent education policy.* **San Francisco: Jossey-Bass.**
Fuhrman's chapter provides a good introduction to the movement to make education in the United States more systematic and internally consistent.

Kaestle, C. F. (1983). *Pillars of the republic.* **New York: Hill & Wang.**
This book provides a balanced discussion of the schools of the Young Republic era and how that system was replaced by the Common School movement.

Lortie, D. C. (1975). *Schoolteacher.* **Chicago: University of Chicago Press.**
Lortie's classic study still offers one of the best introductions to teaching as an occupation.

Murphy, J. (1990). *The educational reform movement of the 1980s.* **Berkeley, CA: McCutchan.**
This book provides a handy overview of the policy reforms of the 1980s, especially those that sought to perfect the old Common School model.

Perkinson, H. J. (1991). *The imperfect panacea* **(4th edition). New York: McGraw-Hill.**
Perkinson's history of education in the United States focuses on how

Americans have sought to solve broader social problems by reforming education policy.

Ravitch, D. (1983). *The troubled crusade.* **New York: Basic Books.**

Written from a neoconservative perspective, this history recounts the changes in education policy in the United States during the period from 1945 to 1983. The chapter on progressive education is especially fine.

Spring, J. (1989). *The sorting machine revisited.* **New York: Longman.**

This book provides a good counterbalance to Ravitch's history of policy during the same period.

Spring, J. (1994). *The American school, 1642–1993.* **New York: McGraw-Hill.**

This is a good overview of the history of education in the United States, written from a radical perspective.

Tyack, D., & Cuban, L. (1995). *Tinkering toward Utopia.* **Cambridge, MA: Harvard University Press.**

In this book, two of the eminent education historians of our time discuss several education reform movements of the past, analyzing them in order to suggest their implications for today's reform movement.

Glossary

agenda Those policy issues that politicians and other influential people are seriously considering.

agenda setting The process of deciding which policy issues will be on the agenda; the second stage of the policy process.

bill A draft of a proposed statute law which has been introduced into a legislature for its consideration, or is about to be introduced.

budget process The steps involved in proposing a budget for the federal government or a state government, negotiating its content, and getting it passed into law.

capacity building A policy instrument that involves investing large sums of money in developing over time the ability of individuals or groups to act more effectively.

case law The body of opinions written by judges to explain how they have interpreted or applied the law in specific cases.

cost analysis A procedure for estimating all the tangible costs of a policy.

cost-effectiveness analysis A procedure for comparing alternative policy options to determine which of them offers the best combination of effectiveness and reasonable cost.

evaluation A form of applied research designed to determine how well a policy is working; the sixth stage of the policy process.

federalism A system of government in which the central government and subsidiary governments share sovereign power; the United States, Canada, and Germany have federal governments.

foundation An endowed organization that sponsors policy research and its dissemination.

hortatory policy A policy instrument that involves the government using various methods to persuade citizens to perform a desired action.

ideology A systematic, but rather simplified understanding of how the economy, the political system, and society actually work and should ideally work.

implementation Putting a policy into practice; the fifth stage of the policy process.

inducement A policy instrument that governments use when they offer special funds or privileges to citizens in order to get them to behave in a desired way; grants are inducements.

interest group   An organization that actively works to influence policy.

issue definition   The process by which a problem is transformed into an issue that a government could address; the first stage of the policy process.

lobbying   The process of trying to influence policy, especially a legislature.

mandate   A policy instrument that requires everyone to perform a desired action or suffer some kind of penalty.

mobilization of bias   The institutionalization of power in organizations, traditions, and customs in such a way that people are differentially empowered and disempowered without any individual acting overtly to influence them; the second dimension of power.

policy actors   People and groups who are involved in the policy process.

policy adoption   The process by which a legislature, an agency, or a court approves a written version of a policy.

policy analysis   A systematic procedure for describing a policy and making its implications clear.

policy formulation   The process by which a legislature, an agency, or a court develops a written version of a potential policy.

policy issue   A public controversy over how the government should act in a particular instance.

policy maker   Any policy actor who has the authority to approve or promulgate a policy.

policy network   Loose national coalitions of organizations that work to influence policy in a specific area; the Education Commission of the States is a policy network.

political culture   A collective way of thinking about politics that includes an understanding of the political process and beliefs about how politicians should act.

power   The ability to influence the behavior or beliefs of others.

program   An institutionalized project.

project   A short-term activity, often associated with a grant.

rules   Regulations developed by administrative agencies that interpret or provide details to go with a statute.

shaping of consciousness   The systematic inculcation of a set of ideas about the general worth and proper role of another person or a group of people; the third dimension of power.

statute   A law passed by a legislative body.

system change   A policy instrument that involves shifting power and/or resources from one set of people to another.

termination   Ending a policy because it has accomplished its purpose or is ineffective; ideally, the final stage of the policy process.

think tank   Policy planning organizations, often funded by private money, that do research or disseminate their positions in an effort to affect policy, especially issue definition and agenda setting.

APPENDIX A

USEFUL WEB SITES FOR FOLLOWING EDUCATION POLICY

U.S. Government
House of Representatives—*http://www.house.gov/*
United States Senate—*http://www.senate.gov/*
U.S. Department of Education—*http://www.ed.gov/*
U.S. Supreme Court—*http://www.supremecourtus.gov/*
White House—*http://www.whitehouse.gov/*

Education Organizations
American Association of School Administrators—*http://www.aasa.org/*
American Federation of Teachers—*http://www.aft.org/*
Association for Supervision and Curriculum Development—*http://www.ascd.org/*
Council for Exceptional Children—*http://www.cec.sped.org/*
National Association for Elementary School Principals—*http://www.naesp.org/*
National Association for Secondary School Principals—*http://www.nassp.org/*
National Education Association—*http://www.nea.org/*
National School Boards Association—*http://www.nsba.org/*
Parent–Teacher Association—*http://www.pta.org/*

Foundations, Think Tanks, and Policy Research Institutes
American Enterprise Institute—*http://www.aei.org/*
Brookings Institution—*http://www.brook.edu/*
Carnegie Corporation of New York—*http://www.carnegie.org/*
Cato Institute—*http://www.cato.org/*
Consortium for Policy Research in Education—*http://www.cpre.org/*
Economic Policy Institute—*http://www.epinet.org/*

Ford Foundation—*http://www.fordfound.org/*
Heritage Foundation—*http://www.heritage.org/*
Hoover Institute—*http://www.hoover.Stanford.edu/index.html*
RAND—*http://www.rand.org/*
Rockefeller Foundation—*http://www.rockfound.org/*
Urban Institute—*http://www.urban.org/*

Interest Groups

American Civil Liberties Union—*http://www.aclu.org/*
Americans United for the Separation of Church and State—*http://www.au.org/*
Children's Defense Fund—*http://www.childrensdefense.org/*
Christian Coalition—*http://www.cc.org/*
National Association for the Advancement of Colored People—*http://www.naacp.org/*
National Council of Churches—*http://www.ncccusa.org/*
National Council of La Raza—*http://www.nclr.org/*
U.S. Conference of Catholic Bishops—*http://www.nccbuscc.org/*

Intergovernmental Organizations

Education Commission of the States—*http://www.ecs.org/*
National Association of State Boards of Education—*http://www.nasbe.org/index.html/*
National Conference of State Legislators—*http://www.ncsl.org/*
National Council of Chief State School Officers—*http://www.ncsso.org/*
National Governors' Association—*http://www.nga.org/*

Business Groups

Business Roundtable—*http://www.brtable.org/*
Committee for Economic Development—*http://www.ced.org/*
Farm Bureau—*http://www.fb.com/*
National Alliance of Business—*http://www.nab.com/*
National Association of Manufacturers—*http://www.nam.org/*
U.S. Chamber of Commerce—*http://www.uschamber.com/*

Media

CNN—*http://www.cnn.com/*
C-SPAN—*http://www.c-span.org/*
Education Week—*http://www.edweek.org/*
New York Times—*http://www.nytimes.com/*
NPR—*http://www.npr.org/*
PBS—*http://www.pbs.org/*
Washington Post—*http://www.washingtonpost.com/*

Appendix B

How to Locate Government Web Sites for Specific States

Go to: The search directory, *Yahoo* (*http://www.yahoo.com*)

Select: Government

Select: U.S. Government

Select: State Government

Select: The specific state that interests you

References

Abanes, R. (1996). *American militias.* Downers Grove, IL: Intervarsity.

About national PTA. Available. *http://www.pta.org* [2002, April 22].

About NEA. Available. *http://www.nea.org/aboutnea/* [2002, April 22].

About us. Available. *http://www.stopopts.org/us.html* [2000, September 3].

Abraham, H. J. (1986). *The judicial process* (5th ed.). New York: Oxford University Press.

Abrams, M. H., Donaldson, E. T., Smith, H., Adams, R. M., Monk, S. H., Ford, G. H., & Daiches, D. (Eds.). (1962). *The Norton anthology of English literature.* New York: Norton.

Alexander, K., & Alexander, M. D. (1985). *American public school law* (2nd ed.). St. Paul, MN: West.

Alexander, K., & Alexander, M. D. (1998). *American public school law* (4th ed.). Belmont, CA: Wadsworth.

Almond, G. A. (1990). *A discipline divided: Schools and sects in political science.* Newbury Park, CA: Sage.

American Federation of Teachers. (1995). *What college-bound students abroad are expected to know.* Washington, D.C.: Author.

American heritage dictionary of the English language, The (3rd ed.), [CDROM]. (1992). Available: Houghton Mifflin.

Anderson, J. E. (1984). *Public policymaking* (3rd ed.). New York: Holt, Rinehart & Winston.

Apple, M. W. (1985). *Education and power.* Boston: Ark Paperbacks.

Apple, M. W. (2001). *Educating the "right" way.* New York: Routledge Falmer.

Archer, J. (2001, July 11). NEA agrees to new alliance with AFT. *Education Week on the Web.* Available. *http://www.edweek.org* [2002, April 22].

Arendt, H. (1986). Communicative power. In S. Lukes (Ed.), *Power* (pp. 59–74). New York: New York University Press.

Bachrach, P., & Baratz, M. S. (1962). Two faces of power. *American Political Science Review, 56,* 947–952.

Bachrach, P., & Botwinick, A. (1992). *Power and empowerment.* Philadelphia: Temple University Press.

Baker, K. (1991). Yes, throw money at schools. *Phi Delta Kappan, 72,* 628–631.

Ball, S. J. (1990). *Politics and policy making in education: Explorations in policy sociology.* London: Routledge.

Bardach, E. (1977). *The implementation game*. Cambridge, MA: The MIT Press.

Bartlett, B. R. (1981). *Reaganomics*. Westport, CT: Arlington House.

Baum, L. (1993). Making judicial policies in the political arena. In C. E. Van Horn (Ed.), *The state of the states* (2nd ed., pp. 103–130). Washington, D.C.: Congressional Quarterly Press.

Baum, L., & Kemper, M. (1994). The Ohio judiciary. In A. P. Lamis, (Ed.), *Ohio politics* (pp. 283–302). Kent, OH: Kent State University Press.

Baumann, E. A. (1989). Research, rhetoric and the social construction of elder abuse. In J. Best (Ed.), *Images of issues* (pp. 55–74). New York: deGruyter.

Baumgartner, F. R., & Jones, B. D. (1993). *Agendas and instability in American politics*. Chicago: University of Chicago Press.

Beatty, J. K. (1990). The Iowa judicial system. In L. A. Osbun & S. W. Schmidt (Eds.), *Issues in Iowa politics* (pp. 104–133). Ames, IA: Iowa State University.

Bellah, R. N., Madsen, R., Sullivan, W. M., Swidler, A., & Tipton, S. M. (1996). *Habits of the heart* (updated ed.). Berkeley, CA: University of California Press.

Bendix, R. (1960). *Max Weber*. Garden City, NY: Doubleday.

Benveniste, G. (1986). Implementation and intervention strategies: The case of 94–142. In D. L. Kirp & D. N. Jensen (Eds.), *School days, rule days* (pp. 146–163). Philadelphia: Falmer Press.

Berliner, D. C., & Biddle, B. J. (1995). *The manufactured crisis: Myths, fraud, and the attack on America's public schools*. Reading, MA: Addison Wesley.

Berman, P., & McLaughlin, M. W. (1976). Implementation of educational innovation. *The Educational Forum, 40*, 345–370.

Berman, P., & McLaughlin, M. W. (1978). *Federal programs supporting educational change, Vol. VIII: Implementing and sustaining innovations*. Santa Monica, CA: Rand.

Bernstein, B. (1996). *Pedagogy, symbolic control, and identity*. London: Taylor & Francis.

Best, J. (1989a). Afterword. In J. Best (Ed.), *Images of issues* (pp. 243–253). New York: deGruyter.

Best, J. (1989b). Claims. In J. Best (Ed.), *Images of issues* (pp. 1–3). New York: deGruyter.

Best, J. (1989c). Dark figures and child victims: Statistical claims about missing children. In J. Best (Ed.), *Images of issues* (pp. 21–37). New York: deGruyter.

Beyer, B. K. (1995). *How to conduct a formative evaluation*. Alexandria, VA: Association for Curriculum and Program Development.

Beyle, T. L. (2001). *State and local government, 2001–2002*. Washington, D.C.: Congressional Quarterly Press.

Blank, R. M. (2000). Strong employment, low inflation: How has the US economy done so well? *Canadian Public Policy 26* (Special Supplement), S175–S186.

Bootel, J. A. (1995). *CEC special education advocacy handbook*. Reston, VA: Council for Exceptional Children.

Bowman, A. O., & Kearney, R. C. (1986). *The resurgence of the states*. Upper Saddle River, NJ: Prentice Hall.

Bowman, D. H. (2000, January 19). Lawmakers seek to abolish disdained Kansas board. *Education Week on the Web*. Available. *http://www.edweek.org/ew/ewstory.cfm* [2002, February 3].

Boyd, W. L. (1984). Competing values in educational policy and governance: Australian and American developments. *Educational Administration Review, 2,* 4–24.

Boyd, W. L. (1988). Policy analysis, educational policy, and management: Through a glass darkly. In N. J. Boyan (Ed.), *Handbook of research on educational administration* (pp. 501–522). New York: Longman.

Boyd, W. L., & Kerchner, C. T. (1988). Introduction and overview: Education and the politics of excellence and choice. In W. L. Boyd & C. T. Kerchner (Eds.), *The politics of excellence and choice in education* (pp. 1–11). London: Taylor & Francis.

Boyd, W. L., Lugg, C. A., & Zahorchak, G. L. (1996). Social traditionalists, religious conservatives, and the politics of outcome-based education. *Education and Urban Society, 28,* 347–365.

Brainard, E. A. (1996). *A hands-on guide to school program evaluation.* Bloomington, IN: Phi Delta Kappa Educational Foundation.

Brewer, G. D., & de Leon, P. (1983). *The foundations of policy analysis.* Homewood, IL: Dorsey.

Brouwer, S. (1998). *Sharing the pie.* New York: Henry Holt.

Brunner, C. C., & Björk, L. G. (Eds.). (2001). *The new superintendency.* Kidlington, Oxford, UK: Elsevier Science, Ltd.

Bryson, J. M., & Crosby, B. C. (1992). *Leadership for the common good: Tackling public problems in a shared power world.* San Francisco: Jossey-Bass.

Buchholz, T. G. (1989). *New ideas from dead economists.* New York: New American Library.

Burbules, N. C. (1986). A theory of power in education. *Educational Theory, 36,* 95–114.

Burke, F. G. (1990). *Public education: Who's in charge?* New York: Praeger.

Burron, A. (1994). Traditionalist Christians and OBE: What's the problem? *Educational Leadership, 51*(6), 73–75.

Callahan, R. E. (1962). *Education and the cult of efficiency.* Chicago: University of Chicago Press.

Carl, J. (1994). Parental choice as national policy in England and the United States. *Comparative Education Review, 38,* 294–322.

Carter, G. R., & Cunningham, W. G. (1997). *The American school superintendent.* San Francisco: Jossey-Bass.

Casey, C. (1996). *The hill on the net.* Boston: AP Professional.

Chelimsky, E., & Shadish, W. R. (1997). *Evaluation for the 21st century.* Thousand Oaks, CA: Sage.

Cherryholmes, C. (1988). *Power and criticism.* New York: Teachers College Press.

Chrispeels, J. H. (1997). Educational policy implementation in a shifting political climate: The California experience. *American Educational Research Journal, 34,* 453–481.

Christian Coalition. (1995). *Contract with the American family.* Nashville, TN: Moorings.

Chubb, J., & Moe, T. (1990). *Politics, markets, and America's schools.* Washington, D.C.: Brookings Institution.

Cibulka, J. G. (1995). Policy analysis and the study of the politics of education. In J. D. Scribner & D. Layton (Eds.), *The study of educational politics* (pp. 105–125). London: Falmer Press.

Clark, E. (2000, December 16). School leaders advocate state testing reform. [Hamilton, OH] *Journal-News*, pp. A1, A2.

Clune, W. H. (1994a). The cost and management of program adequacy: An emerging issue in educational policy and finance. *Educational Policy, 8,* 365–375.

Clune, W. H. (1994b). The shift from equity to adequacy in school finance. *Educational Policy, 8,* 376–394.

Cobb, R. W., & Elder, C. D. (1972). *Participation in American politics: The dynamics of agenda building.* Boston: Allyn & Bacon.

Cohen, D. K., & Spillane, J. P. (1993). Policy and practice: The relations between governance and instruction. In S. H. Fuhrman (Ed.), *Designing coherent education policy* (pp. 35–95). San Francisco: Jossey-Bass.

Congress A to Z. (3rd ed.) (1999). Washington, D.C.: Congressional Quarterly Press.

Consortium for Policy Research in Education. (n.d.). *Research agenda and recent publications list.* N.P.: Author.

Cook, D. (2001, August). *Regime disruption: The case of public education and the Reagan Administration.* Paper delivered at the Annual Meeting of the American Political Science Association, San Francisco.

Cookson, P. W., Jr. (1994). *School choice: The struggle for the soul of American education.* New Haven, CT: Yale University Press.

Coombs, P. H. (1984). *The world crisis in education.* New York: Oxford University Press.

Cooper, B. S., Fusarelli, L. D., & Carella, V. A. (2000). *Career crisis in the school superintendency?* Arlington, VA: American Association of School Administrators.

Coplin, W. D., & O'Leary, M. K. (1981). *Basic policy studies skills.* Croton-on-Hudson, NY: Policy Studies Associates.

Coplin, W. D., & O'Leary, M. K. (1998). *Basic policy studies skills* (3rd ed.). Croton-on-Hudson, NY: Policy Studies Associates.

Corson, D. (1993). *Language, minority education and gender.* Clevedon, United Kingdom: Multilingual Matters.

Corson, D. (1995). Discursive power in educational organizations: An introduction. In D. Corson (Ed.), *Discourse and power in educational organizations* (pp. 3–15). Cresskill, NJ: Hampton Press.

Coulter, E. M. (1991). *Principles of politics and government* (4th ed.). Dubuque, IA: Wm. C. Brown Publishers.

Cronin, T. E., & Loevy, R. D. (1993). *Colorado politics & government.* Lincoln, NE: University of Nebraska Press.

Cusick, P. A. (1973). *Inside high school: The students' world.* New York: Holt, Rinehart & Winston.

Dahl, R. (1984). *Modern political analysis* (4th ed.). Upper Saddle River, NJ: Prentice Hall.

Dahl, R. (1986). Power as the control of behavior. In S. Lukes (Ed.), *Power* (pp. 37–58). New York: New York University Press.

Davey, C. (1995, December 3). Ohio lawmaker pay rated average. *Cincinnati Enquirer*, B1, B9.

Davies, S., & Guppy, N. (1997). Globalization and educational reforms in Anglo-American democracies. *Comparative Education Review, 41*, 435–459.

Davis, L. J. (1974). *The emerging democratic majority.* New York: Stein & Day.

Deal, T. E., & Kennedy, A. A. (1982). *Corporate cultures.* Reading, MA: Addison-Wesley.

DeBray, E., Parson, G., & Woodworth, K. (2001). Patterns of response in four high schools under state accountability policies in Vermont and New York. In S. H. Fuhrman (Ed.), *From the capitol to the classroom: Standards-based reform in the states* (pp. 170–192). Chicago: University of Chicago Press.

deKieffer, D. E. 1997. *The citizen's guide to lobbying Congress.* Chicago: Chicago Review Press.

Delpit, L. D. (1988). The silenced dialogue: Power and pedagogy in educating other people's children. *Harvard Educational Review, 58*, 280–298.

Detwiler, F. (1993/1994, December/January) A tale of two districts. *Educational Leadership, 51*(4), 24–28.

De Witt, K. (1994, December 19). Have suburbs, especially in south, become the source of American political power? *New York Times*, p. A13.

Dobson, J. C. (January, 1995). Fund-raising letter for focus on the family.

Dubnick, M. J., & Bardes, B. A. (1983). *Thinking about public policy: A problem-solving approach.* New York: Wiley.

Dunlap, D. M., & Goldman, P. (1991). Rethinking power in schools. *Educational Administration Quarterly, 27*, 5–29.

Dye, T. R. (1990). *Who's running America?* (5th ed.). Upper Saddle River, NJ: Prentice Hall.

Ebbing, L. (2000, September 6). Proficiency tests create additions to school curriculum. [Hamilton, OH] *Journal-News*, p. A7.

Edelman, M. (1964). *The symbolic uses of politics.* Urbana, IL: University of Illinois Press.

Edlefson, C. (1994). The substance and politics of education reform: A view from a governor's office. *Planning and Changing, 25*(1/2), 41–55.

Education Commission of the States. Available. *http://www.ecs.org* [2002, April 22].

Elazar, D. J. (1994). *The American mosaic.* Boulder, CO: Westview Press.

Elling, R. C. (1996). Bureaucracy: Maligned yet essential. In V. Gray & H. Jacob (Eds.), *Politics in the American states* (6th ed., pp. 286–318). Washington, D.C.: Congressional Quarterly Press.

English, F. W. (1994). Politics in the nation's schools: The battle for the principalship. *NASSP Bulletin, 78*(558), 18–25.

Fairclough, N. (1995). Critical language awareness and self-identity in education. In D. Corson (Ed.), *Discourse and power in educational organizations* (pp. 257–272). Cresskill, NJ: Hampton Press.

Federal register. January 18, 2002.

Federal register. February 28, 2002.

Fenby, J. (1986). *The international news services.* New York: Schocken Books.

Fillingham, L. A. (1993). *Foucault for beginners.* New York: Writers & Readers Publishing.

Firestone, W. A. (1989). Educational policy as an ecology of games. *Educational Researcher, 18,* 18–23.

Firestone, W. A., & Corbett, H. D. (1988). Planned organizational change. In N. J. Boyan (Ed.), *Handbook of research on educational administration* (pp. 321–340). New York: Longman.

First, P. F., Curcio, J. L., & Young, D. L. (1994). State full-service initiatives: New notions of policy development. In L. Adler & S. Gardner (Eds.), *The politics of linking schools and social services* (pp. 63–73). Bristol, PA: Falmer Press.

Fleet, M. (1993). Christian democracy. In J. Krieger (Ed.), *The Oxford companion to politics of the world* (pp. 136–137). New York: Oxford University Press.

Ford, P. (1992). American Enterprise Institute for Public Policy Research. In C. H. Weiss (Ed.), *Organizations for policy analysis* (pp. 29–47). Newbury Park, CA: Sage.

Fowler, F. C. (1985). Why reforms go awry. *Education Week, V*(10), 24, 17.

Fowler, F. C. (1987). The politics of school reform in Tennessee: A view from the classroom. In W. L. Boyd & C. T. Kerchner (Eds.), *The politics of excellence and choice in education* (pp. 183–197). London: Taylor & Francis.

Fowler, F. C. (1992). Challenging the assumption that choice is all that freedom means. In F. C. Wendel (Ed.), *Reforms in empowerment, choice, and adult learning* (pp. 15–28). University Park, PA: University Council of Education Administration.

Fowler, F. C. (1995a). The international arena: The global village. In J. Scribner & D. Layton (Eds.), *Politics of Education Association 1994 commemorative yearbook.* London: Taylor & Francis.

Fowler, F. C. (1995b). The neoliberal value shift and its implications for federal education policy under Clinton. *Educational Administration Quarterly, 31,* 38–60.

Fowler, F. C. (1996, April). *Meaningful competition? A study of student movement under interdistrict open enrollment.* Paper presented at the annual meeting of the American Educational Research Association, New York.

Fowler, F. C. (2000). Converging forces: Understanding the growth of state authority over education. In N. D. Theobald & B. Malen (Eds.), *Balancing local control and state responsibility for K-12 education,* pp. 123–146. Larchmont, NY: Eye on Education.

Frahm, R. A. (1994). The failure of Connecticut's reform plan: Lesson for the nation. *Phi Delta Kappan, 76,* 156–159.

Friedman, M. (1962). *Capitalism and freedom.* Chicago: University of Chicago Press.

Frohnmayer, D. (1986). Legislatures and the courts: Guarding the guardians. *State Government, 59* (1), 7–11.

Frumkin, N. (1987). *Tracking America's economy.* Armonk, NY: M. E. Sharpe.

Frumkin, N. (1994). *Guide to economic indicators* (2nd ed.). Armonk, NY: M. E. Sharpe.

References   361

Fuhrman, S. H. (1993). The politics of coherence. In S. H. Fuhrman (Ed.), *Designing coherent education policy* (pp. 1–34). San Francisco: Jossey-Bass.

Fuhrman, S. H. (2001). Introduction. In S. H. Fuhrman (Ed.), *From the capitol to the classroom: Standards-based reform in the states* (pp. 1–12). Chicago: University of Chicago Press.

Fullan, M. (2001). *The new meaning of educational change* (3rd ed.). New York: Teachers College Press.

Galbraith, J. K. (1994). *A journey through economic time.* Boston: Houghton Mifflin.

Gargan, J. J. (1994). The Ohio executive branch. In A. P. Lamis (Ed.), *Ohio politics* (pp. 258–282). Kent, OH: Kent State University Press.

Garvin, J. R., & Young, A. H. (1994). Resource issues: A case study from New Orleans. In L. Adler & S. Gardner (Eds.), *The politics of linking schools and social services* (pp. 93–106). Bristol, PA: Falmer Press.

Gaventa, J. (1980). *Power and powerlessness.* Urbana, IL: University of Illinois Press.

Gerth, H., & Mills, C. W. (Eds.). (1946). *From Max Weber: Essays in sociology.* New York: Oxford University Press. Quoted in D. H. Wrong, *Power* (New York: Harper & Row, 1979), 230.

Gewirtz, S. (2000). Bringing the politics back in: A critical analysis of quality discourses in education. *British Journal of Educational Studies 48*, 352–370.

Gewirtz, S., Ball, S. J., & Bowe, R. (1995). *Markets, choice and equity in education.* Buckingham, United Kingdom: Open University Press.

Giroux, H. A. (1999). *The mouse that roared.* Lanham, MD: Rowman & Littlefield.

Goode, E. (1994). *Site-based management in public education: A challenge for critical pragmatism.* Unpublished doctoral dissertation, Miami University, Oxford, OH.

Graber, D. A. (1994). Swiss cheese journalism. In T. L. Beyle (Ed.), *State government* (pp. 69–72). Washington, D.C.: Congressional Quarterly Press.

Grace, G. (1995). *School leadership.* London: Falmer Press.

Grady, D. O. (1991). Business group influence in state development policymaking. *State and Local Government Review, 23*(3), 110–118.

Gray, V. (1996). The socioeconomic and political context of states. In V. Gray & H. Jacob (Eds.), *Politics in the American states* (6th ed., pp. 1–34). Washington, D.C.: Congressional Quarterly Press.

Gronn, P. C. (1983). Talk as the work: The accomplishment of school administration. *Administrative Science Quarterly, 28*, 1–21.

Gross, N., Giacquinta, J. B., & Bernstein, M. (1971). *Implementing organizational innovations.* New York: Basic Books.

Growth spurts. (2000, September 27). *Education Week on the Web.* Available. *http://www.edweek.org/ew/ewstory.cfm* [2002, February 25].

Guba, E. G., & Lincoln, Y. S. (1989). *Fourth generation evaluation.* Newbury Park, CA: Sage.

Guthrie, J. D., Garms, W. I., & Pierce, L. C. (1988). *School finance and education policy* (2nd ed.). Upper Saddle River, NJ: Prentice Hall.

Guthrie, J. W., & Koppich, J. (1987). Exploring the political economy of national education reform. In W. L. Boyd & C. T. Kerchner (Eds.), *The politics of excellence and choice in education* (pp. 25–47). London: Falmer Press.

Haddad, C. (2001, May 21). Congratulations, grads—you're bankrupt. *BusinessWeek*, p. 48.

Hagan, J. P. (1988). Patterns of activism on state supreme courts. *Publius: The Journal of Federalism 18*(1), 297–315.

Halberstam, D. (1986). *The reckoning*. New York: Morrow.

Hall, E. T. (1966). *The hidden dimension*. Garden City, NY: Anchor Books.

Hall, L. (1988). Bending the rules: Negotiating rules in administrative agencies. *Policy Studies Journal, 16*, 533–541.

Hamm, K. E., & Moncrief, G. F. (1999). Legislative politics in the states. In V. Gray, R. L. Hanson, & H. Jacob (Eds.), *Politics in the American states* (7th ed., pp. 144–190). Washington, D.C.: Congressional Quarterly Press.

Hamrin, R. (1988). *America's new economy*. New York: Franklin Watts.

Hanna, J. (2000, May 19). Fighting within Kansas GOP continues as campaign season revs up. The Associated Press State & Local Wire. Available. *http://web.lexis-nexis.com/universe/docum* [2002, February 3].

Hannaway, J., & Kimball, K. (2001). Big isn't always bad: School district size, poverty, and standards-based reform. In S. H. Fuhrman (Ed.), *From the capitol to the classroom: Standards-based reform in the states(* pp. 99–123). Chicago: University of Chicago Press.

Hanson, R. L. (1996). Intergovernmental relations. In V. Gray & H. Jacob (Eds.), *Politics in the American states* (6th ed., pp. 35–77). Washington, D.C.: Congressional Quarterly Press.

Hanushek, E. A. (1989). The impact of differential expenditures on school performance. *Educational Researcher, 18*(4), 45–51, 62.

Hanushek, E. A. (1994). A jaundiced view of "adequacy" in school finance reform. *Educational Policy, 8*, 460–469.

Harragan, B. L. (1977). *Games mother never taught you*. New York: Warner Books.

Hatch, J., & Clinton, A. (2000, December). Job growth in the 1990s: A retrospect. *Monthly Labor Review*, 3–18.

Heclo, H. (1978). Issue networks and the executive establishment. In A. King (Ed.), *The new American political system* (pp. 87–124). Washington, D.C.: American Enterprise Institute for Public Policy Research.

Heilbroner, R. L. (1985). *The nature and logic of capitalism*. New York: Norton.

Hendrie, C. (1996, April 17). Deteriorating race relations shake Denver. *Education Week*, 1, 8.

Hilgartner, S., & Bosk, C. L. (1988). The rise and fall of social problems: A public arenas model. *American Journal of Sociology, 94*, 53–78.

Hirschman, A. O. (1970). *Exit, voice, and loyalty*. Cambridge, MA: Harvard University Press.

History of Ohio proficiency tests. (n.d.) Available. *http://www.stopopts.org/histotybocy.html* [2000, September 3].

Hobbes, T. (1958). *Leviathan*. Indianapolis: BobbsMerrill. Quoted in Wrong, D. H. (1979). *Power* (p. 218). New York: Harper & Row.

Hodgkinson, H. (2000/2001). Educational demographics: What teachers should know. *Educational Leadership 58*(4), pp. 6–11.

Hoff, D. J. (1997, September 3). Riley offers test control concession. *Education Week*, 1, 34.

Hoff, D. J. (1999, April 28). Eminent science group reiterates importance of teaching evolution. *Education Week on the Web*. Available. *http://www.edweek.org/ew/ewstory.cfm* [2002, February 3].

Hoff, D. J. (1999, October 20). Kansas to revise standards without citing evolution. *Education Week on the Web*. Available. *http://www.edweek.org/ew/ewstory.cfm* [2002, February 3].

Hoff, D. J. (2000, March 8). State capitals stirred by evolution. *Education Week on the Web*. Available. *http://www.edweek.org/ew/ewstory.cfm* [2002, February 3].

Hoff, D. J. (2002, June 12). Panel to examine standards-based math curricula. *Education Week*, p. 5.

Hofstede, G. (1987). Cultural dimensions in management and planning. In D. R. Hampton, C. E. Summer, & R. A. Webber (Eds.), *Organizational behavior and the practice of management* (pp. 401–422). Glenview, IL: Scott, Foresman.

Hogwood, B. W., & Gunn, L. A. (1984). *Policy analysis for the real world*. London: Oxford University Press.

Huberman, A. M., & Miles, M. B. (1984). *Innovation up close*. New York: Plenum Press.

Hudgins, H. C., Jr. (1970). *The Warren court and the public schools*. Danville, IL: Interstate Printers & Publishers.

Hulten, C. R., & Sawhill, I. V. (1984). *The legacy of Reaganomics: An overview*. Washington, D.C.: Urban Institute.

Hunt, S., Tortora, A., & Mrozowski, J. (2000, September 3). High-stakes state tests raise stress, controversy. *Cincinnati Enquirer*, pp. A1, A10.

Husen, T., Tuijnman, A., & Halls, W. (1992). *Schooling in modern European society*. Oxford: Pergamon Press.

Iannaccone, L. (1988). From equity to excellence: Political context and dynamics. In W. L. Boyd & C. T. Kerchner (Eds.), *The politics of excellence and choice in education* (pp. 49–65). London: Falmer Press.

Iannaccone, L., & Lutz, F. W. (1995). The crucible of democracy: The local arena. In J. D. Scribner & D. Layton (Eds.), *The study of educational politics* (pp. 39–52). Washington, D.C.: Falmer Press.

Illinois State University, College of Education. (1997). Status of school finance constitutional litigation. Available. *http://www.ilstu.edu/depts/coe/boxscore.htm* [1997, January 12].

The immigration wave. (2000, September 27). *Education Week on the Web*. Available. *http://www.edweek.org/ew/ewstory.cfm* [2002, February 25].

Isaak, A. (1987). *Politics*. Glenview, IL: Scott, Foresman.

It's all relative. (2000, September 27). *Education Week on the Web*. Available. *http://www.edweek.org/ew/ewstory.cfm* [2002, February 25].

Jackson, J. E., & Kingdon, J. W. (1992). Ideology, interest group scores, and legislative votes. *American Journal of Political Science*, 36, 805–823.

Jacob, H. (1996). Courts: The least visible branch. In V. Gray & H. Jacob (Eds.), *Politics in the American states* (6th ed., pp. 253–285). Washington, D.C.: Congressional Quarterly Press.

Jacobs, J. A. & Gerson, K. (2000). Who are the overworked Americans? In L. Golden & D. M. Figart (Eds.), *Working time* (pp. 89–105). London: Routledge.

Jacobson, L. (2000, November 8). Census finds fewer young children being cared for by relatives. *Education Week on the Web*. Available. *http://www.edweek. org/ew/ewstory.cfm* [2002, February 25].

Jennings, J. F. (1998). *Why national standards and tests?* Thousand Oaks, CA: Sage Publications.

Jensen, D. N. (1985). Judicial activism and special education. (Project Report No. 85-A10, sponsored by the National Institute of Education, Grant No. NIE-G-83-0003.)

Johnson, S. M. (1996). *Leading to change: The challenge of the new superintendency.* San Francisco: Jossey-Bass.

Joint Committee on Standards for Educational Evaluation. (1994). *The program evaluation standards* (2nd ed.). Thousand Oaks, CA: Sage.

Kaestle, C. F. (1983). *Pillars of the republic.* New York: Hill & Wang.

Kagan, R. A. (1986). Regulating business, regulating schools: The problem of regulatory unreasonableness. In D. L. Kirp & D. N. Jensen (Eds.), *School days, rule days* (pp. 64–90). Philadelphia: Falmer Press.

Kahne, J. (1996). *Reframing educational policy.* New York: Teachers College Press.

Kalodner, H. I. (1990). Overview of judicial activism in education litigation. In B. Flicker (Ed.), *Justice and school systems* (pp. 3–22). Philadelphia: Temple University Press.

Kaplan, G. R., & Usdan, M. D. (1992). The changing look of education's policy networks. *Phi Delta Kappan, 73,* 664–672.

Kaplan, M., & O'Brien, S. (1991). *The governors and the new federalism.* Boulder, CO: Westview Press.

Keller, B. & Coles, A. (1999, September 8). Kansas evolution controversy gives rise to national debate. *Education Week on the Web*. Available. *http://www.edweek.org/ ew/ewstory.cfm* [2002, February 3].

Kelman, S. (1988). Why public ideas matter. In R. B. Reich (Ed.), *The power of public ideas* (pp. 31–53). Cambridge, MA: Ballinger.

Kenworthy, L. (1995). *In search of national economic success.* Thousand Oaks, CA: Sage.

Kerwin, C. M. (1994). *Rulemaking.* Washington, D.C.: Congressional Quarterly Press.

Kimbrough, R. B. (1982). Do political ideologies influence education in the United States? *Educational Administration Quarterly, 18*(2), 22–38.

King, J. A. (1994). Meeting the educational needs of at-risk students: A cost analysis of three models. *Educational Evaluation and Policy Analysis, 16,* 1–19.

Kingdon, J. W. (1995). *Agendas, alternatives, and public policies* (2nd ed.). New York: HarperCollins.

Kirp, D. L. (1982). Professionalization as a policy choice: British special education in comparative perspective. *World Politics, 34,* 137–174.

Kirp, D. L. (1986). Introduction: The fourth R: Reading, writing, 'rithmetic—and rules. In D. L. Kirp & D. N. Jensen (Eds.), *School days, rule days* (pp. 1–17). Philadelphia: Falmer Press.

Kirst, M., & Jung, R. (1980). The utility of a longitudinal approach in assessing implementation. *Educational Evaluation and Policy Analysis 2*, 17–34.

Kowalski, T. J. (1995). *Keepers of the flame*. Thousand Oaks, CA: Corwin Press.

Kowalski, T. J. (1999). *The school superintendent*. Upper Saddle River, NJ: Prentice Hall.

Kruschke, E. R., & Jackson, B. M. (1987). *The public policy dictionary*. Santa Barbara, CA: ABC–CLIO.

Kuttner, R. (1984). *The economic illusion*. Boston: Houghton Mifflin.

Lagemann, E. C. (1989). *The politics of knowledge*. Middletown, CT: Wesleyan University Press.

Lamare, J. W. (1994). *California politics*. Minneapolis, MN: West Publishing.

La Morte, M. W. (1993). *School law: Cases and concepts* (4th ed.). Boston: Allyn & Bacon.

Largest foreign-born populations in the U.S. (2000, September 27). *Education Week on the Web*. Available. *http://www.edweek.org/ew/ewstory.cfm* [2002, February 25].

Lawton, M. (1997, August 6). Feds position national tests on fast track. *Education Week*, 1, 34.

Lemke, J. L. (1995). *Textual politics*. London: Taylor & Francis.

Levin, H. M., & McEwan, P. J. (2001). *Cost-effectiveness analysis* (2nd ed.). Thousand Oaks, CA: Sage Publications.

Lewis, D. A., & Maruna, S. (1996). The politics of education. In V. Gray & H. Jacob (Eds.), *Politics in the American states* (6th ed., pp. 438–477). Washington, D.C.: Congressional Quarterly Press.

Lind, M. (1996). *Up from conservatism*. New York: Free Press.

Lindblom, C. E. (1968). *The policymaking process*. Upper Saddle River, NJ: Prentice Hall.

Lipset, S. M. (1996). *American exceptionalism*. New York: Norton.

Loomis, B. A. (1994). *Time, politics and policies*. Lawrence, KS: University Press of Kansas.

Lorch, R. S. (1987). *Colorado's government* (4th ed.). N.P.: Colorado Associated University Press.

Lortie, D. C. (1975). *Schoolteacher*. Chicago: University of Chicago Press.

Louis, K. S., & Miles, M. B. (1990). *Improving the urban high school*. New York: Teachers College Press.

Lowi, T. J. (1964, July). American business, public policy, case studies, and political theory. *World Politics*, 677–715.

Lowi, T. J. (1979). *The end of liberalism* (2nd ed.). New York: Norton.

Lowi, T. J. (1995). *The end of the Republican era*. Norman, OK: University of Oklahoma Press.

Lowi, T. J., & Ginsberg, B. (1994). *American government* (brief 3rd ed.). New York: Norton.

Lugg, C. A. (1996). *For God and country*. New York: Peter Lang.

Lukes, S. (1974). *Power*. Houndsmills, United Kingdom: MacMillan.

Lutz, F. W., & Merz, C. (1992). *The politics of school/community relations*. New York: Teachers College Press.

Madaus, G. F., Stufflebeam, D. L., & Scriven, M. (1983). Program evaluation: A historical overview. In G. F. Madaus, M. Scriven, & D. L. Stufflebeam (Eds.), *Evaluation models* (pp. 23–43). Boston: Kluwer-Nijhoff.

Madsen, J. (1994). *Educational reform at the state level.* Bristol, PA: Falmer Press.

Makin, J. H. (1996). How low should inflation go? *AEI Economic Outlook* [Online serial]. Available: *http://www.aei.org/eo/eo6981.htm.*

Makin, J. H. (1997). Perils of prosperity. *AEI Economic Outlook* [Online serial]. Available: *http://www.aei.org/eo/eo8270.htm.*

Malen, B., & Ogawa, R. T. (1988). Professional patron influence on site-based management. *Educational Evaluation and Policy Analysis, 10,* 251–270.

Mann, M. (1992). *The sources of social power. Vol. 1.* Cambridge, England: Cambridge University Press.

Manzo, K. K. (2001, May 16). Protests over state testing widespread. *Education Week,* pp. 1, 26.

Marshall, C. (2000). Policy discourse analysis: Negotiating gender equality. *Journal of Education Policy, 15* (2), 125–156.

Marshall, C., Mitchell, D., & Wirt, F. (1989). *Culture and education policy in the American states.* New York: Falmer Press.

Martin, J. M. (1994). *Lessons from the hill.* New York: St. Martin's Press.

Mazmanian, D. A., & Sabatier, P. A. (1989). *Implementation and public policy.* Lanham, MD: University Press of America.

Mazzoni, T. L. (1993). The changing politics of state education policy making: A 20 year Minnesota perspective. *Educational Evaluation and Policy Analysis, 15,* 357–379.

Mazzoni, T. L. (1995). State policymaking and school reform: Influences and influentials. In J. D. Scribner & D. H. Layton (Eds.), *The study of educational politics* (pp. 53–73). London: Falmer Press.

McCarthy, M., Langdon, C., & Olson, J. (1993). *State education governance structures.* Denver, CO: Education Commission of the States.

McCarthy, M. M., & Cambron-McCabe, N. H. (1998). *Public school law: Teachers' and students' rights* (4th ed.). Boston: Allyn & Bacon.

McDonnell, L. M. (1991). Ideas and values in implementation analysis. In A. R. Odden (Ed.), *Education policy implementation* (pp. 241–258). Albany, NY: State University of New York Press.

McDonnell, L. M. (1994). Assessment policy as persuasion and regulation. *American Journal of Education, 102,* 391–420.

McDonnell, L. M., & Elmore, R. F. (1987). Getting the job done: Alternative policy instruments. *Educational Evaluation and Policy Analysis, 9,* 133–152.

McGann, J. G. (1995). *The competition for dollars, scholars, and influence in the public policy research industry.* Lanham, MD: University Press of America.

McGivney, J. H. (1984). State educational governance patterns. *Educational Administration Quarterly, 20,* 43–63.

McLaughlin, M. W. (1976). Implementation as mutual adaptation: Change in classroom organization. *Teachers College Record, 77,* 339–351.

McLaughlin, M. W. (1987). Learning from experience: Lessons from policy implementation. *Educational Evaluation and Policy Analysis, 9,* 171–178.

McLean, J. (2000, July 30). Primary highlights GOP feud. *Topeka Capital Journal.* Available. *http://web.lexis-nexis.com/universe/docum* [2002, February 3].

Mead, T. D. (1994). The daily newspaper as political agenda setter: *The Charlotte Observer* and metropolitan reform. *State and Local Government Review, 26*(1), 27–37.

Meade, E. J., Jr. (1991). Foundations and the public schools. *Phi Delta Kappan, 73,* K1–K12.

Miles, D. (2000, November 8). Gamble, Rupe, Wyatt win Board of Ed seats. The Associated Press State & Local Wire. Available. *http://web.lexis-nexis.com/universe/docum* [2002, February 3].

Miles, M. B., & Louis, K. S. (1990). Mustering the will and skill for change. *Educational Leadership, 47*(8), 57–61.

Miller, D. (Ed.). (1987). *The Blackwell encyclopaedia of political thought.* Oxford, England: Basil Blackwell.

Mintrom, M. (1997). Policy entrepreneurs and the diffusion of innovation. *American Journal of Political Science 41,* 738–770.

Mirel, J. (1994). School reform unplugged: The Bensenville New American School project, 1991–93. *American Educational Research Journal, 31,* 481–518.

Miron, L. F., & Wimpelberg, R. K. (1992). The role of school boards in the governance of education. In P. F. First & H. J. Walberg (Eds.), *School boards* (pp. 151–175). Berkeley, CA: McCutchan.

Mitchell, D. E. (1984). Educational policy analysis: The state of the art. *Educational Administration Quarterly, 20,* 129–160.

Mixed needs of immigrants pose challenges for schools. (2000, September 27). *Education Week on the Web.* Available. *http://www.edweek.org/ew/ewstory.cfm* [2002, February 25].

Morken, H., & Formicola, J. R. (1999). *The politics of school choice.* Lanham, MD: Rowman & Littlefield

Morrison, P. A. (2001). *A demographic perspective on our nation's future.* Santa Monica, CA: Rand.

Muller-Hill, B. (1988, December 22). Heroes and villains. *Nature,* 721–722.

Murphy, J. (1990). *The educational reform movement of the 1980s.* Berkeley, CA: McCutchan.

Murphy, J. T. (1971). Title I of ESEA: The politics of implementing federal education reform. *Harvard Educational Review, 41,* 35–63.

Muth, R. (1984). Toward an integrative theory of power and educational organizations. *Educational Administration Quarterly, 20,* 25–42.

Nagel, S. S. (1984). *Contemporary public policy analysis.* University, AL: University of Alabama Press.

Nakamura, R. T., & Smallwood, F. (1980). *The politics of policy implementation.* New York: St. Martin's Press.

Nathan, R. P. (1993). The role of the states in American federalism. In C. E. Van Horn (Ed.), *The state of the states* (2nd ed., pp. 15–32). Washington, D.C.: Congressional Quarterly Press.

National Alliance of Business. (2002.) Available. *http://www.nab.com* [2002, April 22].

National Governors Association Online. (n.d.) Available. *http://www.nga.org* [2002, April 22].

Nelson, R. H. (1991). Economists as policy analysts: Historical overview. In D. L. Weimer (Ed.), *Policy analysis and economics: Developments, tensions, prospects* (pp. 1–21). Boston: Kluwer Academic Publishers.

Neustadt, R. E. (1960). *Presidential power.* New York: Wiley.

New York Times, The. (1996). *The downsizing of America.* New York: Times Books.

Nielsen, W. A. (1985). *The golden donors.* New York: Dutton.

Nuttall, D. L. (1994). Choosing indicators. In K. A. Riley & D. L. Nuttall (Eds.), *Measuring quality* (pp. 17–40). London: Falmer Press.

OEA Online News. (n.d.). Available. *http://www.ohea.org/news/news.htm* [2000, September 3].

Ogawa, R. T. (1994). The institutional sources of educational reform: The case of school based management. *American Educational Research Journal, 31,* 519–548.

Ohio Department of Education. (1995). *Venture capital in Ohio schools: Building commitment and capacity for school renewal.* Columbus, OH: Author.

Ohio State University. (1991). Department of Policy and Leadership. Policy Research for Ohio Based Education. *How to lobby the legislature: An interview with Representative Michael Fox.* Produced by Robert Donmoyer. [Videotape].

Okun, A. (1975). *Equality and efficiency: The big tradeoff.* Washington, D.C.: Brookings Institution.

Okun, A. M. (1982). Customer markets and the costs of inflation. In M. N. Baily & A. K. Okun (Eds.), *The battle against unemployment and inflation* (pp. 35–39). New York: Norton.

Oleszek, W. J. (2001). *Congressional procedures and the policy process* (5th ed.). Washington, D.C.: Congressional Quarterly Press.

Olson, L. (2000, September 27). Minority groups to emerge as a majority in U.S. schools. *Education Week on the Web.* Available. *http://weww.edweek.org/ew/ewstory.cfm* [2002, February 25].

Olson, L. (2000, September 27). School-age 'millenni-boom' predicted for next 100 years. *Education Week on the Web.* Available. *http://www.edweek.org/ew/ewstory.cfm* [2002, February 25].

Oregon. (2002). *Oregon Administrative Rules, 2002 Compilation.* Available. *http://arc.web.sos.state.or.us/rules/OAR* [2002, May 23].

Paris, D. C., & Reynolds, J. F. (1983). *The logic of policy inquiry.* New York: Longman.

Patterson, S. C. (1996). Legislative politics in the states. In V. Gray & H. Jacob (Eds.), *Politics in the American states* (6th ed., pp. 159–206). Washington, D.C.: Congressional Quarterly Press.

Peck, M. S. (1978). *The road less traveled.* New York: Simon & Schuster.

Penner, R. G., Sawhill, I. V., & Taylor, T. (2000). *Updating America's social contract.* New York: W. W. Norton & Co.

Perkinson, H. J. (1991). *The imperfect panacea* (4th ed.). New York: McGraw-Hill.

Perot, R. (1993). *Not for sale at any price.* New York: Hyperion.

Peschek, J. G. (1987). *Policy-planning organizations.* Philadelphia: Temple University Press.

Peshkin, A. (2001). *Permissible advantage? The moral consequences of elite schooling.* Mahwah, NJ: Lawrence Erlbaum Associates.

Peters, C. (1983, May). A neoliberal's manifesto. *The Washington Monthly,* 9–18.

Peterson, P., Rabe, B., & Wong, K. (1986). *When federalism works.* Washington, D.C.: Brookings Institution.

Peterson, P., Rabe, B., & Wong, K. (1991). *When federalism works.* Washington, D.C.: Brookings Institution.

Phillips, K. (1994). *Arrogant capital.* Boston: Little, Brown.

Pipho, C. (1990). State departments: Change on the way. *Phi Delta Kappan, 72,* 262–263.

Placier, M. (1996). The cycle of student labels in education: The cases of *culturally deprived/disadvantaged* and *at-risk. Educational Administration Quarterly, 32,* 236–270.

Pliska, A. M., & McQuaide, J. (1994). Pennsylvania's battle for student learning outcomes. *Educational Leadership, 51*(6), 66–69.

Plotkin, S., & Scheuerman, W. E. (1994). *Private interests, public spending.* Boston, MA: South End Press.

Popham, W. J. (1988). *Educational evaluation* (2nd ed.). Upper Saddle River, NJ: Prentice Hall.

Porter, A. C., Archbald, D. A., & Tyree, A. K., Jr. (1991). Reforming the curriculum: Will empowerment policies replace control? In S. H. Fuhrman & B. Malen (Eds.), *The politics of curriculum and testing* (pp. 11–36). London: Falmer Press.

Porter, M. C. (1982). State supreme courts and the legacy of the Warren court: Some inquiries for a new situation. In M. C. Porter & G. A. Tarr (Eds.), *State supreme courts* (pp. 3–21). Westport, CT: Greenwood Press.

Porter, M. C., & Tarr, G. A. (1982). Introduction. In M. C. Porter & G. A. Tarr (Eds.), *State supreme courts* (pp. xi–xxvii). Westport, CT: Greenwood Press.

Portner, J. (1996a, May 11). Minn. student leaders push for place at policy table. *Education Week,* 11.

Portner, J. (1996b, June 19). Study tracks violent deaths at school or related activities. *Education Week,* 10.

Portz, J. (1994). Plant closings, community definitions, and local response. In D. A. Rochefort & R. W. Cobb (Eds.), *The Politics of Problem Definition* (pp. 32–49). Lawrence, KS: University of Kansas Press.

Prestine, N., & McGreal, T. L. (1997). Fragile changes, sturdy lives: Implementing authentic assessment in schools. *Educational Administration Quarterly, 33,* 371–400.

Problem is politics. (1999, May 16). *Topeka Capital Journal.* Available. *http://web. lexis-nexis.com/universe/docum* [2002, February 3].

Przeworski, A. (1993). Socialism and social democracy. In J. Krieger (Ed.), *The Oxford companion to politics of the world* (pp. 832–839). New York: Oxford University Press.

Putnam, R. D. (2000). *Bowling alone.* New York: Simon & Schuster.

Putnam, R. D. (2002). Bowling together. *American Prospect 13* (3), 20–22.

Questionable clout. (1994, September 28). *Education Week, 30*.

Ravitch, D. (1983). *The troubled crusade*. New York: Basic Books.

Ravitch, D. (1995). *National standards in American education*. Washington, D.C.: Brookings Institution.

Rawls, J. (1971). *A theory of justice*. Cambridge, MA: Harvard University Press.

Ray, C. A., & Mickelson, R. A. (1990). Business leaders and the politics of school reform. In D. E. Mitchell & M. E. Goertz (Eds.), *Education politics for the new century* (pp. 119–135). London: Falmer Press.

Reich, R. (1991). *The work of nations*. New York: Knopf.

Reid, K. S. (2001, March 21). U.S. census underscores diversity. *Education Week on the Web*. Available. *http://www.edweek.org/ew/ewstory.cfm* [2002, February 25].

Reif, J., Whittle, J., Woznick, A., Thurmond, M. E., & Kelly, J. (1997). *Services: The export of the 21st century*. San Rafael, CA: World Trade Press.

Robelen, E. W. (2002, January 9). ESEA to Boost Federal Role in Education. *Education Week*, pp. 1, 28–29, 31.

Roberts, S. (1993). *Who we are*. New York: Times Books.

Robertson, D. (Ed.). (1985). *A dictionary of modern politics*. London: Europa Publications.

Robinson, V. M. J. (1995). The identification and evaluation of power in discourse. In D. Corson (Ed.), *Discourse and power in educational organizations* (pp. 111–130). Cresskill, NJ: Hampton Press.

Rochefort, D. A., & Cobb, R. W. (Eds.). (1994). *The politics of problem definition*. Lawrence, KS: University of Kansas Press.

Rosenblatt, R. A. (1996, March 14). Latinos, Asians, over-50s top growth groups for U.S. *Cincinnati Enquirer*, p. A14.

Rosenthal, A. (1981). *Legislative life*. New York: Harper & Row.

Rothman, S., & Lichter, S. R. (1982). *Roots of radicalism*. New York: Oxford University Press.

Rubin, I. S. (2000). *The politics of public budgeting* (4th ed.). Chatham, NJ: Chatham House.

Russo, C. J., & Lindle, J. C. (1994). On the cutting edge: Family resource/youth service centers in Kentucky. In L. Adler & S. Gardner (Eds.), *The politics of linking schools and social services* (pp. 179–187). Bristol, PA: Falmer Press.

Sabatier, P. (1975). Social movements and regulatory agencies: Toward a more adequate—and less pessimistic—theory of "clientele capture." *Policy Sciences, 6*, 301–342.

Sabatier, P. A., & Jenkins-Smith, H. C. (1993). *Policy change and learning*. Boulder, CO: Westview Press.

St. John, E. P. (1992). Who decides educational policy? Or how can the practitioner influence public choices? In P. F. First (Ed.), *Educational policy for school administrators* (pp. 96–103). Boston: Allyn & Bacon.

Sarason, S. B. (1996). *Revisiting "The culture of the school and the problem of change."* New York: Teachers College Press.

Sargent, L. T. (Ed.). (1995). *Extremism in America*. New York: New York University Press.

Schattschneider, E. E. (1935). *Politics, pressures, and the tariff.* New York: Prentice Hall. Cited in Lowi, T. J. (1964, July). American business, public policy, case studies, and political theory. *World Politics,* 677–715.

Schattschneider, E. E. (1960). *The semisovereign people.* New York: Holt, Rinehart & Winston.

Schor, J. B. (1998). *The overspent American.* New York: Basic Books.

Schroeder, R. (1992). *Max Weber and the sociology of culture.* London: Sage.

Shafer, B. E. (1983). *The quiet revolution.* New York: Russell Sage Foundation.

Shafritz, J. M., Williams, P., & Calinger, R. S. (1993). *The dictionary of 20th century politics.* New York: Henry Holt.

Sidoti, L. (2000, September 5). Schools feel pressure from test-driven ratings. [Hamilton, OH] *Journal-News,* pp. A1, A2.

Skrla, L. (2000). The social construction of gender in the superintendency. *Journal of Education Policy, 15,* 293–316.

Smith, A. (1976 [1776]). *An inquiry into the nature and causes of the wealth of nations.* Oxford, England: Clarendon Press. Quoted in Buchholz, T. G. (1989). *New ideas from dead economists* (pp. 21–22). New York: New American Library.

Smith, J. A. (1991). *Brookings at seventy-five.* Washington, D.C.: Brookings Institution.

Solomon, R. P. (1992). *Black resistance in high school.* Albany, NY: State University of New York Press.

Sommerfeld, M. (1996, April 24). California parents target math frameworks. *Education Week,* 1, 11.

Spring, J. (1989). *The sorting machine revisited.* New York: Longman.

Spring, J. (1994). *The American school, 1642–1993* (3rd ed.). New York: McGraw-Hill.

Spring, J. (1997). *Political agendas for education.* Mahwah, NJ: Lawrence Erlbaum Associates.

Sroufe, G. E. (1995). Politics of education at the federal level. In J. D. Scribner & D. H. Layton (Eds.), *The study of educational politics* (pp. 75–88). London: Falmer Press.

Stone, D. A. (1989). Causal stories and the formation of policy agendas. *Political Science Quarterly, 104,* 281–300.

Stufflebeam, D. L. (1983). The CIPP model for program evaluation. In G. F. Madaus, M. Scriven, & D. L. Stufflebeam (Eds.), *Evaluation models* (pp. 117–141). Boston: Kluwer-Nijhoff.

Stufflebeam, D. L., & Webster, W. J. (1983). An analysis of alternative approaches to evaluation. In G. F. Madaus, M. Scriven, & D. L. Stufflebeam (Eds.), *Evaluation models* (pp. 23–43). Boston: Kluwer-Nijhoff.

Summers, L. H. (1984). The long-term effects of current macroeconomic policies. In C. R. Hulten & I. V. Sawhill (Eds.), *The legacy of Reaganomics: An overview* (pp. 179–198). Washington, D.C.: Urban Institute.

Susser, B. (1995). *Political ideology in the modern world.* Boston: Allyn & Bacon

Swanson, A. D. (1989). Restructuring educational governance: A challenge of the 1990s. *Educational Administration Quarterly, 25,* 268–293.

Tapper, J. (2001). *Down & dirty: The plot to steal the presidency.* Boston: Little, Brown.

Tennessee Code Commission. (1995). *Tennessee code annotated: 1995 supplement. Vol. 9.* Charlottesville, VA: Michie.

Thomas, C. S., & Hrebenar, R. J. (1999). Interest groups in the states. In V. Gray & H. Jacob (Eds.), *Politics in the American states* (7th ed., pp. 113–143). Washington, D.C.: Congressional Quarterly Press.

Thurow, L. C. (1985, November). The "big tradeoff" debunked: The efficiency of a fair economy. *The Washington Monthly,* 47–54.

Thurow, L. C. (1992). *Head to head.* New York: Morrow.

Thurow, L. C. (1996). *The future of capitalism.* New York: Morrow.

Toch, T. (1996, February 26). Why teachers don't teach. *U.S. News and World Report,* 62–71.

Tripp, R. T. (Ed.). (1970). *The international thesaurus of quotations.* New York: Crowell.

Trotter, A. (2001, May 23). Census shows the changing face of U.S. households. *Education Week,* p. 5.

Turner, D. W. (1995). Building legislative relationships: A guide for principals. *Here's How, 13*(5), 1–4.

Tyack, D. (1974). *The one best system.* Cambridge, MA: Harvard University Press.

Tyack, D. (1986). Toward a social history of law and public education. In D. L. Kirp & D. N. Jensen (Eds.), *School days, rule days* (pp. 212–237). Philadelphia: Falmer Press.

Tyack, D., & Cuban, L. (1995). *Tinkering toward utopia.* Cambridge, MA: Harvard University Press.

Tyack, D., & Tobin, W. (1994). The "grammar" of schooling: Why has it been so hard to change? *American Educational Research Journal, 31,* 453–479.

Unfulfilled promises: School finance remedies and state courts. (1991). *Harvard Law Review, 104,* 1072–1092.

U.S. Department of Education. (1999). *A back to school special report on the baby boom echo: No end in sight.* Available. h*ttp://www.ed.gov/pubs/bbecho99/index.html* [2002, February 25].

Van Horn, C. E. (Ed.). (1993). Preface. *The state of the states* (2nd ed.). Washington, D.C.: Congressional Quarterly Press.

Verba, S., & Orren, G. R. (1985). *Equality in America.* Cambridge, MA: Harvard University Press.

Verstegen, D. (1994). Reforming American education policy for the 21st century. *Educational Administration Quarterly, 30,* 365–390.

Vinovskis, M. A. (1996). An analysis of the concept and uses of systemic educational reform. *American Educational Research Journal, 33,* 53–85.

Viteritti, J. P. (1999). *Choosing equality.* Washington, D.C.: Brookings Institution.

Vobejda, B. (1995, April 24). 24% of kids in fatherless homes. *Cincinnati Enquirer,* p. A6.

Waite, D. (1995). Teacher resistance in a supervision conference. In D. Corson (Ed.), *Discourse and power in educational organizations* (pp. 71–86). Cresskill, NJ: Hampton Press.

Weaver, S. W., & Geske, T. G. (1995, April). *Educational policymaking in the state legislature: Legislator as policy expert.* Paper presented at the annual meeting of the American Educational Research Association, San Francisco.

Weber, M. (1968). *Economy and society.* Three volumes. New York: Bedminster Press. Quoted in Wrong, D. H. (1979). *Power* (p. 21). New York: Harper & Row.

Weber, M. (1986). Domination by economic power and by authority. In S. Lukes (Ed.), *Power* (pp. 28–36). New York: New York University Press.

Weeres, J. G. (1988). Economic choice and the dissolution of community. In W. L. Boyd & C. T. Kerchner (Eds.), *The politics of excellence and choice in education* (pp. 117–129). New York: Falmer Press.

Weimer, D. L., & Vining, A. R. (1992). *Policy analysis: Concepts and practice* (2nd ed.). Upper Saddle River, NJ: Prentice Hall.

Weiss, C. (Ed.). (1992). *Organizations for policy analysis.* Newbury Park, CA: Sage.

Weiss, C. H. (1988). Where politics and evaluation research meet. In D. Palumbo (Ed.). *The politics of program evaluation,* pp. 47–70. Newbury Park, CA: Sage.

Weiss, C. H. (1992). Helping government think: Functions and consequences of policy analysis organizations. In C. H. Weiss (Ed.), *Organizations for policy analysis* (pp. 1–18). Newbury Park, CA: Sage.

Welsh-Huggins, A. (2000, September 5). State tests raise angst. *Cincinnati Enquirer,* pp. B1, B4.

Welsh-Huggins, A. (2000, November 30). Overhaul of Ohio's proficiency test procedure may be forthcoming. [Hamilton, OH] *Journal-News,* p. A7.

Wiget, L. A. (1995). *Effective government relations for public education.* Bloomington, IN: Phi Delta Kappa Educational Foundation.

Wildavsky, A. (1988). *The new politics of the budgetary process.* Glenview, IL: Scott, Foresman.

Williams, B. R., & Palmatier, M. A. (1992). The RAND Corporation. In C. H. Weiss (Ed.). *Organizations for policy analysis* (pp. 48–68). Newbury Park, CA: Sage.

Wilson, J. Q. (1989). *Bureaucracy.* New York: Basic Books.

Wirt, F. M., & Harman, G. (1986). *Education, recession, and the world village.* London: Falmer Press.

Wodak, R. 1995. Power, discourse, and styles of female leadership in school committee meetings. In D. Corson (Ed.), *Discourse and power in educational organizations* (pp. 31–54). Cresskill, NJ: Hampton Press.

Wolf, R. M. (1990). *Evaluation in education* (3rd ed.). New York: Praeger.

Wrong, D. H. (1979). *Power.* New York: Harper & Row.

Yanow, D. (2000). *Conducting interpretive policy analysis.* Thousand Oaks, CA: Sage.

Zitterkopf, R. (1994). A fundamentalist's defense of OBE. *Educational Leadership, 51*(6), 76–78.

Author Index

Detwiler, F., 132, 137
DeWitt, K., 68
Dobson, J., 125
Donaldson, E. T., 240
Drake, Lisa, 105
Driscoll, D., 104–105
Dubnick, M. J., 8
Dunlap, D. M., 28
Dye, T. R., 174

Edelman, M., 10
Elazar, D. J., 80, 97, 98, 100
Elder, C. D., 180, 185
Elling, R. C., 154
Elmore, R. F., 250, 252, 253–254, 256, 258

Fairclough, N., 29
Fenby, J., 158
Fillingham, L. A., 34
Firestone, W. A., 8, 13, 271, 293
First, P. F., 94
Fleet, M., 131
Ford, G. H., 240
Ford, P., 177
Formicola, J. R., 184
Foucault, M., 34
Fowler, F. C., 6, 15, 109, 116, 118, 120, 128, 149, 152, 299n, 341, 342
Fox, Herb, 104–105
Frahm, R. A., 122
Franklin, B., 111
Friedman, M., 123, 184
Frohnmayer, D., 215
Frumkin, N., 61
Fuentes, E., 324n
Fuhrman, S. H., 14, 15, 17, 85, 86, 87, 345
Fullan, M., 271, 278, 279, 280, 281, 283, 284, 289, 291, 296
Fusarelli, L. D., 152

Galbraith, J. K., 56, 57, 63
Gargan, J. J., 209
Garms, W. I., 116
Garvin, J. R., 93, 94
Gaventa, J., 30, 31, 35, 40–41
Gerson, K., 124
Gerth, H., 47
Geske, T. G., 146
Gewirtz, S., 38–39, 119
Giacquinta, J. B., 271, 272, 274, 286–287, 288, 292
Ginsberg, B., 205, 215, 216, 217, 240, 241, 243, 244, 246, 328
Giroux, H. A., 39
Goldman, P., 28
Goode, E., 7
Graber, D., 158
Grace, G., 297
Grady, D. O., 155
Gray, V., 82
Gronn, P. C., 28
Gross, N., 271, 272, 274, 286–287, 288, 292
Guba, E. G., 311, 312, 317
Gunn, L. A., 184, 318, 320, 321
Guppy, N., 329
Guthrie, J. D., 116
Guthrie, J. W., 71

Haddad, C., 64
Hagan, J. P., 216

Halberstam, D., 119
Hale, E. E., 330
Hall, E. T., 124
Hall, L., 211, 212, 213
Halls, W., 75
Hamm, K. E., 144, 145
Hamrin, R., 57, 58, 63, 64
Hanna, J., 139
Hannaway, J., 17
Hanson, R. L., 81, 85
Hanushek, E. A., 74
Harman, G., 329
Harmon, M., 78
Harragan, B. L., 38
Harrington-Lueker, D., 132
Hatch, J., 59
Hays, C., 201
Heilbroner, R. L., 64
Henry, W. A., III, 69
Hernandez, D., 45–46
Hilgartner, S., 182, 186, 190
Hirsch, E. D., Jr., 16
Hirschman, J., 185
Hobbes, T., 47
Hodgkinson, H., 66, 68
Hoff, D. J., 18, 138, 139, 256
Hofstede, G., 87, 94, 111
Hogwood, B. W., 184, 318, 320, 321
Hoxby, C. M., 193–194
Hrebenar, R. J., 153, 154, 155, 156
Huberman, A. M., 275–276, 277, 283, 287, 288, 293, 296, 297
Hudgins, H. C., Jr., 216, 219
Hughes, S. K., 78n
Husen, T., 75

Iannaccone, L., 86, 108, 116, 120, 124, 327, 343
Isaak, A., 81, 87, 124

Jackson, B. M., 8
Jackson, J. E., 109
Jacob, H., 151
Jacobs, J. A., 124
Jacobson, L., 69
Janklow, W., Governor, 148
Jefferson, T., 82, 331
Jencks, C., 174, 184
Jenkins-Smith, H. C., 176
Jennings, J. F., 14, 16
Jensen, D. N., 219
Johnson, S. M., 7, 33, 34
Johnson, W., 164–165
Jones, B. D., 170, 186
Jones, Lyle, 256

Kaestle, C. F., 331, 333n, 334, 336
Kagan, R. A., 212, 213
Kahne, J., 116, 119
Kalodner, H. I., 219
Kaplan, G. R., 92, 156, 178, 185
Kaplan, M., 83, 148
Kearney, R. C., 82, 83, 84, 85, 86, 145, 146
Keller, B., 139
Kelly, J., 63
Kelman, S., 109
Kemper, M., 215
Kennedy, A. A., 95
Kerchner, C. T., 5, 72, 120, 343
Kerwin, C. M., 210, 211, 212, 213

Subject Index

Page numbers with *f* indicate figures; page numbers with *t* indicate tables.

AASA. *See* American Association of School Administrators (AASA)
Accelerated Schools, 75
Administrative agencies
  influencing, 222–225
  policy formulation and adoption in, 210–215, 211*f*, 212*f*
  as source of legislative proposal, 198
Administrative Procedures Act (1946), 213–214
Administrative rules, 210–211
  making, 212–213
  need for, 210–211
  process of writing, 211–212
Administrators. *See also* School administration
  in following policy issues, 21
  implications of political culture for, 99–102, 100*f*
  in policy implementation, 21
  in policy influence, 23
  in policy making, 20–21
Advisory councils, 101–102
AFL-CIO. *See* American Federation of Labor-Congress of Industrial Organizations (AFL-CIO)
AFT. *See* American Federation of Teachers (AFT)
Agendas, 34–35
  governmental policy, 181, 182, 183–186
  of media, 158, 182
  policy, 158, 181–187, 183*f*
  relationship between, 182–183
  setting, 16
    influencing, 189–190
American Association of School Administrators (AASA), 179, 220
American Center for Law and Justice, 132
American Enterprise Institute, 173, 177
American Federation of Labor-Congress of Industrial Organizations (AFL-CIO), 154
American Federation of Teachers (AFT), 154, 178, 345
America Online (AOL), 61
Amicus curiae, 151
Anti-Defamation League, 155
Appellate courts, 217
Applied research, 175
Appointed officials and groups, identifying, 161–163, 161*t*
Appropriations Committee, 204
Arenas, 92–93
Articles of Confederation, 82
Aryan Nation, 128
ASCD. *See* Association of Supervision and Curriculum Development (ASCD)

Association of Supervision and Curriculum Development (ASCD), 226, 306
Authority, 31–32
  charismatic, 32
  competent, 32
  legal, 32
  patriarchal, 31–32
  reallocation of, 5–6

Baby Boom, 57
Baby-boom echo, 67
Baker v. *Carr*, 83, 145
Balance, search for, 121
Basic research, 175
Basic Skills First Program (BSF) in Tennessee, 298–299
Benefits, 260
Bennett, W., 16, 74
Bias
  mobilization of, 35–39
  in school choice, 38–39
  against women in school administration, 37–38
Bilingual education, 72, 323–324
Bills, 200
  drafting of, 200–201, 201*f*
  movement of, through legislature, 201–204, 202*f*
Boards of education
  local, 151–152
  state, 148–149
Brief *amicus curiae*, 233
Broad appeal, issue definition and, 180
Brookings Institution, 173–174, 174, 175
Brown v. *Board of Education of Topeka*, 12, 218, 219
Budget Day, 207
Budgeting
  policy and, 11
  process of, 207
  at state level, 209–210
Bureaucracy, 328
Bush, G. H. W., 5, 17, 58, 147
Bush, G. W., 5, 58, 118
Business conservatism, 125–126
Business cycles, 59–60, 60*f*
  implications of, 70–72
  monitoring, 61
Business lobby, 155
Business Roundtable, 155, 185

California Learning Assessment System (CLAS), 257
California Teachers Association, 164–165
Campaign contributions, 234
Capacity building, 253–254
Capitalism, emergence of, 56

networks, 156
noneducation interest groups, 155–156
planning organizations, 156–157
Nonregulatory licensing, 241, 242f
Northwest Ordinance, 331
NSBA. *See* National School Boards Association (NSBA)
Numbers, 34

OERI. *See* Educational Research and Improvement, Office of (OERI)
Olin Foundation, 173
OMB. *See* Management and Budget, Office of (OMB)
Ongoing assistance in policy implementation, 289–290, 290f
Online service, 158
Opinion Day, 218
Opinions, 215, 217
Opportunity cost, 260
Order, 133
    freedom and, 121
    as general social value, 110–111
Organization of Petroleum Exporting Countries (OPEC), 58
Output maximization, 116
Override vote, 203

Paramilitary organizations, 128
Paraprofessionals, 299–300
Parental involvement, 36–37
Parental Rights Act, 126
Parents' Coalition to Stop High-Stakes Testing, 185
Parent Teacher Association (PTA), 27, 37, 46, 154
Partisan activity, 234
Party machine, 98
Patriarchal authority, 31–32
Patronage, 33
Peak, 59
Pennsylvania Association for Retarded Children v. *Commonwealth*, 219
Per capita gross national product (GNP), 61
Perot, H. R., 58, 63, 64
Personal visits in lobbying public officials, 232–233
Personnel
    in cost analysis, 261
    in policy implementation, 285
Persuasion, 32–33
    manipulative, 33
    in policy implementation, 295–296
    rational, 32
Pew Charitable Trusts, 174
Phi Delta Kappa (PDK), 305
Physical force, 31
Plessy v. *Ferguson*, 11
Political culture, 80
    defining, 94–95
    education policy and, 98–99
    implications for school administrators, 99–102, 100f
    individualistic, 98
    moralistic, 97
    traditionalistic, 95–97, 96f, 96t
Political equality, 113
Politically controlled study, 310
Political party affiliation, policy activity and, 91
Political situations, anticipating, 246
Political strategies in policy implementation, 291
Political system, 80, 95
    federalism in, 81–84
    focus on elections, 86–87

fragmentation of governance, 84–86
    implications of, for school leaders, 87–94
    judicial review in, 87
    separation of powers in, 84
    in U.S., 80–87
Politics, 196, 329
    basic values in U.S., 109–119
    distributive, 241–242
    of educational policy evaluation, 314–316
    of getting policy adopted, 204–206
    redistributive, 245
    regulatory, 244
Poor, gap between rich and, 64–65, 65t
Posse Comitatus, 128
Power
    assessing, 44
    building, 45–46
    as contested concept, 27
    dangers of, 47
    defining, 27–28
    discourse and, 28–30
    discursive, 34–35
    in educational settings, 41–46, 42t
    education policy and, 26–49
    ethical issues surrounding, 47–49
    explicit uses of, 30–35
    as means and end, 47–48
    as self-interest value, 109–110
    three-dimensional model of, 30–41, 30t
    types of, 31
Power relationships, analyzing, 41, 43–45, 43f
Power resources, 33, 33t
Precedents, 215
President of the Senate, 144
PRINCE system, 41, 43
Priority, assessing, 44
Privatization, 241
Privatizing, school services, 236–237
Problem coping in policy implementation, 290–291, 290t, 291t
Problems
    distinguishing, from policy issues, 170
    transformation into issue, 169–170
Professional agenda, 182
Professionalization, 328–329
    of evaluation, 305–306
Professional staff members, 145
Professional values, policy implementation and, 295–296
Programs, defined, 304
Progressive Movement, 86
Projects, defined, 304
Pseudo-evaluations, 310
Psychic force, 31
PTA. *See* Parent Teacher Association (PTA)
Public agenda, 182
Public Law, 94-142, 71
Public leadership, 7–8
Public officials and agendas, 184
Public policies, 8, 55
    analysis of, 259–260
    value-free analysis of, 107
Public relations evaluation, 310

Qualitative methodologies, 311–312, 311f
Quality, 118–119, 120f, 133
    efficiency and, 123
    freedom and, 122
Quantitative research designs, 310–311